A ROUGH PASSAGE

Volume I

Author and wife, St Catharine's May Ball, 1953

A ROUGH PASSAGE

Memories of Empire

Volume I

Kenneth Barnes

The Radcliffe Press
LONDON • NEW YORK

Published in 2007 by The Radcliffe Press
6 Salem Road, London W2 4BU

In the United States and in Canada
distributed by Palgrave Macmillan, a division of St Martin's Press
175 Fifth Avenue, New York NY 10010

ISBN: 978 1 84511 263 9 (Volume I)
ISBN: 978 1 84511 264 6 (Volume II)

A full CIP record for this book is available from the British Library
A full CIP record for this book is available from the Library of Congress

Library of Congress Catalog card: available

Typeset in Sabon by Newgen Imaging Systems (P) Ltd
Printed and bound in the UK by TJ International, Padstow

To

Lesley,
lover, wife, mother of our children,
my stay and support until her death

and to

The Colonial Administrative Service
in which
I was privileged to serve

Contents

Illustrations

Figures

Maps

Glossary, acronyms and abbreviations

ACB	African Continental Bank
ACP	African, Caribbean and Pacific states
Action Group	AG, Western Region of Nigeria political party
ADB	African Development Bank
ADO/ADC	assistant district officer (W. Africa) or commissioner (E. and S. Africa): lowest rung in hierarchy
Ama uke (Efik/Ibibio)	'What do you want?' ('Your money or your life?')
amah (Chinese)	child's nurse
ARP	air raid precautions
ASP	assistant superintendent of police
ayer (Malay)	water, lake
Baas-Kaap (S. African)	White man's rule
bajus (Malay)	jackets
baleen	filter in a whale's throat
barathea	lightweight suiting material
BAT	British-American Tobacco Company, linked with Imperial Tobacco ('Imps')
BBWA	Bank of British West Africa
BHC	depending on context, either the person of the British High Commissioner (i.e. ambassador to a Commonwealth country) *or* the entire office, buildings and staff supporting same
bilal (Malay)	caller to prayer, a *muezzin*
BIS	Bank of International Settlements (Basle)
boma (Swahili)	government offices
bukit (Malay)	hill
cantinas (Portuguese)	bar, restaurant, bottle-shop
Carley float	simple raft for emergency rescue at sea when ship's boats are unusable
caveat (Latin)	*warning*

CDC	Commonwealth Development Corporation, government-funded parastatal to help fund economically viable projects
CDFC	Commonwealth Development Finance Corporation
CD&W	Colonial Development and Welfare (money voted by the UK Parliament to help the economic development of colonies, for apportionment by the Colonial Office)
CO	Colonial Office (located in Church House, Great Smith Street after original office was bombed in 1941 – sometimes the address was used as an alternative name)
COR	Calabar, Ogoja and Rivers State Movement in E. Nigeria
CRO	Commonwealth Relations Office
de minimus non curat lex	Latin tag, 'the law ignores the smallest matters as too trivial'
'Developing country'	another mealy-mouthed way of saying 'poor'
'Devonshire'	name of Colonial Administrative Service training courses
DG VIII	Directorate-General 8 of the European Commission responsible for overseas aid
DO/DC	district officer (West Africa) or commissioner (E. and Southern Africa): the member of the Administrative Service responsible for the good government of a territorial area known as a division or district. The key figure in governing the Empire
ECOWAS	Economic Community of West African States
EDF	European Development Fund – money given or loaned by EU to ACP for development aid
EEC/EU	European Economic Community (also Common Market) now known as European Union
EIB	European Investment Bank, located in Luxemburg, responsible for loans for industrial projects at commercial interest rates
El Dorado (Spanish)	Untold wealth awaiting discovery
ESCOM	Electricity Supply Commission

ExCo	the Executive Council that advises the governor
exeat (Latin)	permission to be absent
FCO	Foreign and Commonwealth Office
Federated Malay State	Negri Sembilan, Selangor, Pahung, Perak
FMB	Farmers Marketing Board
Fort Johnson	Mangochi
Fort Manning	Mchingi
GATT	General Agreement on Tariffs and Trade
Gorsuch	slang for a salary increase
gully-gully man	a juggler or magician, usually Egyptian
gyp	college servant (Cambridge)
hantu (Malay)	ghost
HE	His Excellency
IBRD	International Bank for Reconstruction and Development (UN), commonly known as the World Bank
ICS	Indian Civil Service on which the Colonial Administrative Service was modelled
IDA	International Development Association, 'soft' loan face of World Bank
IFC	International Finance Company
IMF	International Monetary Fund, commonly 'the Fund'
juju	West African religious belief
kampong (Malay)	Malay village
kamuzu (Chichewa)	chief, leader
KAR	The King's African Rifles was the name of all the E./Central African infantry, the First and Second battalions being recruited from Nyasaland. The First battalion became the Malawi Rifles on independence
khonde (S. African)	veranda
lappas	voluminous W. African women's wear
latterite	red soil, suitable for road making
LDC	less developed country – another mealy-mouthed way of saying 'poor'
LegCo	the Legislative Council in a colony, sometimes known as a House of Assembly
Lomé	Capital of Togo where aid agreements between EEC and ACP were signed,

	commonly used as shorthand for these agreements
Lumpers	slang for 'lump sum compensation for loss of career' paid to pensionable colonial service officers when the colony in which they were serving became independent
machete	crude but effective cutting implement sometimes made from car-springs. Similar to the naval cutlass which it is in fact called in the West Indies
mata-mata (Malay)	policeman
MBTA	Malawi Buying and Trade Agency
MCP	Malawi Congress Party
MCS	Malayan Civil Service
MDC	Malawi Development Corporation
Mems (Malay)	white women
MO	medical officer
NCNC	National Council of Nigeria and the Cameroons. Tried to combine attributes of Ibo National Party and Universal Party for all Nigerians
NGO	non-governmental organisation
night soil	untreated human excreta
NPC	Northern People's Congress
OAU	Organisation of African Unity (with reputation for impracticality, inefficiency and disunity)
ODA/ODM	Overseas Development Administration/ Ministry
ODI	Overseas Development Institute: colonial economic think tank
padang (Malay)	grassy, flat, open public space
Palm Beach	lightweight gentleman's suiting
PC	provincial commissioner – the governor's representative in a province
PIDE	Polícia de Intervenção e Defesa do Estado (Portuguese Secret Police under Salazar regime)
poilu (Fr. slang)	soldier
polio	formerly known as infantile paralysis. Paralysis of motor nerves in spinal cord by a virus; transmitted by contaminated water

	Preventive vaccine discovered 1955, disease now largely eliminated
Port Herald (Nyld)	now Nsanje
poule (Fr. slang)	prostitute
PWD	Public Works Department: responsible for designing, building, furnishing and maintaining permanent government buildings, roads, bridges, water supplies, etc.
RADAR	Royal Association for Disability and Rehabilitation
resident	the governor's representative in a province (Nigeria); also provincial commissioner (for Nyasaland)
Rome, Treaty of	treaty creating EEC
sais or *syce* (Malay)	chauffeur
stadthuis (Dutch)	government building/offices
STD	sexually transmitted disease
Straits Settlements	Singapore, Malacca, Penang
tong (Malay)	large earthenware jar
topi	a hat; name given to the pith helmets, white or khaki, worn by Europeans in the tropics as a protection against sunstroke
tukang (Malay)	workman
UFP	United Federal Party
ulat (Malay)	snake
UMCA	Universities Mission to Central Africa
UMNO	United Malay National Party
UNI	Unilateral Declaration of Independence (Rhodesia)
UNIP	United National Independence Party
UNDP	United Nations Development Programme
Unfederated Malay States	Johore, Kedah, Kelantan, Perlis, Trengganu
UPE	universal primary education
veldtschoen	a very sturdy waterproof leather shoe
WAFF	West African Frontier Force: became the parent of the armies of Ghana, Nigeria, Sierra Leone and the Gambia

Author's note

Aware of the dangers of over-reliance on memory I have tried to check my recollections with others who were present at the events described or who were aware of them.

My brother, Geoffrey Barnes, CBE, was with me from his birth in 1932 almost continually until October 1943, when he returned to our prep school and I went to Dover College (where he later joined me); his own recollections of those early years are contained in *Mostly Memories*. He has also read all the later chapters of this book in which he makes periodic reappearances. Anne Deveson, AO, was also a passenger on the *Viceroy of India* and subsequently lived in Perth at the same time as me; she has seen both relevant chapters. Air Commodore Dr Michael Pallister has read the chapters dealing with my life in Australia and my subsequent meeting with him again in London and Cambridge. Judge David Anderson who was at Hale School, Perth, WA has read the section dealing with my life there. Mr J. M. Clayton has read the sections describing our bicycle holidays while we were at Dover College, as has Brigadier Michael Doyle with reference to the holiday in the New Forest.

Messrs R. Graham, A. J. Shepherd and M. G. Smith were contemporaries of mine on the Overseas Service course and subsequently in E. Nigeria and have read all the 'Nigerian' chapters. The late Robert Varvill, DSC, read my recollection of the Nya/Oniong feud. The Rt. Rev. Michael Mann who was my DO at Uyo has read that chapter and Dr Kenneth Rowden, once Medical Officer i/c the Annang Joint Hospital at Ikot Okoro, has read the chapter dealing with my time as DO, Abak.

Hamish Robertson, CB, worked with me in Zomba, Nyasaland/Malawi between 1963 and mid-1965, and he has read the chapters dealing with these years. Mr K. J. Neale, OBE, who was a home civil servant in the Colonial Service and the Central Africa Office has read the sections dealing with 1963/4 during which time he was responsible for those departments in Nyasaland/Malawi. Mr K. Windsor, OBE, a home civil servant, was seconded from ODM to the British High Commission in Zomba from 1967 until my departure and has been most helpful in giving the view 'from the other side of the hill'. Mr C. W. Collins, CBE, worked with me during the period 1966 to 1970, and has seen the chapters dealing with these years. Professor Colin Baker, who was on the Colonial Service course in 1953, and subsequently my colleague in Nyasaland/Malawi has read all the chapters concerning Malawi, and has been most helpful in providing comments as well as information.

'Terry' Barringer has been an outstanding researcher and general guide, critic and friend while Sheelagh Lowes has typed and retyped the manuscript without complaint. To both I give unstinted thanks. The indexes have been compiled by Michael Solomons to whom I express my very sincere thanks.

Finally, I wish to thank Tony Kirk-Greene, MBE, CMG, to whom all writers on the Colonial Administrative Service are indebted for having ensured that the Colonial Administrative Service is not forgotten.

Currency value

Nigerian and Federal currency and subsequently Malawi currency was at par to sterling during the period. During the years 1954–71 inflation was low but nevertheless over the 17 years purchasing power probably fell by a third.

It would be about right to multiply all monetary figures, in sterling or Nigerian or Malawi currencies, by 24 to bring them up to present-day equivalents.

Part One
Early Years

Chapter 1
A childhood in Malacca, 1930–7

Tristram Shandy's life begins with the process of his birth – or is it his conception (?) – and I can well believe that the first few months or years of one's existence affect much of later life even though there may be no conscious memory of them. Be that as it may, my first conscious memory, and that when I was already 27 months old, is itself far from clear, a picture in a mist of unknowing. I am standing by the entry-post to a driveway, leading up a small hill to a bungalow, and am being told that Mummy was in the bungalow – the old Malacca European Hospital – with a baby brother for me. Geoffrey, that brother, was born on the 18 August 1932.

How 'real' is this memory? Could it be that there was once a photograph of this scene and that it is the photo rather than the event that has remained in my mind? I don't know, for, if there was ever such a photo, it was lost during the calamitous events of January 1942. Nevertheless, it is entirely appropriate that my memory of life should begin with my brother's birth as his life and mine have since intertwined so closely; and still so remain, closer than most brothers, as we both enter our post-Biblical span.

It is appropriate, too, that the memory should be misty. The 70 years that have passed saw more changes than in any other similar period of the world's history. The society into which I was born, that of the British Empire at what still seemed its zenith, has gone; the British Empire is one with those of the Seleucids, of the Romans, of the Mongols and of the Pharaohs, a bit, no more, in the muddle of the past. Yet since, as a historian by formation, I feel that an understanding of the past remains important for the present, it may be that what I have to recount of my experiences of this past will interest those professional historians who will try to interpret this turbulent age.

Malacca, where I had been conceived and where my brother was born, was a quiet sleepy town on the peninsula of Malaya, which juts down from and is the most southerly point of the great Eurasian landmass. An English civil servant in Malaya at this time wrote of it, 'No other place in Malaya has such monuments of its past – Portuguese fortifications and churches, Dutch buildings (my office is in what is still called the Stadt House) and picturesque Chinese streets. Portuguese and Dutch names are common, although the blood is mixed, and while Dutch speech has vanished the earlier Portuguese has survived and is still spoken.'[1]

British it had remained, although, by the time of which I am now writing, Malacca's former commercial importance had long departed; her port had largely silted up; the traders had moved to Raffles's new creation of Singapore. The town had charm, and it had antiquity. It was a convenient and pleasant shopping centre for the British rubber planters who managed the rubber estates in the neighbouring – but independent and Malay – States. Malacca was different from these; it was British in perpetuity, a colony of the Crown whose Resident Commissioner represented the King himself.

It was impossible, even for a small boy, to be unaware of the past; its evidences were all too obvious. I have already mentioned some of the buildings of the earlier centuries that reflected the differing architectural styles and cultures of past rulers. There were mosques from whose minarets the *bilal* would call the faithful – the Malays – to prayer; Chinese temples – the Cheng Hoon Teng Temple (Abode of Merciful Clouds), dedicated to the Goddess of Mercy and dating from the seventeenth century, was only one of many – and those of the Hindus; the towers and bells of the Roman Catholic Cathedral; the austere Calvinist line of Christ Church.[2]

On the crowded streets and in the shops the differing styles of dress – Malays in *bajus* (jackets) and sarongs, Chinese, sometimes in traditional long robes, sometimes in Western-style clothing, the poor in singlets and khaki shorts, European men in white duck suits – proclaimed the many different national strains in the population. Predominant in the township were Chinese, some rich traders belonging to families established since before Marco Polo made his travels,[3] some the owners of small shops, some, not-yet-arrived at the latter status, street peddlers and market-hawkers. There would be a few newly arrived poor, also, who made a bare living pulling the prosperous in rickshaws. There might be a few Malays; in general Malays did not much care for town life, preferring to farm or to fish but a few earned a graceful living by driving motor cars or as smartly dressed *mata-mata*'s (policemen), pride-fully directing the traffic. Outside the Stadthuis bewhiskered Sikhs stood guard, already big men whose stature was further increased by their turbans so that they seemed to be veritable giants. In contrast to these proud men there were dark-skinned, almost blue-black, Tamils from South India who formed the bulk of the labour on the neighbouring rubber estates and who were also the gardeners and sweepers.

Mixed in with these, there were a smaller number from other races, for example, a few Japanese (one of whom, a photographer named Ishi, was later reputed to have been an officer in the Imperial Navy and to have spied for them in addition under the cover of his quite legitimate business). There were also a considerable number of Eurasians, their ancestry sometimes complex, some with Portuguese names whose families had lived in Malacca for centuries and who clung to the Roman Catholic faith of their ancestors. These lived, for the most part, in the 'Portuguese Town', outside the circumference of the former walls – maybe the Dutch had considered them a security risk in the first years of their rule – although they worshipped within the town at the twin-towered Cathedral of St Francis Xavier. There must have been, also, some 'Burgher Dutch' and, no doubt, there were also descendants of the illegitimate offspring of the British who had lived there during the past century.

But it was the 'Europeans' – the generic name given in the East and in Africa to all white people including Americans (just as in South America Europeans proper are thought of as a sub-species of the North American genus) – who were the apparent undoubted masters of this microcosm. Well fed, well built, self-assured, with servants and motor cars, they lived – at least for the most part – in spacious houses outside the crowded and noisy old town, which seemed now to have no purpose but to be their backdrop. If the 'Europeans' were pre-eminent amongst other races, within the category of 'Europeans' the British were first. Malacca was 'their' town, the Royal Navy ruled the seas where once Portuguese, Dutch and French had sailed, the British Empire covered a quarter of the world. There seemed to be no likely end to their 'Empire on which the sun never sets'.

My father, as a bachelor, made a first, and brief, visit to Malaya in 1920 (already he had worked for some years for the Dunlop Rubber Company, at that time one of the world's greatest companies). He had then returned to work in their London headquarters but I believe that there had ensued some boardroom dispute amongst the company's directors, that he had been thought to be in the camp of those who lost the argument and that he had considered his career prospects in England would be prejudiced in consequence. Accordingly, when the opportunity arose for him to move sideways within the organisation into the position of company secretary to its subsidiary, Dunlop Malayan Estates, he felt that it was a chance not to be missed.

He was in England, however, in early 1928 and it was probably at this time that he became engaged to my mother. They had known each other, I think, for some time; both came from south London; both from the educated lower echelons of the middle class; they were of approximately the same age, both in their mid-thirties.

My father returned to Malaya alone in mid-1928; mother voyaging out in 1929 to join him and to be married in Christ Church, Malacca. It must have been something of an ordeal for her, that first journey, a month aboard a coal-burning steamer – and, as she herself was always to admit, she was 'no sailor', succumbing to seasickness almost as soon as the ship untied from the jetty. Neither her family nor my father's had any tradition of living or working abroad upon which she could draw, although she and her sisters had spent several holidays in France and once she had even been to Algiers. Effectively, though, her voyage to Malaya was her first time out of Europe.

Fortunately, my mother was a woman with great strength of character as she was to demonstrate on many occasions subsequently; in addition Malaya, even then, must have ranked pretty high on any list of 'comfortable' tropical colonies. Admittedly it was very close to the equator and with a rainfall of over 80 inches a year – more than twice the average in Britain – the climate was always hot and humid.

European housing, though, was generally of a high standard with airy spacious rooms and wide external verandas to shield them from the glare and heat of the sun's direct rays (of course there was no such thing as air conditioning at that time). There were also hill stations at Cameron Highlands and at Fraser's Hill, both on the mountainous central spine of Malaya, where those well enough off could find relief from the continual enervating heat and enjoy the luxury of sitting by a wood fire in the evenings and being grateful for its warmth.

Food was no problem. There was an abundance of fruit – limes, green-skinned oranges, pomelos (a kind of rather large and coarse grapefruit), rambutans (a red-fleshed fruit), *buah sousou* (passion fruit), *buah chiku* (pineapples), durians (which I have never tasted but which have been described to me as having a flavour as delightful as the smell of the fruit is vile), bananas and papayas or pawpaws (an almost invariable 'starter' for breakfast, delicious with freshly squeezed lime juice). Vegetables were available in a Chinese profusion. Fish was abundant; nowhere in Malaya was far from the sea and the high rainfall meant that there were many rivers and lakes. Chickens appeared to live everywhere, running wild in every Malay *kampong* (village). The tsetse fly, the scourge of tropical Africa, had never spread to Asia so that local meat was available (and in Malacca the municipal authorities maintained a high standard of hygiene in what was sold from the market). If one wished to spend freely, imported Australian meat could be bought from the Cold Storage Company whose shop, selling ice creams – one favourite of ours was called Eskimo Pie – was usually full of '*mems*' (white women) and their children. The only thing unobtainable, as I recall, was fresh milk – dried milk was the norm, 'Klim' being the brand we used, although evaporated milk diluted with water was an alternative. Water itself was always boiled and filtered before drinking, although whether this was really necessary in the towns I cannot say.

Generally health was good. Great care was always taken against going uncovered into the sunlight – even a few minutes' exposure was rumoured to lead to illness(!), Europeans universally wore white pith topis. The high level of humidity encouraged the development

Figure 1 Christ church, Malacca.

of prickly heat and athlete's foot, but there were very few tropical diseases apart from malaria; even from that Malacca itself was free, although, being on the coastal plain and surrounded by paddy fields, mosquitoes were an inescapable torment every nightfall.

Medical services were far superior to those obtaining in any African colony but my mother was comparatively old to bear a first child and her doctor must have decided that, since it was likely to be a difficult birth, it would be safer in England. So, within a few months, she was back on board ship 'homeward-bound'. It was the first of the many separations she was to experience during her married life.[4] Her doctor had been correct in his diagnosis. Mother had a difficult accouchement and the use of forceps was necessary to pull me out; their mark on my temple is still visible and my right eye has never closed easily. So it was that I was born in London in May 1930 (much to my regret as a child – I thought an overseas place of birth much more unusual and interesting!).

While I have an abundance of memories of the next seven years I have difficulty in fitting them into any sort of accurate time frame. Geoffrey's birth in August 1932 puts me firmly in Malaya at that time. During 1934 the family returned to England on home leave. As the ship steamed through the Mediterranean to Marseilles, we went past Stromboli[5] one evening when it was in eruption, red-hot lava streaming down the sides of the cone which itself seemed to rise straight from the dark sea. Above, red-gold clouds reflected the flames. In November that year a photograph shows both of us small boys – well wrapped up – in Bournemouth. Christmas was spent with my mother's family and I remember my older boy cousin promising me that next time I was in England for Christmas he would give me his toy soldiers' fort as by then *he* would be too old to play with them!

Early in the New Year, however, we sailed once more for Malaya aboard the Blue Funnel Line steamer *Sarpedon* and the menu of a children's tea party (for children a very sumptuous meal indeed) while on board is dated 12 February 1935.

My next 'datable' memory is of the Silver Jubilee celebrations in May 1935, of the King-Emperor, George V, which we watched from a veranda in Bastion House. There were floats, Chinese dragon-dancers twisting and writhing, a march past by a detachment of the Malay Regiment. The climax consisted of the Chinese and Malay schoolchildren, uniformed all in red, white or blue, being so drawn up on the grass of the Padang in Malacca as to compose an enormous Union flag. 'God Save the King' was then sung and 'three cheers' called and given. Two years later at the

Coronation of King George VI RI (originally planned to be that of his brother King Edward VIII: I have a souvenir handkerchief commemorating this non-event) there were similar celebrations. These included a pageant enacting the Changing of the Portuguese Guard of two centuries before, a Song of Portugal, a Dutch song and a staging of the handing over of the keys of the Fort by the Dutch to the British. Finally, in August 1937, my mother, Geoffrey and I returned to England where I was to go to school.

England was, of course, 'home' during these years just as it was 'home' to many who never touched her shores, but it was 'home' only in name. My own memories of England at this time are sparse – understandably so given my age and the short time I spent there. There are rather vague recollections of a holiday in lodgings at some seaside resort where the beach was stony (Worthing, perhaps?) and, as I have mentioned, of another holiday at Bournemouth. There, looking across the bay to the line of the Purbeck Downs, I was told the story of the siege of Corfe Castle, of its defence by Lady Bankes and of its betrayal to the Roundheads. But, for the most part, while in England my parents and Geoffrey and I lived with my mother's parents in a Victorian house, at first one just off Clapham Common and later another by Wandsworth Common. An aunt lived there too, so we must have been all rather squashed together!

I have rather more recollections of our sea voyages. On one, to or from Malaya it is no matter which, our ship was caught in a great storm in the Gulf of Lyon; my toy soldiers fell from the upper bunk to the cabin floor and it was this that fixed the occurrence in my mind. Another memory is of my mother's hat being caught by the wind at Marseilles, escaping our chase after it and of her proudly worn headgear finally being blown into the filthy waters of the dock.

In general, though, Malaya was the country to which I really felt attached. And in fact those seven years of my childhood were probably the calmest and most settled of any single period of my life – at least up to the present time of writing this memoir. In these Malayan years we lived only in Malacca, in two homes: the first, a flat at Bastion House, above the Dunlop offices; the second, a bungalow at Bukit Sebukor, just outside the town. This latter was to be my parents' home for 15 years. The contrast to the innumerable moves my own children were to experience in their childhood could not be more marked.

Shortly after my parents' marriage there had occurred the Great Crash of 1929 on Wall Street, followed by the slump. The rubber industry, itself highly cyclical, was plunged into recession. The price of rubber fell from 73 cents per pound in 1925 to 28 cents in 1928 and then to less than 3 cents in 1932. Salaries were cut or, at best, frozen; I can remember overhearing worried conversations between my parents about their finances. My father felt that, with his non-public school background, he would be amongst the first to be made redundant should that become necessary (although he had greater skills and ability by far than most of the public school men who normally occupied commercial posts in the colonies).

As a consequence we lived modestly, although comfortably enough. Daddy smoked a pipe on occasion. Neither he nor my mother drank alcohol habitually, my mother very rarely indeed although my father would drink a beer from time to time with other men at the Malacca Club. The Club building with its onion-topped towers, vaguely Moorish in style, had been the setting of some of Somerset Maugham's short stories; it was the centre of European social life in the colony, its convivial bar a magnet that attracted the young planters in town for the weekend, escaping from an often lonely life on the surrounding rubber plantations.

At Tanjong Kling, a few miles north of Malacca, were the two other social requisites of Europeans in the tropical colonies, golf and swimming clubs. I do not think my parents belonged to the golf club – my only memory of it is seeing a small biplane sitting on the grass; it had used the fairway as a landing strip (quite a normal thing with planes of that era). The swimming club, though, we would visit every Sunday, driven by our Malay *syce* (chauffeur) who, being a Muslim, would have attended his mosque on the previous Friday. Neither my father nor my mother drove a car at this time: they learned only when they returned to England in their late fifties.

Our Chinese *amah* (nurse) would accompany us and once there join her sister *amahs*, sewing, embroidering and gossiping, each one extolling – or so I trust – the perfection of her own charge(s) and his or her superiority to those being cared for by her fellows (this superiority reflecting – or so it was of course implied – the *amah*'s own greater abilities and virtues than those possessed by her sisters). While they were thus occupied, we little children would play on the sandy edge of the swimming pool (really no more than a small square of the Malacca Strait, bounded to seaward and on either side by concrete and rock walls). Babies and small children thus became accustomed to the water; as they grew more sure they would be taken by their mother to a small raft-like structure – thatched, of course, one had to be careful that the fierce sun did not burn delicate white skin – around which they could drift in rubber rings. Geoffrey, at the age of 2 or 3, once jumped into the water off the plank floor of the raft, slipped through his ring and could have been in trouble except that I, two years older and by then an experienced swimmer, was there to rescue him.

We would lunch at the Club (so giving our cook some free time) and also have tea there – fizzy Orange Crush, accompanied by Huntley & Palmer's digestive or ginger biscuits, crisp for a few hours only once their sealed tin container was opened. If we had been good we might be allowed to stay for supper as well, eating sardines or baked beans on toast while the sun set out to sea, beyond the fishing stockades surmounted by frail little huts of the Malay fishermen. Then, as the tropical darkness descended, the lighthouse would begin blinking its message of caution to the shipping sailing down the Strait as ships had done for centuries.

The Dunlop flats at Bastion House faced across the Padang[6] looking out to sea and may have caught the breeze in the morning and evening. They were, no doubt, very suitable for a bachelor or

Figure 2 Author aged 4.

for a couple without children living with them – the Allens, who occupied the other flat, had only one daughter who was at school in England and whom I do not recall ever meeting – but they were far from ideal as a home for two young boys. We were allowed out to play on the Padang only when accompanied by Amah or Mother, while the courtyard at the back of the building was forbidden ground since the servants' children played there (it was, of course, unthinkable to adults that white children should mix or play with 'natives' although we ourselves felt no such inhibition).

My main, indeed my only, memory of the years we spent living in Bastion House is of constantly being told not to be noisy, either because we might disturb our neighbours Mr and Mrs Allen,[7] or because we might disturb the work going on in the offices below. Since we were normally noisy children the need for quiet cannot have been easy to enforce.

By the mid-1930s the rubber industry was recovering from the worst of the slump and Dunlops built four bungalows for its European staff at Bukit Sebukor a few miles outside Malacca Township. This was much more suitable for us; we had a large garden and beyond its boundary hedge and around all four bungalows was a small golf course, the grass browsed by cattle belonging to the local kampongs. In turn beyond that were rubber plantations and rice paddy fields.

Our bungalow at Bukit Sebukor seemed enormous to the eyes of a small boy but it must have been actually quite small, even though it was not a true 'bungalow' being a two-storied building. On the upper floor, there were two airy bedrooms, within each of which wire gauze enclosed a sleeping area for beds (thus obviating the need for mosquito nets). Each bedroom had its own bathroom (my parents' bedroom had two, one for each of them). In the bathroom opening off the bedroom I shared with Geoff I do not think there was initially a porcelain bath; we washed with water from a *tong*, a great earthenware jar full of water which was cooled by evaporation: to wash, one dipped a jug into this and poured the water over one's sweaty body onto the tiled floor.

At the back of the house was a veranda from which an open staircase led to the servants' quarters and up which coolies would carry water to fill the *tong* or buckets of hot water heated over the kitchen fire. Above the car-porch was an evening sitting room, the internal side of wire gauze, the windows similarly covered and provided, also, with wooden shutters to keep out the torrential rain. The wire mesh, although reasonably effective as a barrier against mosquitoes (provided that these did not accompany one through the door – swift entry and egress were essential), was inclined to make the room hot. The alternative, if we stayed downstairs in the sitting room, was to light a coiled wick, which smouldered, giving out fumes which, it was hoped, would deter mosquitoes. The ground floor comprised little more than one very large room, a projecting part-wall dividing the sitting and dining areas. Behind the latter was a small pantry containing the refrigerator, the water filter and small kerosene stove on which Mother would make cakes and fudge from time to time. From this pantry a covered way led to the kitchen and servants' quarters. Pillared verandas ran all round the ground floor. Here mother grew plants in great Chinese pots. One of these 'kung wah' ('queen of the night') would flower at full moon, white waxen blooms with a heavy cloying scent.

Located where we were, the dark of the night can hardly be guessed at by a Western European. The European bungalows were lit by electricity but there was no service to the villages where the only light came from fires or from oil lamps; as a consequence there was no reflected glow in the sky from city lights.

There was no traffic noise; indeed, there was no traffic as we would judge it today. There were few cars or lorries and still fewer public buses. The normal transport of the Malays and Chinese was by bicycle, loads being carried on high-roofed bullock carts, their only noise being the creak of the wooden axle and the scrunching of the wheels in the laterite roads, their only illumination the yellow glow of a small oil lamp.

The sounds with which we grew up, then, were rural ones. There were bird songs at morning, gradually dying away as the sun rose in the heavens and the heat of the day increased. In the evening there was a beating of wings as bats took to the sky – a colony lived in the attics of our house, on occasion causing our Malay houseboy to say that there was a *hantu* (ghost). At night we experienced the deafening croak of the thousands of frogs that lived in the paddy fields, and the infuriating whine of the mosquitoes, which bred in the fields or in the irrigation ditches (we would watch the little *chichiak*, as geckos[8] were called in Malay, clinging to the ceiling or the walls, patiently stalking these and occasionally catching their supper!).

Our garden at Bukit Sebukor was filled with tropical flowers, shrubs and trees. There were great bougainvillea bushes, red and purple flowered; there were red- or yellow-flowered 'bean' shrubs; there was a frangipani tree with its waxy white flowers, yellow centred. Garden flowers themselves were mostly orangey-yellow marigolds or zinnias; the heat and high humidity were far too great for English flowers to grow.

A lime tree grew by the steps leading down from the bungalow to the servants' quarters, seemingly always covered with small green limes. Pineapples grew at the back of the servants' quarters. There was also a *buah chiku* tree, whose fruit looked rather like a potato. There may well have been other fruit trees, rambutans or papayas (pawpaws), certainly there always seemed to be these fruits available but whether they actually grew in our garden or were purchased, I cannot say.

The bamboo hedge that separated our garden from the golf course was 'out of bounds' to us as it formed a very suitable habitat for snakes. We were constantly warned of the danger from these, although I do not recall anyone actually dying from a snake bite. The existence of snakes, though, was graphically instanced to us by the following incident.

One afternoon we were lying down on our beds. Amah, coming up the main stairs, saw a cobra sunning itself on the coconut matting of the corridor outside our bedroom. She cried out in alarm, '*Ulat, ulat*' (snake, snake); my father, coming out from his bedroom to investigate the disturbance, saw the snake between him and the head of the stairs. He jumped over it and rushed down the stairs to find a suitable implement with which to attack it, followed by the cobra. He picked up a golf club and had the good fortune to hit the creature with his first blow; he missed with his second swipe and could have been in trouble had the reptile not been partly stunned by the first. The third swing again caught it squarely and, its neck broken, it was soon finished off. The servants measured its length, over four foot long.

Amah or Mother kept us two boys constantly under their eye and even in the garden our play was supervised. In part this was no doubt due to the very real worry about snakes to which I have just referred – seeing the play and subsequent death from snake bite of the small English boy in Jean Renoir's beautiful film *The River* one can easily understand this; in part too, though, it stemmed, I suspect, from a more general anxiety.

The Europeans in the colonies might appear confident: all too often even to the point of arrogance. Their white skin, their Western lifestyle, their superior economic position, all combined to reinforce their feelings of self-worth and lack of respect for the other races of Malaya. But their conspicuous white skin also emphasised how few they were, how many times they were outnumbered by the yellow, brown and blue-black peoples around them and of whose religious beliefs and social customs they were largely unaware.

Malays, it was known, would from time to time run amok when with a drawn kris[9] they would kill anyone who came into their path. It did not happen very often, it was true, but when it did the consequences were bloody and the deaths numerous. The Chinese, far from being the controlled and inscrutable people of popular Western belief, were hot-tempered and quarrelsome – I can remember a cook chasing another servant with a great carving knife and Geoffrey recalls seeing our Amah being half-throttled after some dispute. That particular cook was thereafter summarily dismissed but his successor, Ah Fong, would chase us boys from 'his' kitchen with a flaming brand of firewood (no doubt we were being pests and we did not really think he would hurt us, but there was always an element of apprehension).

Again, when on one occasion in Malacca town we boys – separated from whoever was looking after us – were caught up in a Chinese procession with excited crowds, the banging of cymbals and the noise of firecrackers – both necessary to frighten away demons – I recall being very frightened even though we were not at all in any danger.

On another occasion, visiting a British family managing a rubber estate outside Malacca, I remember hearing the grown-ups talking about a strike by Tamil rubber tappers, that these had put barricades across the roads and that there was talk of the 'Volunteers' (a European armed militia) being called out. Here again, I do not think that there was in fact any actual violence but when we were driven back home that evening through the shadowy darkness of the rubber plantations I could sense my parents' uneasiness. The law and the power of Britain seemed a long way away.

My parents were always careful to avoid wounding the susceptibilities of others. On Bukit China, the highest of the hills around the town, where the rich Chinese had their elaborate graves and where they flew kites on festival days, we were allowed to run, but always with the exhortation that the tombs themselves were to be respected as one would a Christian churchyard. Comments about skin colour, however innocently meant, were also frowned on lest they caused offence.

Since the existence of the British Empire depended upon British control of the seas, a visit to Malacca by Royal Navy ships of the China Squadron was very much welcomed. The ships themselves, the destroyer *HMS Delight* and a submarine, *HMS Perseus*,[10] lay at anchor off the port as there was insufficient draught to allow them to tie up at the jetty. Visitors were received, taken out in a launch and shown over the great ships. The brass work, including the caps over the gun muzzles, shone brilliantly in the glaring sunlight, the wooden decks had been holystoned to dazzling whiteness, the crew were immaculate in 'tropical whites', a tightly stretched awning provided welcome shade and cool drinks and cakes were served by way of refreshment. A highlight of the visit was being taken aboard the submarine and being permitted to look through the viewfinder of the periscope and to see the shaft retracted. I determined that my ambition would be to become one of these demigods myself when I grew up, to join the Navy and to command a ship like these. It was an ambition I retained until circumstance irrevocably prevented its achievement.

In the Malacca Club there were copies of the *Illustrated London News* that I would look at with fascination. The edition for 19 July 1936 showed silhouettes of the new warships (including seven cruisers and two aircraft carriers) it was proposed to add to the Fleet, while a photograph taken from a seaplane over Alexandria showed the Mediterranean Fleet lying at anchor. Another issue (6 February 1937) contained the famous photograph of HM's ships *Resolution* and *Ramillies*, both battleships of the Home Fleet, steaming through heavy seas. Other photographs and drawings of new German and Italian warships brought home the need for increased British military strength on sea. British worldwide commitments on land were demonstrated by photos of British troops guarding the roads in Palestine (issue of 12 August 1936) and of the expedition against the Fakir of Ipi who was leading a rebellion on India's Northwest frontier.

Photographs of the fighting in Spain and of the damage caused there by bombing raids were balanced by a display (featured in the issue of 9 May 1936) of Britain's anti-aircraft defences, guns, searchlights and sound-locators. Another issue (11 July 1936), under the title 'A Queen Mary of the Air' depicted an artist's impressions of the new flying boats, the 'Canopus Class', being developed for Imperial Airways. These planes with a dining saloon and a spacious passengers' lounge were aimed at the luxury trade. Each night they would land at some prearranged port of call, their passengers would disembark, change into evening dress for dinner and pass the night in comfort in a luxury hotel before re-embarking the next day. Such civilised and aristocratic travel is a far cry indeed from the modern package holiday!

However comfortable air travel might be becoming for the few, voyaging by sea was to remain the norm for most for another twenty or more years. Sea was also the usual medium for most postal traffic, particularly in the case of any item that was weighty or bulky such as newspapers or journals. My parents used to receive the *Daily Mirror*, a fortnight's copies being bound together in book form (as sea mail took about a month before arrival, this meant that the first issue in each batch received would be six weeks old!). I recall the comic strip cartoons that I used to follow avidly but nothing else in the paper has remained in my mind.

Daddy was a member of the Overseas League, which published a monthly journal. On the cover of this journal a stylised galleon was depicted, sailing through tropic oceans, with below a quotation from Tennyson,

> We sailed wherever ship could sail.
> We founded many a mighty State.
> Pray God our Greatness may not Fail
> For craven Fears of being Great.

I was attracted to the picture and the sentiments of the verse that accorded with my own feelings on the subject – although to my 6-year-old mind the end of the Empire was inconceivable – but otherwise the contents of the journal I labelled dull. I preferred books of romance, preferably illustrated, such as the Tales of King Arthur, saddened almost to tears though I was by a black and white drawing of Arthur, pierced through and through by Mordred's spear, yet making one last desperate exertion of his strength to hold Excalibur aloft and cleave the traitor to his death.

We were the only white children living on Bukit Sebukor and on most days we would have had no European children to play with except each other but I cannot remember feeling any sense of loss at this; we played well together, Geoff and I.

When it rained – on about 180 days in the year – we would float toy boats in the open concrete storm drains that ran round the house and race one against another, whooping them on as the waters carried them round to the rear of the house where they poured like a cataract down an incline. The lawns around the house would have been transformed into pools of water, meanwhile, by the downpour – not only did it rain often but the annual total exceeded 80 inches – but within minutes of the rain ceasing and of the reappearance of the sun, the waters would have evaporated. No wonder then that the humidity was a constant 90 degrees!

In and around Malacca though there must have been in all a dozen or more 'suitable' boys and girls of Geoff's and my age, while a few others lived even more isolated lives on the rubber plantations. The individual composition of this little European world, though, was constantly in a state of flux, government servants in particular rarely serving more than one 3- to 4-year tour in the same place; childhood friendships, therefore, were particularly evanescent and I can recall the names of few of my playmates. One, whom I was to meet again many years later, was Margaret Willan, the daughter of the bank manager. She was unique in that she had an English nanny, who must have found her social position difficult – Chinese *amahs* normally, and very efficiently, carried out the tasks for other children that she had to perform for Margaret; an English nanny being white could not mix with 'natives' but as 'a servant' was of a different class to most of the Europeans.

Margaret's Nanny usually came with her when Margaret visited my house to play. I do not recall her presence though except once when we were both invited to a party for a child living on a rubber estate some miles off. That particular day is marked in my memory by a number of incidents. It was at this estate that the tiger incident occurred which I refer to below; the boy's mother, too, was sick of malaria and we were all invited in to her bedroom to see her, lying on her bed looking very pale and drawn. Returning home that evening, the road was flooded from recent torrential rain – my father had recently bought a Standard 10 with a Union Jack on its bonnet badge and we were concerned whether it would be able to get through the surging brown waters.

On either this occasion or on another visit we were warned to be especially careful to keep near the house as there was reputed to be a man-eating tiger in the rubber trees which had attacked some of the Tamil rubber tappers. A few days later, I saw the skin of this or another tiger, pegged out to dry on the Padang at Malacca. For many nights thereafter, my dreams were made restless by fears that some great tiger would jump up from the dark of the garden onto the open veranda around our bedroom – separated from us only by the flimsy metal gauze of the mosquito cage – and seize us two small boys.

There was a steady stream of children's parties – birthday parties, Christmas parties – as, except at these and at visits to the swimming pool, all children lived a somewhat isolated life. Occasionally, though, picnics were organised – a favourite spot was Tanjong Badara, where some huge, smooth, round rocks protruded from the surface of the water. One had to be careful, though, as jelly fish – Portuguese men-of-war – were plentiful and their long trailing tentacles could give a most unpleasant sting! At one of these picnics, Geoff suffered in another way. Chasing each other wildly along the beach, he failed to notice the glowing red, and still hot, embers of our picnic fire and trod directly into its centre. His foot was badly burned and he was in considerable pain. Fortunately, amongst our party was Ivor Parrish who owned the dispensing chemist business in Malacca; he was able to advise on first aid before we drove back hurriedly to the town to obtain more adequate emollients.

During these years, Mother had been in charge of my education, teaching me to read and to write, following a copybook, and the rudiments of simple arithmetic. Once a knowledge of reading had been obtained, a subject I mastered quickly, then there followed simple History lessons, the books for English History being two Victorian manuals *Little Arthur's England* and Charles Dickens's *Child's History of England*. There was also a globe showing the political divisions of the world, the countries of the Empire (of course) being pink, and Mandates white with a pink border. It covered an impressive amount of the surface. I studied also Egyptian and Mesopotamian History – possibly because of their connections with Bible Studies?

Some time after my sixth birthday it was felt that I needed some more formal education and I was sent to the Convent School in Malacca. This was not a success. The great majority of pupils were Eurasian – and I had absorbed the general prejudice against those of a mixed blood. Also, the nuns who taught were not English and the combination of their being female, French and Roman Catholic (Charles Dickens had dwelt long on the wickedness of 'Bloody Queen Mary', the burning by her of Protestants at Smithfield and of the need for all right-thinking English boys to be wary of Popish practices) was too much for me. I was a very chauvinistic child.

All this came to a head when I was taught French: a language for which I could see no use since surely all people of intelligence spoke English. Only two or three formed our particular class (one of them being the very blonde daughter of the Danish Consul – her long, flaxen plaits and blue eyes seemed to me the epitome of beauty) and, no doubt, a wish to 'show off' encouraged me to behave badly. What form this misbehaviour took, I cannot recall. What I do remember is being told that I had made one of the nuns cry because of my rudeness and being forced to apologise, which I did with gritted teeth and with tears in my eyes, tears not at all of remorse but only of injured pride.

On Bukit Sebukor, also, I was beginning to run rather wild. Taunted by some small Malay children, I pursued them into their own quarters and, to horrified screams, through the women's quarters, which, since Malays were Muslim, were very strictly forbidden. A complaint was made to my parents who, as I have mentioned earlier, were always much concerned that there should never be any racial incident.

At the same time Japan's aggressive aims in Manchuria and North China were becoming increasingly more overt. The Marco Polo Bridge 'incident' of 7 July 1937 and the subsequent capture by the Japanese of Beijing – events that were the first steps in Japan's objective to conquer and occupy all China – may have been little noticed in Europe where attention was focused on the Civil War in Spain, on the Italian aggression against Ethiopia and on the steps Hitler was taking to incorporate Austria into his Third Reich. In the Far East, though, and particularly in Malaya with its large and influential Chinese population, the warning signals were noted with apprehension.

This combination of events probably influenced my parents into deciding that I should be sent back to England to prep school. Accordingly, shortly after my seventh birthday, it was decided that Mother, Geoffrey and I should sail for England. Of my own feelings on this I have no recollection; I was not of an age to understand – Malaya, Malacca, Bukit Sebukor, these were my home. Our parents had given Geoffrey and me a happy home, one where Duty had pre-eminence over Will but where there was always love and the ordered routine of daily life so essential to a child's need for security. It was, too, a very Christian upbringing, where Church attendance and worship was the norm rather than the exception, whether under the form of attendance at Christ Church on Sundays (where Daddy often took the service in the absence of a Colonial Chaplain) or of Mother hearing our childish prayers each night. God, our Family and the Empire made up our own personal Trinity; no children could have been given a sounder foundation.[11]

Chapter 2
England, prep school and the war, 1937–40

In August 1937 my mother, Geoff and I went aboard the little steamer that would take us down to Singapore and then to England. Our *Amah* came to see us off giving us each parting presents of a gold tiepin and cufflinks (this must have represented a comparatively large outlay given the low level of wages): I, although fond of her who had always looked after us with devoted care, was embarrassed as small boys are by displays of tears and emotion and stayed in my cabin refusing to go on deck for the last farewells.

Another farewell present had come to me from my childhood sweetheart, Margaret Willan, a book called *A Thane of Wessex*, a story of covetous duplicity, of young romance and of love, of an England invaded by the terrifying Danes, at first victorious but ultimately defeated. This book I still possess. The picture of Anglo-Saxon virtues has remained with me.

At Singapore we transferred to the *Diomede*, a Blue Funnel Line cargo ship of about 6,000 tons and carrying only 12 passengers, for the month-long passage back to England. We were the only youngsters aboard and, accordingly, were made much of; on one occasion (Geoffrey's birthday?) we were allowed on to the bridge where for a brief moment we held the steering wheel (with the regular helmsman ready to take over immediately in case of any difficulties); even so, the ship's wake became decidedly wobbly!

At Aden we coaled and there was strong advice to keep our cabin portholes securely fastened and cabin doors locked to prevent any theft by the Arabs who hefted the coal sacks on to the ship. However, coaling was a filthy business and the dust would get in everywhere, even if these precautions might have stopped casual pilfering.[1]

There was a whale in the Red Sea, keeping station in our ship's shade and seeming to be of equal length. Probably it was there, too, that a canvas swimming pool was erected on the foredeck, where we could cool down from the baking heat. One young woman let me read one of the first Penguin books (a novel about the massacre of Glencoe by Elizabeth Bowen, although I think mother thought it a bit 'adult' for a 7-year-old). It may have been this same young woman (the ship's passenger-list shows a young couple, accompanied by a Chinese *amah*) who sat with me in a deckchair, conjuring magic pictures from the cloud shapes in the sky above.

At Port Said we visited Simon Artz's famous emporium and, aboard ship, were mystified by an Egyptian *gully-gully* man who conjured live chicks out of one's ear and performed other marvels of mystification. On sailing, no doubt we performed the ceremony of throwing our topis in the ship's wake to signify our leaving the East. I am sure, though, that when doing so I did not realise that it was meant to be for the last time and that the school plans for my brother and me could have resulted in this being a last farewell.

In England, we three stayed with my mother's family in their Victorian house just off Wandsworth Common and for a month or two I attended a private day school in Nightingale Lane. I was not happy there. I found England an alien place, nor was it easy to determine an academic level appropriate to me. My reading skills were advanced, as was my knowledge in such fields as History where I had read widely. But the other boys did not have the same outlook as I. Nor was I used to being taught in this way. I can remember being given dictation at far too fast a speed for me so that I ended by writing only the initial letters of each word in the hope that I would remember enough afterwards to reconstruct the entire piece – which, of course, I could not! Mother, seeing how upset I was that evening spoke to the teacher and I rather think that I was moved down a class to one more appropriate to my age.

It is difficult nowadays to imagine how quiet the streets were in London suburbs such as Wandsworth. There were, I think, two garages for cars at the top of the street but cars themselves were hardly ever seen. House owners kept themselves very much to themselves; they might greet each other formally if they met in the street but there was no easy social intercourse. There was another boy who lived in the street of about our age but the idea that we might ask each other informally to play in our respective homes was not welcome – indeed, I think my grandmother regarded our manners and general behaviour as dangerously free and easy, it just showed the dangers of living abroad. My grandmother, of course, was thoroughly Victorian. My grandfather, recently retired, was more relaxed and his main hobby was playing bowls at the local club on the Common, a game that he played with some skill.

At a street corner at 11 a.m. on the 11 November there was a sudden hush as all traffic stopped. Pedestrians, too, stood at attention, as the country remembered the Great War and its dead. The mutilated living were still to be seen, begging outside Underground stations.

January 1938 marked the next stage of my education; I began boarding at Hollingbury Court Preparatory School, situated on what was then almost open downland looking out to the sea (now a built-up suburb of Brighton). Like most such schools it was privately owned. The headmaster and his wife would fawn on parents and be nice to their children while the former were present: the attitude could change abruptly when they left. The headmaster, again as was usual, taught, while his niece, 'Maidie'[2] (aged perhaps 18 and loved by the boys) was one of the three assistant teachers. Another of these was an ex-army officer, shell-shocked in the Great War, who was teased unmercifully.

To enter a school other than at the beginning of an academic year always causes problems; boys, new, lost and lonely themselves only a few months before have made friends, learnt the customs of the place, the quirks and habits of the teachers, and unite suspiciously against the stranger. In my case I was doubly strange, a boy from overseas (although there was another boy at the school from Malaya, he was some years older than I and so was in a different world!). As a result I felt very isolated and while in time I made my friends amongst the 35 boys I was never particularly happy there; the headmaster had favourites of whom I was never one. On the other hand, there was no actual ill treatment, the food was adequate and the teaching sound, if conventional.

The clothing list was long and complex: Marlborough suits with stiff collars (front and back neck studs which delayed still further the business of dressing) and long trousers for Sundays,[3] a best suit of grey corduroy (with short trousers), shorts and a blazer for daily wear, whites for cricket in the summer, 'house shoes' for indoor wear (and woe betide any boy found indoors with outdoor shoes or out of doors in his house shoes, although boys being boys this was a fairly constant occurrence). On the instep of each shoe the owner's number was marked in nails. All clothes, of course, were labelled with Cash's nametapes.

Good manners were stressed, continually. At mealtimes we had to queue to go into the dining room, showing our hands to which ever of the staff was on duty so that they could be seen to be clean. Any recalcitrant ink-stain was a sufficient bar to entry; the boy would be sent back to wash his hands once more and on his return would have to show them to the headmaster. The matron, though, was kind to us small boys; she used to read the *Just So Stories* for a few minutes before we were put to bed. Even so, the new boys' pillows were usually wet with tears.

One Sunday early in my second term I was changing in my dormitory after morning chapel and feeling particularly low – it was my eighth birthday and I was missing my parents especially badly – when I was told to go down to the headmaster's sitting room. I was terrified, wondering what I had done wrong, but when I went in I saw my father standing on the other side of the room. With a strangled cry of 'Daddy' I rushed across the room and threw myself into his arms; I did not even know he was back in England! Then the headmaster's wife, all smiles, told me to go up to change again into my best suit as I was being taken out to lunch.

My parents came down several more times that term – I remember lying in the sun on my school rug one day while my father and the headmaster made regular trips indoors to find out from the wireless how Len Hutton was amassing his record-breaking score. As I wrote above, the headmaster and his wife were always as nice as pie on these occasions; they depended on parents' good will in subscribing to buy extras such as a cine-projector (*with sound*!) to provide entertainment in the winter terms!

The school, unusually at that time, had a swimming pool: open air, of course, and small, but still a proper pool. In summer the boys could swim there daily and at swimming – because the years spent in Malaya had given me opportunities English-bred boys did not have – I thought that I should be able to excel[4] (in any game which needed dexterity or the co-ordination of hand and eye I was to be sub-average all my life, unlike Geoffrey who possessed a natural grace and gift for these games). But, my hopes were to be dashed. At the school swimming sports I came first in everything all right, but, because I had not stayed in my lane of water (as marked by lines on the bottom of the pool), in each event I was disqualified!

On another occasion, either I dived too deep or the water in the pool was too shallow. Either way, I cracked my scalp on the bottom and emerged with blood running down my forehead. The small scar and a distinct ridge on the bone can still be seen and felt, but in those days the possibility of consequent brain damage would never have been considered.

There was a Roman camp just outside the school gates and in the winter terms there was a daily 'run' around it, following its earthen bank. On misty days one could imagine a Roman soldier materialising out of any thick patch.

The holidays that summer we spent as a family together in lodgings in Falmouth, visiting the castles of Pendennis and St Mawes, which guard the entry to the harbour, St Anthony's in Roseland, the Lizard and many of the other local sites. One day we visited Mousehole Cove where Margaret Willan and her parents, also home on leave, were taking a holiday, although I was shy at this re-encounter after a separation of more than a year. On another day, in company with my father's brother Jim and my cousin Winnie (at 15 years of age almost a grown-up in my eyes) we took a pleasure cruise up the Fal to Truro and saw the rusting ships lying idle at anchor, a visible symbol of the slump of the early 1930s, which was still casting its shadow.

In September the holidays were over. We two boys went back to school (Geoffrey aged just 6, starting as the youngest boy in the school and, for a time, as such being made much of by the headmaster and his wife) while our father returned alone to Malaya. Mother remained with us, to see that Geoff settled down happily (she was certainly aware that I had found this difficult), but presumably with the intention of joining him early in 1939.

As I have made clear, I was never happy at Hollingbury (on one occasion a year later the headmaster's wife stormed at me for making my mother worry with my 'unnecessary' complaints), nor was I ever popular with the staff. But I must emphasise that it was not a *bad* school, probably a lot better than average; and it had some very good points. The school library, for example, although quite small was well stocked. I had been an early reader and there were in practice no restrictions on what I could take out. The 'Brigadier Gerard' books of Conan Doyle were an early favourite, followed by his other historical novels, *The White Company*, *Micah Clarke* and *The Refugees*. There was an adventure story about the Great Pacific War between Chile and the Peru/Bolivian Alliance and one, which I did not completely understand, about an uprising of serfs in Russia. This must have been set in Alexander II's period and told of desolate steppes, a beautiful dark-haired, ivory-skinned countess, the threat of a civilised order being overthrown by savage, barbaric force. At night I would smuggle a book up to my dormitory and, in the summer, as my bed was by a window and I could twitch aside the curtain, would read in the evening light ('lights-out' was 8 p.m.).

It was extraordinary how much information could be obtained even from such run-of-the-mill stories. One, centred on airships, had the hero flying over Balkan League lines during the siege of Adrianople in 1912 – for a long time this represented all I knew about this Balkan War. A naval story about the Great War taught me about the sinking of the armoured cruisers, *Cressy*, *Agincourt* and *Hogue*; another described the German invasion of Belgium, the defence of the forts of Liege and the burning of Leuven. The 'Cadet Alan Carr' series by Percy F. Westerman featured a Merchant Navy Cadet in his voyages around the world and from them I learned of the Yokohama earthquake of 1923, the New Zealand floods and earthquakes of the same period, of how China was modernising itself and 'within a few years' would be a serious rival of Japan.

G. H. Henty was another favourite author whom I continued to reread until my early teens. Masters who regarded them as an acceptable ancillary to History lessons always approved of his books with their plans of past battles and their very Victorian expositions of the past. Although their strong emphasis was that English was best (Scots and Welsh being a bit inferior), they were not wholly bigoted; pretty girls, if aristocratic, could be assimilated into the English race, even if Catholic and French or Spanish, provided that they saw the light and in the end married the brave, free, honest Englishman who had saved them from some terrible fate such as being savaged by a dog (in Haiti), run away with by a wild horse (England), pursued by wolves (Russia), bitten by a cobra (India) or murdered by French peasants (anytime in the thirteenth, fifteenth and eighteenth centuries). They would, naturally, then bring with them a substantial dowry to make up for their non-Englishness!

But my two favourite books were my own. Reading *Bevis* by Richard Jefferies, given to me by my father's mother (of whom I have no conscious memory as she died in 1931) was at first more a duty than the pleasure it became later. These were much better than those rather sissy 'Swallows and Amazons'. Then there was *Java Ho* by Fabricius, and its tale of (fictional) Peter Hajo's voyage with (real) Captain Bontekoe on the *Nieuw Hoorn* to Batavia in 1621 – a book now, sadly, out of print in English, but which can still be rejoiced over in the British Library Reading Room.[5]

At this time my father was in Malaya by himself. We exchanged letters every week, but in those days when the normal method of carriage was by sea, a letter would take a month to reach its destination and another before a reply to it could be received; letter-writing – which all boarding-school children find tedious – became even more stilted as a consequence. Daddy tried, nevertheless, to make his letters as lively as possible, although I have since learned that he himself at that time was deeply worried about his own future.

Normally, by this time, six months after the ending of his leave, mother would have been making preparations to join my father in

Malaya. However, I suppose that the worsening international situation persuaded my mother to stay on in England longer than must have been planned and the three of us spent part of the summer holiday of 1939 at Saundersfoot in South Wales. It was there on the morning of Sunday 3 September that we heard on the wireless Chamberlain's announcement that Britain was at war with Germany.

At first, the coming of war had no effect on us at all. We read of the sinking of the *Athenia* (which did not surprise me; had not I read many boys' books about German 'frightfulness' in the Great War and of the killing of simple fishermen?). We had to carry gas masks at all times, which had been issued earlier in the year but, because our school was on the outskirts of the supposedly 'safe' town of Brighton, the evacuation of children from London passed us by.

Newspapers, as they had done during the Great War, published maps of Western Europe so that tiny flags could be stuck in to show changes in the front line. But after the defeat of Poland, there were no changes to be made. Everyone knew the Maginot Line was impregnable – that Christmas the famous toy-shop Hamleys had an enormous display model showing the deep tunnels and shelters that would protect the soldiers manning it from shellfire, the underground railways to transport supplies and ammunition, the cunningly sited machine gun posts and gun cupolas, the gallant French *poilus* in their blue-grey uniforms and distinctive helmets.

Although the sinking of *The Royal Oak* at Scapa Flow was a shock there was the destruction of the pocket battleship *Graf Spee* to exult over and the thrill of patriotic joy evoked by hearing of the release of prisoners on the *Altmark* with the words, 'The Navy's here . . .'.[6] Accordingly, since England (and we two boys) seemed secure, in March 1940 mother arranged to return to Malaya to rejoin my father – their separation had been unduly prolonged.

Before she left England, though, I explained my bad marks at some subjects by saying that I could not see the writing on the blackboard. My mother had my eyes tested, short sight was diagnosed and thereafter I had to wear glasses (which were constantly getting broken in the day-to-day scuffles that are an inseparable part of a small boy's communal life). My hope of getting into Dartmouth and the Navy was ended.

Soon after that I suffered a very severe attack of German measles, so bad, in fact, that my mother was summoned by the school down from London and stayed for a night at Brighton until the crisis was passed. However, thereafter I made a rapid and full recovery and she was able to stick to her plans, travelling overland through France to catch a steamer from Marseilles.

The Easter school holiday (it is always quite a short one), therefore, was passed with both our parents out of England. In part we spent it at the school – there were two or three other boys similarly placed and we were allowed considerable freedom – part staying with my mother's family at Wandsworth Common where our two aunts took it in turns to take us out (as in many years ahead they were to do again for my children and also for Geoff's).

While in Brighton we were taken to see a film *The Real Glory* set in the period of the early American occupation of the Philippines; its theme that the representatives of the civilised occupying power, in this case Americans, must be prepared to suffer treachery, mutilation and death before winning their glorious reward (on the way, incidentally, the hero won his girl as well). There is more than a hint here, I fancy, of Rudyard Kipling and of his much-misunderstood poem 'The White Man's Burden'. In London, an aunt took us to see another film, *Drums along the Mohawk*, with Red Indians attacking (with the support of some nefarious British redcoat) a heroic American colonial village, scalping maidens, etc. It was thrilling enough, but my understanding of the American Colonies and of their lamentable Rebellion was sketchy. Nor could I relate the history depicted here to the situation shown in *The Last of the Mohicans* where it is a British Army which, surrounded and outnumbered, surrenders Fort William Henry in good faith and, retreating peacefully through the North American forests, is treacherously set upon by the Indians and almost all killed. All three films, though, helped to set the cast of my mind.

Shortly after, the 'phoney war' ended.

Germany invaded Denmark and Norway, the *Glorious* was sunk, *Warspite* steamed into Narvik Fiord and wreaked havoc on the German destroyer force. But then the Netherlands, Belgium and France were invaded; there were reports of paratroops descending from the sky dressed as nuns and Fort Eben Emael[7] fell to a *coup de main*. Naturally, as a 10-year-old, the implications were lost on me. There were articles about General Weygand – a saviour from the East – who might retrieve the situation in France, radio bulletins about a new British plane, the Boulton-Paul Defiant, which had a rear turret to surprise German fighters attacking from the rear.

In mid-June, Mr Churchill – now prime minister – broadcast to the nation, advising it of the 'terrible misfortune' that 'the gallant French people' had fallen and that Britain had now become the 'sole champion in arms'. News of the proposal for an Anglo-French

Union must also have become common knowledge at this time; I remember being astounded that anyone could possibly refuse the privilege of being joined to Britain!

Very shortly after these momentous events, we were told that our prep school was to be evacuated to Wiltshire, and billeted on Dauntsey's School, Devizes, a school at which our headmaster had once taught and whereto many ex-Hollingburians subsequently went.

Geoffrey and I were to be at Dauntsey's for only a few days. I can remember, rather dimly, a big dormitory where most of us were installed and I must have sent at least one letter telling my grandparents of our new address, since the latter has stuck with me to this day. Unbeknownst to us, alarmed at the sequence of disasters, my father had put in train arrangements for Geoff and me to be evacuated to Malaya. The first that we knew of this was being told by the headmaster that we were to go up to London with all our clothes and possessions. A young officer, the fiancé of Maidie, the headmaster's niece, was returning to his regiment and escorted us on the Great Western Railway express.[8] There my grandfather met us and, probably the next day, we were taken to Dunlop's head office in St James's Square.

A young planter, aged 24, named Rennie, who worked on one of Dunlop's rubber estates was due to go back to Malaya on leave and we were introduced to him by our grandfather. He was to look after us on the journey out to Malaya. Whether he had any choice, I cannot say, but it was quite a responsibility and not one that would have enchanted many bachelors. But it was wartime, Hollingbury had taught us good manners and no doubt we were well turned-out by our grandmother.

We had to obtain passports – we had previously travelled on mother's. The new passports are dated 17 July 1940, and carry a splendidly worded introduction, 'I, Frederick Edward Lindley, Viscount Halifax, Baron Irwin, etc., His Majesty's Secretary of State for Foreign Affairs . . . Request and Require in the name of His Majesty all those whom it may concern to allow the bearer to pass freely without let or hindrance and to afford him or her every assistance and protection of which he or she may stand in need' (compare that with the almost obsequious wording of the present document!).

I have no other memory of the next few days. My grandmother must have bought us white shirts, socks and shorts for we certainly had these on the voyage, but where we got these, and all the other details that must have taken so much trouble to arrange, I cannot recall at all. Somehow, though, they must have been achieved as by 21 July my grandfather took us north to Liverpool, found Mr Rennie and handed us over,

> Item: Two small boys in good health,
> Clean and Tidily dressed, will say
> 'Please' and 'Thank you' without the need for prompting
> Able to wash, feed and dress themselves
> And accept the world's complexities with wide-eyed tranquillity.

I am sure we said, 'Goodbye, Grandpa. Thank you.'

Then through 'Emigration'; into the organised apparent chaos of a great passenger liner about to sail, companionways full of people with baggage, looking for their cabins, looking for their cabin steward, looking for the bathrooms, looking for the public rooms, asking when dinner or tea would be served. One 10-year-old girl confided to her mother that she thought Geoff and I were '. . . . Lords or something, so beautiful were their manners'. They did not last, of course.

Then, just after midnight on 22 July, the *Viceroy* slipped her moorings and crept silently out to sea.

Chapter 3

The *Viceroy of India* to Malaya, 1940

Having handed us over to Mr Rennie, Grandpa returned to London, while Mr Rennie and we two boys now had a rather better opportunity to assess each other: we unpacked our cabin bags, and began to find our way round the great ship. The *Viceroy of India*, a 19,645-ton P&O liner, had been built in 1929 and had then been regarded as, a 'bench-mark ship'. She had proved 'immensely popular' from her first introduction into service due to her 'new levels of opulence and comfort',[1] speed and quietness. This opulence was greatest, naturally, in the 'First-Class' areas, which were out of bounds to second-class passengers, but these also were much more spacious than was customary. Certainly, the *Viceroy* dwarfed the Blue Funnel steamers by which we had previously travelled – three times the tonnage of *Diomede* and almost twice that of *Sarpedon*.

The next morning we awoke to find ourselves at sea and when, after breakfast, we, with other boys we had met at the breakfast table,[2] went out on deck, it was to find ourselves already far out in the Atlantic. There were tossing seas, seagulls swooping overhead and, in company with us, three other passenger ships (the names of which I have been unable to discover).

From time to time our escorts would appear; tiny little ships they seemed in comparison to our great liner, always in a tearing hurry, flashing signals or breaking flags. They never came close enough to enable me to identify them at the time but the Naval Staff (Historical Section) have since told me that HMS's *Vanquisher* and *Westcott* left Liverpool on the same day so I presume that they were our two escorts. Both were sunk later in the war; their logs have not survived.

Aboard the *Viceroy* were 321 adult passengers and 57 children below the age of 12 years, some like us travelling in the custody of a more or less reluctant temporary guardian, some families, wives with children going out to join their husbands, single Indian Civil Service (ICS) or Malayan Civil Service (MCS) men, planters or other 'civilians' going back to what were regarded as essential jobs. There were also a largish number of young RN sailors being sent out to bases overseas – I recall a sing-song on one of the main staircases with sailors and us children all sitting matily together and singing such songs as 'The Quartermaster's Stores', where 'butter, butter, was running down the gutter'; verses which we learned very rapidly and joined in with gusto. We were clearly not meant to be 'fraternising' though, and Mr Rennie, who had been looking for us, was horrified to find us in such company; we were forbidden to mix again.

Although my brother and I may have made a fairly good first impression on him – as I wrote in the last chapter our prep school had so hammered home good behaviour and correct speech that young Anne Deveson had commented on it to her mother – this veneer did not last long. When we went ashore at Gibraltar our temporary guardian was most upset when we climbed on some old cannon and got our spotless whites filthy. He insisted that we return immediately to the ship, as he was not going to be seen in the streets with a couple of urchins!

Before this landfall the *Viceroy* must have sailed far out west into the Atlantic to avoid possible U-boat attack – she could have easily covered the direct distance between Liverpool and Gibraltar in three days. Then, once out of the most hazardous waters, we left the other ships and steered south and east, back towards the Mediterranean. We reached Gibraltar, guarding the entry to this Middle Sea, on the morning of 27 July.

Three months later, after the voyage had been completed, but when it was still fresh in my memory, I wrote as follows:

During
The Voyage
*To Maylaya (*sic*)*

<u>*Gibralter*</u> *(*sic*)*
On the morning of the 26th of July, 1940 we sighted Gibralter. I had never seen Gibralter before, and it looked very impressive. On one side was the coast of Africa, on the other was the Rock. In Gibralter was a scuttled Italian steamer. Also there were A. A. guns, six inch pompoms and a multitude of warships. There were the Hood, the Warspite, a battleship of the Royal Sovereign Class, the Emerald of the E class cruisers, and about twenty destroyers.

When we went ashore it seemed as if at least 7/8ths of the population were soldiers, sailors and airmen. While we were there the Ark Royal (which has been sunk at least seven times) came in. We had a lot of sailors and F.A.A. men on our boat and we cheered like mad. We left Gibralter that night.

Although I knew that I could not now enter the Navy through Dartmouth my intense interest remained. My Bible was a copy of *All the World's Fighting Fleets* by Lt. Commander Talbot-Booth (a cheaper 'Jane's'), its ship photographs, silhouettes and detailed descriptions studied with the same devotion that Sir Walter Elliot in *Persuasion* gives the Baronetage. Most of the ships mentioned above, therefore, are fairly correctly identified. *Hood* – the largest warship in the world at that time and Britain's pride – was there, *Warspite* was not but *Valiant* of the same class (the 'Queen Elizabeth') was. *Resolution* was the Royal Sovereign class battleship mentioned, the anti-aircraft cruiser was *Enterprise* not *Emerald* which was a sister ship. At that time, it must be remembered, Gibraltar had a position of extreme importance – it had been the base from which operations had been undertaken to cripple the French fleet at Oran and Mers-el-Kebir earlier that month – which must account, in part, for the very large number of ships then in harbour.

About 80 of the servicemen aboard left the *Viceroy* here and, this done, we sailed from Gibraltar that same night. Sailing south, we next called at St Vincent in the Cape Verde Island for refuelling. We were not allowed ashore, possibly on security grounds, so my only memory is of what we could see from the ship's rail: a flat, sandy, landscape shimmering in the fierce sunlight. The 'greenness' promised by the name was not at all apparent!

Pre-war standards were still adhered to aboard ship – for example, quiet was required for an hour after lunch (presumably so as to allow pink gins and curry lunches to be slept off!). This naturally caused problems with so many young children on board and a passenger decided therefore that it would be a good thing to organise a Cubs troop to keep us young boys out of mischief. At first, I, Ewan Tyler, a boy with whom I had made friends (his father worked in Borneo as a geologist) and my brother treated the whole thing with derision and turned up to jeer from concealment rather than to watch. We rapidly became aware, however, that it was we who were being left out, so we too joined and were soon shouting 'A-a-kela' with the rest of our peers. We learned some knots, as well, which appealed as a useful sort of thing to know, although after the voyage I forgot everything except a reef knot.

At some stage we were told to write letters to our grandparents back in England for posting at Cape Town. I wrote, also, to a friend at Hollingbury, the school we had left so hurriedly three weeks before. I asked about the results in the school athletic sports, about how our 'House' had done. I never received a reply – I doubt if I had remembered to give my friend my Malacca address.

In the afternoon of 11 August there was great excitement as the ship's speed increased noticeably. News spread rapidly that we were steaming to the aid of another ship whose SOS we had received. Then, two other ships came into sight, one a warship (I am told that this was probably *HMS Cumberland*, a County Class cruiser similar to *Cornwall*, the ship whose visit to Malacca before the war had sparked my interest in the Navy).[3] The other was a liner, without way, rolling gently in the long slow swell. As she rolled we could see a great hole in her side, in my memory as big as two London buses. Bobbing around in the sea (fortunately calm), were a number of white lifeboats, full of people, the boats looking very small and vulnerable in the wide expanse of sea.

At first, we youngsters aboard the *Viceroy* thought that the damage must have been caused by enemy action, a torpedo from a submarine, but we soon learned that it was more mundane: a collision the previous night with another ship. The lifeboats drew alongside; the passengers, white-faced from seasickness, shock and cold (it was mid-winter in the South Atlantic, although the day was fine) but relieved, climbed aboard. There were 279 of them, a large number of extra bodies to accommodate and there were few vacant berths. 'Doubling-up' was necessary and Geoff and I did so, freeing one bunk in our cabin for a boy from the damaged ship (the White Star liner *Ceramic* had sailed from Liverpool on about the same date as us). Three years later, returning to England, I was to share a cabin with a boy who had been on the *Ceramic* at the time; indeed, it might even have been he for whom we made space at the time, although Geoff's opinion is to the contrary.

The rescue completed, we resumed our voyage, arriving at Cape Town in the morning of 13 August. The original purpose of the call would have been to refuel and take on supplies of water and food, but now we had also to disembark the rescued passengers. Accordingly, there was time enough to allow ashore those who wanted to stretch their legs, an opportunity that was very welcome after nearly three weeks at sea.

Mr Rennie, presumably fearing that there could be a repetition of the Gibraltar incident, played safe and took us to the cinema. My recollection is that the feature film was called *The Silver Fleet* about a Dutch submarine captain foiling the Germans' intention to steal the Netherlands's bullion reserves by transporting these in his submarine to England (the analogy is with the famous Dutch sailor of the seventeenth century, Piet Hein, who captured the Plate fleet on its yearly voyage from the Indies and thus crippled Spain's last efforts to reconquer the Netherlands). If this memory is accurate – and certainly such a film exists – then it must have been one of the quickest ever to be made since Holland had been conquered only four months before.

At some stage in the voyage there was a ship's Ball. I had been asked by Anne Deveson,[4] who knew that I had had dancing lessons at my prep school, to be her partner, but I knew also that I danced very badly, having very little sense of rhythm and being much given to standing on my partner's toes. It was bad enough to have to do this in public with another boy's mother, but with a girl! Well . . . I grew steadily more and more terrified at making a fool of myself, as first the day, and then the hour of the Ball approached. Eventually I 'funked' it, hiding behind some deckchairs on the darkened promenade deck so that the girl would not find me and force me to join her. Ungallantly I did not think of her own feelings at being so unceremoniously let down; even when I heard her and a friend (Phillipa) talking only a few feet away while looking for me.

Even with such excitement, however, the voyage was beginning to pall. The food was becoming monotonous – I invented a mixture of rice, peas and lots of tomato ketchup which for a time became 'the dish' for all children to eat, although hardly haute cuisine! Each child had only a limited number of books and toys as cabin space was limited (although I had my favourites – *Bevis* and *Wood Magic* by Richard Jefferies, and *Java Ho* by Fabricius), and swapping or borrowing was the norm. I remember a 'Chums' Annual, a publication I have never since heard of. We must have had some toy lead soldiers as well, since I remember Ewan Tyler being very scornful of cavalry which he asserted were useless, tanks being the thing, while I was romantically attached to these splendidly caparisoned horsemen.

We tried making papier-mâché but not very successfully – there was a shortage of paper and also grown-ups objected to our leaving paper to soak for hours in handbasins! Very unreasonable, we felt – washing could always wait. Finally, Ewan Tyler – my hero – and I decided, or more likely had it suggested to us, that we should organise a school to teach the young ones. Discipline was strictly kept and, while I do not suppose anyone learnt anything very much, at least it kept us out of mischief.

We arrived at Mombasa at about midday on 21 August and I later wrote:

> *Mombasa*
> <u>*25th of August 1940*</u> (sic)
> *As we approached Mombasa we saw an aeroplane take off. As it approached we saw it was a German Junkers in British colours. After a time we found it had been bought before the*

war. We went down to lunch, I think I was about the only one who had a decent lunch, all the others were looking out of the portholes and running about. When we went ashore we went for a tour of Mombasa. We saw an old castle and batteries for guns old and new. We left Mombasa that evening.

This entry reflects either a lack of sensibility to the vividness of the green foliage and the excitement of seeing land sliding past – almost within touching distance it seemed (after weeks at sea when there had been nothing to look at except sky and ocean) or a wish to pretend to be 'grown-up' and untouched by childish emotions! The castle referred to was Fort Jesus, originally built by the Portuguese to be the Western bastion of their East Indian Empire. The Arabs, who had previously dominated the Indian Ocean, besieged it on at least one occasion, and were to do so again in the nineteenth century, but while its thick walls were a security against human enemies, they were valueless against mosquitoes; fever was to be the deadliest foe of the European in Africa.

We were not allowed ashore at Bombay (which we reached on 29 August) because of a cholera epidemic, so, after disembarking 80 India-bound passengers and 50 servicemen, we continued south to Ceylon. As we approached we saw fishermen using out-rigger canoes, a device that allowed these small craft to operate far out in the Indian Ocean.

Colombo, the capital of colonial Ceylon (now Sri Lanka) was reached on 1 September.

At Columbo we saw a converted auxiliary cruiser with a seaplane and four 6 inch guns. We went ashore, and went to Mount Lavinia. On the promenade we saw eight 9.2″ guns. They were terrific. There were AA. Guns as well. At Mount Lavinia we had a lovely time. We all baked when we got back to the ship. As we left we saw the Hindustan.[5]

Mount Lavinia, just outside Colombo town, was a noted tourist centre with a famous hotel by the sea. There we swam, sunbathed and had an enormous, and gorgeous, curry lunch at the hotel, served by turbaned waiters on great silver trays loaded with *sambols*.[6] There was an aquarium at Mount Lavinia as well but I do not recall visiting it. As for the other remarks in the essay quoted above, I do not know how I determined on the calibre of the guns – 9.2″ guns had certainly been produced at one stage before the First World War but were already obsolete then.

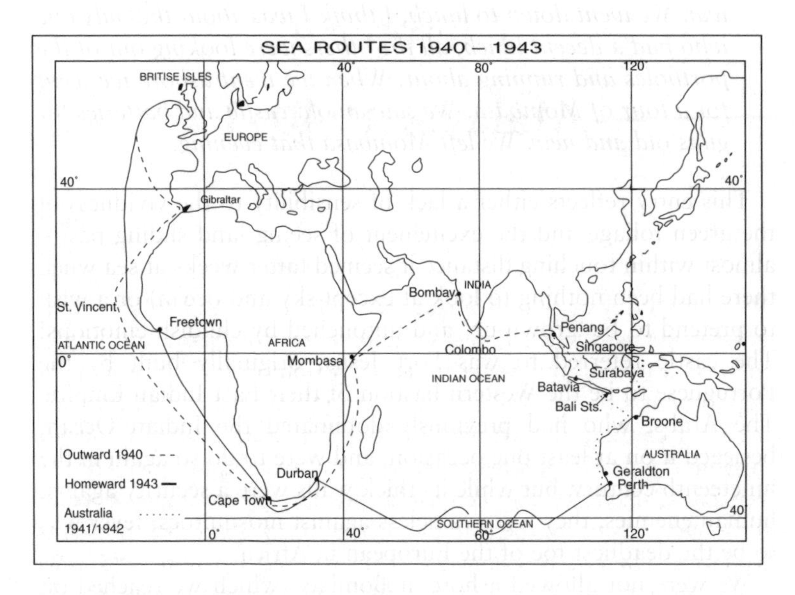

Map 1 Voyages, 1940–3.

Note: Routes shown are indicative only; in wartime the hope of avoiding submarines or aircraft could cause wide divergencies.

Source: By permission of G. Barnes

During the voyage across the Bay of Bengal Geoff fell quite seriously ill, possibly from sunstroke. He had a high fever and was moved to a separate cabin where the mother of one of our friends nursed him. I remember reading to him as he was too sick and his head ached too much to read for himself. He was only just 8.

The voyage that all on board were beginning to feel tediously protracted was drawing to an end. The island of Penang at the northern entrance to the Malacca Strait was our next port of call but this, reached on 5 September, was simply to disembark some 200 passengers; those remaining were not allowed ashore. The ship's companionways, previously thronged with passengers, now seemed deserted in contrast. All minds were concentrated on packing, on saying farewells. We bought presents at the ship's shop, a present for our long-suffering temporary guardian (whose enjoyment of the voyage can hardly have been added to by being responsible for two young brats) and for each of our parents. Then Singapore (7 September), about seven weeks after we had left England, the joy of being again in Malaya and, even more intense, of being reunited with our parents.

Chapter 4
Malaya, 1940–1

We spent a day or two in Singapore – where toy lead soldiers were bought for us, French Foreign Legionnaires for Geoff and French infantry for me, and some books at Robinsons. This was a big department store as well stocked as anything in London (perhaps even better than in wartime London) that used also to publish a large and glossy Christmas catalogue full of temptations. Then, it was back, up the Malay Peninsula (possibly by train as we would have had with us on the ship our school trunks and tuck boxes) to Malacca. There, we resumed the life we had led until 1937. We occupied the same house; we had the same servants (except for the fact that we no longer had an *amah* as we were thought old enough to look after ourselves); there was the same well-ordered routine.

Because we were older, however, something had to be done about our schooling, at least in our parents' eyes (I am quite sure that neither Geoff nor I felt any pressing need for this). The Convent School, which I had gone to, rebelliously, three years before was not a real option, but there was no other remotely suitable local school.[1] Fortunately, there were some other British parents with children in the same position as we were. One of these, a Mrs Nankivell, whose husband was district engineer in the Public Works Department and who had trained as a teacher, was also the mother of two recently arrived daughters, of almost exactly the same age as Geoff and me. An arrangement was thus reached between our mother and Mrs Nankivell under which she would teach us in the mornings, along with her own two children and another boy, David Bearblock, whose father was a doctor at Malacca General Hospital.

Accordingly, each morning we would be driven with Daddy to Malacca, dropped off at Mrs Nankivell's house on Peringit Hill where we would do our lessons seated around her dining table – English, Geography (concentrating on Australia where it was planned we should go to school), History and Arithmetic. At lunchtime we would be collected to return with Daddy to Bukit Sebukor.

As far as Geoffrey and I were concerned, it was a very successful arrangement, although much less so for David – indeed, while I could remember his presence his very name had been long forgotten by me until it was recalled to me recently by Mrs Nankivell. In our group of five, David was the odd one out, rather left on the sidelines whilst I paired up with Valerie – who was cleverer but whom, as a girl, I somehow felt *ought* not to do better at her lessons than me, a boy – and Geoff with Janet. These two latter, both about 8, took the 'play-school' rather less seriously than did Valerie and I.[2]

I had the mildest of flirtations with Valerie (although I doubt if my 'tenderness' to her was at all reciprocated!). Not that our younger siblings would ever leave us together in peace, threatening to tell our respective mothers about us (which certainly filled me with embarrassment – love and romance at that age were 'soppy', of course, while sex was something so unknown that I probably didn't even know that the word existed). So it was all very, very innocent; I doubt if we even held hands, although this did not stop the feeling of self-consciousness. On one occasion, retreating, as we thought, to the security of a cupboard under the stairs, Geoff and Valerie's sister Janet poured rice and sugar on us through the cracks in the staircase boards, to their great mirth and our discomfiture.

I do not know how many European, i.e. 'white', children of the 7 to 12 age group were living in or around Malacca at that time, but perhaps a dozen or so would meet fairly regularly at the swimming club or at each other's homes. At birthday parties the giving of a present was, of course, normal and I remember vividly one occasion when Geoff and I went to a party without one. The invitation had not specified that it was a 'birthday' party and our parents, not wishing to incur unnecessary expense, had decided that there was no need. Our shame, when we found that we alone were not provided with this courteous acknowledgement, was very great; we sat alone, or felt alone which was as bad, on the edge of the party, imagining as children do that the others were all talking about our meanness. When our mother came to collect us I, feeling most humiliated, rushed to tell her; fortunately, she, swiftly understanding, then told the mother of the boy concerned that the present ordered from Singapore had not arrived – something that happened quite often and a story that was readily accepted. The next day presents which had actually been bought for *us two* for Christmas were solemnly handed over to the birthday boy as if they had just arrived: our 'face' had been saved!

As when I was younger, Sundays were normally spent at the swimming club at Tanjong Kling where tiffin (lunch) could be obtained, thus giving our servants some time off. The swimming club was sited about two miles off the far side of Malacca, perhaps four miles away from our bungalow at Bukit Sebukor so visits during the week were rare; use of the car was necessary and this was also Daddy's transport to the office.

Mother and Daddy bought us a dog, a mongrel puppy, which, rather unimaginatively, we named Spot. Spot had to be walked, which in turn meant being bathed – the *lallang* (long, coarse grass) was the home of ticks from the cattle that grazed on the golf course around the house. On these walks, care had to be taken since Spot would bark furiously at the great water buffaloes used by the Malays in the cultivation of the rice paddy fields – enormous beasts, whose grey hides were streaked with brown mud. They were placid enough normally but one still had to take care with them: which Spot did not understand! He was devoted to us two boys, though; on one occasion our family and another went on a picnic to a nearby lake, Ayer Kroh. The whole party went out in a sampan, leaving Spot on the shore. He went frantic, struggled furiously and barked pitifully. Eventually he escaped from his keeper, rushed into the water and swam out to us. He had never been swimming before and very nearly drowned before we could reach him and pull him into our boat. In return for being rescued he shook himself energetically, thoroughly wetting the ladies' dresses.

The life I describe sounds very peaceful, and so indeed it was. The war was a long way away, in Europe. In the Far East there was still peace (although one was aware of the continuing Japanese invasion of China). Even so, all adults knew that Britain was fighting for its life, every morning the wireless would be switched on so as to catch the latest news broadcast by the BBC. The Battle of Britain was being fought in September and the announcements of ever increasing numbers of German planes being shot down were greeted with pride as well as relief.

More sombrely, I can remember one evening when, seated downstairs around the burning anti-mosquito coil, we read in the *Straits Times* of the torpedoing and sinking of the *City of Benares* in the North Atlantic and of the death by drowning and from exposure of many of the children aboard. This must have brought home to our parents the good fortune that had been with Geoff and me aboard the *Viceroy*; we could all too easily have experienced the same terrifying fate of those drowned youngsters. (After this disaster, the British government ceased to authorise the evacuation of children

Figure 3 Fishing boat, Malacca.

from Britain; the likelihood of an invasion of the British Isles by the Germans had, in any event, much decreased).

Mrs Nankivell decided that the five of us would put on a 'do' to raise money for the Red Cross war effort. This consisted of our giving animated recitations of A. A. Milne's verses; I was the King and Valerie the Queen in 'The King's Breakfast', wearing a paper crown obtained from a cracker, while in another piece, I was 'Bad Sir Brian', my battleaxe being of plywood cut with a fretsaw. Mrs Nankivell wrote in 1990 that 'Janet did not like reciting "Have you been a good girl, Jane?" '

With this same fretwork set, I made a tower for Geoff's Foreign Legionnaires, modelled on what I could remember was depicted in the film version of *Beau Geste*. Rather more up to date was a model trench system that we constructed, using a mixture of red laterite earth and cement to imitate the mud of the Western Front, with barbed wire entanglements made by winding cotton thread around dressmaker's pins and puffs of cotton wool to represent the effect of an exploding shell.

Thus it was that the weeks slipped by; we knew that at the beginning of 1941 we would have to leave Malaya once again to go to prep school in Australia, a prospect that we contemplated with resignation but without enthusiasm. Before that, however, my father decided that we would all have a short holiday at Fraser's Hill, a hill station on the mountain spine of Malaya. Here there were wood fires and a cool refreshing air, English flowers, the inevitable golf course and private hotels to provide a welcome break from the steamy humidity of the plains below.

The holiday ended and Christmas celebrated (Daddy was a lay reader and, in the absence of a colonial chaplain, was in virtual charge of Christ Church while Mother played the organ – more from a sense of duty than from enjoyment), it was time to pack our trunks and tuck boxes again. In January 1941, this time accompanied by Mother, we set off for Australia and the next stage of our education.

Chapter 5
Australia, 1941

In mid-January 1941, my mother, Geoff and I sailed from Singapore to Fremantle, the port of Perth, Western Australia, *terra incognita* to us. Our ship was the *Gorgon*, one of Alfred Holt's[1] ships, her name *Gorgon* was derived from Greek mythology; she was small, almost flat-bottomed, built especially for the West Coast route where most ports had only a shallow draft. Even so, I can recall that at one of these the ship, berthed alongside a wooden pier that stuck out into the ocean, was left by the receding tide sitting on the brown mud bottom. *Gorgon*, with her sister ships *Charon* and *Centaur*, represented the main – indeed perhaps almost the only – link between these ports and between them and the outside world.

Of our departure from Malacca and of the voyage south no memory remains – although I am certain that our poor mother, always easily seasick, would have suffered additional torments from the *Gorgon*'s lack of a keel and the resulting loss of stability. Perth, which we reached on 25 January 1941, we found bewilderingly strange; we knew no one there, and, although in those years the city was regarded by Eastern Australians as little more than a sleepy and old-fashioned country town, to us it was both alarmingly large and busy. Australians, too, my mother found brash and eyed with caution: with some reason. The hotel in Railway Street into which we had been booked and where we stayed for the first few weeks may have been respectable enough; nevertheless, it had the usual bar and I have memories of young Australian soldiers being sick in the gutter of the street outside after the routine '6 o'clock swill', the first time that I had ever consciously seen anyone the worse for drink; the sight horrified my mother.

I, also, was sick one day, but from overeating! Breakfast in the hotel in true Aussie style included steak, eggs and kidneys as well as porridge, toast and marmalade, and I, never having seen such a lavish display, was unable to resist, ordered the lot, over-gorged: and justly suffered.

The menu to which I succumbed on this occasion reflected the availability and abundance of Australian domestic food production.

Indeed, apart from the presence of the young recruits, daily life in Australia in 1941, as in Malaya, was little affected by the war; a historian has even written 'its citizens . . . were more aware of a measure of prosperity than of war. . . . Unemployment . . . (was) non-existent, wages were good and petrol and newsprint were the only commodities rationed'.[2]

It was mid-summer in Australia when we arrived but this did not at all inconvenience us. We were used to tropical temperatures and this was a dry heat with none of the debilitating humidity that existed in Malaya. Nevertheless, for a boy with a boy's interest in military affairs at a time of war, there was a profound 'culture shock'; an example of this was the extreme concentration in the daily newspaper and wireless on the Australian contribution to the war, such as the part played by Australian troops (the Second Australian Imperial Force) in the capture of Bardia (which had occurred on 3 January) and in the other victories being won in the Western Desert (as the Egyptian/Libyan border region was then called). Later, and while still in Australia, I was to read an apt comparison between this situation and that in Britain during the First World War when readers of the British press would never have known of the much greater length of line held by the French Army on the Western Front or of their consequentially higher casualties.

There had been long discussions before we left Malacca as to which school we should go to; it was a peculiarity of Australian private (public) school education that schools were all overtly denominational, Church of England (the most 'snob'), Presbyterian (Scotch College), Methodist (Wesley) and Roman Catholic (Aquinas). My father being strongly C. of E., there was really no choice unless we went to Eastern Australia which was less convenient and where, anyway, the end result would probably have been much the same. So, Guildford, the Anglican school, it was to be; we had studied with care its prospectus with photographs of its impressive chapel, very similar in style to that of Lancing College in Sussex, and had been accepted as pupils for the preparatory school attached to it.

A complete new school uniform was naturally needed for both of us, the stockists being the two principal department stores in Perth, Foy & Gibson or Bon Marche (this, said to be the cheaper, being the one that we first used). Another boy was also being outfitted while we were there; we were to meet him again at Guildford. At the time, though, our mother was somewhat reserved in her manner towards this boy's mother; she was a strikingly attractive woman somewhat over made-up (wearing a rather purple lipstick, I think). She was a Eurasian (as people of mixed European and Eastern blood were called at that time) and Eurasians, generally, were treated with a certain reserve (as I have remarked in Chapter 1; this is shown, also, to the heroine in John Masters's *Bhowani Junction*).

The prep school itself, about a mile away from the 'big school', was a lot less impressive architecturally, consisting of one-storey buildings with corrugated-iron roofs. The headmaster was English and did his best to maintain 'English' standards but the general atmosphere and approach was much tougher than at comparable English schools; the Australian boys, too, were, even at that time, very ready to regard 'Poms' as natural sissies.

Fortunately for Geoff and me, there was a very big intake of other English boys at the same time – John Coles and the Barrett boys who had been with us on the *Viceroy* were only a few among many – and in some forms we might have even outnumbered the Aussies; enough, anyway, to enable us to hold our own. Guildford School has recently sent me a list of those at the prep school in this year; 78 boys seem from their home addresses to have been expatriates out of a total enrolment of 170.

The 'tough' approach by the school staff to the boys was not confined to 'Poms': all suffered. One master made a hobby of keeping the whole school standing to attention in the assembly hall, a concrete-floored area roofed with corrugated iron, which became as hot as an oven under the scorching southern sun. Any detected movement would be punished by having to stand motionless for an extra minute; any further movement by another minute. It was pure sadism.

Many of us 'did' riding as an extra. We were keen enough to begin with – the heroes in all boys' books could ride – and about a dozen of the 'English' boys would troop along the road twice a week to the stables; most of the Australian boys could ride already. The instruction was very thorough but quite unsympathetic. I, for one, had never been near a horse in my life and I was terrified of this hulking great beast. No matter, I was put on and away I went.

Many of the horses, also, were not entirely suitable for small boys; one was reputed to be a former Australian cavalry charger and, on one occasion, while I was in the saddle, 'Gunner' took it into his head to gallop off into the bush. I was quite powerless to control or guide him; terrified, I lay as flat as I could on his back as he swept underneath trees, one branch brushing off my school cap (there was no nonsense, here, about safety aids such as riding hats!). I would never ride that horse again, and in the future, so far as was possible, confined my activities to a rather fat, old white mare, which would amble gently around the paddock. We were, however, taught the safest manner to fall off – a very useful bit of knowledge.

I was not a good rider – Geoff was – but I was not alone in having an unhappy experience. Michael Pallister fell off and cried when he hit the ground. He was promptly hoisted back into the saddle and fell off on the other side! He could not control his tears and was sent back to the school as clearly being a bit of a sissy. There, when he complained of a pain, he was merely sent to his bed where he stayed for the best part of a week before it was discovered that he had actually fractured his arm. His father, who was a distinguished doctor in Malaya, was not amused!

At the same time, I can remember also our pleasure in eating bran from the horses' troughs and raw carrots. This may have been a reflection on the quality of the regular school meals, where the food was often particularly unappetising even to hungry small boys – shark and tripe were dishes that I have never since been able to appreciate.

Water, however, was always available. A canvas water bag hung near a tap, keeping the water almost ice-cold through the evaporation process. To tilt the bag and pour the cold water into one's open mouth was like drinking nectar!

All this time Mother was living in a kind of private hotel or boarding house where we two would also stay on our *exeat* weekends. On one of these – it would have been on 25 May – I was sitting in the afternoon in my bedroom making a balsa wood model of *HMS Hood* when it was announced on the wireless that she had been sunk in action against the German battleship *Bismarck*. I was desolated. The *Hood* had occupied a particular place in the affections of the British people. She had been the largest warship in the world, and was a beautiful ship to look at withal. She had symbolised Britain's power in the world and her destruction seemed to be more than the loss of a ship; it was as if it was the end of the era of British naval supremacy going back to Trafalgar.

It may be that I was temperamentally unsuited to boarding-school life; I had not been happy at Hollingbury in England nor was I at Guildford. At the end of *exeat* weekends I would concoct every possible excuse not to return; I had a headache, my eyes hurt – I wore glasses which were constantly getting broken or bent in the daily animal turbulence in which small boys live (and I was as turbulent as any). Mother indulged me up to a point; she too was in a strange land and, doubtless, she could understand my feelings. But she had also a sense of duty and purpose in life. She would make excuses for me to extend the *exeat* for a few hours; but then it was back to school.

However, school life was not at all wholly miserable. There was the brilliance of the stars in the sky, constellations we had never before seen, with the Southern Cross blazing in the clear night air. There was the Aurora Australis. There were 'willy-willies' (small whirlwinds) which would suddenly appear, sucking up the dust and leaves, and moving rapidly over the bone-dry land. There were elaborate games of marbles played in the bare earthen patch outside the main hall. There was occasional swimming in a nearby 'billabong', shared I think with cattle. Small boys are quite resilient creatures on the whole; they live for the moment, which may be of overwhelming excitement or deep despair; the moods may alternate rapidly but normally neither endures for long. Above all else, most small boys find much strength from the company of their equals. I made many friendships, some of which have endured for more than fifty years.

Seeing us gradually settle down, Mother felt that she ought to return to Malaya to be with my father. We two boys would, after all, be coming back to Malaya ourselves at the end of the year for the long summer holidays. (It must have been an expense, also, for her to stay in the hotel, let alone being a very boring existence.) For the next six months our only contact with her was by letter, she writing with the regularity of clockwork a letter to each of us each week; in one letter she described the advent of Australian troops to Malacca (being a Crown Colony Malacca had been chosen as their main base in Malaya; the various Malay States were all independent, of course, linked to Britain only by treaty). Malacca had experienced many foreign invaders in its history but the Australians were something new to its experience, even if the main complaint of the existing white population was that the Australian soldiers forced up prices by paying immediately what they were first asked for an item; long hours of bargaining had been the practice from time immemorial.

As a consequence, though, there was no one with whom Geoff and I could stay during the August holiday (a short one in Australia where it was winter). There were a number of other 'English' boys in the same position, however, and the school arranged for us all to stay in a hotel at Rockingham, a seaside village a few miles south of Perth (now, I am told, engulfed in the swelling Perth conurbation).

My memories of this holiday are of having a marvellous time. There was a stretch of sandy scrub in which we built 'cubbies', boy rabbit burrows that from a narrow entrance would widen out into a large chamber sufficient to accommodate two or three of us. (Geoff remembered Cedric Hall as being the name of another boy in this group). We were very proud of these 'cubbies' and we showed our work to Mr Todd, the headmaster, who was looking after us during the holiday. He, though, was horrified at the danger we were courting should the roofs of unsupported earth cave in and bury those inside. In the future we were allowed to use them only on the condition that the overhead earth was dug away and replaced as a roof by wooden planks.

While playing in this scrub, some boy threw an iron bar that hit Geoff on the scalp. He still has the scar. It was here, too, that a boy threw a stone that hit Geoff in the eye. He could have been blinded but, very fortunately, escaped this. His eye was bloodshot and the lids swollen for some days thereafter.

During the day we would fish, sometimes from a rowing boat out at sea (accompanied by an adult, of course), sometimes from a wooden pier. On the beach there was the rusting hull of an old steamer (the *Kwenana*), her stern still in the sea and her holds full of sea water in which there were baby octopuses; I was a bit wary of clambering about this wreck as I feared that in the dark waters there might be a full-grown octopus whose suckers would be much more dangerous than those on the little ones that boys caught.

At night a kind of 'wide game' was often organised; we boys being divided into two teams, one whose aim was to defend a position, the other to attack it. Any boy among the attacking team who was sighted by one of the defenders was automatically out; the emphasis, then, was on stealthy movement, taking advantage of shadows along the poorly lit streets of the little village, with sudden darts across lighted stretches when reconnaissance had shown no obvious watcher.

There must have been some boys from the main school as well, passing their holiday in a similar fashion. I remember an entertainment evening with humorous sketches including one on the misadventures of a Chinese laundryman that we found hilariously funny. It was a happy holiday but it had to end and we returned, sunburnt, to the preparatory school.

There it was lessons and the old routine again, including French – for the first and only time in my life I was complimented on my French accent (it must have been only by comparison with the Australian boys' French pronunciation: any real French nationals writhe with anguish when they hear my mangling of their language!) and 'English', too, was taught with an emphasis on how to parse.

I cannot have shone at this judging from comments on my present prose style but nevertheless an essay of mine on the Battle of Britain found favour. The headmaster said that he would have it printed in *The Swan*, the school magazine – a great honour. Perhaps it was for this reason that I was given a prize for 'English Studies' at the end of the year – a finely bound copy of Kipling's *Puck of Pook's Hill*.

November came and with it the end of term and the end of my schooling at the Prep School. The next term I would be in the big school, but first there was to be the voyage to Malaya to rejoin our parents for the Christmas holidays.

Chapter 6
The invasion of Malaya, 1941–2

At the end of the Christmas term (about mid-November 1941) Geoffrey and I, with a number of other boys and girls of about our age, sailed from Fremantle to join our parents in Malaya, under the general charge of the ship's Purser. We were told how much pocket money would be allowed us – to buy soft drinks, etc. – and I remember protesting that I, as a boy in the top class of the prep school, should be entitled to more than the 'little ones'; the Purser did not agree: 'I was below the age of 12 and *that* was the rule!'

The *Gorgon*, the same ship on which we had sailed to Australia earlier in the year, made her slow progress up the West Australian coast, calling at the small townships which studded the barren shoreline. These, with their rusty corrugated-iron roofed houses, their 'hotel' – the centre of social life for some hundreds of square miles of mostly unoccupied outback – their few shops selling little more than basic necessities, were dreary places but they gave us youngsters the opportunity to stretch our legs and let off steam.

Gorgon and her sister ships were used to transport sheep from the vast 'stations' (as the outback sheep farms were known) to the Dutch and British tropical dependencies to the north; largely Muslim by religion and densely populated by comparison with the sparse immensities of Western Australia. Michael Pallister remembers a sheep being slaughtered at one of these ports, behind brown hessian screens so that the blood would not upset the young or squeamish. The screens were makeshift affairs and, far from being upset, most of the boys were fascinated; it was easy to peer through and look at the gore.

A girl, Marion Williams, the elder sister (aged 11!) of a friend of Geoff's, was going back to Malaya with her brother and, of course, I became infatuated with her. This, as with my liking for Valerie Nankivell the previous year, caused Geoff enormous mirth; one day Marion, another girl, I and a boy of my age were all in one of our cabins together while the littler ones hammered at the door, jeering and generally being obnoxious. Their threat was that, 'We'll tell Mummy (or rather the individual Mummy of each one of us four)', which – even though there was nothing to tell – was embarrassing enough at that age to persuade us to buy their silence with promises of chocolate bars or soft drinks!

My brother remembers that, while waiting for the sound of the gong that would mark the call to the dining saloon for the next meal, the whole group of youngsters would hang over the ship's rail, chanting,

Oh how the camp does yell
When they hear the dinner bell;
Wallaby stew and onion-smell,
Three times a day.
Ham and eggs we never see,
Butter is a luxury,
That's why we're gradually,
Fading away.

We landed at Singapore on 30 November 1941, where our parents were waiting to meet us. There was a joyful reunion – we had not seen Daddy for almost a year – some shopping for Christmas and other presents (I bought a copy of *The Ghostly Galleon*, by Vice-Admiral Sir E. R. G. R. Evans, a tale of a knightly brotherhood putting down pirates in the Spanish Main). Outside the bookshop the hoardings of newsvendors were proclaiming that the Volunteers were being mobilised. It was 1 December but no one seemed seriously alarmed, everyone knew Singapore was impregnable. The streets were full of soldiers; the shops were busy with the pre-Christmas trade. In Malaya it was business as usual.

Ahmut, our *syce* (driver), then drove us back to Malacca where we were greeted by the servants and, ecstatically, by Spot our dog. Spot, though, was to be the cause of our first heartbreak. During Mother's stay with us in Australia he had been ill-treated by some Chinese (Daddy at work during the day had no time to spare for his care, food and exercise). As a result, while still friendly to white people, Spot had developed a hatred of all non-Europeans, not only of Chinese but also of any non-European; our return appeared to fuel this, almost as if he felt compelled to savage those who, having ill-treated him, might do the same to us. Within days he had achieved a reputation for ferocity over all Bukit Sebukor – although he was still normal with our cook, Ah Fong, and Talip, the Malay houseboy, who fed him. The Tamil postman was attacked twice; the first time he had to be bought off with compensation; after the second incident, though, he vowed never to deliver letters to us while 'the devil dog' lived. My father, with what must have been great reluctance (he was a very tender-hearted man), decided that he had no option but to have Spot humanely destroyed; otherwise he feared that the dog might seriously maim or kill a Malay or Chinese child. We were broken-hearted.

As a consolation to us two mourning boys, therefore, another dog, a bitch rather, was obtained from the Pound, a very young mongrel terrier, emaciated and covered with enormous ticks. Pat (as we named her) was loved by us immediately in spite of her condition. She was bathed in disinfectant, the ticks, bloated with blood, were removed; she was properly fed for the first time in her life. She was a gentle little thing and repaid our care and attention with the usual doggish blind adoration of her human masters. The exact dating of this episode I am not sure of, but I think it must have been within one or two days of our return to Malacca. The next, though, can be dated to the hour.

On the morning of 8 December we heard on the wireless that the Japanese had attacked the United States base in Pearl Harbor. Singapore had been bombed. Worse still, the Japanese had 'attempted' a landing at Khota Bahru on the north-east coast of Malaya. 'Mopping-up operations of stray groups of invaders who had managed to get ashore were continuing' – such was the sanitised official version of the beginning of the debacle that was to unfold with such startling rapidity over the next ten weeks and was to affect our lives so profoundly. Unknown to us at the time, this announcement was to mark the end of the British Empire as we knew it.

Later that day, as we listened anxiously to the news broadcasts, we were astonished to hear an appeal for the return of some secret documents left in a car in Singapore. It sounded unbelievable; we comforted ourselves with the reflection that it must be a coded message meaning something quite different – no one could be so careless as to leave secret papers lying about like that. The news item was repeated several times that day but since then I have never read any reference to it; it remains a mystery.

Then on 10 December we were shocked, indeed stunned, to hear the bleak announcement of the sinking of the *Prince of Wales* and *Repulse* by Japanese aircraft. The arrival of these two ships – *HMS Prince of Wales* was the most modern battleship in the Royal Navy and the *Repulse*, although old, had been extensively modernised – at Singapore only the week before had been the cause of much pride amongst the British community. It had been hailed as an example of British preparedness and of her determination to keep Malaya safe. Now this exultation suddenly soured.

Of course, I did not understand the implications of the disaster although, coming after the loss of the *Hood* six months earlier, I was made miserable by the blows to the Navy that I worshipped. I could sense that the grown-ups, although they put a brave face on it, were now inwardly sombre. Over the next few weeks we were to become accustomed to the almost daily recital that British troops had withdrawn from Japanese forces (the success of whose landing at Khota Bahru could no longer be denied) 'to prepared positions in accordance with prearranged plans'. However, our daily life seemed to continue much as before.

I had been given some golf clubs and practised almost every day and mostly alone on the nine-hole golf course that surrounded the five Dunlop European staff bungalows. Pat had to be walked, and carefully de-ticked afterwards. There was mah-jong to play. Almost daily, with Mother, we would be driven to Malacca for shopping, to the public library and occasionally to the cinema.

It was the life that we had been used to, but after the communal existence of a boarding school, a somewhat lonely one. Geoff and I had each other to talk and play with but there were no other boys and girls living on Bukit Sebukor; even in Malacca itself there were few of our friends of past years – the constant comings and goings of colonial life meant that the expatriate population was an ever-changing one, while the war with Germany, now in its third year, would have resulted in no new faces coming out from England. There was a girl, though, called Hilary Clark, whose parents, Fay and Lister (the latter being in the Malayan Civil Service and responsible, under the Resident, for Malacca), were friends of Mother and Daddy. Another family were the Snells whose younger son, only a few months older than me, was a friend. The Vowlers had a rubber plantation in Malacca colony and a son, Billy, also about my age. We must have been friendly but my mind remains blank on the subject. We met again in the 1990s.

Being below the age of 12 years, the Snell boy and I still used the children's changing-room at the Tanjong Kling swimming club. This was separated from the women's changing-room only by a screen of coconut fronds supported by bamboo verticals and horizontals. It was not difficult to shin up these, and we did, intensely curious to see the occupants undressed. We were heard, though, and one woman looked up to see two boys regarding her 'dishabille'. She screeched; we hurriedly descended. But a complaint was made and in the future we two were told to use the men's changing-room that was a discreet distance away.

In mid-December two of our parents' friends arrived, refugees from Penang – I have no record of the exact date but the island was captured by the Japanese on 17 December, the European population evacuated in somewhat of a panic a day or two before (no thought was given to the fate of the non-Europeans).[1] This couple – their names I cannot remember, but she had fair hair and my father was very gallant to her (which made my mother tighten her lips!) – slept on the back veranda near our bedroom for one, maybe two, nights before continuing their journey to the safety of Singapore. No doubt they told our parents of their experiences in full but Geoff and I were kept in innocent ignorance.

The colony of Hong Kong, off the coast of China, was also under Japanese attack. On Christmas day, after attending church in the morning and a family midday meal, we were invited to dinner with the Allens. A toast was drunk to Hong Kong's continued resistance, but, although we did not know it, the colony had capitulated that very day.

I had decided to keep a diary, which, surprisingly, has survived and this forms the meat of the remainder of this chapter and is reproduced below in italics. Where it seems necessary, I have added notes, these being put in brackets to make clear that they are later additions.

Friday 26th of Dec.
We went to the swimming club with Hilary. Had Xmas Pud for lunch. Geoffrey pinched a charm.
(There is a reference to this swimming club party in the journal of Fay Clark, Hilary's mother, which may be read in the Colonial Records Archive of the Rhodes House Library at Oxford.)

Saturday 27th of Dec.
Finished off the Xmas pudding. The toucan came and boarded up the slats above the stairs. Went to the pictures and saw 'Underground'. It is all about the Freedom Station in Germany. I enjoyed it but Geoffrey didn't.
(The 'toucan' – wrongly spelt, but spelling was not my strong point – was a carpenter.)

Sunday 28th of Dec.
We went to the swimming club in the morning. I finished writing my book list out. We went to church in the evening and then went to the pictures. We saw 'Charlie Chan at the Wax Museum'. It is a very good film and makes you laugh and shiver by turns.

Monday 29th of Dec.
I woke up at 7.15am, instead of 6.45am. We made an incendiary mixture, which burns on the application of a match. It is made

of: ghecragvar, pbggia jbly, fhrycuhe, nag gnyphz abjqre. (turpentine, cotton wool, sulphur and talcum powder). *In the afternoon I practised shooting with Geoff's toy revolver. I had a game of golf in the evening.*

The code was intended to stop the Japanese from learning this vital military secret should the diary fall into their hands. Given my misspellings, I have no doubt they would have been very confused indeed!

Sir Shenton Thomas, the Governor of Singapore and the Straits Settlements, visited Malacca this same day – although I was not of course aware of his visit at the time. In his diary Sir Shenton wrote: 'Arrived in Malacca during air-raid alert. Had long talk with Bryant (Resident Commissioner) who seemed rather at sea and had let all his European women leave – though much too soon. Generally he seemed to be guided by some nondescript junior military officer!'[2]

Tuesday 30th of Dec.
We had a bonfire in the morning. Packed my books and had a game with guns in the afternoon. In the evening I had a game of mah-jong.

Wednesday 31st of Dec. 1941
Mummy went to the hospital in the morning. In the evening we had a walk and Mummy and Daddy went to Auntie Allans to play mah-jong.

Thursday 1st of Jan. 1942
I went shopping with Mummy. In the evening I had a game of golf. Pat slept in our monkey house. V znl abg or noyr gb poagvahr. (I may not be able to continue.)
(That Pat was permitted by Mother to sleep in the 'monkey house' – our name for the mosquito-meshed enclosure in which we slept – is an indication that we two boys must have appeared to be upset by all that was happening around us. Similarly, the next sentence in my amateurish code probably refers to a feeling of impending disaster.)

Friday 2nd of Jan. 1942
Geoffrey went to Cherry to get his bike. In the afternoon Mummy went to the hospital and G. upset the ink. G. and I watched Daddy inspect a shelter and two posts.
(Daddy, too old to be a Volunteer, was an Air Raid Warden. The 'posts' would have been observation posts. I can remember nothing of these but my memories of the air raid shelter are of a small, dark, sandbagged structure.)

> <u>*Saturday 3rd of Jan. 1942*</u>
> *In the morning we packed Mum's glass and silver. In the evening we had a haircut and brought a copy of 'The Navy'.*
> <u>*Sunday 4th of Jan. 1942*</u>
> *In the morning we went to the swimming club. As we were going through Malacca the 'alert' sounded. In the evening we went to the rifle range and found 47 bullets and two cartridge cases.*
>
> <u>*Monday 5th of Jan. 1942*</u>
> *Jr unir tbg gb bb Nhfgenyvn.* (We have got to go Australia and reach Singapore tomorrow. Everything is packed. I am very sad.)

My parents' plan was that we should be driven to Singapore by car – in his diary Sir Shenton Thomas had noted as far back as 30 December that trains from Kuala Lumpur to Singapore were only running at night because of the fear of Japanese air attacks. Ahmut, our *syce*, however, was equally scared and he flatly refused to drive us. My father was hurt – Ahmut had been employed by us for many years and had always been well treated – and also dismayed. 'How could his family get to Singapore without a driver?' He pleaded; Ahmut was adamant. Daddy lost his temper and sacked Ahmut on the spot and many hard words were said between him and my mother about the unreliability of Malays, 'inward cowards'.

In retrospect, though, it is hard not to feel some sympathy with Ahmut. The stories of the Europeans' panic abandonment of Penang and the lack of thought for all non-Europeans would no doubt have spread rapidly amongst the Chinese, Malay and Indian communities.[3] Somehow, though, Daddy must have obtained another driver because we still left for Singapore on 6 January, only a few hours later than planned. At Batu Pahat on the boundary between Negri Sembilan and Johore states (where the Muar River had to be crossed by a ferry) we broke our journey, taking a snatched meal at the rest house before continuing on to Singapore.

Safely arrived, we were driven to a hotel (my brother thinks that it was the Adelphi) where my father had booked a room, just the one – the hotel was crowded with refugees from the north of Malaya – but with a veranda on which two beds had been erected for Geoff and me. That evening we all walked together on the Padang, the grassy waterfront that was such an attractive feature of the city. While doing this, the air raid sirens sounded and we took refuge in a nearby slit trench. Looking up we could see a Japanese bomber in the not-quite-dark sky with another plane apparently in fruitless pursuit – the American-made Brewster Buffaloes with which the RAF was equipped, were hopelessly obsolete and quite outclassed by the Japanese aircraft. (The previous year Sir Shenton Thomas had written in his diary, 1941, 'the best of the Japanese fighters were old fabric covered biplanes which wouldn't stand a chance against the Buffalo fighters'!)

It was, I think, the next night, the last before sailing, that I could not sleep. I felt lost, lonely and afraid and I went in my pyjamas in search of my parents, down to what appeared to me to be a vast, crowded and noisy lounge, to try to find them. They were at a distant table, saying their farewells to friends, but I was directed to them by a 'boy', comforted and, after an interval, when I was calmer, Mother took me back to my bed. Even so, the rest of my night was rather troubled.

Tuesday 13th of Jan.
I have not been able to write up my diary since 5th of Jan. On the 6th we arrived at Singapore and had a raid. On the 7th we saw Mr and Mrs Parish. On the 8th we left S'pore. It was a very rough voyage and Mummy and Geoffrey were both sick. Purves was also sick the first day out, but not again. Geoff was only sick for 2 and ½ days. Jiming and I wer'nt sick at all.

On the 10th we arrived at Batavia and saw n fybbc, n. p. pehfre, naq n qrfgebbre (a destroyer, a sloop, and a cruiser). *In the afternoon we brought some curios. On the 11th we left B'avia. On the 12th it was rough, it is still rough.*

(The Mr and Mrs Parrish referred to had lived in Malacca (see Chapter 1) and had always been close friends of my parents. Geoff's purchase at the curio shop in Batavia was a wooden flute, mine a carved breadboard. It cost me the equivalent of 1 shilling and tuppence! It is still in my possession. After sailing from Batavia, the ship, the *Charon*, called at Surabaya, the Dutch Naval base at the eastern end of Java. Our stay was for a few hours only and there was no question of passengers being allowed ashore but from the ship I saw a flying boat, a 'Walrus', moored nearby: an old-fashioned plane with an open forward cockpit with a machine gun on a ring mounting.)

Wednesday 14th of Jan.
In the afternoon we had a game of 'chassee'. We had a lovely barricade of deck chairs, but an officer told us we were not to play with them, and we had to put them away. Still rough.

Thursday 15th of January
7.56 min 55 sec. It is a little calmer. In the morning I played coits, I am getting on very well and I practise every day. In the afternoon I read a book.

To both port and starboard the *Charon* was streaming paravanes (a torpedo-shaped device intended to deflect sea mines away from the ship). One calm, clear evening we sat at the ship's peak, watching the white bow-waves, brilliantly phosphorescent in the tropical waters, breaking away in a wide V on either side of the bow, and only a few feet below us, while at the extremities of their securing wires the paravanes themselves created similar 'magics'.

Friday 16th of January
In the morning I read and played coits. In the afternoon went down to the hold with Palister.
(Pallister – the correct spelling of his name – was a school friend and was to continue so until we left Australia in 1943. We were to meet again in 1950 when he was at Cambridge as is recounted in Chapter 11.)

Saturday 17th of Jan.
At 2 o'clock we arrived at Geralton and heard that Znyynpn unq orra pncgherq (Malacca had been captured). *The Gorgon was in.*

Geraldton – once again a misspelling – was another of the small, little townships on the Western Australian coastline. Most of the boys aboard the ship went ashore for exercise and it was then that we saw a newspaper headline announcing that Malacca had been captured (this, in fact, had happened on 13 January). I rushed back to the ship carrying the news and, without thinking, blurted it out to the women passengers who had not gone ashore and were sitting talking amongst themselves in the Lounge. One went white, stood up and said to me 'Is this true? If you are making it up I will beat you.' I swore it, confirmation of its correctness was given by one of the ship's officers, and, silent, they went away to reflect, and perhaps to weep, alone.

Sunday 18th of Jan.
We arrived at Fremantle. At 5 o'clock two buses took us to the Memorial Hall, where the Land's department gave us a lovely supper and then took us to a Red Cross building where we slept for the night.

Chapter 7
Australia, 1942–3

I continued to keep a diary for the next two weeks but few of the entries for this period are worth recording. We were in a kind of 'hiatus'. We had left Malaya because of the advancing Japanese but I do not think that we (or at least we children) believed that Singapore itself would fall and that the sudden disruption to our lives would be permanent. The mothers may have been more realistic; as I relate below, my mother seems to have had few illusions.

Even so, we children were 11-year-olds at most. We had had one traumatic upheaval after another over the past three years: schools and homes, relations, friends and family, all the settled pillars of our existence had been removed. Our mothers, too, although trying to present a brave front to the world, must have been in inward torment. They had lost almost all their worldly possessions; they did not know, and were not to learn for many months, whether their husbands still lived; their present financial resources were meagre and their future re-provision an unknown. Nerves frayed; we could not be oblivious to how they felt.

The Australian Red Cross had arranged for us to be accommodated in a kind of children's home, presumably vacant because of the summer holidays. My diary records that the next day, Monday 19 January, *In the morning we made our beds, and then went to town to be registered. In the afternoon our trunks arrived. The Japs are down to the Johore border.*

The next day we moved out of the home to a hotel in Perth, the 'Edward' and the day after that to Glen Forest. Miss Shepherd, a teacher at Guildford Prep School, had invited a number of her pupils and their mothers to stay at her family's farm, Shepherd's Bush. This kindness was much appreciated by the mothers concerned. We children, I think, took it rather as just one more change in a rather turbulent life.

Her family house was quite spacious – it had to be to accommodate, as a minimum, an extra three women and six children – but there was no privacy, no opportunity for the women to give vent to the anxiety that all must have felt: in front of their children mothers had to keep calm. I can remember only one weeping while I was in the room; even then she hurried away, followed by one of the other mothers while mine explained to me that the mother 'was upset'. The sanitation was 'rural': a pit latrine – either a 'two' or a 'three' seater! I found this distasteful; I was accustomed to, and thought quite natural, the lack of privacy in a boys' boarding school but the idea that one might be defecating in the next stall to one's own – or even some other boy's – mother was almost obscene.

We were not used to farm life, to chickens running everywhere, to seeing a newly born calf, to seeing a cow being milked – I remember the boy who was milking squirting us with milk from a cow's teat! We had to be careful also about using water: the farm depended on an artesian well, a pump and a tower-tank. This was amply sufficient normally but our arrival may have trebled consumption.

Towards the end of this first week, Mother took me off for a walk in the woods. During this, she told me that she hoped that she could rely on me, that though I was not yet 12, I would have to try to be the 'man of the family'; if anything happened to her I was to take Geoff to her parents in England as we had no one in Australia. I promised to do so, sincerely, but actually I did not fully understand our position or the possible implications of what she was trying to tell me.

On Sunday my diary tells me that we went to church. What church? I have no recollection. That evening I can remember Miss Shepherd told our fortunes from tea leaves in a cup by a dim lamp, but not what she divined or said she divined in the leaves. The next day we children were taken in a horse and trap for a swim and a picnic in a nearby national park. Coming back we drove through a bush fire, the scrub burning on either side of the road; not a roaring great fire but a steady burn with quite a bit of smoke. It didn't seem very much at the time but the bush was bone dry and the fire advanced steadily and by the evening of the next day had reached the edges of the Shepherd's farm. We joined everyone else in beating, not of course in any place where we were in danger, but ensuring that grass did not catch and let the fire take hold in trees. By the next day the fire was out, leaving a blackened landscape.

At the beginning of the next week my mother received a letter from my father. What he wrote in it, I do not know – nor its date of posting from Singapore – except that she told us that all the glass and silver sent down from Malacca had arrived and had been safely stored in the Dunlop godowns.[1] This was very probably the last letter my mother received from my father before the Japanese took him into internment. Already, by this date (2 February), the British, Australian and Indian troops had withdrawn from the mainland to Singapore Island. (We did not know this, of course, but the mothers in our party, having witnessed the repeated Japanese successes over the past two months, probably feared the worst.)

This was my last diary entry. I have no recollection why I suddenly stopped, whether I had simply lost interest or whether I no longer wanted to record the present for the sake of a very uncertain future. Or, more mundanely but very possibly, we were all now busy in getting ready for the new school term.

The hospitality given to us all by the Shepherds had allowed the adults time both to reflect upon their present unhappy position and to decide what they should try to do to remedy it. The most pressing need was to determine where to live; space dictated that we could not stay indefinitely on the farm. In our case Mother with her friend Renée Parrish, last seen in Singapore, who had also now arrived in Perth (accompanied by her young daughter Cecile), another woman, Molly Webb, and her baby son, Robert (they had been on the *Charon* with us), together rented a small house in Nedlands. Mother moved there immediately we two boys had returned to school. Geoff, aged 9, returned to prep school while I, as planned the previous year, entered the big school, going to Henn's House.

I felt very lonely in the next few weeks. I was no longer in the familiar surroundings of the prep school, although, of course, there were other boys in my house who had been at the prep school with me and whom I knew well. But, whereas there, I had been one of the 'seniors', now I was very much a junior. It is never an easy adjustment, even if it is one that all must make, one which recurs repeatedly in life, but on this occasion the process was made more difficult by the constant disruptions to my life over the past five years.

Moreover, the war news was uniformly bad; Singapore capitulated to the Japanese on 15 February 1942 (just after term had begun): we did not know whether Daddy was alive or dead, and, even if he was alive, when we would ever again see him. I used to walk down the road to the prep school at every available opportunity to talk to my brother; my housemaster warned me that I was doing so far too often, that, while it was understandable to do so at first, I must remember that now I was no longer a prep-school boy and should stick to the company of my peers.

Meanwhile, in Australia there was an apprehension that the Japanese might invade the continent itself in the near future. The country's 'defences were perilously close to collapsing. . . . There was no large military force between the Japanese spearhead and the Australian mainland. . . . (and precious few there – most of the country's seasoned troops were in the Mediterranean or had been captured by the Japanese). . . . Two-thirds of the men between eighteen and forty years of age were called up for service, others being retained in "reserved occupations" necessary for war or civilian life. . . . Shop windows (in Perth) were boarded up, slit trenches were dug in back yards and public parks, a partial black-out was imposed in Perth and other main centres (the "brown-out"). . . . Daylight saving began during the summer months to conserve power supplies and all civilians were issued with ration books and identity cards.'

An air raid on Darwin (19 February 1942) was the occasion of the largest newspaper headlines ever seen in Australia, even though the published casualty list numbered only 17 (in fact 300 died and 400 were wounded but strict censorship was imposed). Other air raids followed – over 100 on the north-western ports, the last being an attack on military installations near Exmouth as late as May 1943, although few of these were made public.

It was thought that Perth would be bombed; a 'brownout' was imposed and many schoolchildren were evacuated to the country. Guildford School was one of those that took the decision to move away to the safety of the south of the state.[2] This was the signal for many ex-Malayan mothers to withdraw their children. Already concerned about their financial position and having lost home and husband, they were not prepared to be separated also from their children. There was a mass exodus, accordingly, from Guildford to one or other of the day schools. In our case, Mother decided that we two boys should transfer to Hale School, although (or so she later told me) Canon Freeth, the headmaster of Guildford, tried his best to persuade her not to do so, offering to waive or at least substantially reduce the fees.

Mother, Renée Parrish and Molly Webb had decided that they would continue to share but a bigger house was needed to accommodate us two boys as well. A suitably sized one was vacant at 71 Malcolm Street which the three decided to rent from two spinster ladies, the Misses Cowan, who were moving out of reach of Japanese bombs.

The Cowan family was one of the 'best' in Perth. Mrs Edith Cowan, the mother (I suppose) of these two, had been elected in 1921 the first woman member of any Australian parliament and a statue to her stood at the top of Malcolm Street. I rather think that there was some family link, also, with the Forrest family – Sir John Forrest had been a famous Western Australia premier at the turn of the century. In any event, their large old house and garden had been immaculately kept until we arrived.

The house has (for I am told it survives still) a 'feature', a little room jutting out of the main house roof and reached by a separate outside open staircase, which had been added as an observatory. This was to be our room, a private bolthole from the world where we could be totally alone. It was bliss; and our school friends all agreed. Here we could do almost as we pleased, away from the eyes of grown-ups. We would scramble over the roofs, cut lead from the guttering (Michael Pallister's idea, I think), melt it down in borrowed saucepans and then cast it for shot for our catapults and generally behave thoughtlessly. The garden contained a slit trench as protection against air raids. We boys thought it needed enlarging and the trench rapidly became a labyrinth of holes and dugouts, the garden being reduced to a wilderness in the process.

Malcolm Street was within a few minutes' walk of Hale School. At the top of the street there was Kings Park, a vast area of natural countryside in which one could happily wander for hours without seeing anyone else. This park was full of Australian flora, the kangaroo paw flower, eucalyptus trees, wattle – all gold when in bloom – bush sticks which grew from 'black-boys' – reputed to survive bush fires, to grow only one inch each year and to be a 'protected' species (not that *that* would have worried us unduly: we had all become proper 'larrikins' in the Australian argot).

There were a large number of ex-Malayan wives and children living nearby, all situated in the same sorry position: Muriel Pallister with her son, Michael, Mrs Morris with her two sons, Peter and Edward (much the same age as me and Geoff), Mrs Drysdale who had a daughter Alison of about my age, and a son Jimmy of Geoff's age; these I remember as being our closest friends. I do not recall the mothers mixing much with the 'native Australians' and as a result we boys, although we made friends with Australian boys at school, usually in our leisure time stayed as a fairly coherent group.

It is perhaps pertinent to remark here that an aftermath of the overwhelming disaster in Malaya had been the customary search for a scapegoat(s), the feeling that there must have been a hidden reason for the catastrophe. The public in Australia blamed the aristocratic and incompetent 'Pommy' generals or the effete gin-swilling, money-mad planters of Malaya (although those who had family members taken prisoner were not slow, also, to impugn the courage of the Australian General Gordon-Bennett who had escaped). The British refugees, in turn, talked of the indiscipline and drunkenness of the Australian troops while those, like us, whose husbands and fathers had worked in the private sector, contrasted their lot unfavourably with the 'government' dependants (although I have been told recently that these also were treated far from generously).

On the whole, though, the wives were mutually supportive. Woe betide, though, one who stepped out of line, who went out with 'men' (and there was one who was alleged to be living well in company with an American submarine commander based in Fremantle!).

We children, too, stuck together although when in March 1942 Geoff and I produced a copy of the *Mars*, a comic containing 'serials, jokes, short stories' we found that there was no 'public demand' for our work. Accordingly, there was only one copy and only one issue (which I still possess).

In the wider world, although there was the first '1,000-bomber raid' on Cologne in May 1942, the war generally continued to go badly. In the Far East the Japanese had decisively defeated the Dutch/British/American fleet in the Battle of the Java Sea (*Exeter* the victor in the battle with the *Graf Spee* in 1939 was sunk here), and went on to occupy the whole of the Netherlands East Indies, to land on Guadalcanal in the Solomon Islands and to occupy the northern shore of New Guinea. In the Western Desert, the Germans under their new commander Rommel attacked. Although the Free French fought gallantly at Bir Hakeim, the British armour was wiped out at the 'Battle of the Cauldron'. The surrender of Tobruk (another supposedly impregnable fortress) and the capture of the South Africans followed within days. Then there was news of the dreary retreat through Derna, Benghazi, Sollum, small towns whose names were by now familiar. Cairo itself seemed threatened.

And yet, against this background, Mother decided that we should attempt to return to England. The dangers of the sea voyage were known. She would have learnt by letters from her parents and her sisters of the bombing from which London was suffering. Nevertheless, she felt that our situation in Australia was intolerable for any long period, being without family, and in financially very reduced circumstances (my father had worked for Dunlop Malayan Estates, which was a separate company from the main Dunlop business and all the assets of which were now in Japanese hands). But, although she had decided on departure, passages in wartime were difficult to come by. It was to be many months, indeed over a year, before one was secured.

The eviction of the Japanese from Guadalcanal and the repulse of their thrust to Port Moresby had rendered unlikely any Japanese bombing of Perth, let alone an invasion of the continent itself. Those who had prudently removed themselves, therefore now returned. Amongst them were the two maiden ladies, the Misses Cowan, who owned 71 Malcolm Street and who wished to return to their own home, horrified though they were at the damage that we had inflicted upon their carefully preserved period piece.

Mother had to find somewhere else for us to live and there were also some disadvantages to sharing with Renée (who was half-French and inclined to be emotional which Mother could bear with, but which I, a rather intolerant young English male, found irksome). Mother selected a bungalow in Robinson Street, Subiaco (a suburb of Perth) for our future home. It was not quite as centrally located an area as Malcolm Street; nor was the house as well furnished – indeed, if I was to see it now, no doubt I would judge it as rather shabby. However, it was entirely suitable for us at that time, the only disadvantage being that the lavatory was outside, at the end of the garden (the *West Australian* torn into squares being used for lavatory paper; giving the opportunity to read peacefully any news items that might have been missed).

Although Subiaco was a suburb, at that time Perth was so small a city we could cycle to school in less than 15 minutes; Kings Park (another side of the park to that approached from Malcolm Street) could be reached on foot within five minutes, as well as local shops where we bought milkshakes and ice creams with a vast choice of flavours, colours and sizes (very cheap too!), a public library and an open air cinema where we saw Charles Laughton playing the lead in *Mutiny on the Bounty*. Perth was well supplied with cinemas, many of them air-conditioned, which made them attractive haunts as the temperatures built up in the Australian summer. In one cinema we would sit in the front of the gallery, eating pomegranate seeds – and sometimes bursting the juice over the heads of those in the stalls below.

We could all swim, of course; Peppermint Grove, on the bank of the Swan River was a favourite resort. More rarely we would take a bus to the coast where great waves would roll in, 'all the way from Cape Town', we would jest, but indeed South Africa was the nearest westerly land. The beauty of Perth in those days was unparalleled. The Swan broadened out here to form a great lagoon, crystal clear and always blue in what seems in recollection to have been an unbroken succession of hot, dry days. The exit of the lagoon was 'The Narrows' with a bluff on the north bank and

Kings Park at the top. The four main public schools would row here, the 'Head of the River' race being a highlight in the schools sporting calendar.

The tide seemed to have turned, also, in the war. The German thrust into Russia, deep though it went, far east and south, was checked at last, and their armies, like the ebbing tide, drew out as fast as that summer they had come in, leaving behind them only the contracting pool which was their Sixth Army at Stalingrad.

There was the great British victory of El Alamein to celebrate as well, quickly followed by news of 'Operation Torch', the Allied landings in North Africa. Lying on the threadbare carpet in our Subiaco sitting room, though, I found the political manoeuvring difficult to follow; Darlan was an admiral and therefore *ipso facto* admirable, even if French, and his assassination consequently to be regretted, but why was there all this fuss about General Giraud? France already had an authentic hero in de Gaulle whose 23 June 1940 broadcast to the people of France placed him firmly in my galaxy of men to die for. Anyway, and fortunately for my young romanticism, all came right about this in the end.

Understandably the war and news of it meant a great deal to us. Every evening Mother, Geoffrey and I would listen to the news, preceded by advertisements for Hoadleys Violet Crumble Bar and a cough linctus made from 'seaweed gathered off the coast of Ireland': then there were the opening bars of Beethoven's Fifth Symphony, 'Dit-dit-dit Dah', the Morse code symbol for 'V' that had become short-code for ultimate victory.

In the Far East, though, Japan still loomed powerful and menacing. The American carrier fleet had won a decisive victory at Midway. In New Guinea an attempted Japanese landing at Milne Bay had been repulsed, the Australian troops were clambering up the Kokoda Trail over the Owen Stanley range, investing the Japanese strongholds at Gona, Buna and Lae. The names of these tiny villages and the battles for them were unknown in England but were as hard fought as any in the war and were pictured in every news film shown in every cinema in Australia. To Australians this had become the 'real' war, close to hand, threatening their homes. Europe and 'Hitler's War' were remote by contrast.

In January 1943, Renée, who had been given the use of a fruit farm near Shepherd's Bush, invited us three to stay with her. A high mesh fence to prevent kangaroos eating and spoiling the crop surrounded the fruit orchards containing peaches, apricots, nectarines and plums. However, high though the fence was, the kangaroos could jump even higher. One of our tasks, accordingly, was to chase away any that we saw. The kangaroos seemed to realise that we two small boys posed no real danger and would wait, calmly eating their fill, until we, shouting and making as much noise as we could, approached quite close. Then, lazily and disdainfully, they would jump away in great bounds until they reached the perimeter fence over which they would sail with effortless ease.

There was a disused tower near the farm buildings erected, or so we were told, as a watch point against the Aborigines in the early days of the settlement of Western Australia. Geoff and I appropriated this as our own special place, where we could be private away from the grown-ups and from Cecile who we thought was a spoilt and rather silly little girl.

Marketing difficulties had resulted in there being a superfluity of milk, far more than could be drunk. Accordingly the excess was scalded each night, basins of cream being obtained. Wheat grain was steeped overnight in milk and then cooked the next morning to make porridge that was served with cream for breakfast. 'Very yummy' as one might say.

Mother had learned, by now, from the Red Cross that my father was alive; or rather, that he had survived the fall of Singapore. Whether he *still* lived was another matter; the news was many months old by the date when she received it and all were aware that conditions in Japanese prisoner-of-war and internment camps were hard and the treatment of their inmates harsh.

I cannot recall my own feelings about this news; indeed, I am saddened now at how little impact it seems to have had. I loved my father dearly but he had already become almost a shadowy figure. This was perhaps inevitable given I had lived under the same roof as him for not more than seven months in the five years since I had left Malaya in 1937 for schooling in England. Inevitable or not though, it is a fact that I have come increasingly to regret as my own life has unfolded; it is, of course, a deprivation in which Geoffrey also shared; other families, too, throughout the whole period of Empire had had to experience this severance of domestic ties – it is ironic that cheap and easy air travel only came about after 'the imperial sunset'.

In Malacca, as I have told, Mother had attended services at the Church of England's Christ Church. In Perth, though, she reverted to the Congregational worship of her own family, the simple, plain, strong service of the men who had been Cromwell's Ironsides, who had established the New England colonies and had died for their faith at Sedgemoor and in the Bloody Assize that followed. I was at an age when religious and sexual feelings are both burgeoning – the Sunday school teacher was perhaps a focus for both – and I am sure that the dose of Puritanism such as the Congregational Church provided was good for me!

The genes transmitted to me through my father from my Barnes ancestors, on the other hand, held romantic and wild strains. My father and his brothers had been attracted as a consequence to Belloc, to Chesterton and to Shaw; I, at the age of 12, found Raphael Sabatini to my taste – the comment about Scaramouche in the novel of that name that, 'He had been borne with the gift of laughter and the belief that the world was mad', has remained with me.

In the little local branch library there were these books; books also about service in the French Foreign Legion which was also 'romantic' – with hinted-at references to upper-class sexual activities – champagne, oysters and languorous '*poules*' – but they gave me in addition some interesting nuggets of fact, e.g. the Druse uprisings in 1922 and the subsequent French shelling of Damascus, the fierce guerrilla war against Abd el-Krim in the Rif, etc.

Hale School I found congenial. I was never top of my class – an Australian boy named David Anderson was streets ahead of the rest of us, combining all-round scholastic and sporting abilities with every good personal quality – but I was a well-placed second or third most of the time. Apart from David, there were other Australian boys with whom I was friendly, Benson and Barnsely in particular, and of whom, and through David, I have recently had news. All have 'done well' in life; throughout mine I have been blessed with good and enduring friends.

Hale School taught *Australian* History. I learned there of the early governors, of Macquarie and of Bligh (a great navigator, possibly a much maligned man, but certainly one who possessed to excess the unhappy ability to alienate his subordinates), of the early explorers, Flinders and Bass, of Sturt and his Stony Desert, of Stuart and his camels, of the gold rushes in Victoria and Kalgoorlie, of the 'squatters mounted on their thoroughbreds', and the lawlessness described in *Robbery Under Arms*. The picture of Australian history, the opinion of Western Australians themselves of their past, that is left with me is rather different from that painted in the highly successful book *The Fatal Shore*. But then Robert Hughes is an 'Easterner', his references to Western Australia inclined to be cursory and rather slighting. Western Australia, at the time of which I am writing, thought of itself still as somewhat separate from the rest of the Commonwealth.

The railway journey from Perth to other capitals took days to accomplish; little was known and no great loss felt at the separation (indeed, a very large majority – 138,653 to 70,705 – had voted in 1933 that Western Australia secede from the Commonwealth; it was a Joint Select Committee of the Imperial Parliament at Westminster which rejected the State's Petition that it be severed from the rest of Australia). Our poetry, also, had an understandable inclination to Australian writers and our anthology, *The Poets Commonwealth* cried,

Give us from dawn to dusk,
Blue of Australian skies . . .
Give us the wattle's gold
And the dew-laden air.

Another Australian writer, Andrew Paterson, eulogised 'The Droving Days', when 'Clancy' had

Gone a-droving 'down the Cooper' where
the Western Drovers go;
As the stock are slowly stringing, Clancy rides
behind them singing,
For the drover's life has pleasures that the
towns-folk never know.

Paterson and his contemporary, Adam Lindsay Gordon, are not names you will find in any English anthology of verse but they imparted to me a little of Australian nationalism and of Australian national pride in their continent. At school I would sing with as much feeling as any born Aussie that

There is a land, where floating free,
From mountain-top to encircling sea
A proud flag flies most gloriously;
Australia, Australia.

In my second year at Hale I made a start with Chemistry and Physics, both of which were taught with some thoroughness, although I was not at the school for long enough to learn much; Latin was taught but was given much less emphasis than in English schools (understandably, by many it was felt to be almost irrelevant to Australian culture and life). Hale did, however, offer a course in 'Commercial Subjects' (including book-keeping) which I opted for, rather against my form-master's wishes as he thought it insufficiently 'academic'; I justified my choice to him by explaining that we didn't have and, given my father's incarceration, might continue not to have any money. Thus I might have to leave school early and start earning my living.

At Hale we played Australian Rules football (probably at Guildford, also, but that I cannot remember). This game must have been derived from some early form of rugby; it is played on an oval pitch, with four goalposts at each end, 18-a-side, 15 of whom are positioned in five lines of three over the whole pitch (marked by their opponents, similarly so positioned), with three players on each side free to roam at large. At least some handling of the ball is permissible but under what circumstances is now beyond my memory. At the time, I played the game with zest but without skill.

Inevitably, given that Hale was predominantly a day school and that much of each day was spent away from it, the routine at Hale School did not dominate its pupils' existence as does that at a boarding school. Perhaps that was its strength. Certainly, I now look back on my year-and-a-quarter at Hale with affection.[3]

Chapter 8
The *Sarpedon*: back to England, 1943

At last Mother heard that we had confirmed passages on a ship sailing for England and expected to leave Fremantle in early June. The school had to be notified of our withdrawal, the acting Headmaster Mr Hadley writing kindly that 'we are very sorry indeed to lose Kenneth and Geoffrey. They are very fine boys and are progressing very well here. We wish them every success in their future lives and trust you will all have a safe trip home.' There was the lease of the house in Subiaco to be terminated, our possessions to be packed. There would have been letters to write – to her parents in England amongst others letting them know that we were on our way (although the date on which we would reach that country could not even be guessed at), financial arrangements to be made, our effects to be packed up. At the time I do not think either of us boys had a thought for all these cares.

We were not to know that in Germany Admiral Doenitz felt himself to be making 'the most difficult decision of the whole war'.[1] U-boat losses over the past six months had been on such a scale that he was unsure as to whether he would be justified in persisting with the Atlantic campaign. After consultation with his commanders he decided to do so. Even so, the numbers of U-boats in the North Atlantic during 1943 fell as follows:[2]

	May	*June*	*July*	*Aug.*	*Sept.*	*Oct.*
U-boats (no.)	186	165	157	131	123	133

The Goddess Chance was allowing us to take our voyage just as the Germans were recoiling.

At the beginning of June we learnt that the ship would be sailing from Fremantle on the 11th. My best friends at Hale gave me presents, a boomerang, a ruler inset with various Australian woods, a pencil-box; there were promises to write letters – somewhat surprisingly kept. My other friends ex-Malaya, Peter Morris, Michael

Pallister and Alison Drysdale, were said goodbye to (I rather think I may have exchanged a quick kiss with Alison while she was getting on her bicycle); surprisingly, I was to meet the first two again some years later back in England.

As an experienced traveller Mother would have known which cases could safely be marked 'HOLD: NOT WANTED ON VOYAGE', which 'BAGGAGE ROOM' and which 'CABIN' – not too many of these latter as the three of us would all be sharing one cabin. She knew, however, how important it was that we had some diversion and she bought a board game called 'Buccaneer' (a kind of cross between 'Tri-Tactics' and 'Monopoly'). Having been told of the need to have warm clothes in case the ship was torpedoed, she also bought herself a 'siren-suit'; I did not much approve as I had never before seen her in trousers!

The *Sarpedon* was an 11,400-ton cargo liner of the Blue Funnel Line built in 1923 and rated to carry 155 passengers in a single class (on this voyage, though, she was carrying considerably fewer, 78 adults and 22 children being shown on her books on arrival at Liverpool). Although it was wartime, a pre-war routine was still very largely observed; there were stewardesses to look after women passengers – just as well as Mother was invariably seasick immediately the ship sailed. There were bath stewards (even on much larger passenger liners private bathrooms 'en suite' were an extreme rarity) who would run a bath, at a previously fixed time, of seawater of course, as fresh water was precious, although a basin of fresh water was placed on a plank tray across the bath so that the salt could be rinsed off, dining-room stewards and a steward in charge of the passenger lounge and smoking-room.

However, one could not hide the existence of war. On the aft-deck was the standard issue 4-inch gun – very old and one of the thousands that must have been made in the early part of the century and then stockpiled; its efficacy must have been doubtful – while on the boat-deck were four little turrets each equipped with two Oerlikon cannon as a protection against aircraft attack (the Oerlikon was a Swedish quick-firing 20-mm gun, of modern design).[3] Also on the boat-deck were rockets which carried a parachute from the corners of which wires would trail, the intention being that any attacking low-flying aircraft would be at risk either from getting a wire tangled round its propeller or from wires cutting into its wings. No case is known, I am told, of these devices (PACs) having been used successfully. On the bridge were Browning machine guns – in the early days of the war many ships had been crippled by low-flying planes machine-gunning the bridge, killing the master and disabling the steering, after which the ship could be finished off at leisure. Finally, aft along with the 4-inch were smoke canisters to hide the ship from any surface attacker. It sounds quite impressive, but the losses the Merchant Navy was suffering showed the pitiful inadequacy of this protection, greatly increased though it was from the early days of the war.

On all decks Carley floats were lashed so that should the ship sink too quickly for boats to be lowered there would be some buoyant object for survivors to cling to. The ship's boats themselves were kept swung out, of course, in readiness for instant lowering; no one could tell when a torpedo would strike from the moment a ship left harbour until it berthed in a safe haven. All passengers had to carry their life jackets (stuffed with kapok not the pre-war cork ones which had been clumsy to put on and which had a reputation for breaking the wearer's neck), each with its red light and whistle – to help searchers locate survivors in the dark – and box of Horlicks tablets (which I am ashamed to say I and many others periodically and very foolishly ate as sweets).

At all times, also, we had to carry a 'scatter bag' of warm clothing: experience had shown that many who had escaped drowning from torpedoed ships died in the boats from exposure. Boat drill was practised regularly; at any time the klaxon might sound and over the tannoy would come the cry 'Boat Stations, Boat Stations', when all passengers had to hurry *immediately* to their muster points.

At night the ship sailed in total darkness, portholes were closed and blacked-out, no lights – not even a cigarette – were allowed on deck, permanent screens outside each door opening on to the deck stopped any internal light from being seen by hostile watchers at sea.

As I was over the age of 12 I was classed as an adult, paying the full fare, and hence I took my meals with Mother and the other 'grown-ups'. We two were seated at a table for four, the others being a Mrs Newman and her daughter Margaret (very slightly younger than me) who had joined the ship some two and a half weeks and nearly 3,000 miles earlier at Melbourne. Before we reached England they would have covered over 20,000 miles!

There were three others of about Margaret's and my age, Tony Hawker, Robin Berens and Sheila Robertson. The two girls naturally went round together while Tony, who shared a cabin with his older brother, and I formed another pair.

Tony was an avid reader of science fiction and owned a number of copies of an American magazine devoted to this 'Astounding

Science Fiction'. It was a new genre to me[4] and I devoured them with fascination. We made up a board game 'Space' in which galaxies warred with each other and where space navies made up of battleships, battle cruisers and destroyers fought their battles with space mines and space torpedoes. Each piece carried a picture – culled originally from the drawings in 'ASF' – of the craft or weapon it was meant to represent, carefully drawn in Indian ink and bearing a number representing its value in the game. It occupied us all – for Geoff as a good drawer and some of the other young were also allowed to participate – for many hours, although I do not remember any game ever being concluded! The girls, Sheila and Margaret, thought the whole thing rather silly and would go off giggling together.

The ship's library was probably quite adequate for normal voyages. It contained a copy of Richard Jeffries *After London*, which I began with enthusiasm but found rather unsatisfactory overall, and there were also copies of John Masefield's classic sea stories *Victorious Troy* and *The Bird of Dawning*, both epic tales of clipper ships returning to England through storm in the waters in which we too sailed. The library, though, had not been intended for such long journeys as ours and for reading matter we had largely to rely on our own resources, sharing, lending or swapping books between us. This was fine to begin with but I was an avid reader and had soon devoured all there was available.

There were deck games to play, tennis and quoits, both played with rope quoits, in the first case thrown in the air by one player over a net to be caught and returned, or hopefully not, by the opponent, and in the second thrown so as to slither and land close to the centre of the concentric circles marked on the deck. I was not very agile or deft and so had no natural aptitude for tennis which in any case soon became impractical as the high winds prevented play; with practice I was not too bad at quoits, at which I would contrive, when returning her quoits to the lady with whom I used to play, to brush her breast with my hand (unobtrusively, as I thought, but no doubt very obvious to her 30-plus-year-old maturity, although she never remonstrated about it!).

Some months before we left Australia, Mother, recognising my pubescence, had obtained and given me a pamphlet on the 'facts of life' which I had read with the normal boy's embarrassed but fascinated curiosity. I had assured her – boys do not like talking about such things to their mother – that I understood it, and so I suppose I did, in a fashion. Peter and Tony Hawker and Robin Berens, however, were at least a year or two older than me, more accustomed to shamefacedly 'talk dirty', while I did not want to let on how little I really understood for fear of being thought still a child. Sex was of absorbing interest but still an unknown terrain; girls, however, I had always liked and Sheila Robertson now held sway over my heart. I would walk the companionway outside her cabin while she was lying inside during the post-lunch quiet hour, waiting for her to emerge, but would go fiery red if laughed at about it; which she did, of course, being a teenage girl.

Most of the time, though, our attitudes to each other were still simple boy/girl; together we would walk the decks for exercise in the howling gales – it was mid-winter in the Southern Ocean and, to avoid submarine or surface raider attack, we would steam south even of 'the roaring forties'. Towering great waves constantly pursued us, ever threatening to overwhelm the little stern gun whose barrel pointed so cheekily at them.

The strength of the gales was such that we could lie back into it and not fall to the deck, lie on the canvas hatch combings billowing in spite of their tight lashings and note that our weight was insufficient to press the canvas back onto the battens covers beneath. It was thrilling as well as being frightening, though our young fears were of the elements rather than of the unseen and even more dangerous human enemy.

At that time it was the custom for the ship's captain to conduct every Sunday the Service of Common Prayer as laid down in the Prayer Book. It was a simple service with well-known hymns, naturally including,

> Eternal Father, strong to save,
> Whose arm hath bound the restless wave,
> Who bid'st the mighty ocean deep
> Its own appointed limits keep,
> Oh hear us when we call to thee
> For those in peril on the sea.

The words had a particular meaning for us at the time. Our position in waters that might contain hostile enemies, our ship having for safety to maintain wireless silence so that no one – whether friend or foe – knew where we were, reminded all how puny and insignificant we and our ship were in this vast world of grey waters.

At last, after more than three weeks at sea – 24 days to be exact – we reached Durban on 5 July. The distance direct from Fremantle is some 6,000 miles but the course we steered would have made that covered much greater; my recollection of the lottery on the ship's daily run is of a winning number usually around 260 to 290 nautical miles. Anyway, it was more than enough; crew as well as passengers were glad this long haul was over.

At Durban we were berthed under the Bluff – the heights of which were a forbidden area being fortified against possible attack from the sea – next to the whaling station. It was not a convenient berth; we were on the opposite side of the harbour to the main port and to the town, both of which could be reached only by long walks and a ferry crossing. Presumably it had been decided on, though, because our stay in Durban was to be protracted; the ship's engines needed repair. So it was that we remained in Durban nearly three weeks, which, had Mother had plenty of money, could have been very pleasant at that time of the year. However, she had to husband what little she had: to obtain any more, in wartime, in a strange country would have been impossible.

Mother recalled that a couple, Railton by name, who had lived in Malacca, were now living in Durban; their son, Mark, a year or so older than me had been my admired friend when I was 6. She got in touch with them and we were invited to visit. Their flat looking over the sea was very smart, we, although clean and tidy, must have looked rather shabby by contrast. I was outgrowing my shorts, for example, which was remedied by the offer of a pair of long trousers that Mark was said to have outgrown – my first and another mark of growing up of which I was very proud. Mark, also, took us swimming from the adjacent beach, protected from shark attack by a curtain of nets out to sea.

The prevalence of sharks in these waters was clear enough from the state of the dead whales towed in to the whaling station. These had been harpooned far out in the ocean by the whalers, tiny ships sometimes not as big as the great whales they were killing but equipped with a harpoon gun against which the whale had no chance; it was no longer the almost even conflict of an Ahab and Moby Dick. Dead these great creatures were an enticing meal for any hovering shark and the males would be towed in to harbour with their penes almost totally devoured and the cow whales with their mammaries ripped. We passed these horrific sights daily when walking to the ferry but I do not think we youngsters made any connection between the torn bodies of these mammals and our fate at the hands of such predators should a torpedo find our ship.

Once at the whaling station the whales' carcasses would be cut up and rendered down for oil; a revoltingly smelly business of which we, in our neighbouring berth, were only too well aware. Whale meat, too, appeared on the ship's menu and, fresh, it did not taste at all bad although later in the war the rather staler meat obtained by the Ministry of Food appealed not at all to the palates of the British public, hungry though they were for almost any red meat. Geoff was sensible enough to obtain as a souvenir a piece of baleen, which he inscribed with the date and the weight and length of the whale from which it was obtained.

Walking through the docks one evening we passed a battleship built in the early days of the First World War. I was astonished to note how low she lay in the water – the side casements housing the secondary armament must have been almost useless in any kind of sea. (I have recently been informed that this was *HMS Revenge* – actually a battle cruiser: she had fought at the Battle of Jutland in 1916, had been modernised in the 1930s and was, in theory, still operational. The sinking by the Japanese of her sister ship, *HMS Repulse*, in 1941, must have raised certain doubts about this.)

At last the repairs were complete and on 23 July we sailed in convoy[5] for Cape Town, six or seven ships, I think, with a SA Navy armed tug acting as escort. The weather was stormy, as so often off this stretch of coast, and a tanker of peculiar construction – built to provide minimum deck space at a time when Suez Canal dues were calculated on this – seemed often to be totally immersed by the waves, only her upper bridge and funnel showing in the wilderness of waters and seeming to be attached neither to each other nor to anything resembling a ship. But she and we survived; indeed, apart from the storm, this passage was without incident.

Cape Town was grey and cold, rainy and foggy with Table Mountain almost perpetually veiled in cloud, not the white tablecloth of repute but rather a soiled and ill-washed cover. My spirits were equally low; I did not wish, I would not go ashore; I didn't want to see the celebrated seventeenth-century Dutch merchant's house; I refused contemptuously suggestions that, with other passengers, I should take the aerial ropeway to the mountain top – Mother and Geoff were sensible and did not let my hump spoil their excursion. At dinner it was, of course, maddening to hear Mother, Margaret and Mrs Newman exclaiming over the interest of the afternoon.

Our stay in Cape Town was longer than envisaged; the ship's engines were again in need of repair. *Sarpedon* had been built well – the Second Engineer, Mr J. S. Keith, had almost been in raptures over the thickness of her plates, 'they don't build them like that, now', he said to me when I expressed a passing interest in Marine Engineering – but she was 20 years old and her boilers had been built to burn Welsh steam coal which was unobtainable. Moreover, her voyage had been a long and arduous one, sailing from Liverpool in the late autumn of 1942, crossing the North Atlantic in gales in a convoy continuously attacked by submarines, ship after ship being sunk (no wonder that the Chinese stokers had deserted en masse in New York, forcing the Master to go against all Blue Funnel principles and recruit afresh in that port from the pool of idle seamen there: never good quality and least of all in that time of desperate shortage when every good man could take his pick). From New York she had sailed through the Panama Canal and across the Pacific, under threat of Japanese submarine attack, to Sydney where again many of the crew had 'run', then round the south of Australia to Fremantle where we had joined (two crew had deserted there, too). At Cape Town it had already been a nine-month and 25,000-mile voyage!

On this occasion, though, the repairs took only about a week and by the beginning of August the ship had left Cape Town en route for the United Kingdom. For this stretch of the voyage Mother, aware that for a $13\frac{1}{2}$- year-old boy to continue to share a cabin with her and Geoff was not very satisfactory, had arranged with another mother, similarly placed, that I and her son, Robin Berens, should have a cabin to ourselves on the promenade deck. (Presumably, some passengers must have disembarked either at Cape Town or Durban; no doubt there was an extra charge as well – which she could ill-afford.) We were, naturally, enjoined by our respective mothers to keep our new quarters tidy, which, also naturally, we undertook to do; but I have never been able to keep anything tidy for long and I very much doubt if I did while sharing with Robin. However, both of us were glad to have a 'room to ourselves', and also quite proud of it, and did our best to make it homely.

The weather initially was reasonable, the ship rolling but not excessively. Three or four days after sailing from Cape Town, on 5 August, the news spread that the chief engineer was missing. The ship was searched from stem to stern; no trace of him was to be found. Accordingly, the captain put about in the forlorn hope that in retracing our course we might find him still floating in the ocean but after five hours' steaming 'all hope of rescuing the Chief Engineer was abandoned'; accordingly, he turned about again and we resumed our course.

A full report of this incident may be found in the ship's official log held by the Ministry of Transport in Cardiff and it certainly reads most mysteriously. There are reports of lights being seen and then extinguished in the chief engineer's cabin, and although, as I have said, the ship was rolling heavily it seems unlikely that he could have gone overboard accidentally. However, if accident is ruled out, one is left with the choice between suicide or murder. This unhappy fact was recognised by all and the reports, no doubt embroidered in the retelling, surrounding the chief engineer's death cast a gloom over the ship. The Master, I learnt at dinner from Mrs Newman (who used to play bridge with him), had spoken very plainly and firmly to the crew and particularly to the engine room staff.

The job of these latter was always both onerous and dangerous in those days of coal-fired ships but the 'black squad' aboard the *Sarpedon* at that time, mainly recruited in New York to fill the vacancies caused by the desertions after the Atlantic crossing I have already mentioned, can be expected to have been a particularly difficult bunch. Working below the water level for long periods when, at any moment, a torpedo striking the ship would lead to their almost inevitable death, either from scalding steam or from the inrush of waters, must have been unnerving for all; the engine breakdowns at Durban and Cape Town must, also, have preyed on the mind of the officers and particularly of the chief engineer whose charge this was.[6]

Shortly after we ran into another patch of bad weather, the ship pitching so violently in the steep seas that, having descended one her bows would be buried deep in its successor while her stern was left high in the air. Then, lying in one's bunk at night, one could feel the whole ship vibrating while the air was filled with the whine of her twin screws racing as the violent pitching of the ship left the blades, deprived of water to bite into, screaming in the air. And if we were not pitching, we were rolling. One night at dinner over she went – over and over. In spite of the 'fiddles' on the dining tables, plates, cutlery, the contents of plates, the waiting stewards, all were thrown to the floor with a crash of breaking crockery. Still she seemed to go over. Then, there was a moment of deathly silence while she seemed to hang, poised, almost on her beam-ends. She hung there for a moment, and then slowly, oh so slowly, began to recover to the upright position, only to go over again to the starboard, not quite so far this time, before again returning. There were a few more rolls, each progressively less violent. The stewards picked themselves up from the floor to which they had been thrown, white faced and shaken, as were we.

All had believed in that half-second that she would go right over and that we would all be lost at sea (many years later, in the National Maritime Museum at Greenwich, a marine engineer told me that the *Sarpedon* class were notoriously unstable and that on one occasion a ship loading in dock almost went over, being kept upright only by the edge of the dock; but of the truth of this I do not know).

It was customary for 'grown-ups' – which for this purpose included Robin and me – to bath about 6 p.m. prior to changing for dinner. On one such evening, returning to our cabin, with only a bath towel wrapped around our loins, we two boys found the two girls, Sheila and Margaret, waiting there. These two promptly stripped us of our towels, leaving us to clutch – or not – (as we chose) our genitals, to their delighted giggles! This became a daily evening pastime of theirs – not unenjoyed by us either, although any attempts on our part to see as much of their bodies as they had of ours were firmly repelled!

On one occasion, at dinner, Mrs Newman, making general conversation, asked what time of the day one found best. I replied, in some innocence, 'The hour before dinner' at which Margaret broke down into uncontrollable giggles. Nor then could I keep a straight face, and I did likewise. Our mothers could not understand what was so funny, of course, and neither of us was prepared, or dared, to explain the cause of our mirth!

The distance from Cape Town to Freetown as shown on the charts is only 3,120 miles but that, of course, is by the most direct route. The fact that it took us nearly three weeks to reach Freetown indicates that we probably sailed far out into the Atlantic, not sticking to the established shipping route (which would have been the favourite resort of German submarines looking for a target). Fresh water from the ship's tanks ran out and we were forced to rely upon water distilled by the ship's condensers, healthy enough but of a rather peculiar taste. The supply of potatoes too became exhausted.

There were compensations, however. As we steamed northwards the storms of the southern hemisphere weather gave way to day after day of blazing sun. Robin and I often slept in deckchairs on the deck outside our cabin and there we could see the dawn break, the pitch dark of the tropic night, the sudden appearance of the sun's rim above the distant horizon, then a blaze of light as it jumped high above the waters.

We reached Freetown on 21 August but our hopes of being able to go ashore were to be dashed. There was a yellow fever epidemic raging and shore leave was forbidden. Instead the ship lay at anchor in the estuary, hopefully out of range of the mosquitoes, which carried the virus. Day after day we lay there, lacking the movement of air caused while on passage, baking in the tropical sun. Tropical fruits, though, could be obtained from local vendors anxious to earn a penny or two for the sale of a bunch of bananas or oranges. African boys would dive for coins thrown into the water (which must have been hazardous since Geoff maintains that on one occasion he saw a crocodile swimming lazily in the estuary waters). Fresh water, though, was obtained and that at least was an improvement. For the rest, though, we were all very bored and very, very hot – the butter fresh from the ship's refrigerator would, within minutes, dissolve into a greasy pool of yellow fat.

Mother alarmed at the length of the voyage had arranged for me to be given some instruction by one of the other passengers, a teacher, in Maths and French, Margaret and Sheila being other pupils. I was in an extremely difficult mood. I questioned and objected constantly – some of Euclid's theorems seemed nonsensical and I said so, probably rather rudely. Anyway, one day a man passenger, a Salvation Army official, took me on one side and gave me a long talking to on the pain I was causing my Mother, how she was paying for lessons for me, which she could not really afford, and how ungrateful I was showing myself to be. He must have spoken very well as I was almost reduced to tears of repentance and I certainly tried harder thereafter.

While we lay there the crew were not idle. The ship had to be coaled and, since we could not use the regular coaling berth, lighters came out to us, laden with sacks of coal, which were carried by the African stevedores, sack by sack, up a plank to a port in the ship's side. It was dirty hard work and quarrels between the labourers were not infrequent, while the coal dust rose in a haze over the ship, coating all with grime. We had to take on cargo, too, and other lighters came out laden with palm kernels that we were to carry to England to turn into margarine and other edible oils. The smell of this is particularly frightful, but in the ship we were unable to get away from it. It permeated everything and was to be with us for a month until the end of the voyage.

The reason for this long wait at Freetown – more than a fortnight – was that we were waiting for a convoy to assemble. At last several ships had collected and in early September we set sail again on the last leg of our journey back to England. The Master had been appointed Commodore of the convoy and he had a Royal Navy officer aboard to advise him. It was our duty to convey instructions to the other merchant ships about keeping a constant, common speed and an exact station, not an easy matter since the convoy's ships varied in size from a few thousand to over

20 thousand tons, and from slow, old, coal-fired tramps to modern oil-burning ships and one motor vessel which kept breaking down (I have never discovered how a motor vessel worked).

As we steamed out into the Atlantic Ocean, other ships joined the convoy until there were approaching 80 in all. The amount of water covered by this vast fleet must have been enormous, at least nine square miles of ocean since there was a fair distance between each column – we sailed in eight – as well as between the ships in each column. This spacing was essential as otherwise there would have been collisions during the hours of darkness between the blacked-out ships.

The convoy was provided with a merchant ship converted to enable a Sea Hurricane to take off in case of attack by enemy aircraft. The pilots of these planes must have been very brave men; the Hurricane, once launched, could not land again and the pilot would have had to eject in the hope of being picked up before he drowned. Also there was a small rescue ship, an ocean going tug, whose duty it was to pick up survivors from any torpedoed ship; the standing instructions were that no merchant ship should delay if another was torpedoed, 'come hell or high water the convoy went on'. This may seem heartless, given the fact that there would be survivors swimming in the water, perhaps without any wreckage to support them, but it was based on the bitter experience that U-boats would always lurk by a torpedoed ship, ready to send off a second salvo of torpedoes to sink any rescuer. On the outskirts of the convoy, rarely seen by us, were escorts, constantly circulating, always searching with their sonar for sound of an attacker.

It was while on this stretch that the news came through that Italy had sued for peace. All ships sounded their sirens and whistles in a great explosion of joyous thanks and relief. At last, it seemed, there might be an end to the war that had begun more than four years before.

The ship's wireless, one day, picked up the broadcast of a speech by Winston Churchill in the Houses of Commons in which he said that even as he was speaking, a convoy was under attack in the Western Ocean;[7] Mother speculated to me that her parents must have been wondering whether it was we who were the victims. But by some miraculous chance we were to come through unscathed.

Submarines must have been in the area, though, since my brother remembers a night when all the passengers sat together in the saloon, hearing the crunch of depth charges in the distance. One old lady took a jewelled ring from her finger and gave it to her grandson saying that he would be more likely to survive than she. If we went to our bunks at all that night, it was fully clothed.

The next day we heard the Commodore hailing from our ship's bridge to one of our little grey escorts 'Well done'. On another occasion, a German reconnaissance aircraft appeared but, much to our relief, thick fog descended almost immediately; the whole convoy was enveloped in it and we did not emerge for some days.[8] A convoy as large as ours, covering about nine square miles of water, would have been not only a tempting but also a very vulnerable target. As it was, though, the Germans lost contact; only the sounds at night of underwater explosions – depth charges we conjectured uneasily, as we lay in our bunks – indicated that we were under a constant danger of attack.

As we sailed north, the weather grew colder although it was only September. Then, almost without warning, there were reports of land and on 28 September, we sailed up the Mersey to the ship's homeport of Liverpool, a sunny day with great fat barrage balloons floating over the city and gleaming silver in the light. All the ships in port sounded their sirens in welcoming recognition. After a circumnavigation of the globe in the past year she was home. So too were we, 38 months and more than 20,000 miles after leaving Liverpool in the *Viceroy* in July 1940. England, at last.[9]

Chapter 9
Dover College I, 1943–5

As the *Sarpedon* was prodded by tugs into her berth, aboard her there was all the hustle and apparent confusion – and also the tedious waiting – attendant upon any arrival, the check to ensure that after four or more months at sea no item had now been left behind, the patient queuing as the passengers were questioned by immigration officers, not the usual perfunctory glance at passports but a thorough examination since this was wartime England. There were the farewells, the exchange of addresses and promises to 'keep in touch', the ending shipboard romances. Baggage, including hold-baggage not seen since Australia, had to be checked and cleared through customs – some of our fellow passengers had quite a lot and one porter made the sour comment, 'Talk about refugees, I have never seen so much luggage.' Mother must have phoned her parents to let them know of our arrival. Then we took the crowded London train with several others. Again we were reminded that Britain was at war when one youth who talked of our voyage was sharply reminded 'Careless Talk Costs Lives'.

And so we returned to my grandparents' home at Wandsworth, which we had left over three years before. The emotion that my mother must have felt at being reunited with her family must have been very great but she was never one to be demonstrative of her feelings. Moreover, her relief at no longer having to carry the full burden alone would have been diminished by the imperative need to deal with other problems that had been shelved during the long voyage.

We still had the identity cards issued in 1938 but we had to obtain ration books and books of clothing coupons (we were I think given an initial extra allowance of these which took some account of the fact that we were 'refugees' from the tropics and needed to kit ourselves out). So she had immediately to register us with the local council and with the local office of the Ministry of Food, to go through all the bureaucratic procedures and fill in all the forms, which were such a feature of wartime Britain.

Then there was the question of schooling where, again, a decision had to be made without too much delay. My brother was of the age when he could return to our old prep school, Hollingbury Court (although even this step cannot have been as simple as it might seem: 'Where was Hollingbury now located? We had last known of it evacuated to Dauntsey's School, Devizes. 'Were there vacancies for an 11-year-old?'). In my case the problems were greater as at $13\frac{1}{2}$ I would have to go to a secondary school (I do not think – but cannot of course now know – whether my entry into a state school was considered: it would have been easier for Mother even if it meant abandoning her and my father's dreams for us children). Mother enquired of Truman and Knightley, a firm that specialised in such matters; they gave her the names of three schools, all in the West Country (all public schools in the south-east of England and from around London had been evacuated to 'safer' areas).

After long, tiring train journeys to inspect these, she settled provisionally on Dover College of which she had heard, which was not too expensive – a very important consideration in view of her precarious finances – and where there were vacancies. The next step was for me to accompany her to the school so that they could interview me; so we had to make the long wartime rail journey to Exeter and then out into the country to Poltimore where the school was housed in a Palladian country house. At the time it looked very grand to me and I felt very small and lost, but Dover College had been badly hit by the evacuation from Kent. So far away from its traditional recruiting ground its numbers were down to only 99 boys. Indeed, I learned later that it was facing closure, so, although the headmaster was appalled at my ignorance of Latin, he was prepared not only to accept me but to reduce my fees until my father was released.

I was not happy there at first. Any boy entering a school other than with his fellows at the beginning of a term is looked at askance by these – boys are very suspicious of anything unusual. In my case, too, I felt and was very alien in England; the school subjects and curricula were not those I had become used to in Australia, the rules of Rugby football were not the same as those of Australian Rules football;[1] and I was unaccustomed to the cold English weather. I knew no one and spent long hours writing letters to my mother – not too depressed ones I hope, but just to pass the time.

The park which surrounded Poltimore had clearly been splendid in its day, with water gardens and Chinese bridges leading to a little temple, with three great walks, one set about with ornamental flowerbeds, another leading through an avenue of noble lime trees.

These were in decay long before Dover had leased the house – to maintain them in their original glory would have required a half-company of gardeners and a heavy purse. The headmaster was determined, however, that decay would not increase and one afternoon a week was spent in 'labour' in the gardens, not felt by us at all as a chore but rather as an enjoyment, although cutting wood and pruning timber in the snow was rather colder than one would have wished.

Cold dominated my life that first winter. The coal ration was totally inadequate to heat the large draughty rooms with marble or paving stone floors. Fires were lit only after 4.30 p.m.; to get warm before that boys would coil themselves around the pipes in the drying rooms in the damp steam given off by washed and drying games kit and rugger socks.

All new boys 'fagged'; this fagging was of two kinds, 'general' and 'personal'. 'General fagging' meant sweeping the floors of the rooms and dormitories, laying the tables for meals and clearing up afterwards, the menial duties that there were no menials to perform. 'Personal fagging' was doing jobs or running errands for one's own personal prefect/fag-master; in a letter to my Hale schoolfriend, David Anderson, I wrote 'I am a fag and have to clean Stroud's boots (I fag for Stroud) and shoes and keep his study tidy. Also whenever he wants anything, say toast, I have to make it. At the end of term, however, I was given a tip'.[2] Such duties as these were accepted without demur; I thought 'my' prefect, Stroud, a young god preparing for future war (in which, alas, he was to die).

Life was dominated by 'the war' to an extent that can be understood only by those who have experienced such a condition. All boys were members of the Junior Training Corps and passed one afternoon a week being drilled, taught how to use a .303 rifle and simple infantry manoeuvres, 'Section in Attack', 'Platoon in Attack'. All senior boys at the age of 17 became members of the Home Guard (as were the masters – elderly and decrepit though these were: the young and fit ones had gone long since. The Home Guard kept night watch over any local militarily sensitive spots – the threat of a German invading raid even at this stage could not be entirely discounted. The newspapers were scanned intently to discover the latest news, at 6 p.m. and 9 p.m. all huddled soundless around the wireless as if the BBC announcer was uttering Holy Writ. From time to time there would be news of the death in action of an Old Boy, or sometimes of a relative of a boy still at the school. 'Before the war' was a fairy-tale age that few could remember clearly; 'the end of the war' was still nowhere near in sight.

In late 1943, it will be remembered, the armies of the Western Allies were bogged down in southern Italy, facing one hotly opposed river crossing after another, and the German armies in the East still held vast areas of Russia. At sea our own unscathed return had clearly been unusual; news of the German discoveries of the *schnorkel* and their use of hydrogen peroxide as a fuel meant that U-boats could remain safe underwater for longer and travel faster, both changes making them vastly more dangerous.

The Christmas season 1943 passed in London at my grandparents', as had always been the custom with our Christmases in England, was punctuated by air raids, usually short, by German hit-and-run bombers. As the sirens wailed we would descend from our attic beds to the coal-cellar as a place of comparative safety. A Canadian subaltern, with whom my cousin Mary was 'walking-out', celebrated Christmas day with us, his uniformed presence being yet another reminder that 'Peace on Earth' was not yet.

As I wrote to David, 'England is crowded out with troops, Canadians, Americans, Free French, Poles, and British, wherever you go you meet a soldier. On the way down to Exeter there was hardly standing room, there were so many soldiers on the train.'

At about this time mother decided that she would go back to work at the Post Office, a move which in the circumstances of the time was not remarkable since almost everyone worked to help the war effort. She could probably have claimed exemption however; that she did not must have been dictated by an imperative need to increase her income. Even though the costs of living with her parents would have been small, school fees for two boys were not.

In my letters to David Anderson I commented on the fact that this and subsequent holidays at Wandsworth Common were rather dull as no other boys at Dover lived nearby. London, itself, by this time was a shabby city, showing clearly the price of four years of war, bombed buildings being numerous. Even those not directly scarred had dirty or peeling paint, windows were criss-crossed with brown paper to reduce the number of glass splinters from bomb blasts, at night the streets were unlit because of the blackout and, indoors, lights were dim so that sufficient electricity was available for the factories. Economy in everything was the rule; even the amount of water in a bath had its 'advisory' level.

In spite of all this, my letters show that I was taken to a number of entertainments, from a pantomime to Agatha Christie's *Ten Little Niggers* and, also, that I went to Madame Tussauds (which did not live up to my expectations). My aunts, who would have organised these things, were always to exert themselves in every way for both us two boys.

A few more boys entered Dover in the Lent term, which meant that I was no longer the junior boy in the school. I had been moved out of the lowest class, where I had been first put, and, even in the next, was regularly top in the fortnightly marking order. I made friends, joined the Scouts; life was brighter.

As winter gave way to spring and summer the pleasures of Poltimore became more evident. The grounds contained many exotic trees, there was abundant wildlife (one prefect, Took by name, had a pet buzzard which he kept in his study; when disturbed by a fag coming in with a message for Took the buzzard would fly angrily round the little room – I found the bird's great beak to be terrifying – before settling again on its master's shoulder, although keeping one alert brown eye fixed on the intruder). At the back of Poltimore House the grounds were laid out around three avenues. One, the lime avenue, was lined with magnificent trees, and connected the house to the parish church so that the Baron Poltimore could ride in his coach from his front door up the avenue to the church where a pew – or rather a group of pews, which resembled a box in the opera rather than a normal church pew – awaited him. The central avenue had been lined with flowerbeds with stone seats engraved with tasteful verses. One of these read:

> The kiss of the sun for pardon.
> The song of birds for mirth.
> One is nearer God's heart in a garden
> Than anywhere else on earth.

As a 14-year-old I would sit on the seat looking out over the now unkempt gardens and think back upon the dandies and ladies of the Regency who might have sat on those very benches in their Corinthian splendour (heavily influenced by the novels of Georgette Heyer).

The shortage of teaching staff was such that there was no master available to run the Scouts so a prefect, 'Jacky' Wicker, did so, doing the job admirably. Once the summer term began we were allowed to camp out almost every weekend, each patrol building its own elaborate camp sites with camp furniture – a washstand, racks for cooking utensils, for cutlery and for crockery, all constructed out of young sycamore thinnings (a large plantation of this tree had grown wild). This enthusiasm was to develop and occupy a major place in my teenage life.

The summer brought with it, too, the opportunity to explore the south Devon countryside, a bicycle ride to Budleigh Salterton or to Sidmouth – each being about 15 miles distant from Poltimore – for a swim being regarded as no more than a pleasant spin. These bicycle rides also brought us into the neighbourhood of the numerous American troop camps (strictly out of bounds to us) and in another letter I wrote, 'There are troops, tanks, lorries and guns everywhere. . . . We are in a banned area now. The Home Guard is in a state of emergency and a platoon is always at the stables. Machine-gun posts have been established about two hundred yards from the edge of the playing fields and we have been warned not to go further. . . . Every morning we hear the sounds of planes revving up their engines . . . (while on 6 May) I saw 90 Dakotas going overhead' – the whole sky was filled with arrowhead after arrowhead of these Allied planes, practising as I can now surmise for the forthcoming invasion of France.

Then on 6 June came the news the country had been waiting for, the Allied forces had successfully landed in Normandy. Euphoria abounded; none now doubted that we were on the road to victory (although a month later, Captain Cyril Falls, writing in the *Illustrated London News*, pointed out that after a month of hard fighting the beachhead occupied no more in area than two French *départements*).

My Scout friend, 'Tubby' Clayton (who was in a different house to me in the school, but this was not much of a differentiation then as we all lived in one building), suggested that at the end of term we two should cycle to visit a cousin of his living at Llanidloes in central Wales. My mother was far from sure that such an expedition was wise – a view shared, no doubt, by Tubby's – but my housemaster and his wife were supportive and so it was agreed. We begged and borrowed a small tent, groundsheets for each of us which doubled as cycling capes should it rain, a rough blanket which with pins would serve as a sleeping bag, haversacks, 'billies'[3] and a frying pan, and, given by relatives from their own tiny rations, a stock of cans of meat, M&V (a ready prepared stew), baked beans and dried egg powder. Then, on our sit-up-and-beg bikes, and laden until we resembled Tweedledum or Tweedledee in a Teniel illustration of *Alice*, we set out.

It was quite an adventure. We would cycle – nearly 70 miles the first day but more like 30–40 thereafter – until evening, ask permission of a farmer or the occupant of any large country house to camp, then cook, sleep, cook breakfast, leave the site of the camp, so far as possible so that it showed no trace of our passing (as laid down by Baden-Powell in *Scouting for Boys*), give thanks to the owner and go on our way. Where there was a 'sight' – e.g. Wells Cathedral or Chepstow Castle on this first leg – we would stop to visit it.

When necessary we would wash our clothes, boiling them in the same billies in which we would cook our evening meal, spreading them to dry on the grass in the sun. We crossed the Severn on the old Aust ferry; we slept one night in a high wind on the Black Mountains (we supped that night on dried-egg omelette with a chocolate-spread filling). It was rare for us to be refused permission to camp; more often the wife of the house would take maternal pity on us two lads and offer us milk or fresh eggs or some other similar treat. The roads were emptier of motor traffic in those days, of course, and cycling was much safer. At no time, either on our bikes or in camp, were we ever afraid – although in one Welsh village we were asked jokingly if we had 'ever read *The Innocents Abroad*? Look at you leaving your packs for anyone to steal.'

At Llanidloes we were welcomed, bathed (I am sure that in spite of our best endeavours we must have reeked of wood smoke) and fed. Our clothes were properly washed and ironed and we slept in beds again, not just separated from the rough ground by a groundsheet and a blanket. We climbed, or rather walked up, Plynlimmon but otherwise we had five days of rest.

We set off on the return ride to London as full of enthusiasm as when we had cycled out of The Balls of Poltimore but this diminished fast. By the time we had reached Oxford we had both had enough and determined to give up and catch a train (with our bicycles of course) to London. It was late evening by the time we arrived at Paddington, so, not knowing the way across town, we left our bikes at the 'left luggage' and, carrying our haversacks, took the Underground to the nearest station to my grandparents' house (where we planned to spend the night). By this time dark had fallen and we were disconcerted to find no one in. 'What to do?' There was a brick air-raid shelter at the end of the road and poking our heads into it we were told that the shelter was full; we should find somewhere else to sleep. We were very tired by now and I knew nowhere else to go, except the Underground station a mile or so away and from which we had just come. Rather than retrace our steps to the Underground we decided to see if there was any window in the house we could force. By chance there was one not properly secured. We entered and, dog-tired, lay in places on the floor where we thought we would be safe from bomb blast and flying glass splinters. We slept.

At dawn next morning my grandparents, mother and aunt entering the house waked us; their amazement at seeing us, tousle-headed, was great. We explained our search for shelter and they then recalled hearing voices from inside the air-raid shelter we had approached; voices that, sleep-dulled and not expecting our arrival, they had not recognised as ours. We were fortunate that the house had not been hit during the night; if it had been the ARP would have been told that there was no one in it and that there was no need to make a search for survivors!

Although France had been invaded and the German army routed, were fleeing north and east, the south-east of England, particularly London, was under steady bombardment by V-1s, pilotless, gyroscopically guided planes loaded with explosives. When the plane's motor cut out, the plane and its deadly load would fall to earth. Although the number of 'doodlebugs' (as the V-1 was known) was limited, the physical damage each caused was considerable and the psychological harm even greater. In consequence, the population of London had reverted to the practice of 'the Blitz', taking refuge in shelters each night. Because of these, Geoff had remained at his school, Hollingbury (then in the relatively safe area of Haywards Heath), for the first weeks of the summer holidays.

Although the progress of the war in Europe was satisfying, in the Far East Japan still held most of the territory she had seized in her overwhelming initial assault – indeed in the battles of Kohima and Imphal it seemed at first as if India itself might suffer a major invasion. The prospect of seeing my father again, therefore, seemed as far off as ever but letters from him were now being received through the Red Cross – short, subject to a delay of over six months, and irregular in arrival, but still some evidence of continued life. In turn we were permitted to send short air letters that were centrally 'photo-ed' and reduced in size to lessen their weight. These communications would of course be subject to censorship, both in Britain and by the Japanese and, inevitably, were left somewhat stilted in construction, conveying little to the recipient of the realities of the life of the sender. To me, my father was becoming a rather insubstantial figure; I had seen him for a total of less than seven months in the past eight and a half years; the change in a boy's outlook growing up in this time is immense.

Christmas 1944, the sixth of the war, marked the last (though this was not known at the time) German offensive in the West which seemed to have come close to splitting the Allied line. This, and the continued bombardment of London, no longer by V-1s (whose launching sites in the Pas de Calais had been overrun) but by V-2s, rockets whose arrival was preceded by no warning, simply the crash of a great explosion, were indications that the war was not yet won. Similarly, at about this time I wrote, 'Potatoes are in short supply here now. All the war they have been trying to make (people eat them) and apparently they have succeeded so well that they have eaten too much. We have been getting quite a lot of eggs and oranges lately.'

That Christmas, also, was the occasion of my first encounter with death. My grandfather, whom I respected and liked, suffered a stroke and died, I think on the day after Christmas. His only son (my uncle Bert) and my cousin Don (a few years older than me) had sat with him (we played cards as we waited for him to die, we two boys pretending to an 'adult' nonchalance we did not really feel).

In the next four months events moved bewilderingly fast. The newspaper headlines proclaimed victory after victory (one cartoon showed a distraught Hitler looking at a map of Europe where 'Westphalia' was spelled 'WestFailure') by the Anglo-American armies in the West and the Russians in the East. Then came 8 May. The war in Europe was over.

At school the occasion was marked by a whole day's holiday. The headmaster could now set in train the arrangements for the school to return to its home in Dover, where the buildings had been requisitioned and occupied by the Navy and where my house, St Martin's, had been seriously damaged by a German shell. The last days of the summer term, therefore, were passed in assembling, so far as was possible while they were still in use, all the furniture, equipment, book and stationery supplies that are the essential adjuncts to such an institution. It was a time, too, for the school, its masters and us boys, to say our farewells to Poltimore House, the village and the villagers which had made the school so welcome over the past five years, and which for many had been the only 'Dover College' they had known.[4]

Clayton, another boy, Doyle, and I had determined to repeat our previous year's excursion, this time going to the New Forest (I suspect that this choice was influenced by the location of *The White Company* which I had just read). We took the train to Salisbury, viewed the cathedral, were advised by the police as to the name of a respectable, and cheap, 'bed and breakfast' (it was still a period when one would as naturally approach a police station as a present-day individual might go to a Citizens' Advice Bureau), and then set off for Lymington.

The New Forest, though, was not what we had envisaged. There were no real 'forests' with grassy glades and bubbling streams where one could camp far from any human habitation. In fact it seemed rather suburban, and owned by individuals, not 'common'. Finding a suitable campsite was dishearteningly difficult. At Beaulieu (whose abbey had featured in *The White Company*), Clayton remembered that a female relation of his had been to school with a Montague girl. So, in our still-clean Scouts uniforms, we cycled up to the front door of Palace House.

The young Baron Montague was in France with the Guards, but his mother, Mrs Pleydell-Bouverie, took us in, gave us tea and suggested that we camp in the grounds of the Dower House which had been occupied until recently by Americans. We said 'thank you', and went off. However, it was getting late so we decided instead of putting up tents etc., we would spend the night in an empty lodge cottage, although its bare boards would be harder than earth. The next day we found a campsite near the vegetable garden, looking over fields to the river, and making ourselves comfortable we went into the village to buy provisions.

Unfortunately, Mrs Pleydell-Bouverie had not told her estate agent that she had agreed to our staying and after a day or two he came up in a foul temper, accusing us of trespass and demanding eviction. He was not much mollified in being told that we *had* asked and been given permission to camp; so, unable to evict us as he would have liked to do, he had to content himself with warning us to behave and to tidy the vegetable garden as compensation for being allowed to camp there. He then went off, swearing to himself under his breath.

So we passed about ten days, swimming, getting burnt in the sun and generally doing nothing. By this time young Doyle was getting a bit homesick so we took him off to Ringwood to go home. That evening I remember a great crimson sunset. Next morning, in the village we learned of the dropping of the first atom bomb and of the probable imminent surrender of Japan. We felt that these momentous events required us to go home; we half expected our fathers to reappear instantly. So, we packed; we tidied the campsite and went to Palace House to say 'thank you' (hearing Capt. Pleydell-Bouverie saying 'its those damned Scouts again'). Then by bike to Ringwood and train to Ewhurst (where Clayton lived) speculating about what the end of the war would mean to us.

In fact, of course, the war was not to end for another day or two. When it did, I joined the crowds in Piccadilly celebrating 'VJ Day'. I can still remember the feeling of mass excitement, the belief that a new era had begun. But like all such feelings, reality was rather different. My mother had to wait another month for news. On

15 September I wrote to David Anderson, 'We had a cable from the Colonial Office today telling us that my father had been released from the Civilian Internment Camp at Singapore. We hope that he will be back here soon, in less than 2 months anyway.' Another tranche of my life had ended.

Chapter 10
Dover College II, 1945–9

I and a number of other boys had volunteered to return to school early to help unpack and carry into their new homes all the school furniture and equipment which had been brought back from Poltimore, partly because we were curious to see the buildings and playing fields, which the school had vacated in 1939 and of which the older masters had talked so often. Accordingly, in early September a group of us assembled at Charing Cross and took the train to Dover Priory station, a journey then new to us but one with which we were to become increasingly familiar.

Dover Town had suffered badly as a result of constant shelling from German gun-batteries on Cap Gris Nez and the streets of the old town near the basin contained as many wholly or half-derelict houses as those which were habitable. The area around Snargate Street, in particular, looked sinister as well as dingy (it was soon declared officially 'out of bounds' to the college, rumour said because of brothels!). Yet, curiously, dominating the town and its approaches whether by land or from the sea, the great castle high on the eastern cliff, the proud key to our 'precious jewel', seemed to have emerged from the war unscathed, inviolate.

The college buildings, also, had been left relatively unharmed; only the front of St Martin's House hit by a shell was in ruins. The thirteenth-century gatehouse, the refectory with its medieval wall-painting of the Last Supper and the chapel where King Stephen was reputed to have lain in death, these witnesses to England's past, and also the nineteenth-century buildings built in a matching style, all were still there, if shabby and rundown like England herself.

Gradually as much was put to rights as could be and all was made ready for the Michaelmas term to begin. We in St Martin's House, however, would have to eat our meals in School House and slept as one big dormitory in the refectory until the war damage to our own quarters had been made good. It was thus that, much to my amazement, I saw Peter and Edward Morris, last seen two years before in Perth, West Australia. They had remained, perhaps sensibly, in Australia until the war's end had made the seas safe again; I had not written to Peter in the past two years and it was pure chance that we were reunited – we then remained in contact until his death in 2001.

Another 'new boy' was my brother, Geoff, who also entered St Martin's House. At the time, that he should do so seemed normal and automatic to me but, with experience, I am far from sure that so doing is altogether wise, at least as a norm. As it was, however, in our own case, although there were occasional temporary frictions between us two, resulting from our different positions in the school hierarchy, the strong underlying bond of friendship that we had each for the other, and our shared experiences, meant that any disagreements that did take place were short-lived.

My father arrived back in England in November 1945 and Geoff and I were allowed special leave to see him. My memory of that weekend – which should be sharp – is, in fact, very fogged. He had been in the prisoner of war and civilian internee camps at Sime Road and at Changi (Singapore) for nearly four years, kept on semi-starvation rations in a climate always considered most unhealthy to Europeans, forced to do manual labour, subjected to indiscriminate violence from the Japanese guards and almost without news of the world and his family. I, last seen by him as almost a child, was now an adolescent, concerned primarily with my own doings. Nor did he speak much, or at all, of what he had experienced (as it seems was common amongst all those taken by the Japanese, whether they were soldiers or civilian internees).[1] It was perhaps almost inevitable, therefore, that paternal and filial affection should be overlaid with mutual incomprehension. Only in his last years did I get to know him better; only after his death did I begin to appreciate him, as he deserved. Geoff, even though two years younger, also found the act of bridging to be difficult.

Christmas 1945 was passed, as usual, at my grandmother's house, but it cannot have been convenient for my parents. Anyway, shortly after, my cousin Winnie offered to them the use of her grandparents' house in Swanage and it was there that we went for Easter 1946.

I lost my heart to Purbeck that holiday and there it has remained. I say 'Purbeck' here, but in fact it was not all of Purbeck, just that piece bounded to the north by Ballard and Nine Barrow downs, to the west by unbroken downs that reached out to the Channel at Kimmeridge and to the south and east by the grey sea that possessed us (for I think my brother shared equally in this worship). We had spent our young lives travelling the wide world and known no place as ours but here the bounds were drawn clear and within them lay an area comprehensible to the mind, pleasing to the sight and redolent with all those images of England's past that entranced a romantic imagination. There, on the downs, dwarfed by the radar towers that jutted against the sky, were the burial mounds of those who lived in Britain before Rome, while hillside after hillside showed the strip lynchets where those early men had planted their crops.

At Corfe, the entry into this land, the castle, its ruins like jagged teeth upon its hill, was witness to seven hundred years of history, treachery, but also courage, the murder of Saxon King Edward by his godmother, the death by starvation of Arthur's Breton knights, Lady Banke's heroic defence for the King in the Civil War and the weasel treachery that had let in by guile the Parliamentarians who could not enter by force.

In the south there were the sheer cliffs that dropped vertically into the Channel and which were murderous to sailing ships in storm – particularly if the warning beacon on St Aldhelm's Chapel had been extinguished by men anxious for loot and unconcerned for their fellows' lives. Then, even in Swanage Bay, so placid on a windless day, the *Anglo-Saxon Chronicles* told of a Danish fleet wrecked with all hands (fortuitously for Alfred and England).

Writing to David Anderson on 1 May, towards the end of that Easter holiday, I described the house, 'gas-lit' (each lamp had its small pilot and to give a proper light one pulled a small chain). 'It is in lovely country', I wrote, 'looking up the valley to Corfe. Corfe village is full of old houses with thatch or stone roofs and dormer windows. . . . Not far away are several other small villages, Worth Matravers, Langton Matravers and Studland. . . . We have had the most marvellous Easter; the hottest since 1900 and there has been hardly a cloud in the blue sky. . . . All the apple and cherry blossom is out and I can see the branches swaying in the breeze from the window by which I am sitting. Just beyond are gooseberry and current bushes. In fact all the countryside is in bloom and the bluebells and violets and primroses and daffodils are all out. The ground is covered with buttercups and daisies.'

Geoff and I cycled all over these 25 square miles and, in succeeding years, were to walk over most of them as well. We drew a map, part Ordnance Survey, and part our imagination, showing all beyond the perimeter of hills and sea as 'foreign' dangerous and unknown. By doing this, we accentuated further the particularity of the first piece of England we had really come to know – our equivalent of Kipling's Sussex.

As it happened another ex-Malacca family, the Willans (see Chapter 1), were living in Swanage, Margaret, the elder daughter, being almost exactly my age and at Sherborne Girls School. We had played as children and now, not knowing any other girls of my own age, I fell in teenage love with her, a condition in which I remained for the next two years and which further endeared Swanage to me. I was, however, as bashful as any other teenage boy. A boys' public school may have taught many things but not easy intercourse between the sexes.

My father returned to Malaya in the middle of 1946; he had not had long in England to recover from the seven continuous years he had spent in Malaya, but Dunlops was a commercial company and there was an urgent need to make good all that had been left undone during the Japanese occupation. Mother stayed on in England with us two boys.

That summer I took my School Certificate, passing it with a respectable number of credits and distinctions. In my two Latin papers, however, I secured marks of 2 and of 0 respectively (the '2' in the first paper must have been for writing my name; even that I neglected to do in the second). George Renwick, Headmaster of the College during these years, was a man of integrity and character who had the total respect of both colleagues and boys. He had represented Great Britain as a hurdler in the Olympic Games of 1924, was a Classicist and a respectable amateur musician, one of those few schoolmasters to whom Kipling's 'Let us now Praise Famous Men' could be applied without any qualification (except that he found few occasions to need the use of the 'rod'). Now he was filled with fury at my miserable showing, which he regarded as disgracing the school. The next term his wife gave me personal coaching for a 're-sit' of the Latin papers in December (in which I passed with credit). Latin, at that time, was still regarded as important, indeed a credit in the subject was an essential requirement for entry into Oxford or Cambridge universities; since my career ambition was now to enter the Colonial Service, which meant going first to one of these two, my performance in the July exam was really rather silly. But the sun had shone on the days of the Latin exams, I was weary with my desk and with writing papers, and the fresh air called!

At the end of term Clayton and I went on another cycling holiday, on this occasion to the Norfolk Broads. As in the past, we had no difficulty in finding campsites on the upward journey – one country gentleman personally showed us his walled fruit garden, supplying us with nectarines and other fruits picked from bushes fan-shaped against old pink brick walls. He, or rather an ancient gardener, also gave us a demonstration and some practical instruction in the 'art of the scythe', how to cut great, even swathes with the minimum of exertion – and, also, with safety!

When we reached our destination, though, we had the same difficulties in finding a permanent campsite as we had met with the previous year in the New Forest. Eventually we settled on the level top of a dyke, a river on one side and a drop to rather soggy meadowland on the other. By the time we had pitched our tent, of course, there wasn't much room for anyone else to pass; however, as no one attempted to do so during the week we spent there, this was no great matter.

We fished regularly but with no great reward by way of a catch, save for eels, which were abundant. Neither of us had ever eaten eel before, nor had we any idea either how to clean or cook them. We learnt, although we found rather disconcerting their habit of continuing to writhe wildly after their heads had been cut off; cut in steaks and fried they made quite respectable eating.

The weather, however, was inclement and the narrow strip of land and the small tent in a wet early August was not a particularly attractive abode. We swam whenever it was fine – boat traffic on the Broads at that period was very light – we read; but that was about all we could do. Finally, bored, we decided to go home and in continuous rain (against which our cycling capes were no great protection) we did the 80 miles to London.

It was the last holiday we were to take together. The three journeys that we had made in 1944, in 1945 and now in 1946 had shown us much of the diversity of southern England and Wales; we had developed our self-reliance. Finally, and also of importance, we had had a thoroughly good and healthy time for about eight weeks at a minimal cost.

Mother, Geoff and I spent the rest of that holiday back in Swanage. We did some 'stooking' of corn sheaves, we joined the excited crew of boys and men that gathered in every field as the binder reduced the area of standing wheat to a small central patch, until not a stalk of corn was cut without a terrified rabbit breaking and bolting for the cover of the hedgerow. In the path of that safety, though, was the line of men and boys with sticks, and, should the rabbit escape that ring, the village dogs, shouted on by their owners. Not many got through, but, such was the size of the rabbit population in those days before myxomatosis, the few who did would ensure that there would be just as many greedy predators by next year's harvest.

On one occasion Geoff and I gleaned the fields after the wheat had all been cut, gathering sufficient heads of grain to make, once they had been husked and ground (in an ordinary mincer), a flat cake of coarse bread.

We swam on Swanage beach, between the still-standing anti-invasion defences, barriers of steel scaffolding designed to stop enemy landing-craft getting close enough to shore to discharge their burden of men or armoured vehicles. (On the beach itself were concrete 'teeth' to block the advance of German tanks, while in the rising land behind were pillboxes and gun emplacements; all these were, perhaps, amateurish compared to those built three years later, and with infinitely greater resources, by the Germans to form their 'Western Wall', but they represented the best that could be improvised in haste in the dangerous days of 1940 and 1941.)

The winter of 1946/7 was amongst the coldest England had experienced in the century, made crueller by a breakdown in coal production and distribution. Tories (and almost every master and boy at the college was a Tory), still bitterly resentful of their overwhelming defeat in the 1945 General Election, were able to say, 'Look, it takes Socialist planning to produce a coal crisis in an island built on the stuff', but this did not keep them any warmer. The snow fell thick and stayed. January, February, March, even early April saw England covered in a thick white blanket, while in the homes and offices the people shivered.

No one shivered more than we. Bedroom windows still had to be kept wide open at night and the jugs of water kept in the room for the morning to wash with were frozen, sometimes solidly. Flannels were of course frozen every night and using them was like wiping one's face with a piece of rigid sandpaper. Boys went to bed wearing every sweater that they had while the inadequate blankets were supplemented by dressing gowns, 'Corps' greatcoats, anything possible that could be used. The daily mid-morning PT was continued unless the snow reached the knee. Games were impossible, the ground was too hard and the snow too thick. But cross-country runs *were* still practicable, and so we ran. At least, while running one was warm.

It was during this winter that Russia had imposed a blockade on land access to Berlin, hoping to starve that city into submission; an aim they would have achieved had it not been for the success of the Allied airlift of supplies. Even before this, in March 1946, I had written to David Anderson of Churchill's Fulton speech (in which he had warned of 'the Iron Curtain') that it was 'the best he has ever made'.

My School Certificate results had been sufficiently promising to lead the school authorities into thinking that there was a chance that I might be able to succeed in obtaining a 'Higher' Certificate in one year instead of the normal two. My abilities in French were a bar, however, but it was hoped, rather optimistically, that a visit to Paris with a school party in April 1947 might give me the extra edge. It did not; but the visit, admirably organised by the master teaching me, was of such value to my general education that it was worth every one of the £15 it cost.

From the moment we stepped off the ferry at Calais we were 'abroad' in a way that never before had I experienced. Port Said, Colombo, Malaya, Australia, South Africa, even Batavia, all these had seemed little more than rather exotic bits of England; France, though, was *different*. The crowded trains had different dimensions, the stewards summoning us to '*Première Service*', or '*Deuxième*', or even '*Troisième*' (in point of fact we never got served at all, which did not entirely surprise us), the 'hole-in-the-floor' lavatories in the *Lycée*, the wooden bowls from which we drank our breakfast coffee, the notices on the walls of all official buildings – '*Pas d'afficher*' alongside '*Pas de pisser*' – the cafés, the animation, and the amazing fact that no one was speaking English, all these filled us with exhilaration.

In fact Paris that year, not yet the third since her liberation, was in a state of crisis. The continent had experienced temperatures even lower than those in England, while the transportation system, wrecked by years of deliberate Allied bombing, was unable to function. Food was in short supply; France experienced her first bread riots since the years of Napoleon. Inflation was reaching levels experienced before only in the Germany of 1919; and it was still rising. Department store windows, indeed those of every shop, which didn't wish to be labelled 'Capitalist extortioner', bore in large white letters the slogan, '*A bas les haux de prix. Moins 10%*', but like all such populist slogans, by itself, this achieved nothing of lasting benefit.

Against this background, Leo Wright – the master in charge of our little group – organised a brilliantly comprehensive tour of the city. We went to the Louvre and saw the Mona Lisa, the Winged Victory, the sphinx Napoleon had brought back from Egypt, the Venus di Milo and the great portrait of Richelieu, dominating the gallery in which it was hung as the Cardinal alive had dominated early seventeenth-century Europe. We visited the Rodin museum, Les Invalides and the Pantheon. We went up the Eiffel Tower and gaped at the Arc de Triomphe, strolled in the Bois de Boulogne, looked at Notre Dame and were amazed by the delicacy of stone and beauty of glass in St Louis's Sainte Chapelle.

We sat in cafés in the *Boule Miche* and ordered '*Bière, Garçon, s'il vous plâit*', feeling very grown up, went to the Opera – the first time I am sure that any of us had done so – and were present at a state performance at the *Comédie Française* where the *Guarde Républicaine*, rigid at attention, splendid in their gleaming cuirasses, massive helmets and long horsehair plumes were in full fig, while President Vincent Auriol entered and mounted the grand staircase to the passionate sounds of the 'Marseillaise'. How glorious was France, in spite of all.

And how innocent we were. Two of us were walking one evening near the Gare St Lazare, and were accosted by some young women. We could not understand what they wanted – their idiom was not included in any of our textbooks – and we struggled to explain with courtesy our non-comprehension: much to their amusement, they were tarts.

In that same Easter holiday the Reverend Fortescue-Thomas (the eccentric but agreeable vicar of a parish near Dover who augmented his stipend by teaching English) proposed that Peter Morris and I should accompany him on a tour of 'Hardy Country', *Tess of the d'Urbervilles* being a set book for HSC. Fortescue-Thomas stayed in a B&B in Swanage, Peter and I camped; he drove us round all identified locations, 'F-T' on his motorbike, one of us riding pillion and the other in a sidecar. 'F-T' was an eccentric, not a particularly good disciplinarian but the kind of character who used to enrich school life. He was a man to be remembered with affection.

The summer holiday was again spent at Swanage. Geoff and I cycled down from London, spending the night in a haystack, waking with the sun and reaching Corfe Castle just as the freshly baked bread was being taken from the oven in the village bakery (now closed, after what it is reasonable to assume had been an existence of a thousand years). Freshly picked tomatoes were bought as well. Then we took the narrow little road that climbs halfway up Nine Barrow Down and then follows the contour east until it descends into Ulwell. Little rivulets edged or crossed the road, providing fresh, crystal water and this with bread and tomatoes in the early morning sun provided a breakfast that could be surpassed nowhere on earth.

At the end of the summer Mother sailed to join Daddy in Malaya, which seemed outwardly to be restored to its pre-war peace, although the Communist rebellion – known as the 'State of Emergency' – was to begin the next year. Geoff and I were now old enough to be left on our own, indeed, at the beginning of the next school term I became head prefect. I had failed my French (in spite of the Paris trip). I would need to work harder at that if I was to go up to university, but otherwise school life went on as before.[2] With some prompting I started a small literary society which aimed to introduce its members to a little more 'culture' than was obtainable from the curriculum; although it was certainly not 'high-brow', a paper I gave was on Chesterton's poetry and prose – *Lepanto, The Flying Inn* and *The Napoleon of Notting Hill* are still sympathetic to my romantic taste; the latter indeed should probably be prescribed reading for all leaders of post-Soviet states.

Christmas we spent at Granard Road, not a very lively holiday, and at the end of which Geoff developed acute appendicitis which was caught in the nick of time. Apart from that, I have no memory at all of the next six months until, in August, exams over, I was at a harvest camp organised by 'F-T'. Here I received news that my grandmother had died, which gave me an excuse for leaving the harvest camp 'F-T' had organised for a second year more 'stooking', an occupation of which, in any event, I had had enough.

The funeral over, a severance with my last link with that generation, Geoff and I went down to Strete in Devon where an old friend of my father's 'took in' a few boys whose parents were abroad. It is perhaps necessary to explain here for the benefit of present-day generations accustomed to cheap and easy air travel that at the time of which I am writing the problem of what to do with children in this situation was a very real one. The slaughter of so many in the First World War had diminished enormously the numbers of people of my parent's generation. Those working abroad, therefore, had fewer 'family' members to take in the children left behind at school, the houses of those they had were likely to be smaller than those which had belonged to an earlier generation and their circumstances more straitened. Sea travel still took too long to permit school holiday visits while air travel was too expensive, there were fewer destinations served less frequently and with much slower planes than now (1993). So, just as Kipling's parents had to find some home for the young Rudyard, my parents sought out their friends. (The analogy is not particularly exact; Geoff and I were much older than the young Kipling and the Butlers with whom we stayed were infinitely kinder and more sympathetic than the horrid people Kipling suffered.)

While staying at Strete Geoff and I received the news of our exam results, School Certificate in his case and Higher in mine. Both were satisfactory, to our great relief. In the normal course of events I would then have left school to do my national service.

However, my parents had agreed that if there seemed a reasonable chance of my winning an 'Oxbridge' college scholarship, I should stay on to sit these further exams. It now seemed that there was such a chance, even if a slim one. Accordingly I returned with Geoff to Dover for the Michaelmas term 1948.

At that time the Oxford and Cambridge colleges had formed themselves into groups, each group setting its own entry and scholarship exams, and not all being held at the same time. The exams of the first group for which I would try were to be held in the first week of December and so when the time came I went up to Cambridge – my first choice in this group was St John's. I was nervous; the competition, from all over England, was very stiff; I did not disgrace myself and was offered a place (in itself an achievement); but I did not win an award.

The next group was of Oxford colleges in early January, my first choice here being Christchurch; the result was the same as before – I had just missed an award. (Looking back, it may be just as well that I did not get one there. Christchurch, which features in Waugh's *Brideshead Revisited*, was a snobbish college and most who went there expected their parents to make them very generous allowances, which mine would certainly have been unable to match.)

Things were beginning to look rather desperate but one more chance existed; a third group, of Cambridge colleges, had their exam in February. So, it was to Cambridge that I made my way again, my first choice here being St Catharine's College, an ancient and 'sound' foundation, middle-of-the-road socially and with a reputation for attracting and producing good games-players. I sat the exam, was interviewed, and then, without any knowledge of the outcome (the experience I had obtained of the competition prevented me from over-sanguinity), I left Dover College to begin my national service and another stage in my life.

Chapter 11
National service: the RAF, 1949–50

At Dover all boys had to be members of the 'Corps' but when one passed 'Certificate A: Part I' (meaning that one had assimilated basic military training) there was the option of choosing to continue in the Air Training Corps (ATC) or of remaining with the 'brown jobs' (JTC). I had taken the former option, mainly because I was poorly co-ordinated on the drill square and thought that the ATC, and subsequently a choice of the RAF for my national service, would suit me better. So, on leaving Dover College, I caught the train north to the RAF recruit reception centre in Lancashire.

At this vast camp, over a thousand bewildered, homesick, 18-year-olds arrived each week, to be medically examined, numbered and kitted out, to sign papers giving the names of next of kin and of their religion (the only recognised religious faiths were Church of England, Roman Catholic and Jewish). All these steps were taken in groups, whose only common feature was the date and time of their arrival at the camp, shouted at constantly by NCOs (whose screamed orders no one could possibly interpret), moving uncomprehendingly in shambling squads from one Nissen hut or disused hangar to the next. No wonder many of these young men were homesick; most had never been away from home before. Certainly their parents had never shouted at them in the manner that they were now perpetually shouted at, by beings almost unrecognisable as human, with their cap-peaks low over the eyes.

Although at school I had taken the soft option of transferring to the ATC, I had learned the basic drill *and* I had learned how to polish brasses. The brass work on the uniforms and webbing we had been issued with was filthier than any I had ever seen – I think some pieces might well have seen service in the First World War, so thickly were they corroded. No other recruit in my flight possessed my knowledge of how to clean them; immediately, therefore, I was in demand as the imparter of knowledge on the respective merits of Brasso and Duraglit and the adviser on the need to polish the *back* of buttons and belt brasses as well as the front, the better to outwit the bullying flight corporal!

It was just as well that I had this knowledge since, within three or four days of being called-up, I received a telegram inviting me to an interview at St Catharine's College, Cambridge, whose scholarship exam I had sat a few weeks before. It was unusual, to say the least, for a raw 'erk' like me, to get a telegram, but to ask for leave so soon after enlistment was even odder. Nevertheless, in spite of the obvious doubts of the NCOs, I was given a leave pass and a rail warrant (I had no money for the fare) and, dressed in my 'best blue', was carefully inspected to make sure that I would not bring discredit on the station, and then allowed out, past the guardroom.

Thus it was that I turned up for the crucial interview at St Catharine's (or Cat's), not a schoolboy but an Aircraftsman (Second-Class), dressed in my 'best blue', with boots and brasses gleaming even more brightly than the antique silver which shone in the candlelight of the senior common room. It probably did me no harm to appear clad in this manner. The Master of the College had been a colonel and, at this date, almost every don present would have held a commission during the war and have experienced enemy fire. Moreover, this particular exhibition did not lay stress only on academic ability (although the ability to read was alleged to be of help) but was given at the college's entire discretion to 'those who were thought likely to contribute to the general life of the College'. Usually, this condition was used by the fellows (who governed the college) as a way of getting in the not so clever who were thought to be of 'blue' potential, Cat's having a high reputation as a games-playing college. Not being even remotely in the 'blue' class myself, my brasses had to dazzle instead.

A few days later, back within the confines of the recruit reception centre, another telegram arrived, this time to inform me that I was through and could take up a place when I 'got my demob' in 18 months' time – much relief, by all. Three days later my intake was split into four groups, one for each of the recruit training centres spread around the country. At these we would endure 12 weeks of square-bashing (eight for those who had been in the ATC or JTC at school).

As I had already discovered one of the less obvious advantages of having attended a public school was that no future regime could ever shock. One could endure being screamed at by uneducated corporals, the inanity of polishing a metal stove black so that when the time came for it to be lit the whole hut was filled with the stench of boot polish, eating the uneatable and saluting everything that moved. Life was like that.

Unfortunately for them, my colleagues had not had this advantage. Not only did they not know how to polish brass buttons (back as well as front, remember), they did not know how to put permanent creases into the trousers of one's best blues (soap the inside of the trouser crease, then iron), how to burnish a pair of perfectly good boots to produce a mirror-like surface in which the inspecting officer could see his own features. To prevent the flexion of marching from cracking this glassy surface one had to be carried to the parade ground. They did not know how to wash their socks, their hankies and themselves in cold water, or to clean a rifle barrel so that looking up it would dazzle any inspecting officer. Sometimes, I wondered what they had learnt at school: they could not even peel potatoes or muck out a porridge bin (although I found this pretty repulsive, too, while as for fat buckets . . . well, ugh!).

When I had been called-up I had been under the impression that the RAF did not have an officer cadet training scheme for national service recruits. However, it had recently been decided that this policy should be changed and, well before the recruit-training course was completed, I was told to report to my Flight Commander. Like a guilty schoolboy, I cast my mind back to see what I might have done wrong to be ordered to report, could think of nothing in particular, and was then taken aback to be asked if I would like to be considered for a commission. I said 'Yes, Sir'. There followed a string of interviews, Squadron, Wing, Station and Command, where other candidates were winnowed out and, eventually, I learned that I had been duly selected. To my surprise, however, another man, George Edmondson, also aiming for the Colonial Service, and whom I thought to have the edge on me, had not. (We were to meet again four years later, however, on the Colonial Service course in London. He was to be posted to Uganda where he caught, and died, of polio at the same time as I contracted that disease. He left a young and pregnant wife.)

At the end of eight weeks of being shouted at, of wheeling and marching, of repeating my air force identification number so often that it is still etched into my brain, I passed out as an Air Craftsman Grade 2, spent a few days with my aunt and reported to RAF St Athan for the next stage of my training. So began one of the most unproductive years of my life.

The RAF, or at least such was my impression, had not given much thought to the use that could be made of national service officers, since the 18 months call-up period was adjudged too short to train them to fly. All they could do, therefore, was to be taught to help administer the vast numbers of aircraftmen that the recruit training schools were producing (and which the service did not know how to use either). At St Athan we started learning this; our main duty there was to be inconspicuous.

About a dozen cadets had preceded me to St Athan at the time of my arrival in May, billeted in a hut outside the main camp as if to emphasise our semi-detached status. We had to appear reasonably tidy when we went for meals; otherwise, however, I do not remember appearing at all for anything. Most of my fellows were from the larger public schools, two from Eton and one each from Rugby, Harrow, Winchester, Stowe and so on. Almost all were going to either Oxford or Cambridge. I thought them very sophisticated and wanted very much to be accepted into their group, as I suppose I was, since some I have remained in touch with until now. Subsequently, one became a bishop, one a successful novelist, one a prominent solicitor; none, so far as I know, did badly judged by worldly standards.

For the next five months, at St Athan, at Bircham Newton in Norfolk and at Spittlegate near Grantham, we were cadets, and at the two latter stations were kept quite busy. We learned RAF law and Air Council Instructions, how to fill in forms, to shoot and to dig a slit trench (I am not quite sure why these two skills were thought appropriate), to drill others without causing chaos – which it is very easy to do on a busy parade ground, and how to behave like a 'gentleman' in an officer's mess. But my personal memories are quite other, of visiting Caerphilly Castle, of a church service at St Athan's small, old parish church commemorating the fourth-centenary of the Prayer Book, of walking (a pilgrimage, perhaps?) from Bircham Newton to Walsingham, of a class in hand-bell ringing by the Rector of Sandringham – a nice combination of associations with royalty and Dorothy Sayers's *The Nine Tailors*.

November came, and with it a grey day for our 'passing-out' parade, all clad in our blue barathea (second-hand of course, we were only 'temporary' officers even if we might aspire to be permanent gentlemen). My mother, recently returned from Malaya, came up, to talk with some mutual embarrassment to other parents, an occasion reminiscent of parents' day at a prep school.

Three of us were to be posted to RAF stations in Lancashire,[1] so I know that the idleness with which I spent the next ten months was not exceptional. I was posted as adjutant to a non-existent Squadron of a non-existent Wing in a camp devoted to demobbing those whose service had come to an end. As one might imagine in such circumstances, morale amongst the men was low while the permanent officers – to use the word 'regular' is to give them an unwarranted air of professionalism – were mostly elderly 'passed-overs'.

I played rugger for the local club (Third XV, I expect) and for a RAF team made up of players from the stations in the area. I also boxed – equally inadequately. I had neither the weight nor the nimbleness to be any good as a boxer but I could take quite a lot of punishment and would sometimes surprise an opponent at the end of a fight when he had got tired of hitting me.

In late February 1950, I suggested to a group of airmen that we go for a walk in the foothills of the Pennines. They, as bored as I, were agreeable and, with another officer, we set out. We had ample food with us; my plan was to keep away from people and to sleep out. So, having walked about ten to fifteen miles, we found a deserted valley with plenty of wood for fuel and a small stream. We fed. All were cheerful. But after dark a bitter wind swept along the Trough of Bowland. Windward, the great fire I had built was useless; to the lee, the wind blew great tongues of flame in an erratic quarter circle, so that those sheltering there were alternatively either burnt or frozen. And, the fire, roaring as if blown by bellows was consuming in minutes the fuel I had counted on to last for hours.

We had to find proper shelter before it got too late so I abandoned my ideas of roughing it and we made our way to the nearest road and then to the next village. The pub there was dark but it was not overly late and the landlord and his wife were not yet asleep. They opened up willingly, relit the fires in the bar, gave the men beer and we two officers rum – the memories of wartime comradeship were still recent and my chaps were all very young and well-behaved – a big double bed upstairs for us, while the men made themselves comfortable around the fire.

Next morning, rested and fed, they were all cheerful but clearly thought that there was no place like the camp. So, we let them go – it was a weekend and they were free to do as they wished – while the other officer and I continued walking by iced-over streams. Later, the sun gave enough warmth to melt the frost on the grass and, tired from walking, we sprawled by another stream, eating bread and cheese and drinking the cold fresh water.

With more time available than I could fill on any RAF duty, I decided upon translating into English the *Memoirs of the Maréchal du Plessis*, a copy of which I had bought when visiting Paris in 1947. The Marshal, who was kin to Cardinal Richelieu, appears from these memoirs to have been a competent but not particularly distinguished – save in his own estimation – general, whose seventeenth-century campaigns, against the English and the

Huguenots, against the Spanish in Roussillon, Catalonia and Savoy, attract no mention in any general histories of the period. That was, perhaps, part of his attraction for me; he was 'mine', someone no one else knew about, although I have yet to make any use of this particular bit of knowledge.

In the spring of 1950 my father retired from his job in Malaya. Malacca itself had escaped attacks from the Chinese Communists, who had forced the 'Malayan Emergency' of 1948, but some Dunlop planters had been killed, and Bukit Sebukor was far enough out of town to be vulnerable. So we were mightily relieved at his return home.

Later in the year I was told to take a team to Bisley to shoot in the RAF Championships. This again was fun, sleeping in bell tents and spending the days on the ranges. I was not, even by Air Force standards, a good shot, nor were any of my team, but there is a certain magic about Bisley and we shot sufficiently above our normal to leave us well pleased – and my station commander, also, on our return.

July came; my own demob was only six weeks off, and on the wireless we heard of the invasion of South Korea, of early American defeats and of their forced withdrawal towards Pusan. The United Nations Security Council – the USSR seat on which was temporarily vacant because of a Russian boycott – acted decisively. The UK promised to send troops. War, maybe another world war, seemed imminent. My concern, though, was personal. There was talk of the length of national service being increased to two years. Would I get out in time to go up to Cambridge in September? Yes, I would.

There were six weeks to fill before the start of the Cambridge term; for the first two of these Geoff was still on holiday before the Dover term began, so we followed our usual practice and went walking, in Surrey. This time, though, we were just going to walk and not to camp so we took with us only clean clothes and our washing things, begging accommodation from farmers in any barn that was available. I have a photo of myself wringing out a pair of slacks, wet from falling in a river, so clearly we had some adventures.

During my years at school I had kept in touch with Michael Pallister who, like Geoff and me, had been at Guildford and Hale schools in Perth, whose father – a doctor – had been in Changi with mine. (Michael was already at Cambridge reading Medicine and as a result his national service had been deferred until he had qualified.) He, too, having no firm English base, was short of friends in

London, so we decided to visit Brighton. There we walked along the pier, watched fishermen watching their lines and eventually drifted in to a palm reader's booth on the pier. We were only there for a lark, as the lady knew full well, but looking at my hand and prophesying a long life she added that I would shortly experience an emotional upset. 'You don't believe me, I know, but it's there.' I laughed and paid my half-crown.

A few days later Michael invited me to go canoeing with him and another friend on the Thames – his friend who lived in a riverside house had two canoes. So, we paddled off (in the vicinity of Chiswick Eyot I think). By the time we reached the middle of the river it was clear that the canoe, which Michael and I were using, was leaky – only the fact that there had been some water swishing around from the beginning had prevented this being obvious before. We made for the bank, but it was too late and the wretched thing went under beneath us.

Both of us were good swimmers so that, even though we were fully clothed, we were in no real danger from drowning. But on the other hand there was a lot of barge traffic. These looked huge from the viewpoint of a swimmer, while we, on the other hand, must have been almost invisible to any lookout on a barge, even though our friend with his canoe (and our floating but waterlogged craft) kept us company. And, of course, in those days before the cleaning-up of the Thames, the water was filthy and smelt. At last we reached the south bank of the river where, the tide being low, there was a stretch of malodorous mud to wade through before we could climb up the nearest embankment steps. The small crowd that had gathered, as they do, gave a desultory cheer and gradually disbursed, probably disappointed at the less than dramatic conclusion. It was, however, chilly in the wind and an elderly and respectable lady invited us back to dry off in front of her kitchen fire. We were glad to do so; glad also of the hot tea she gave us. And, when we made to leave, her husband offered to drive us home, 'My vehicle's just outside.' We followed him to the door: 'There it is', he said, pointing to it proudly. It was a hearse!

Chapter 12

St Catharine's College, Cambridge, 1950–3

St Catharine's (or Cat's as it was known in my day) was not modern – it was in fact a fifteenth-century amalgam of several small medieval student lodgings – but nor was it a college whose past members had left it richly endowed. The eighteenth-century weathered red-brick buildings which formed three sides of the main court – money had run out so that the fourth side had never been built – were open to the world, friendly rather than impressive. The undergraduate body, distinguished at games (during my time there were never less than three in residence who had won Rugby International caps from one or the other Home Countries) was 'middle-of-the-road' socially, decidedly less 'smart' than, say, Trinity or Magdalene, and less 'aesthetic' than King's.

This suited me very well as I still felt rather gauche socially and would not have been much at ease in a more scintillating or wealthy environment. Even so, I felt the need to make some kind of gesture and decided that I would write a fine hand using a quill! So, before 'going up', I bought a beautiful peacock feather from a shop in the Burlington Arcade, intending to attract the attention at lectures. However, quills, although picturesque, I did not find practical: the nib required constant trimming; so the feather remained only as an ornament.

At the time of which I am writing it was Cat's practice for freshmen to spend their first year in digs – college-approved lodgings – and for most men to be in college for their second and third years (although the shortage of rooms in college was such that a few, of whom I was to be one, passed two years in digs). This practice, the opposite of that generally followed in other colleges, while ensuring a final year in which one was able to enjoy college life to the full, had a disadvantage. Living 'out' of college in one's first year made it more difficult to integrate into college life and to make friends.

I was fortunate, however, Stephen James, a former fellow RAF officer cadet at St Athan and Bircham Newton, was also a freshman at Cat's. He too was reading History. Another freshman, Michael

Hughes, who had rooms in the same digs as Stephen, was also reading History and the three of us had all been placed under the supervision of a newly appointed young don, Oliver MacDonagh. For the next two years the three of us were to meet each week during term in MacDonagh's rooms to share a tutorial.[1]

Another freshman, John Armstrong, shared digs with me, each of us having our own sitting and bedrooms. The landlady, Mrs Bull, provided us with breakfast, cleaned our rooms and did our washing and was also responsible to the college for seeing that we observed university regulations. Landladies must often have had problems with 'their' young men, and some were reputed to be tartars, but John and I were fortunate in ours. I was fortunate, too, in that John was reading English and so, through him, I met yet another group of freshmen.

No doubt others were having the same experience, of finding by surprise acquaintances from the past, some even from the same school, so it was, that when we all grouped together outside the hall on our first night of term, wearing our 'new' (usually in fact second- or third-hand) short gowns, there was already the loud buzz of gossip and the exchange of greetings. The buzz made the louder no doubt by the underlying nervousness that all would be feeling as they contemplated the three exciting years that lay ahead.

At our first tutorial we were told what subjects we would be examined in at 'prelims' the next summer, given a list of books we should buy (or at least look at) and the lectures to which we should go. Somewhat naturally, at first most freshmen did as they were advised and the lecture theatres were thronged for the initial few weeks. One soon found, however, that there was no check on attendance and thereafter attended or not at one's own choice.

Some lecturers delivered the same course year after year and borrowing the notes taken by one's predecessors was quite as useful and much less restrictive than attending in person. Sometimes, too, the lecturer would have written a book on the subject, so that often he would do little more than regurgitate: here again attendance was often irrelevant. Few lecturers, in my experience, were inspiring in delivery or illuminating in their language. Inevitably, though, there were a few undergraduates who attended every lecture, perhaps because they were unable to read the set books or because they wished to attract to themselves favourable notice by the lecturer. There were also some lectures in specialist topics which might attract only a few and then the small size of the group could lead to a real communication between the lecturer and his audience, such as Dom David Knowles's lectures on Medieval Political Philosophy. On this matter, my conduct was that of the majority, but as I liked history as a subject I was pretty conscientious over reading the recommended books and, as I did not wish to be shown up in the weekly tutorials by Stephen or by Mike Hughes, I took considerable pains over the set weekly essay.

I soon discovered that history at Cambridge was a very different thing from that I had done at school. There it had been the 'Whig interpretation' (without being explicit). At Cambridge this was regarded as pretty old hat while there was, if anything, even greater scorn for 'universal' theories such as that which underlay Arnold Toynbee's enormous opus. The 'Marxist' interpretation, even less scientific, not surprisingly however was exempt from this blanket condemnation! Namier's methods, building from the bottom up which placed the emphasis on detailed research prior to the construction of general conclusions was the 'preferred' view. This accorded with my own character and is one which I have tried always to act on – in other spheres as well as that of history.

Cat's was a great rugger college at that time – Glyn Morgan had been a brilliant Welsh fly half and John Smith an outstandingly fast wing who had come within a yard of winning the 1949 Varsity match for us and had almost done the same for England in an international. They were to be followed by many others in succeeding years, Freddy Berringer (Ireland), Ian Beer (England), Ken Dalgleish (Scotland), to name only a few. Both the College First XV and the Second XV (the Kittens) were star-studded (although in my second and third years I was occasionally chosen for one or the other). My normal home, however, was the Third XV where the general wealth of talent meant that we could beat other college's Third XVs (or their Seconds, or even some Firsts, come to that) by cricket-match scores. However, I would have liked to have been a better player and envied my friends Dicky Dawes and Kit Wenban (the latter had been at King's School, Canterbury, and I had played against him in the past – Dover being always the losing side) who regularly turned out for the senior games.

At squash I expended a lot of energy without often hitting the ball. Rowing I tried, but was no good – no rhythm or balance. My last excursion in the water ended when I upset a whiff in the path of the blue boat, which was doing a trial. This was an unheard of disgrace. I was not much better in a punt. In my first summer my college was entertaining some elderly ladies from the East End of London where they ran a 'mission'; I volunteered to take them in a punt. All went well to begin with and I was showing off splendidly – throwing the pole in the air with a flourish, basking in the compliments and thinking myself no end of a fellow. Alas, I was not looking where I was going. I had just put the pole into the Cam and given a shove when I saw that we were about to go under Trinity Bridge. There was no time to withdraw the pole: nor had I the presence of mind to let it go, and so I felt the punt slipping away from under the soles of my shoes, while I went from a vertical to a horizontal and then to a splash! The Cam water was cold but I could swim well and followed the punt downstream to a dock just below the Bridge of Sighs where the ladies, much excited at (delighted by) their adventure were rescued and where I could get onto dry land. Then having made sure they were OK, I made tracks for the nearby rooms in St John's College's New Court of Michael Pallister.

There was a wind and I was damned chilly, uncomfortable and in haste to change. I did not notice therefore that his oak was 'sported', and entered without invitation. Michael and a girl were on the floor before the gas fire and were disconcerted, although I swear I have no recollection of their state of dress or undress, but went hastily and a bit confusedly to his bedroom. There, when they had collected themselves, I was supplied with dry clothes and, most charitably under the circumstances, with tea.

Bridge I played regularly but my friends Ron Simson (very clever) and Gerald Potts were far more reliable players. Both were in college while I was in digs and so most games ended with me climbing out; it was fun and we played for token stakes only, so that losing, as was my invariable lot, was never a major pecuniary disaster. My landlady, who in theory was meant to inform the college authorities of late-night escapades, invariably turned a blind eye to them.

Climbing into – and out of – colleges was a normal feature of most graduates' lives. An impromptu party in one college might move en masse to another, gowns often being ripped in the process of climbing over spikes. Occasionally, of course, they might be quite forgotten in the exhilaration of the evening, but those who did so risked being stopped by the proctors and having their names taken and given to their college Dean. This would mean a lecture, and worse a fine, the amount according to the frequency of the offence.

The editor of the undergraduate newspaper *Varsity*, Paul Rudder, was in his second or third year at Cat's, and I tried my hand at being a reporter, but lacked any journalistic flair and never found anything sensational or scandalous to report on; so that avenue dried up.

In a further attempt to be distinctive I helped found a wine society, knowing nothing about the subject but thinking, as no doubt many other young men have done, that knowledge of wine gave a social cachet. A marvellous don, Sydney Smith, encouraged us in our attempts to learn and love wine and let us taste some superb bottles – a Richebourg 1923, I remember, and a Kabinet hock from a Prussian State vineyard bearing a Hohenzollern eagle crest. At that time outstanding wine was not overly expensive and my records of 1933, 1934 and 1937 vintage clarets that I drank (and my memory of a Schloss Bockelheimer Trockenbeeren Auslese of 1947) – and of their fantastically low prices – amaze me.

Similarly, I helped a bit with the college revue in my first year – there was a very talented man called Barney Miller who was the main star, but my assistance would have been in some very minor capacity. I had first met Barney when I was climbing out and he in, one or other side of a gently pitched, snow-covered roof against which we were horribly conspicuous in our black dinner jackets. Each could hear, but not see, the other and each thought the other a 'bull dog' or university policeman, so that at the slightest sound from one, the other froze (in both senses of the word), spread-eagled on the roof. All of this, we learnt later, was being watched with some amusement from the senior common room by a group of dons mellow with port.

In my last year Peter Hall produced *The Duchess of Malfi* for the college dramatic society; his first production I think. I was stage manager and, with my brother, helped design the set (he painted the scenery and made the bloody hand sufficiently realistic to produce the right shudders in the audience). The production was a great success and helped lay the foundation for Peter's entry into university drama and also for his subsequent career.

Almost all undergraduates were short of money and found jobs in the vacations. At Christmas the usual one was to work for the Post Office helping deliver the Christmas mail. Often there would be three or even four deliveries a day, and I discovered how many ways architects had designed letter flaps in doors so as best to trap the deliverer's fingers and to crush letters and cards. I also discovered how kind and generous old people could be, concerned at our loads in the cold and wet, anxious to offer tea (or even something stronger) to refresh and to give a 'Christmas box' by way of thanks – which one did not like to accept from those clearly in need themselves, but which it was sometimes difficult to refuse without giving offence.

Fruit picking in summer was well paid, but very hard work. Teaching in a prep school was a doddle by comparison. It was astonishing to discover how much some of them resembled Evelyn Waugh's caricature of such institutions in *Vile Bodies*: it made one wonder how parents could be so gullible as to trust their offspring to such peculiar institutions.

With the proceeds I and another undergraduate (he reading languages) holidayed for a month on the continent for £15, hitch-hiking with a Union Jack stitched to my rucksack, a practice that was regularly deplored in the 'Letters to the Editor' of both the *Daily Telegraph* or *The Times* as bringing the good name of Britain into disrepute. Maybe, but it was already clear to me that continentals had no picture of the British being in any way superior beings; our comparative economic decline had already begun, although there were still many traces of wartime goodwill.

Austria was interesting, still occupied by the victors (I was travelling in the French sector and did not think much of the turnout of the *poilus* I saw). Around Innsbruck railway station the devastation was total, but the trains ran punctually and were clean.

In my second year, the University Air Squadron formed a Ground Control of Interception Unit, which Peter de Rougemont (another who had been at OCTU with me, now at Clare and reading History) suggested I join with him. Our duties were not onerous; we had to spend one or two weekends a month in term and as long as we liked in vacations (for which we were paid as Pilot Officers, RAFVR, this being the attraction for impecunious undergraduates!). After initial training we were put in 'cabins', watching radar screens in case 'bandits' from the East appeared (this was all very, very Cold War). I never knew of any such incursion actually taking place but we constantly practised the drill in case it did: scramble Sabres – piston-engined fighters with a top speed of little more than 400 mph (much less than that of any current civilian jet) but which were then high tech – and 'vector' them on to the intruder, aiming to intercept at right angles at a range of about 200 yards. It is lucky there was no war; we were a pretty frail line of defence.

My involvement in this did not mean that I was hyper-patriotic; rather it was symptomatic of the era. Many of my year had fought in Korea, my brother was doing his national service fighting, with his usual bravery and competence, communist guerrillas in Malaya where, until his retirement in 1950, my father too had been at risk. War was something we had grown up with but the fear of the use of atomic bombs was real even if not to the extent of the total annihilation of humanity later to be popularly evoked by Nevil Shute in his novel *On the Beach*. To us the situation was quite simple. Communism was an enemy, as Nazism had been, and it had to be fought; there was no tortured mind-searching amongst most of my friends.

We knew that Britain was not as important as it had been. India and Pakistan had been given a bloody independence, but most of the map was still coloured pink. While I read about the development of political parties, in Malaya, for example, which was naturally of particular interest to me – it was the time when the United Malay National Party (UMNO) under Tun Razak was getting established – but while I read, even approvingly, about this it did not lead me to think that the end result of this political activity would be an early end of empire. Instead I joined the Royal Empire Society (founded by Joseph Chamberlain, the great Secretary of State for the Colonies in Queen Victoria's reign, as the Colonial Institute).

I was like many undergraduates of those years, conservative, reacting to what we saw as the bureaucracy and incompetence of the latter days of the Labour government. Cambridge was still overwhelmingly pre-war in its values, at least socially. Even though I doubt if at home the parents of any of my friends kept servants (apart from a 'daily'), we took for granted the pleasures of having 'gyps' and 'bedders' when in college, while even in digs the landlady would be expected to bring a cooked breakfast to one's rooms and generally wait on one in a way that would nowadays be almost inconceivable.

However, at the same time life was still full of wartime restrictions. We were still meant to carry identity cards and there were ration books. There was no bathroom in my digs in Abbey Road, and to get a bath I had to cycle into college, remembering to take with me a towel, soap and clean underwear! In college too, of course, while most staircases had running water on them it was mostly in the form of a communal tap. To go to the loo might mean descending several flights of stairs, an excursion into the main court and often a walk (or run) of some 20 or more yards!

Women visitors to college were even worse catered for, but then, male undergraduates still lived surprisingly celibate lives, having very little to do with women, since there were only two women's colleges and the only other 'acceptable' source of girls were Adenbrooke's for trainee nurses and Homerton for graduate teachers. This makes my own outstanding good fortune in this field all the more surprising.

A few days after I had gone up, and when we were still feeling pretty strange, Paddy, Stephen James's girlfriend (and later his wife) came to Cambridge looking for digs. Probably to act as a kind of chaperon and make their relationship look respectable (landladies were terribly prim in those days) I was asked to go with them both to inspect some rooms advertised near Castle Hill. They seemed suitable and a deal had just been done when there was another ring on the door and a tall slim girl came on the same errand, wearing a green and white college scarf ('I remember it well' and now there is no one to say that my memory is awry). She was clearly most disappointed to learn that Paddy had forestalled her and that she was too late, so we four had tea together, as a kind of way of making up.

I was attracted by the newcomer at first sight and made it my business to find out her address. Within a few days I had been round to see her in a rather depressing bedsitter, and I did not let the acquaintance drop, much to the amusement of Stephen, Paddy and their friends. For I still felt rather unsure of myself socially. My parent's absence from England, the resulting lack of a home base with its attendant social circle and also my boarding-school education had meant that I had had virtually no contact with any girl or woman of my own age. Lesley to me seemed very beautiful (which she was), very mature and very self-possessed (which she was not). In her turn – quite mistakenly – she ascribed these two attributes to me. She was in fact a newly qualified, indeed still on probation, primary school teacher who had never been away from home until she entered her training college. She was also very hard up and a bit lonely in Cambridge – the other teachers in her college being quite a bit older than her.

We met regularly, and she found rooms in a vicarage not far from mine. At the end of that term I was no sooner home than I was writing to her, much to my parent's dismay. I was, for example, quite unable to give satisfactory answers to questions such as what her parents did, where she was at school, how old she was and so on. What did such things matter to me: we loved each other, and she used a whole week's ration to buy me a steak (which she then overcooked!).

So we went on together, not meeting every evening, since we both had our own friends and interests to keep up and indeed develop. Lesley, of course, as a working girl, had lessons and projects to prepare each evening for her next day's activities, her flat – for after the first year she would rent one and share it with one or two other compatible young women – to keep clean. As a primary school teacher she was not at all well paid, and the payment of rent on a flat – even if shared – made a big hole in her earnings, so she was perpetually short of money. Being skilful, therefore, she taught herself dressmaking and made most of her own clothes (she used Vogue Couturier patterns for ball dresses), even a scarlet winter coat on one occasion with a great Russian-style collar, but this, too, took time.

When we were able to meet it was rare for us to have much privacy. While I was in digs my landlady made it clear that she did not approve of her young gentlemen entertaining ladies in their rooms; she 'kept a respectable house', she told me, 'and wasn't prepared to have any goings on'. Similarly, in the flats Lesley shared, although the girls would draw up a roster between them of the evenings when each would be able to have a boyfriend round and have the flat to themselves for an hour or two, such evenings were irregular and were dependent on the other girls' engagements – or the lack of them.

So my first two years flew past. Having obtained a 2:1 in prelims (somewhat to my supervisor's surprise, I think) I had achieved the same result in part 1 of the tripos, my supervisor writing 'warmest congratulations on carrying off a 2:1 again. It was a fine performance and perhaps we may hope for even better things next year'. It was a kind wish but I was quite satisfied with a 2:1; to have striven for a first would have meant working very much harder and probably unavailingly – 'firsts' are not obtained by hard work alone, and it would have meant a complete change in my way of life.

As it was I continued to put in about 25 hours a week on my books and essays. My special subject for part II of the tripos was 'Sino-British Relations, 1839' (the year of the First Opium War), the lecturer being Victor Purcell, a former 'Chinese Protector' in the Malayan Civil Service, knowledgeable and sympathetic to the Chinese side but not inspiring. However, I found the topic absorbing and read every contemporary document in English on the issue, regretting as I did my lack of knowledge of Chinese, which limited understanding of 'their side of the hill'.

As a consolation for having spent two years in digs instead of the normal one, I had been allowed my choice of rooms for my third year. I chose an attic, which though very draughty was spacious. Lesley made curtains and covered cushions to provide splashes of colour. The college kitchens were indulgent in cooking special dishes for private dinner parties; my gyp, Gus, a refugee Pole, was an exceptionally nice man (later becoming college butler).

Geoff had now come up also and was with me at Cat's, having spent his national service fighting Chinese Communists in Malaya – it was the height of the 'Emergency' there and he had been in the jungle for long periods, which he had done with his usual ability, but which had left him subject to malaria. He and his friends mingled with mine, and Lesley was at home with them all.

My supervisor persuaded me to restart the college history society that like many undergraduate activities had gone dormant. Oliver invited a number of the younger and livelier dons from other colleges to give talks, meetings were held in my rooms, and it was quite a success. Adrian Cowell, a scholar, and later to be a distinguished television film-maker (Triads, Golden Triangle, the Brazilian rain forest were all fields in which he was to lead the way) took the society over when I went down.

In March 1953 there were The Floods. The Ouse burst its banks and along with hundreds of other volunteers I filled sandbags and dumped them in the great gash in the embankment. Gradually the gap narrowed. At last it was closed, but as we stood on the sandbag wall, the cry went up 'Steady, she's going'. A small tug in mid-stream backed up as close as she could get and we, on the barrier, jumped for it as best we could. I was one of the last and could feel the bags slipping away under my feet, but made my escape safely just as with a roar the wall we had built with such labour was swept away by the flood pouring into the low fields. The tug captain raced his engines to the full, but for a moment it looked as if tug, crew and we undergraduates would all be carried away by the water, but at last the screws overcame the flow and we were safe in mid-stream. Frightening.

Great Yarmouth where Lesley's mother lived was also hard hit. Her mother's house was flooded and her mother (her father being away at sea) had to be rescued by a rowing boat from a first-floor window.

During these undergraduate years there was no discussion of future marriage between Lesley and me. I had no money and was dependant on my parents, who of course had met Lesley early on and who had invited her to stay several times. They liked her, but they, themselves, had married late and would have counselled caution had they been asked. I, too, was frightened of the responsibility and would have probably just let things go on without taking a decision – a characteristic of Barnes males!

However, if I was to join the Colonial Administrative Service, which was my continuing but never properly thought-through wish, it was now time that I, in my last year at Cambridge, made application to the Colonial Office. Lesley agreed. My interviews went well, and 'subject to exam results' I was through. I drew out all I had in National Savings Certificates, we chose a ring and she made me propose to her kneeling on the floor of the taxi, which was driving round Hyde Park. It was springtime. (Later, Lesley told me that if I had gone down without proposing she would have gone out to Tanganyika as a woman education officer: but she did not let on at the time that that thought was in her mind.)

Well, part II was sat, the May balls were danced through and the champagne was drunk. We decided to get married immediately so that we could live together (though we had absolutely nowhere to do so, nor money to get anywhere) until my preliminary training course began in September at London University. Lesley had wished the marriage service to take place at the Round Church, but found that her flat was five yards outside its boundary. My college rooms, however, fell in the parish of St Botolph and it was there, in a small and little-used old church, on 27 June 1953, that we were married quietly, by an ancient don of Queen's College who held the living. My brother, who was about to leave for Ethiopia, took a few hours off from his preparations to drive up from London, to give me the ring – he was best man – and later to wish us well and to set off on his journey 'Into the Blue'.[2]

We were married. I had a degree and a (future) career. Life could begin.

Chapter 13
A little interlude in London, 1953–4

Lesley and I were married, and to our great delight. However, we had no roof over our heads or the money to acquire one. It would be a month before Lesley's school term ended and she was also committed to her friend Joan with whom she shared a flat. We didn't have the money to pay for a place for us both to live in so we agreed that Lesley would continue living where she was and I would find digs in Cambridge for myself – and a job to pay for them – until the end of July. It was not a normal way of beginning a married life, but it was better than not being married at all.

I cannot remember exactly what shifts we contrived, but Lesley's friends were very understanding and helpful and somehow we managed. Lesley spotted an advertisement in the *Cambridge News* by Pye[1] for temporary staff and although I had no knowledge of physics except what I had learned for School Certificate (and had forgotten the day after the exam), I was taken on. Pye were experimenting with colour television and my job was to wind wire on resistance coils, maintaining a steady tension. What part this played in the workings of a TV set I do not know but my colleagues – permanent staff – were knowledgeable and good fellows and my work seemed to be judged satisfactory. Anyway it brought in enough money to keep me in the same town as Lesley and that we both judged was sufficient for the time being.

I was required to spend a 'probationary' year at London University attending the Colonial Service course[2] so Lesley had applied and been accepted for a post at a primary school in Morden in south London. We had to find somewhere to live from which both of us could commute. Accordingly, as soon as possible after the ending of her term at Cambridge, we visited London to look for a flat for the next year.

As a married man I would receive an allowance of £44 a month (I think) while Lesley's salary amounted to about another £40. It seemed a lot but we did not know what our living expenses would be, and during the year we would have to buy the clothing and household equipment needed to set up house in Nigeria. So flat hunting had to be done carefully; we judged ourselves fortunate after a week to find one in Raynes Park at five guineas a week, on the first floor of a house with two elderly ladies living below. Heating was by coal fires; there was a refrigerator and a spare bedroom. Money troubles were not over though – indeed, they were with us for almost all our married life. Lesley's new appointment began in September, so we had to be in our flat by the beginning of that month, but my course did not begin until October and my first month's allowance would not come in until the end of that month. Until then we would have to be on short commons.

At the beginning of October I reported to the house in Tavistock Square which was the Colonial Service course base, was welcomed by the officer in charge, Angus Robin, a district officer (DO) on secondment from Eastern Nigeria and made the acquaintance of my fellow probationers. One of these was George Edmondson, destined for Uganda, whom I had met in the RAF at Bridgenorth[3] when we were both recruits being interviewed for selection as officer cadets; our future lives were to exhibit another and more tragic similarity.

Of more immediate – and future – interest, however, were the other three probationers and the two women education officers destined for Eastern Nigeria. Robert Graham, fresh from Hertford College, Oxford, was also provisionally earmarked for Calabar Province and he and I would be studying Efik/Ibibio together. The other four, Tony Shepherd from Pembroke, Cambridge, Alan Ferguson from Oxford, Jenny Nias from Oxford and Marion Weaver were all to study Ibo, the dominant tribal and language group in the east. Although destined for different provinces, however, the fact that we were all bound for the same general geographic area gave a certain cohesiveness to our group – we would all be experiencing the same climate, our living conditions would be similar, the constitution under which we would work, the politicians and political parties we would encounter and suffer would be the same.

Unlike the vast majority of the 40 or so probationers, however, I was married: indeed only two others were in this category – one destined for Gambia, the other for Fiji. Most of the people on the course were in lodgings – there was a hostel in Hans Crescent behind Harrods, which housed many of them – and, naturally, their social life was largely spent with their fellow course members. A few lived at home like Robert Graham whose parents lived in Worcester Park not far from the flat Lesley and I were renting. By contrast, we three couples, two only just married and the third, although in duration longer married but until then mostly separated (he had been in the Merchant Navy), were fixated on our partners.

My mother, and circumstances, had brought me up not to be domestically useless, a condition which in any event I do not think Lesley would have tolerated for long. Moreover, she was working as well – indeed on most days she left the flat before me. As a consequence, from the beginning I was a 'New Age man', sharing all chores; she mostly cooked, I washed up; I took the laundry to the 'launderette' on Saturday mornings, she did the ironing; I brought in the coals and cleared the grate, she cleaned the bathroom.

Lesley's parents having been fairly poor and her income having been small she had no large accumulated trousseau and having married economically we had had no great stock of wedding presents. We had the essentials, but there was most still to buy. After the war and the immediate post-war years of shortages the shops were beginning to have a steady supply, even a choice, of goods and – while we had to be extremely economical – the selection, purchase and accumulation of household possessions was a novelty into which we entered together with pleasure: the scanning of 'personal ads', the visit to the first day of the sales.

Which[4] appeared and was an inestimable help to those who knew nothing and whose purses were as short as their needs were long. Two specialised books, *A Household Book for the Tropical Colonies* and *Dearest Priscilla* by Mrs Bradley, the wife of a colonial civil servant[5] contained a wealth of useful lore (although *Dearest Priscilla* we felt even at the time was rather 'twee'). An old 'Mrs Beeton', picked up in a jumble sale, was to prove invaluable – the cast-iron 'Dover Stove' which had been the normal feature of a Victorian kitchen was just beginning to find its way into Empire outposts while instructions on such disparate matters as the role of different servants and the instructions on how many different ways table napkins could be folded to grace a dinner table were all to prove helpful to us who had such knowledge!

Over the three years we had known each other Lesley had taught herself quite a lot about the art of cooking but, sharing a flat with other young women, she had never cooked a whole meal except for me (and, on one occasion as he reminds me, for my brother as well). This she soon changed. Robert Graham, our near neighbour, was probably the first guest we entertained, joined fairly soon by my brother – when, later than planned, he returned from Lake Tana; my parents (visiting to see how we were settling into married life) and my aunts Agnes and Trissy (whose eating tastes were for plain and simple food). Ron Simson and Kit Wenban from Cambridge (both of whom from the first days had witnessed our burgeoning love affair) stayed with us as soon as we had bought spare bedlinen and the young couple bound for Gambia and who had rented a flat in Kingston were other guests.

Elizabeth David was the new and brightest star in the apprentice cook's firmament. Her evocative language made her recipes a delight to read even for the non-cook. '*Bon Viveur*' (Fanny Cradock and husband), who wrote in the *Daily Telegraph*, was another, perhaps even more immediately useful source, since they wrote against the background of austerity and rationing that still – and quite unnecessarily – prevailed in England *eight years* after the war had ended. It may seem unbelievable nowadays, but the replacement of standard 'national' margarine by individual brands such as Stork was a matter of great moment at that time, the respective resemblances, nay superiorities, of each brand to butter being whispered about in the news columns for weeks before they were launched with tremendous advertising *éclat* on the starved taste buds of the Great British Public.

We wished our conversation at dinner parties to be 'meaningful' and accordingly read *The Listener* (then easily the most interesting of the weekly journals) with a view to deciding on suitable topics to be discussed. In those days before mass TV conversation was expected to be about matters other than the doings of characters in the latest 'sitcom' and, while the *Daily Telegraph* provided a surprising amount of detail in its reporting of cases in the law courts, the sexual peccadilloes of the Establishment were not thought of as being necessarily the most important of the events of the day.

This probably sounds intolerably priggish but few can be as earnest as young marrieds trying to establish their position. Moreover, Lesley and I were avid for culture; I would queue for hours to buy one shilling(!) gallery slip tickets for the opera at Covent Garden. On one occasion we were rewarded by the debut of Joan Sutherland who, as the stand-in, played a large but splendid Aida, staggering the rather small tenor singing Radames. In this same performance, too, peering over the gallery rail from our positions high under the cupola, we could see the troops of the Egyptian Army who marched so grandly while on stage in front of the audience, behind the 'flats', hurriedly exchange their spears for bows, their bows for clubs, and then scurry round the rear of the stage to reappear before the audience. Their change in weaponry gave the illusion of an uncountable army to those seated in the expensive stalls.

We visited the exhibition of designs for a monument 'To the Unknown Political Prisoner' (it was suggested in all seriousness, I think I recall, that the prize-winning design should in some final and colossal form be erected on the cliffs of Dover). We went to the Royal Academy Summer Exhibition; rather more enterprisingly we admired an exhibition of replicas of the mosaics in Ravenna and resolved to see the originals – an aim never achieved. Ron Simson, when visiting us, took us in contrast to *The Love of Four Colonels* at Her Majesty's in the Haymarket starring Peter Ustinov – then young, multilingual, talented and witty, not the patriarchal sage rôle he was later to adopt with such success. These diversions were normally confined to the weekend; the working week was taken up with work!

The Colonial Service course curriculum was designed in true English fashion to teach embryo administrators a little bit about each of an enormous range of matters. The language of the bit of pink we were destined for was an obvious one, Efik/Ibibio in the case of Robert Graham and myself, a tonal, semi-Bantu, language spoken only in the extreme south-east of Nigeria, known as Calabar Province. It was hard to learn unless one had a naturally good ear (which I certainly did not), although not as difficult, I am told, as Ibo. Robert and I did adequately, he not being helped at all by a bad stammer; we were relieved to learn in due course that few administrative officers ever became fluent in either, Tony Shepherd being one such *rara avis*.

Law lectures came second in the time they took up. I am sure that they had been useful in the past but, at least as far as was to concern Eastern Nigeria, they were to prove almost valueless. On arrival in that territory the following year we were gazetted as 'Magistrates, 3rd Class' to be sure, but constitutional change meant that our appointments lapsed on 30 September 1954 (although we remained justices of the peace). This was a pity as it was one of the subjects I was good at.

We studied Anthropology in general, learning with interest about the sexual habits of the Samoans as recorded by Margaret Meade and sex and slavery on Brazilian plantations by Frere. Of just slightly more use was the work of Professor Daryll Forde who had studied in detail the customs of the Yakur – a very small, secluded tribe – on the Upper Cross River which there ran into Calabar Province, but, as I never went to that area nor heard of anyone who had, I cannot pretend that this was any future use. Supervisions under Phyllis Kaberry[6] were much more attractive, not at all dry.

Then we studied Imperial History and Geography and Economics. We were lectured to by Ronald Wraith on the subject of Local Government which, it had been decided, would be introduced into the colonial territories following the English model, quite oblivious of the social and historical factors which had been responsible for the latter's evolution. Lucy Mair, a left-wing lecturer in something-or-another at the London School of Economics lectured us too – although all I can remember is having a sharp disagreement with her on the subject of the Report of the Commission of Inquiry into the Enugu coalfield shooting of 1949; intuitively I felt that she was wrong and she *was*, but I can no longer remember why, how or where! Many years later I was to meet the unfortunate policeman who had been in charge at the time (happily it had not ruined his subsequent career – in another territory).

A book *The Preservation of Health in Tropical Climates*, the cover of which had been treated with a insect-repellent solution(!), and a somewhat perfunctory lecture on the need to wash all salad vegetables in potassium permanganate, to boil and filter all drinking water, to insist on a cook's personal cleanliness and that of his kitchen, to take reasonable precautions against the sun (although the days when 'topis' were deemed essential had gone with the Japanese victories in Malaya) formed the staple of the Tropical Health and Hygiene course. The dangers of an excessive alcohol intake and the importance of taking a regular prophylactic against malaria were emphasised; polio was not referred to.

Figure 4 Ken before polio, 1954.

A splendid retired district commissioner from East Africa taught us how to build roads and install culverts, how to build earth dams, to erect and roof buildings and all sorts of other really useful accomplishments that made the maximum use of local materials and that didn't require the employment of 'professionals'. His book must have been read by hundreds of administrative officers over the years – and should have been read by most architects and engineers as well.

Looking back I am a bit surprised that there was no instruction at all in such office skills as writing letters and reports, in filing systems, etc. 'Paper work' is not romantic but it was a part – an increasing part – of every administrative officer's life and the smooth functioning of the district office was an essential part of administration. I was fortunate in that my brother had given me a lightweight portable typewriter as a twenty-first birthday present and so I was accustomed to typing even if only of the two-fingered variety. It was a great help – there were no secretaries in the bush.

As colonies progressed to independence more and more administrative officers were being needed in the Secretariat[7] of each colony and would then find their hard won 'bush skills' were of little value. With the appointment of ministers the need for *officer wallahs* would become even greater while ministers, unsure of themselves and unaware of how long things took, became ever more demanding. I am sure that some special training would have been invaluable.

The Great Smog had lain over London the previous year, alarming the capital to a determination that the atmosphere must be cleaned. Within a year little could be achieved and 1953/4 was almost as bad as the previous year. White shirts donned in the morning had by dusk a black tarry deposit on the collars and cuffs, a filth almost impossible to remove with the still primitive soaps and detergents that was all we had. Buildings were filthy; so, in spite of our best endeavours, were we.

The Easter vacation 1954, we spent at Wye College in Kent, learning agriculture and surveying in a fortnight. Lesley came down for a long weekend, spending one night with me in an inn in Wye (the landlady clearly suspected that we were not married: maybe we were clearly more in love than she was accustomed to); the next two nights we spent at the George Hotel in Rye, exploring the picturesque old town, walking over to Winchelsea, lunching there in the rain and finding, on our way back to Rye, big puddles in the road over which I carried Lesley in my arms (as it was to happen, it was the last occasion on which I was to be able to do so).

Meanwhile, Lesley, apart from her teaching work, was attending talks given by the Women's Corona Society to guide wives and others going abroad through all the social and other minefields they could expect to encounter, from the rules of precedence at dinner parties to the effects of heat and humidity on the menstrual cycle. She would come up to the Tavistock Square house in the evenings from time to time, as well, to meet my colleagues or to attend the occasional social function.

Angus Robin, the course supervisor, organised a debate on the motion that 'The decline of Empire was inevitable'. I was to propose this, another probationer was to oppose and each of us was to be seconded by a Member of Parliament: Fenner Brockway, well-known Socialist anti-imperialist, MP for Slough (which would have much pleased John Betjeman) was on my side and a Tory MP, Edward Wakefield,[8] on the other. It was the first time I had ever met an MP and I was not much impressed by Fenner Brockway (who left before the end much to his colleague's disgust). The motion was won, surprisingly. Mr Wakefield congratulated me, Lesley was pleased and we went home feeling pretty content.

We were of course aware of the increasing speed of political development in West Africa. Ghana had achieved independence in all but name in April, using the occasion to take a full page in *The Times* of advertisements for qualified British professional and technical staff! But, of course, it was claimed that Ghana was a 'special case'; it was rich; it had had an institution of higher education for many years. Thus, Ghana's independence was not thought of as creating a precedent: but it was, and it was folly to think otherwise.

As the course year drew to an end, we were deluged with invitations from tropical outfitters to mortgage if not our souls then several years' future salaries in the purchase of tropical evening and day kit, 'Rhoorkee' chairs (collapsible and extraordinarily comfortable), camp beds and mosquito nets, Aladdin and tilley lamps, a tin bath with lid and wicker lining in which clean clothes could be kept dry however torrential the tropical rains, paraffin, charcoal or plain ordinary flat irons, waterproof uniform cases, sensible *veldtschoen* for both of us and ladies canvas mosquito boots for Lesley's evening wear. Some firms preyed on the gullibility of the inexperienced; one – Hawes Bros., a small firm in poky offices in Farringdon Street – was honest enough to advise that some items were not necessary, that others could be purchased more cheaply elsewhere, and, while granting credit, tried to keep purchases down to a figure that could be repaid by their clients without financial distress. All have now gone, closing with the Empire that they had supplied.[9]

My father gave me an old 'Palm Beach' suit, I bought another lightweight one, white dinner jacket and trousers, shorts and knee-length socks (khaki both of these, much more sensible than the pristine white used in the Secretariats of Zomba and Lusaka which earned for their wearers the sobriquet of 'white ants'). Lesley made cotton dresses for herself, bought lengths of cotton material for future making-up, matching buttons and thread from Marshall & Snelgroves (they made a speciality of helping colonial wives in this manner – the sales lady telling Lesley impressively of a recent despatch to Lady Templer in Malaya). The ladies of the Corona Society, however, all by this time *grandes dames* by virtue of their husbands' ascent into Colonial Service heavens, advised that she should have white gloves and a wide-brimmed hat for garden parties; we saw a beauty in black straw trimmed with a full-blown fabric rose from Bentalls in Kingston, bought it and a big 'Revelation' hatbox to contain this creation. Alas, I do not think it was ever worn.

Rather late in the day we were told that cadets for Nigeria had to obtain the permission of the Governor to be accompanied by a wife and we were unhappy until this gubernatorial approval was received. Even then we found official obstacles. The Crown Agents were not accustomed to booking the passage of the wife of a cadet, indeed they insisted that this was impossible, there were no available cabins. I pleaded and, reluctantly, they agreed to make an air booking (first class, of course, which was more expensive than the sea passage) to arrive the day after my ship was expected to dock at Lagos.

Another indication of our approaching departure was that we all had appointments for injections for TAB (typhoid A and B), yellow fever and smallpox. Of these, the TAB gave the worst reaction unfailingly. Lesley and I had ours on the same day, and I remember us spending a miserable evening in bed together with our arms throbbing and our heads aching while we listened to Richard Burton reading *Under Milkwood* on the wireless.

Our end of course exams were sat, Robert Graham and I passed our Efik/Ibibio, I obtained distinctions in other subjects (doubtless Lesley had made me work rather more assiduously than my bachelor colleagues), the course photo was taken and in July 1954 the unsuspecting Empire awaited its latest naive administrators.

Part Two
Nigeria

Nigeria

We were an excited group of young men when we gathered at the Elder Dempster Dock, Liverpool at the end of July 1954. We were sad, yes, to say goodbye to wife or sweetheart (although in my own case this was made much easier by knowing that Lesley and I were due to meet again in Lagos in less than a fortnight). But the future awaited, we had passed more than a year waiting for this day.[1]

What happened, however, it was all something of an anti-climax. A [illegible] prevented sailing that day. That evening I think we all phoned home to relate the news. The next day's weather was the same. Again, that evening I phoned to tell Lesley that we were still in Liverpool at this rate it looked as if she was likely to arrive in Nigeria before me.

Lesley meanwhile, was staying with my parents, a bit worried. She had never been out of England before, had never flown. Now she would be doing both on her own, saying 'farewell' to everything she knew and with the possibility that I might not be there to meet her (as, in fact, I was not). She wrote to me at Takoradi, not even sure where Takoradi (the port of Accra, capital of the Gold Coast) was in relation to Nigeria, but hoping that the letter would be forwarded. My mother who had similarly left England on her own in 1929 told her that she had written a letter from Malta to my father in Malacca that reached him three weeks after she did. Whether this was any comfort to Lesley I doubt.

Altogether there would have been almost 20 of us new Administrative Service cadets sailing in the *Accra* for the three regions of Nigeria (including one going to the Western Region which had actually already stopped regular recruiting). In addition there were a number of newly appointed women education officers. All of us felt very raw with very little idea of what in fact we would be doing. It was not surprising, therefore, that we were eager to listen to the views of 'old coasters' – and our future seniors – returning from leave.

Also aboard was the Sardauna of Sokoto, the leader of the biggest political party in the Northern Region, an impressive figure

Chapter 14
The country and the job, 1954

We were an excited group of young men when we gathered at the Elder Dempster Dock, Liverpool at the end of July 1954. We were sad, yes, to say goodbye to wife or sweetheart (although in my own case this was made much easier by knowing that Lesley and I were due to meet again in Lagos in less than a fortnight). But the future awaited, we had passed more than a year waiting for this day.[1]

As it happened, however, it was all something of an anti-climax. A storm prevented sailing that day. That evening I think we all phoned 'home' to relate the news. The next day's weather was the same. Again, that evening I phoned to tell Lesley that we were still in Liverpool; at this rate it looked as if she was likely to arrive in Nigeria before me.

Lesley, meanwhile, was staying with my parents, a bit worried. She had never been out of England before, had never flown. Now she would be doing both on her own, saying 'Farewell' to everything she knew and with the possibility that I might not be there to meet her (as, in fact, I was not). She wrote to me at Takoradi, not even sure where Takoradi (the port of Accra, capital of the Gold Coast) was in relation to Nigeria, but hoping that the letter would be forwarded. My mother who had similarly left England on her own in 1929 told her that *she* had written a letter from Malta to my father in Malacca that reached him three weeks after she did. Whether this was any comfort to Lesley I doubt.

Altogether there would have been almost 20 of us new Administrative Service cadets sailing in the *Accra* for the three regions of Nigeria (including one going to the Western Region which had actually already stopped regular recruiting). In addition there were a number of newly appointed women education officers. All of us felt very raw with very little idea of what in fact we would be doing. It was not surprising, therefore, that we were eager to listen to the views of 'old coasters' – and our future seniors – returning from leave.

Also aboard was the Sardauna of Sokoto, the leader of the largest political party in the Northern Region, an impressive figure of a man attended by a miniature court. The fact that he, a Muslim, spoke affably to one of the newly appointed women education officers destined for 'his' region was regarded as an unusual condescension!

The voyage followed the normal course of such events. As we sailed south we unpacked our new tropical dinner jackets and lightweight suits, we played deck-games, we speculated about our future ('What would we be actually doing given the rapidity of political change?). At the first port of call on the coast we were also told of our posting (this was always the custom: but why could we not have been told before we left England?').

We had a short stop at Las Palmas, at that time a quiet sleepy town, with an obvious police presence that would be unrecognisable in the package-tour days that would soon begin. Then there was Lagos with Lesley on the wharf to greet me. We had been separated for only a fortnight but it was bliss to be reunited. We had been billeted on a youngish couple, Reg and Netta Clarke, and he had come down to meet me and to take us back to his house. This was a modern, two-storey concrete building which I thought on the small size; how little did I know! With three bedrooms it was luxurious by colonial housing standards.

Reg Clarke was working in the Financial Secretary's part of the Lagos Secretariat (the equivalent of the Treasury in the UK Civil Service), was ambitious,[2] he had served in the Eastern Region as ADO, Arochoku where he gained a reputation of 'being good with figures' (although not personally popular) and now, having showed his ability in the field, was carving out a career in the Secretariat. He gave me much good advice and in the two days we spent in Lagos his wife, Netta, introduced us to shops and people, told us what to do and what not to do; generally, in fact, they tried to send us off less raw than we had arrived.

One of my abiding impressions of Lagos, though, apart from the heat and humidity, was the rather sullen non-cooperation of the customs clerks when we were all clearing our baggage. I had I suppose subconsciously expected some respect from them, but my vibes were that they thought our day, the day of young Europeans coming out to administer the country, was done.[3]

On the other hand, all of us cadets, our hosts and a sprinkling of the Lagos 'great and good' were invited to a 'drinks' party at Government House. This was a suitably splendid affair and I felt that Netta Clarke considered their invitation a distinct social plum. The occasion for the 'do' was that the Governor, Sir John Macpherson, had been having a conference with his Lieutenant-Governors of the

Eastern, Western and Northern regions to discuss the new Constitution which would come into force in less than two months' time. The arrival of so much new enthusiastic young blood (nearly 30 administrative officer cadets and half a dozen young women education officers) was an 'extra'. Here, we were assured that Nigeria needed us, and that if we chose we could still look forward to a lifetime's career! We were in neither the place nor the mood to argue or even question.

In retrospect this assurance might appear to have been blind to the point of stupidity but it was not quite so. The senior ranks of the civil service were almost all filled by the British and there seemed no prospect of qualified Nigerians being available to take all their places for many years. The Nigerian politicians were vocal but disunited. The National Council of Nigeria and the Cameroons drew its strength from the Igbo East, the Action Group from the Yoruba West. In the largely Muslim North, the great traditional rulers stood aloof. Indeed, their leader had said in the House of Representatives less then two years before that if the British were to leave the North would 'resume its onward march to the sea'.

The next day we boarded the 'Up-Limited' train to Kaduna where it divided, one half carrying on to Kano and the other becoming the 'Down-Limited' to Port Harcourt. Our loads safe in the baggage wagon, with bottles of filtered water, which Netta insisted we took, we thanked the Clarkes and with our colleagues as enthusiastic as ourselves took the next step in our career.

Lesley and I were lucky. Our compartment was modern, with a little lavatory, hand basin and shower, a folding table by the window which itself was fly-screened as well as having blue glass to keep out the glare. The bachelors however fared less well, in coaches that seemed that they might date from the time when Major Henri de Beaujolais told George Lawrence the story of 'Beau Geste'. The train's speed seemed to date from roughly the same era, too, often appearing to travel no faster than a walk while on only one occasion did it reach speeds of 30 miles an hour, as if in this simple society greater speeds would be an affront. Halts, when they came, were lengthy with the Nigerian passengers, squashed in incredible numbers in their coaches, getting out to stretch their legs, to buy food from vendors, to urinate and to talk. Beggars made beelines for the first-class compartments, as if sensing that here they would find some inexperienced victims who might be prepared to buy off a feeling of guilty compassion with a coin.

Gradually the train made its way north, while we talked, stared at the flat almost unchanging scenery, went for periodical meals in the dining car, and, as station succeeded station, saw our numbers diminish, as one cadet after another arrived at that nearest to his posting. At Kaduna, a big group left us, and then, much depleted, those of us destined for the Eastern Region began the slow down-journey to Port Harcourt. This was made uncomfortable by the fact that the train water supplies had not been replenished, so that water closets and taps stopped functioning (except in our modern compartment, which vastly increased the number of visitors!).

That night, we found there was no electricity either. Nevertheless, somehow, working in the dark, the cooks managed to produce something to eat on their wood fires – though what we did not know as some seven or eight of us were sharing a single torch which, passed from hand to hand, provided our only light. It all seemed pleasantly pioneering, sufficiently uncomfortable to be romantic but not upsettingly so.

Enugu, the capital of the Eastern Region of Nigeria, we reached in the small hours of the morning, several hours late, much to the disgust of the administrative officer who had been deputed to meet us and show us where we were being put up. Lesley and I found that in our case this was Government House, where a sleepy ADC showed us to our room, wished us welcome and bade us goodnight.

The Lieutenant-Governor, Sir Clement Pleass (affectionately known throughout the service as 'Clem') was still in Lagos discussing the new constitutional arrangements – under which, *inter alia*, he would become a full Governor). In his absence his wife, Lady Sybil, presided. She was a woman of strong character who had first come out to Nigeria in the mid-1920s and had walked on foot most of the way to the station where 'Clem' was posted. She was very kind to Lesley who was finding her first experience of tropical heat to be exhausting.

At that time, although still constitutionally one unit, Nigeria was divided for administrative purposes into three regions, which in the past few years had developed almost as separate entities. The Eastern (with its capital at Enugu), in which I would serve, was in its turn divided into five provinces, two being the homeland of the intelligent, industrious and acquisitive Igbo tribe – who were to be found also as groups of unloved traders in the townships of the other three provinces, in Lagos, in the Northern Region and throughout the civil service. Robert Graham and I, however, were to be posted to Calabar Province in the south-east corner of Nigeria, the home of the Ibibio peoples.

Enugu had come to prominence because there were coal seams there, the only ones in Nigeria. Consequently it had been natural when the railway line was built for Enugu to be a major station (although the coal was not of high quality it was all that was available in Nigeria). This had led to Enugu, rather than the great African market town of Onitsha on the river Niger becoming the centre of the south-eastern provinces. Relatively however, it had remained a fairly small town. The coalmine managers (European) and the African miners formed one obvious grouping; a fairly small number of senior government officers formed another.[4]

During the next few days I and the other new cadets were sworn in as administrative officers, to be faithful lieges of Our Sovereign Lady Queen Elizabeth, so help us God, as Magistrates, Grade 3, and as Justices of the Peace. Lady Sybil took Lesley and me to open an account at the Kingsway Store, old fashioned and dark, where customers walked behind the counters and where one was advised to buy staples such as flour, salt and sugar, in quantities sufficient to last three months.

On this first visit there was too much 'new' to be seen and not enough time in any event for sightseeing. We did not see, nor did anyone mention, the rapidly expanding African town, a magnet to the rural peasantry who dreamed (as had Dick Whittington in fourteenth-century London) that the streets of the regional capital would be paved in gold. For most newcomers there were neither jobs nor housing yet still they came, hoping in the town to escape the hard, monotonous life of the village. The unceasing battle to ensure that this African area did not end up as a squalid, crime-ridden shantytown was only partially successful. We would see all this in the years to come.

We had been advised to leave the hiring of servants to arrival at our future station and had been given plenty of warnings about the unreliability of 'recommendations' from previous employers – there was the well-known so-called biblical reference which, when consulted, read 'I was a stranger and he took me in', while others would be stolen, forged or simply bought for cash from the original recipient. Lady Pleass, however, the Governor's wife and whose guests we were, felt that we ought not to delay and assured us that her steward would find someone suitable. We felt we could hardly refuse but the two, a cook and a steward, proved to be unmitigated rascals who had almost certainly 'dashed' (i.e. bribed) Lady Pleass's steward to obtain the posts and who had no wish to live in the bush among 'strangers' and not even in Igboland.

At the time, however, the fact of having got servants seemed to us to be one more step in establishing ourselves, and when we once more got on the train which would take us to Aba,[5] I felt very pleased with myself, and sure that my talents, backed up by my wife, would rapidly be recognised – a feeling that no doubt I shared (and as groundlessly) with many nameless predecessors.

My first district officer, or DO ('Frankie' Davies), who was practising his golf-swing with a large umbrella on the station platform while waiting for the train's arrival, had probably noticed this feeling among cadets before. He was polite enough but plainly irritated that we had taken on servants without consulting him (although we explained our difficulty in not doing what Lady Sybil wanted in this matter), and lost no time in doing some cutting down to size. He put us up for a couple of days but his wife and child were in England, he was due for leave and was very little interested in having a new and married cadet on his hands at that stage.

The Government Station at Uyo consisted of a large cleared area accommodating six 'Senior Service'[6] bungalows with large gardens, a nine-hole golf course, the prison, the district offices, a police station and the police lines for the 40 constables. Their commander, an Assistant Superintendent of Police (a 'Senior Service' post) was a Nigerian who occupied one of the six bungalows.

Our house was situated about 400 yards away from the DO's and the first sight of it was quite enough to dispel any dreams of glory. It was sizeable enough, and attractively sited at the beginning of a ridge with the ground dropping away on either side so that it would benefit from any breeze. It was in a poor state by any standards, and particularly so to me with half memories of my parents' comfortable bungalow in Malaya. The roofing was of matting made from palm fronds (which looked ragged and unkempt), which was cool and waterproof if in good repair: ours was not. There were obvious holes in one wing; the roof of the other it was clear at the first rainfall was almost equally useless. Within, the whitewashed mud-block walls were marked with mould and the mattresses smelt. The servants' quarters were even worse, while the kitchen (a few yards away from the house because of the danger from fire) consisted simply of a room with a high, wide mud block against one wall; we learnt that the fire was lit on this, that one bought four-gallon petrol tins (empty) from the market for ovens and begged a piece of expanded metal sheet from the Public Works Department (PWD); this, when placed on the petrol tins, acted as a kitchen range, with the smoke drifting where it willed. The day Lesley managed to cajole the local inspector of works into supplying us with a proper old-fashioned wood-burning stove, such as Mrs Beeton might have used, she was very happy!

Inside the house there was a proper water closet (a newly installed and still uncommon comfort), the water for its use – carried up the hill from the nearest stream by prisoners on their heads – was thick, muddy and containing every kind of refuse; it was stored in a 44-gallon drum mounted on a low concrete pillar to provide a 'head' sufficient to feed the lavatory cistern, the handbasin and the bath (although it was so dirty that Lesley found it necessary to knot nylon socks over the taps to act as a filter to catch the larger bits). Hot water came in a bucket heated on a wood fire, and poured by the steward into the bath just before one was ready; the water, of course, had to be shared between the two of us and I really do not know that one was much cleaner at the end of bathing than at the beginning. The joy of getting rid of the day's sweat with hot water though, even if it was dirty, was almost indescribable.

The ceiling was of some kind of coarse hessian cloth, nailed to beams, with holes and tears in it. Rats and snakes lived on this and pattered about and once we saw a rat looking at us suspiciously from one of the larger holes. We attacked it with a broom and it withdrew, but the various noises continued.

We soon discovered the reason why in the bedroom the bed occupied the position it did: one day we moved it, it rained and the only part of the roof that did not leak was that above the bed's old position, so we had no recourse but to move it back, while the water accumulated in pools and rivers on the cement floor, lapping at the bricks on which our trunks stood as a precaution against this very possibility.

There was a refrigerator we were glad to see. In the absence of electricity it was powered by kerosene – I never understood the scientific principles involved. I was simply told that the wick had to be kept evenly trimmed if the coolant was to work effectively and that every now and again it was advisable for the 'fridge to be put into the back of a Public Works Department lorry and taken for a drive to shake everything up a bit!' The rubber seals of the doors were of course perished and, in spite of its legs being stood in bowls of water, small sugar ants could always get in. When all was going well, however, it kept things cool and could even make ice.[7]

One thing the house lacked, though, which was speedily remedied was a secure storeroom/cupboard. This was an essential feature since it was advisable to keep in some months' supplies of stores such as sugar, salt and flour, tinned or powdered milk, tinned meats or vegetables, which were often unobtainable except from shops in the big towns such as Aba. An apparently large supply, however, had the habit of 'evaporating' if a servant had access to it; it was better to keep stores locked up, to issue each day enough to meet that day's needs (plus a calculated excess to provide for ordinary waste and the cook's customary perk).

Anyway, this was to be our dwelling. The chief prison warder got prisoners to make palm-leaf 'mats' to mend the holes in the roof (although the dilapidated wing of the bungalow remained unusable throughout our occupancy). Meanwhile, Lesley settled down to turn it into a home. Our 'loads' had arrived without too many breakages (although the crates into which our possessions had been packed were far too large: the sight at Aba station of one very big rectangular crate being moved by being stood upright, pushed over onto the platform and then stood upright again to repeat the process, had made me wonder how many of our possessions would arrive intact; I was on my way to learning that the 'load' that porters could carry, of about 44lbs, was a sensible maximum). Curtains were an immediate need to give a woman some privacy and Lesley ran these up on the sewing machine she had bought in Cambridge. She remembered, also, to make all these curtains six feet long as a precaution against future changes of quarters (curtains could always be 'taken-up' if too long but if made short might be useless in a different house). It was advisable, also, to have a deep bottom hem in which pennies could be placed to keep the thin cotton material hanging straight when there was a breeze.

The district offices were about a quarter of a mile away, an unimpressive huddle of single-storey buildings, roofed with corrugated aluminium which shone brightly in the sun, was cheaper to maintain and less likely to let in the rain than palm mats, such as I had on my house, but was conceded to be hotter. At first I sat in with the DO himself, the better to receive instruction, but later I was given a little box of my own in a separate building a few yards away, from which I could be summoned whenever it was thought I should see something or was otherwise needed.

And I read, as instructed, the 20 volumes of the Laws of Nigeria (!) – which, although necessary as cadets were required to pass law examinations before being confirmed in their appointments, was a pretty useless waste of time as things were turning out, however good it may have been for our souls. I also read the Nigerian Service General Orders that laid down the rules and regulations governing the running of the civil service.[8] To add to all this reading, there were district files and Reports of Commissions, and anything and everything else handy that the DO thought relevant.

I should explain here that the division was the basic administrative unit of the colonial empire and the district officer (or commissioner as he was termed in East Africa) was the representative of 'government', for most people the only one they knew. He was responsible for keeping the peace in its broadest sense, for the collection of taxes and for acting as the local agent of the central authority in all activities. Sometimes there would be in a division specialists in a particular field, an agricultural or education officer, an engineer or doctor, usually a police officer and, increasingly common, a Nigerian qualified at one of the Inns of Court and newly appointed as a magistrate. Each of these, watchful of their own preserves and jealous of any trespass on them, would be working under the orders of their own department, but the co-ordination of the whole, indeed even the performance of the part in the absence of the appropriate specialist, was the task of the district officer. If there should be any new function to perform, whether, as a few years earlier, it was the redemption of the 'manilla' – the former local currency – or the organisation of elections, which was to be an increasing preoccupation in the future, it was invariably on him that it devolved.

Uyo Division was fairly typical. It was densely populated – at the time its official population was about 300,000 but in actual fact this estimate almost certainly grossly underestimated the true figure, which might have been in excess of 400,000 – but only about 500 square miles in area, traversed by a single narrow tarred road. Leading off this road, however, and criss-crossing the division, were several hundred miles of earth roads, dusty in the dry weather, thick mud in the wet, rutted and potholed, which nevertheless gave access to almost every village and on which there was a constant stream of traffic, children walking to school, women to market, traders on bicycles, and, on the wider ones, lorries known as 'mammy wagons', collecting palm-oil or nuts, bringing in dried cod (known as 'stink-fish' from the smell) or loaded overflowing with humanity.[9]

Although the high average temperature – which fluctuated between 85°F and 90°F – and a very high humidity – about 90 per cent for nine months or so of the year – meant that vegetation was luxuriant and its growth rapid, the high density of population meant that the division was heavily reliant on food imports. As it was in the tsetse belt no cattle could be pastured locally, beasts imported by train from the north would be walked the 40 plus miles from Aba in the hope that they would not die before they were slaughtered (the sight of their ribs almost piercing their dusty hides was an indication of how narrow was this interval). Pigs were usually infested with worms; sheep and goats were plentiful, almost indistinguishable in appearance from each other, and tough to eat. Chickens were ubiquitous but scrawny and the freshness of any egg was conjectural.

Pawpaws were plentiful, okra and various beans also; tomatoes were usually green in colour and bitter in taste, and lemons and oranges were green even when ripe. The local staple, though, had been yam, a kind of coarse potato, but this was becoming scarce since it was a greedy feeder and was to an increasing extent being replaced as the daily foodstuff by cassava. Even this was now imported from less populous areas, imports paid for by the produce of the oil-palm trees which covered the division and the province.

After slaves, it had been palm oil, which had attracted European traders to this part of the West Coast and had caused the British government to establish a Protectorate over the oil rivers. At that time Calabar had been the home of a British Consul (the most well known being Sir Roger Casement), although Opobo[10] also had been a well-known port. The area had come down in the world since then, its inhabitants, Efik/Ibibios, now a minority tribe in a Region dominated by Igbos. However, as it had been exposed to European influence for up to three quarters of a century,[11] and more or less effectively administered for 50 years, it had been 'missionised' almost to excess. Every village had its mud-walled school, its beds of red canna lilies (even these were rather tatty) and its playing fields, a welcome clear break after the deep and gloomy shade of the omnipresent palm trees.

Although there had been many changes since Britain had established its rule, schools and communications being obvious ones for example, the general pattern of administration had not altered very much during the first 40 or 50 years of British administration. The district officer was the key figure in this. In his division, he was the face of 'government'; his was the responsibility for ensuring peace and obedience to the law. The Native Authorities operated under his eye. Since April, however, all had been in turmoil.

For years, the District Administration had been the target for abuse by Nigerian nationalist politicians, but in the bush, immersed in their day-to-day tasks and with their enormous range of responsibilities, district officers had been able (to an extent) to ignore what was happening in the wider world and even in the larger towns. They believed that their people were far from 'ready' for independence (rightly by Western European analogy).

The British government, however, had recognised that, in the post-war world of cold battle between the West and the Soviets,

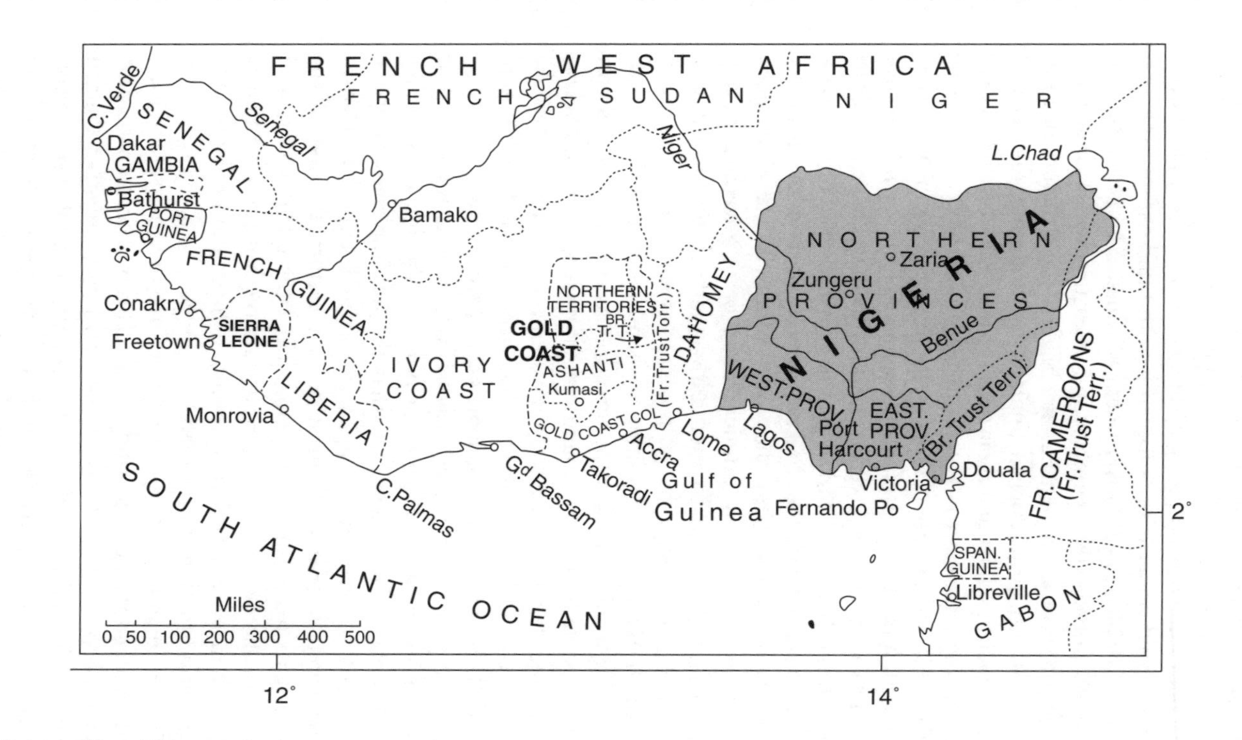

Map 2 British West African colonies.

Note: Calabar province was situated in the South-east of Nigeria.

a step had to be made towards eventual democratic self-government. 'Local government' seemed an area where a start could be made without too much risk. This then came to be 'the flavour of the month' and some officials, as happens, seeing in 'local government' a path to rapid preferment, adopted it with blind enthusiasm.

Early in 1954 a Local Government Ordinance had been passed, an almost unbelievably cumbersome measure which sought to reproduce almost exactly in Eastern Nigeria the structure of local government then prevailing in England, with county, district and parish councils each having their own separate responsibilities over a single geographical area. The result was disastrous.

Villagers – and the population of the Eastern Region was overwhelmingly rural, however politically significant the town dwellers – were used to one authority, represented for them in the person of the district officer. Now they had three, their own people but not necessarily persons for whom they had any respect, nor ones of any ability or integrity. Understandably they were confused. The councillors, too, had no experience of administration or of government, very often having little or no education. Now, suddenly, they had power, its extent not yet tested, its purposes unknown, and its duration uncertain. In West African tradition, and understandably, they cashed in while they could. At the same time, the district officer, not a part of the new system, suddenly found himself no longer responsible for much of the day-to-day work of government. He now lacked the power to ensure its effectiveness but his office and name were retained. There remained, too, some generalised charge and authority, an expectation that in any crisis he could still keep government going. Almost overnight, though, his time was slipping away.

All this was so new, however, that the full implications of the change had not yet become apparent when I arrived in Uyo in August 1954. It creaked, almost from the start, because of the arrangements made for its financing. The consequences of these I describe in the next few paragraphs (although it must be understood that in them I anticipate events a little; the full unfolding took a period of almost two years).

Copying England exactly, there was a three-tier structure of local government: county, district and village. This was accompanied by a system of 'precepting' funds up or down by the district council (the rate collection authority) to the county or the village to meet the costs of the services for which these had responsibilities (village councils, in fact, can be forgotten – they never did anything and soon faded into obscurity). The county council was responsible for primary education, which meant paying the teachers, and this was the most expensive single service.

The district councils, then, were faced with the responsibility of collecting rates, always an unpopular task, so that money could be passed on to a county council of which they were jealous and whose members had the patronage of teacher appointments (always exercised with profit). Somewhat naturally, therefore, they collected only the minimum that they needed for themselves. 'Why should they risk certain unpopularity for nothing or at least for no personal benefit'? The county councillors on the other hand, free from the responsibility of collecting the money themselves, could let funds go in providing new services with which to win popularity.

It was not long before this conflict of interest became all too obvious. Teachers, whose salaries were the largest single expenditure item, began not to be paid. The missions which were very strong in Calabar Province and were the agents responsible in the past for having established and run most schools, made cash advances to those teachers working in them. As the months went by, however, and the missions found that the council was unable to reimburse them, their own resources became overstrained. Naturally then, missions, teachers and any other unpaid local government staff turned to the DO who had always been responsible. The latter still sat in his office with the Union Jack flying from the flagpole outside; but the DO could only listen sympathetically, telephone or write to his superior, the Resident at provincial headquarters, who, in his turn, could only let the Ministry of Local Government and the Governor know the position.

Not that I was aware of this at the time, while my DO, although experienced, was not one to reflect much on the long term nor the kind of man who would discuss his reflections (if he had them) with his junior; he was able enough but near the end of his tour; his wife was coming out to join him for the last month; the training of a new ADO was a chore he could do without. So I read the files and, if the DO was away, signed whatever needed to be signed (except financial vouchers; while the Nigerian clerks were generally very reliable it might have been tempting them too much if a new ADO was able to sign these). I was also put in charge of the prison (a job which the latest ADO on any station always seemed to be given), which required regular inspection to prevent abuse.

Every station had a prison, holding between 100 and 200 prisoners, for periods of a few days up to a year or so. They lived in huts within a fenced enclosure, with a guard at the gate, under the day-to-day supervision of warders who were probably no softer than such men anywhere, but the prisoners did not suffer overmuch. They were fed regularly – records showed that there was almost always a gain in weight during their stay in jail – their work, cutting firewood and carrying water for the station, cutting grass and doing any odd jobs needed, was not unduly onerous and while from time to time one would run away to 'bush', the infrequency of such an occurrence, given the lightness of supervision, made clear that there was no great dissatisfaction.[12] Nevertheless, things could go wrong, brutality was possible, an eye had to be kept on the chief warder, however genial he might seem.

There was no particular social stigma attached by the peasant to a spell in jail and most inmates were in for relatively petty offences, non-payment of tax being frequent, theft fairly common and minor bodily harm also. More violent crime such as murder would result in a spell in one of the more formal town jails, but much may have gone unheard of. It was a society, after all, which had been 'pacified' less than 50 years before, where men always carried machetes, for use primarily to cut their way in the bush, but whose use when tempers were high was as natural and as common as in the Europe of the Middle Ages.

Meanwhile, if in these first few weeks I sometimes wondered what exactly I was doing, Lesley was also having problems adjusting. There was no other European woman on the station, so she had no one to talk to during the day, and our house, as I have indicated, was not up to much. However, the chief warder provided prisoners to dig new flower beds with soil from the valley (and I expect mixed with night soil as a fertiliser) and she planted Carters Selected Tropical Seeds (all done up in a little airtight tin box which we had brought out from England) and which, in that climate, produced in a matter of weeks the most gorgeous French marigolds and zinnias, as well as useful vegetables. Lesley made curtains, covered the biggest mildew stain in the dining room with a colourful Egyptian cloth bought from an itinerant Hausa trader, and generally did her best to make the bungalow attractive.

The servants we had taken on in Enugu, however, were beyond redemption. They were rogues, and they stole. Moreover, as we were to discover to our cost, Nigerian servants had perfected the art of being so difficult that one was forced into dismissing them (usually at the most inconvenient time to oneself) and then they demanded a month's wages in lieu of notice, thus adding pecuniary injury to personal insolence. It was all very trying when one had come out with such ideals about helping the African and serving the Empire.

One went, then another, others were obtained (with difficulty, there was no pool of well-trained domestics in the bush!) and proved almost as bad. At Christmas we were burgled and the police insisted that our then steward, a rather raw youth obtained from a missionary, was involved. We were sure that such a pious lad could not be concerned. But I suspect we were wrong, especially as some months later the police picked him up wearing my socks!

Uyo Division was full of missionaries, Roman Catholic (mostly Irish) jolly men who played golf and were partial to whisky – there was also a Roman Catholic hospital at Anua staffed by nuns and with a highly respected Sister doctor. There was a Methodist manned hospital (there was no government hospital or medical officer on the station). About ten miles away was a large contingent of American Lutherans, many of whom were married and with whose wives Lesley could talk. These missionaries, though, for all their dedication, often lived much more comfortably than we did, having electricity from a small generator and clean water pumped from the ground rather than the dirty brown liquid we had to make do with. There were many, many others: 'The Church of Christ', 'The Church of Jesus Christ', 'The Church of God', 'The Church of the Cherubim and the Seraphim' are only some that come to mind, and many apparently operated out of shabby, broken-down huts. There were also – as throughout Africa – Jehovah's Witnesses who did not recognise any earthly governments, would not pay tax or take the oath in court.

Heavenly salvation thus came in many different forms. On earth, however, we had other tribulations. Take snakes for example. I had had a fear of snakes inculcated by my childhood days in Malaya but the numbers and types of snake prevalent in this south-eastern corner of Nigeria beggared belief. These were everywhere, small black ones or great cobras on the earth, mambas in the trees. Happily, however bad a servant might be in every other respect, I never found one not adept at killing these. There was never any thought given as to whether or not a snake was dangerous: all were assumed to be so. To kill first, with the ever-handy machete[13] or with a long bamboo stick, was the only sensible thing to do.

We had been warned of the dangers of scorpions, which could hide in shoes and give a very serious sting if the shoe was not given a shake before being put on, but in fact I only ever saw two or three and never met a European who had been bitten by one. On the other hand, mosquitoes were as plentiful as in any tale, appearing before dusk and settling on any exposed bit of skin. Women wore 'mosquito boots', knee-high canvas things as a protection, a spray would be used liberally, but still one was bitten. When one came to go to bed, however carefully tucked in, one could hear their whine and await their bite, in a pitch dark as humidly hot as the day.

In Europe, of course, nights are very rarely completely dark these days; there is almost always, even in the heart of the countryside, some faint glow in the sky of light from some town, and a glimmer from some house. In Africa the night fell swiftly and thereafter the darkness was almost unrelieved. We had two pressure lamps – 'tilley lamps' they were called – but these were fiddly things, difficult to light, requiring constant pumping if they were to give a good light, and giving out unwelcome heat. Ordinary oil lamps, 'Aladdins', were better, but of course were cumbrous to carry round, so we had a number of little 'bush' lamps – hardly more than a burning wick – which gave just enough light to see by. (All oil lamps attracted insects; in season 'flying ants' would flock to them in swarms, dropping their wings, and then crawling around the base).[14] By European standards our houses were dark; an African village, however, would normally show no light at all, becoming one with the darkness of the bush.

The 'bush' was the common term for the countryside, meaning also the wild, the untamed and the savage. It was also the feared unknown, where spirits lived, sometimes in a tree, in a stream or generally in a patch of uncleared land, not necessarily malevolent beings, but requiring propitiation; the missions, in spite of their number and 50 years of proselytising, had only given the thinnest of veneers of Christianity (just as in medieval Europe Celtic, Roman and other beliefs lingered long after the formal adoption of Christianity as a state religion). The services of the *juju* man, often a hereditary office, were still needed and by many a great tree there would be a small gourd or pot, with some feathers smeared with dried blood as a sign that some offering had been made to the local spirit.

There was not in fact much true bush left in Eastern Nigeria – the population was too dense; silk cotton trees, with great buttress like ribs, were the most striking trees, soaring up 50 feet or more without a branch; there were, too, occasional slim coconut palms, but most species were much lower, and, of course, the dominant feature were the squat wild oil palms. Sunlight rarely penetrated this dense foliage, but the humid heat meant that the shrub vegetation growth was so prolific that within a few months of a path being cut or a patch of ground cleared there would be no sign of what had been done. So, while there were very few large wild animals extant – leopard, for example[15] – there were still a surprisingly large number of smaller beasts and some men remained hunters; a much larger number laid claim to the title.

The dominant species however was the ant. Termites built enormous underground cities, threw up vast mounds (earth from termite hills was rock-hard, like cement), could eat their way through concrete and would reduce any item of wood to a paper-thin shell, in fact eating their way through everything. Then there were the red soldier ants advancing in columns, unstoppable, eating everything that came into their path. Stories about encounters with soldier ants were common. One, I remember, concerned a recently married couple motoring to visit friends who stopped on the road for a while, which was long enough for a battalion or two of ants to climb in the car. When in position they struck and the man and woman found themselves being bitten everywhere. One piece of clothing after another was torn off in vain attempts to get at their tormentors, so that on arrival their friends were surprised to see the couple jumping almost naked from the car and demanding a bath.

Less dramatic perhaps, but one I can vouch for as a personal experience although one that took place a few months later, is that one evening we were chatting to the district engineer and his wife (who were even more recent arrivals than us), unable in the dark to see that we were in the path of a great column. Almost simultaneously the ants began to bite; unceremoniously we fled to our respective houses and removed all we were wearing; but the ants died with a bulldog grip: kerosene was the only thing to get them off.

One of our first actions was to buy a car (with a government loan; no way could we have done so, otherwise!) and we settled on a Ford Consul, which cost £600 – a huge sum for us. A car though was essential for me to get around the division as there was no official transport on the station; necessary also, for shopping in Aba, or even the market about one and a half miles away. Lesley had had lessons in England; I gave a few more, but she would have to take a test.

This test was given by the local Assistant Superintendent of Police, a big Nigerian named Okafor (who was later to show himself a handy man in a riot). Like all learners, Lesley was inwardly terrified, and she drove with extreme caution and rather slowly, though without making any mistakes. 'Now' he said on a straighter bit of road, 'go faster, faster, faster.' He was right, of course, almost anyone can drive safely doing 15 miles an hour: the real test was of skill and nerves that lay in avoiding an accident when doing 60. She passed.

Driving in Nigeria was a terrifying experience for anyone. The few tarred roads were narrow, maybe 12 feet wide at best, so that there was not room for two passing lorries to keep all their wheels on the tar. One would have to give way and drive on the verge, but the drivers would play 'chicken' with each other, waiting to pull over until the last possible moment; the wrecks of lorries that lined the roads showed how often they had left it too late and that the colourful mottoes on their vehicles 'Trust in God Alone', and 'The Ever Hopeful' had not saved them on that occasion.

Earth roads, rutted and pot-holed, were no easier. Bridges too were narrow, usually at the bottom of a little valley with steep approach roads on either side. Coming down on one side and seeing a jam-packed lorry thundering down the other, brakes almost inadequate and with the driver opening his cab door so that, in the event of a crash, he, at least, would be able to jump free, was enough to frighten the most experienced of drivers.

There were other hazards too. Chickens, sheep and goats could break from the undergrowth without warning, often almost from under the vehicle's wheels, damaging the suspension if hit and provoking demands for compensation from any self-alleged owner. And because the Ibibio were a highly fragmented people, living in small groups rather than clearly defined villages, houses and bicycle tracks were everywhere and cyclists might appear at any time (dusk was a particularly dangerous period as lights were almost unknown and the blackness of the cyclist's skin made him even less visible).

If one was hit, the driver was strongly advised not to stop to see how serious was the injury, but to drive fast to the nearest police station to report the incident; the local inhabitants were inclined to take immediate and violent retributive action – only that year a Nigerian magistrate had been killed, near a big town, on the main road, by a crowd who had seen a neighbour run over and who had dragged the wretched driver from the church where he had taken shelter and battered him to death (the story being made worse by a whispered report that, when it was discovered that the victim of the accident was not actually dead, the inflamed crowd thought it best to finish off what the magistrate's car had begun).

In the rains, bogging down was normal. Lorries would sometimes try to make detours in the adjacent bush to avoid the worst sloughs (just as they did in Europe before the roads were metalled) so that the way might be a hundred yards across, a sea of thick brown mud festooned with lorries. On smaller roads I would find that driving slowly but steadily, reversing immediately to get out of any particular bad patch, rather than racing the wheels ever deeper, was usually enough. Carrying a spade and some chicken wire was advisable, however; but if one was stuck, well, it would not be long before people would pass by and four were usually enough to push the car clear with sixpence as their reward.

The British had established a system of local courts to administer justice according to 'native law and custom insofar as this was consistent with natural morality' (I thought that 'the Christian religion' was also a constraint but I am told that out of deference to the Muslim North there was no direct reference to it). The judges were local elders with a literate appointed clerk. Appeals from sentences went to the district officer and these were frequent since bribery in the first instance was often alleged. The fee charged for the case being reviewed was small, and the delay before the DO heard the case was likely to be long.[16] Ibibios and Igbos were also very litigious people, particularly in land cases, and actions would often go up the line, from the DO to the Resident, to the Governor, and even to the Privy Council in London.

One day the DO told me that the Resident wanted a plan of a piece of land which was the subject of a case that had been referred to him. I was to go out in the morning, the court clerk would take me to the area, and then the two parties would each take me round the land, showing me the boundaries, as each believed them to be (and each of course quite distinct from the other's version). This sounded fine, but, knowing that Lesley was anxious to get out, I asked if she could come too. The DO looked surprised that any wife would want to do such a thing, but agreed.

We drove out as arranged, picked up the court clerk and drove along muddy paths, barely wide enough to take a car, with rain pouring down, to the nearest approachable spot to the site. The two parties were assembled, a little apart, wet but not put off by the rain. Both came up and began talking fast, and way beyond my knowledge of Efik/Ibibio. All I could think of was to tell the clerk that one group, selected at random, should take me round the area, and then that the next group should do the same, and that my map would show the claims of both parties. 'DO would then decide'. This seemed perfectly acceptable, and off we went, Lesley dripping wet, frightened of treading on a snake and of being left behind, followed. To the villagers this was traditional enough a place for a woman to offset in part their surprise that a white female should be there at all.

I had learnt, of course, the elements of surveying, but between what I had learnt in England and making a plan in the Nigerian bush in the pouring rain there was a great gulf. We were on a path, certainly, but narrow and winding, with thick undergrowth so that one could see clearly nothing to left or right. To take compass bearings as I had been taught would have meant taking a new bearing every few yards; measurements could only be by paces, with one's counting interrupted by villagers pointing out this 'economic' tree as having been planted by one ancestor, this ditch as having been made by another. At last we got back to our starting point and then we went off with the other group along a path which at points coincided, at points differed, which sometimes had the same tree planted by a different ancestor, at other times by, apparently, the same one. My paper got wetter (at least I had had the sense to use pencil not ink); my mind more confused.

Back again to the start. I thanked the parties, dropped the court clerk at his court, and went back to the office where I tried to make sense of my notes and measurements (which did not seem to coincide so that according to them I never got back to the place I started from). However, I produced a lovely map. 'I don't suppose', said the DO, 'that Lesley will want to do that again.' She did not, but at various times she did all sorts of other things.

I accompanied the DO several times when he was reviewing cases so as to get some idea of what could be expected. The procedure was that the parties would be warned in advance of the date the case would be heard so that they could present themselves and their witnesses (the reviewing officer had wide discretionary powers; he could hear the case right from the start again or confine himself to one or two points of fact). The night before one would read the record made by the court clerk of the original hearing (and many of these, although the great majority of clerks might not even have had six years of primary school education, were surprisingly complete – especially having regard to the circumstances under which they would have been compiled, perhaps with the aid of a guttering oil lamp on a rickety table).

On the day of the hearing the court[17] would be full – there might be five or six cases listed for the day, each one having its quota of plaintiff, defendant and witnesses for each party and idle bystanders who would be attending as much for the entertainment as for any other reason. There would also be the native court judges, elderly men usually, with little or no formal education but who had been chosen as influential representatives of the local people. There was no question of any professional representation by lawyers.

Cases were held in the local language and so one had to rely heavily on the government interpreter; most district officers had only enough knowledge of the local language to grasp the bare bones of an argument, while since Ibibio (and also Igbo) was a 'tonal' language – the meaning of a word being dependant upon its intonation – it was a brave man who was sufficiently certain of his pronunciation and speech sounds to make a judgement other than in English.

The party asking for the case to be reviewed would be asked to give his reasons, these usually being that his opponent's witnesses had lied, that some of his own had not be present at the original hearing or that the judges at it were biased, stupid or had been bribed. Then began the long and difficult search through these allegations to seek to determine the truth, a search often helped by observing the attitude of the crowd thronging the court that knew the participants and the likely circumstances far better than an outsider could hope to do.

This DO was good at court work, quick-witted and able to produce a jest. I remember a case where by sending a plaintiff and his witnesses out of earshot, and then interrogating each separately, he obtained so many contradictions, to the wild delight of those present, that the case collapsed, even the plaintiff agreeing, wryly, that it could not be sustained. Others were less suited to it; some agonised over the cases before them, spending hours in prior study, further hours in court and often then being unable to make up their minds for sure. I, myself, was not particularly good, I think, having difficulty in 'getting into the skin' properly of the people (speaking of which, I had one case where a sheep was presented in all seriousness as the witness of an event, and was so accepted by those attending: I hope, although I cannot now be sure, that I interpreted his 'Baa-ahs' accurately!).

Unless a woman was involved in a case, most of those attending would be men, simply because women were generally far too busy to spend their time in this way. Women carried, on their heads, the water that was needed by a household, often a mile or two, in spite of the fact that heavy rainfall meant that Calabar Province had an abundance of small streams (there were very few wells in the bush, of course, and no piped water supplies) and very often with a baby slung on their back; women cooked, kept the houses (relatively) clean and tidy, and did most agricultural work such as hoeing. Women went to the local markets – held generally every four or five days – to sell surplus produce and to buy, often in minute quantities such as four matches at a time, whatever they could not produce themselves, transactions that would be haggled over at length, this being half the fun.

The men were the warriors: only now there was no war allowed; the men were the hunters: only now there was little game. In fact men were relative parasites, although they still had a role in cutting bunches of palm fruit from the trees that provided the main source of money income. These bunches had to be handled with care to prevent the fruit being bruised – bruised fruit developed a higher percentage of free fatty acid (FFA) in its oil which made it less valuable. The fruit were then boiled up in great caldrons to extract the oil that was sold for export, the money belonging to the men. Women, however, had extracted, as a right, their ownership of the kernels of the nuts, which were sold separately and, when steam-powered mechanical mills had been introduced a few years before,[18] had rioted and destroyed some of these fearing a loss of 'their' income. Women in fact were a highly organised section of society with their own societies and mysteries from which men were excluded. The fact that 'bride-price' was payable by a suitor to the woman's family before marriage, certainly did not mean that she was in any way a chattel or dependant on her husband. Women had great and independent economic power; women owned most of the lorries – hence the soubriquet of these as 'mammy wagons' – and were the great traders, carrying fortunes in notes hidden in the *lappas* or cloths that covered their massively fat bodies.

A different species of palm tree, when its crown was tapped, produced a clear liquid that if left to ferment turned strongly alcoholic. This was the palm wine most famously celebrated in Amos Tutuola's novel *The Palm-Wine Drinkard* and which in the ceremonial life and mythology of southern Nigerians played the same part as does wine in that of continental Europe or Scotch among Highlanders. The act of tapping, however, killed the tree (itself a mythological touch), and so, even in 1954, drinking of palm wine was mostly done at ceremonial occasions such as funerals.

These were generally celebratory affairs, an important, or 'big', man's coffin being followed by a long crocodile of singers and dancers, the highly decorated and painted coffin itself, often with little panels of glass inset in the wood,[19] being tossed in the air as the procession went on its way – an unusual sight! Such processions would always be quite 'high', although the amount of palm wine drunk by most would have been limited to a ritual slurp (in my view ample; I thought palm wine tasted of low-quality soap). Locally distilled – and often lethal – spirits or, in the classier funerals, smuggled gin or Spanish brandy from Fernando Po, would fuel the exhilaration.

Another feature peculiar to Calabar Province was the custom of erecting commemorative concrete figurines and crosses by the sides of the main road, stylised figures, sometimes with white faces. I do not know whether this was meant to show power, Europeans being people of power and having white skins, or whether, as with the Chinese, white was the colour of death.

Death was of course an ever-present feature. Statistics were lacking – there was no registration of births nor of deaths – and without these one can only make guesses at the average life expectancy, but something between 35 and 40 years would appear to be probable. There was very little outright hunger at this time – the suckling of children well into their second year of life was possibly used more as a way of avoiding too frequent pregnancies than because of any shortage of food[20] – but diseases were everywhere. Yellow fever, filaria, intestinal diseases of every kind, leprosy and polio (about which I write rather more fully in subsequent chapters) were all endemic. The greatest killer and even greater debilitation, though, was malaria.

In the townships, such as Uyo, it was possible to take some prophylactic measures, although these amounted to little more than gestures, by clearing stagnant pools of water, ditches or any similar breeding site of the anopheles mosquito. The use of portable sprayers that covered the surface of any water with an oily film, killing the larvae, was also becoming more common. In the bush, however, nothing like this was possible given the tremendous rainfall and that this was a normal climatic feature for nine months of the year. The new drugs which had become available in the nine years since the war – Paludrine, Nivaquin and so on – had largely replaced quinine as a cure and also as a prevention against contracting the fever, but they did not affect the prevalence of the mosquito. Moreover, they were still fairly expensive when measured against a peasant's income (even if the benefits in improved health and *ability* to work more than outweighed the money cost). The drugs were new, and prejudice had to be overcome (a fear that sexual 'power' might be reduced). Advertising, on hoardings, in newspapers; education in schools; these methods were used but it was slow work.

The medical services were hardly existent outside the towns. The two mission hospitals I have mentioned may have provided 150 beds between them (for a population, as I have estimated above, of 400,000). There might have been four doctors, at best, working in these: there were no others in the division. The nursing sisters in the two hospitals would be European, the assistant nurses would be local women, not trained to any very high standard and, though better than their average colleagues in government-run hospitals, not above charging patients direct for such services as bringing them a glass of water (1d). There were also local dispensaries and maternity units, now run by the district councils, and which because of the new local government organisation, I was barely aware of at the time.

While the act of a nurse demanding payment before supplying an essential need (particularly as the water was not 'hers' initially in any event) may seem outrageous, within the context of African society it was perfectly normal. Thus, in the Post Office the counter clerk needed to be 'dashed' before he would allow a customer to withdraw money from his savings bank account; a 'dash' to him would be advisable also if one wanted to be sure that a telegram was sent (I am writing, of course, of transactions between two Nigerians; Europeans, at that time, were not subject to these exactions, although it is now general knowledge amongst travellers to that country that they too must pay – or suffer).

The traffic police and magistrates' clerks were commonly thought of as the greatest beneficiaries of the 'dash', the possession of either post guaranteeing a comfortable competence, and for doing nothing, just looking the other way or miscounting by half the number of passengers on a 'mammy wagon' (which was probably not licensed to hold any at all).

Haircuts were a problem. African barbers could cut men's hair after a fashion (although Lesley decided that she could do better and more cheaply, and so bought hair-cutting scissors for the purpose of cutting mine). Women though were in a much more difficult position, and they had to rely upon the skills of another European wife, who would be able to 'snip' without devastating the coiffure. In the towns there might be enough European women for one to have been trained as a hairdresser, and she would be a 'pearl beyond price' amongst the women, able to dictate virtually whatever terms she liked.

This then formed the backcloth to the life Lesley and I had embarked on, although in the above few pages I have done no more than touch on a few of its principal features. The unrelenting heat, the violent tropical storms with rain falling so thick that sight and sound were both obliterated only to end as abruptly as they had begun and for the glaring sunlight to dry up in moments the puddles that had lain so thick; the noise, all these were a complete antithesis to the comfortable compromises, the quiet restraints, the *moderation* of both the life and climate of England.

As I have tried to indicate, the life lived by the Nigerians was equally violent and hard. By contrast, we Europeans had it comparatively easy, great as was the contrast with life in England, and we were very, very few on the ground. Uyo was close to two other divisional headquarters, Abak and Ikot Ekpenne, so that there was some social coming and going, although the total number of European government officers in all three divisions probably did not exceed a dozen (and about five or six Nigerians who held 'Senior Service' posts that had once been confined to expatriates). Perhaps half of these would be accompanied by a wife – in those days before cheap and frequent air travel was the norm, children went back to England for school at the age of 7 and the wife/mother was faced with the choice of staying with husband or offspring.[21]

There was usually a tennis court, surfaced with red termite mound earth, by the district officer's house (on which other staff could play by invitation) and a golf course with 'browns' instead of 'greens' with fairways cut by a gang of prisoners, using machetes and cutting to a rhythmic tune, watched benignly by a half-slumbering warder. At Abak there was a small pool near the station, which had been cleared and fenced with palm mats, although the water was almost certainly heavily polluted. Otherwise, 'entertaining' consisted of lunch parties on Saturdays or Sundays, the main dish at which was almost invariably a curry or its local variants, 'palm oil chop' or ground nut stew. Chicken served as the basis of any of these three, with rice, peppers, hard-boiled eggs and any vegetable or fruit that could be served as a side dish, e.g. coconut, okra, tomato, pawpaw, mango, slices of orange, cucumber, aubergines and many more. It was preceded by several hours of drinking gin or beer. These would be drunk, also, with the meal which itself might not start until four in the afternoon.

A meal such as this was within the competence of African cooks and the 'steward' or head servant (the title coming from the ships on which European traders in palm oil were once based and had lived) would preside over them with great efficiency. This was not the case with other dishes or other meals, a shortage of basic supplies, the poor cooking facilities and the difference in cultures meaning that most food coming from African cooks working in bush kitchens bore little relation to the dishes described in cookery books.

Wireless reception was generally poor due to the thick cloud cover and the violent electrical storms, so news of events in the outside world was erratic. English newspapers would take about a month to arrive by sea, although letters by air averaged not more than ten days from posting to delivery at the district office. There was a surprisingly efficient delivery service of the *Daily Times*, printed in English in Lagos (the publishers being the Mirror Group in Britain) and distributed all over Nigeria through the use of 'mammy wagons'. This was usually received on the day after publication; damned as it was by many for its inaccuracies and its politics, it was nevertheless good and professional journalism of a quality not seen before in West Africa.

Like all newspapers, however, it published what it thought its reading public wanted. This readership was almost all urban. It wanted – or thought it wanted – 'independence', and that very soon. So did almost all the politicians in the Eastern and Western regions (and if some had doubts they found it politic to conceal them). They wanted to be 'big men'. They wanted to have power. Ministers wanted total control of their ministries (I revert to this point in a later chapter). They wanted their importance to be clear, not only in the Legislative Council but in the 'bush' from which most of them had originated and by whose residents they were elected. In their eyes the prestige of the British Resident, the administrative officer in charge of each province, detracted from their own. So, in October 1954, Sir Clem Pleass was warning the Colonial Office, 'Certain of the Ministers are . . . quite determined to secure an alteration in the set-up of the Administration. They want to abolish the system of administration by Provinces. This, of course means in effect the abolition of Residents'.[22]

Country and job were changing at a speed that bewildered all.

Chapter 15

Constitutional change and the Federal Election, 1954[1]

I have mentioned in the previous chapter that my arrival at Lagos had coincided with a meeting that the Governor had called to discuss with the Lieutenant Governors of the three regions the implementation of the new Constitution. I had read of this, of course. I probably knew that it was to come into effect on 1 October. I am equally certain that I did not understand all the implications (in which I was probably at one with most of my colleagues).

In about mid-September 1954, my DO was telephoned by the Resident[2] who was in Enugu, and told to come to a district officers' meeting at Oron Resthouse.[3] I was to accompany him (Frankie was due to go on leave to the UK within a fortnight, his successor was not known and my attendance was just to provide continuity). Naturally, I was excited: I had only been in the country for just over a month and the meeting was clearly an important 'Event'!

There would have been seven[4] of us at the rest house waiting with anticipation for the Resident's white Rover car flying the Union Jack to come into sight. When it did, Peter Trevorrow wasted no time in explaining the purpose of the meeting. The new Constitution came into force in about a fortnight. This would require a new elected Federal Government with a prime minister. This meant that countrywide elections to the Federal Parliament had to be held in the shortest possible time. The timetable for these provided for about three weeks to proclaim constituencies, to register voters (universal adult suffrage in the Eastern and Western regions,[5] I do not know about the North) and another three weeks to nominate candidates and for them to campaign. There were no margins for error.

In the interests of speed, the division was selected to be the electoral unit. Since divisions varied widely in size and population, these might be multi-member constituencies (Uyo, for example, would return two members to the Federal Legislative Assembly). This meant that in these every voter would have two votes and would receive two ballot papers. However, as he could not use both votes for one candidate, both ballot papers would have the same serial number and when the time came to count the votes cast the ballot papers would be checked to ensure that the voter had not done so.

Because most of the population was illiterate there was no question of voters being required to mark a name on the ballot paper. Instead they were to put the ballot paper in a box marked with the candidate's name, the symbol of his party – the cockerel of the NCNC,[6] the oil palm tree of the Action Group and the oil lamp of UNIP[7] – and his photograph. The symbol was probably the most important of these as it was easily recognisable; the photographs taken by a local photographer with an ordinary camera often bore little likeness to the candidate. This system meant that there had to be a ballot box for each candidate.

First, though, was the question of compiling an electoral roll. To understand the difficulty in preparing this, one must understand that there was no registration of births or deaths so that even the total population of a division was not known. In Calabar Province also, there was no defined village structure, even the names of all the villages were known only approximately. Accordingly, it was agreed that each registration unit would be the native court area and that the court clerk would be the registration officer.

There was a lot more in the way of detailed instructions that we would have to digest and pass on. There was also much discussion of all the detailed work needed. Ballot papers would be printed by the government printer in Enugu and sent out under police escort. Ballot boxes would be made locally. Stationery – vastly more than our normal pitiful supplies – would be issued ad lib, plus pens and ink and indelible ink pads.[8] As much extra money as was needed for transport would be made available. The comparison with the normal skimpy finance was striking. The secrecy of the poll was stressed. This secrecy is, of course, an essential feature of the modern democratic system but, as I recount later, achieving it created its own problems.

We could have continued the discussion for hours but there was no time to do so. DOs had to get back to their divisions and begin the mammoth task of informing the electorate. So, once we were back in Uyo, messengers went out to the native courts telling the court clerks and council secretaries to come to the district office the next day for a meeting.

At this first meeting the DO began by explaining the background to the forthcoming election and the broad outlines of the electoral process. Posters were to be sent out to the villages telling all adults to come to their native court to register. The first problem, of course, was determining who was and who was not an adult.

How did one decide the age of a late 'teenager'? One could not. So pragmatically we accepted anyone who looked 'adult' and left it to the political parties to challenge the decision. Another problem was that people might be chary of registering for fear that this was a government trick to get them to pay tax (all adult males had to pay 15 shillings a year but a very large number did not). If the question was raised, however, all one could do was to assure the enquirer that there was no link between the two.

The role of the court clerk as registration officer was all-important. These men were literate, of course. They knew the area of their court's jurisdiction. Probably none, however, had attended a secondary school nor had any formal administrative training. Yet all depended on their conscientiousness. When after 1 October an applicant came to the court the clerk was to write down (pen and ink, of course, there were no biros then), the name and village and give the applicant a piece of paper as a receipt. Occasionally we could provide an assistant but there were very few literate, trustworthy people in the bush.

As I have mentioned above, villages themselves were not clearly defined entities. In the thick bush there were no marked boundaries. Personal names were another problem. To divulge a 'real' name might anger the spirits. There was no system of first and family names nor, also, was there the wide choice of name to which we are accustomed – there were an awful lot of 'Akpans' (first son)!

I have written earlier that the DO was due for leave (for family reasons he was determined not to postpone this). His successor was to be Michael Mann, a DO of about the same age and seniority but whose previous service had always been in Igbo-speaking provinces. It was not fair on him, of course, to be posted to a province which he did not know and of whose language he knew nothing, particularly at such a critical time and with such a raw cadet as ADO. But no one else was available. Moreover, Michael was an outstanding man, of very strong character and views and a born leader. In fact no one could have proved more suitable for the position; for me, personally, his coming was a boon as he communicated and taught me well.

I drove Michael Mann around the division so that he could get acquainted with his new charge (although I hardly knew it myself and, on at least one occasion, lost us both). The thick bush meant that one could see nothing except the road ahead, each overgrown earth road looked very much like another and signposts were few and not always accurate. Still we got around, calling on the courts to learn how registration was going, listening to problems and wherever possible helping to resolve them.

We also had to get acquainted with the prospective candidates and the party officials. All the politicians regarded Uyo as a particularly crucial area. Both sides saw Uyo with its two seats and central position in Calabar Province as a key constituency. The NCNC wanted to hold onto it so as to strengthen their claim to be the party supported not only by all Igbos but also by all Easterners. The Action Group/UNIP alliance wanted to win because a defeat for the NCNC could be used as an argument that it was only an Igbo and not a national party. In addition, of course, there would be pecuniary advantages to whoever was returned.

In these circumstances we could rely on the politicians to provide publicity for the election in all the bush villages. We, however, had to make clear to them the limits as to what they could or could not do. They could not intimidate the registration officers but they could officially challenge names put on the electoral roll if they had good reason, such as age. They could put up their own posters but not in the registration offices (which would later be polling stations). In due course they could appoint two agents to each polling station to check that the poll had been conducted properly *but* these were in no way to interfere with the voter's use of his ballots.

A slightly later consequence of the bitter party rivalry was that, when it came to the time to appoint presiding officers at the polling stations, neither party would accept a Nigerian. They did not consider any of their fellow nationals sufficiently impartial. This was something we had to accept. There were however only five other British civil servants, an engineer, education officers and so on. We therefore had to plead with missionaries that they help out; most saw it as their duty to do so. Still we were short so the DO's wife and my own wife were dragooned in.

Lesley, we had just learned, was pregnant. Before she had left England the ladies of the Women's Corona Society had told her that the heat and humidity would upset menstrual cycles, so when she missed a period shortly after our arrival in Nigeria we did not assume automatically that pregnancy was the cause. And there had been no European wife on the station to whom she could talk until Jill Mann had come to Uyo with her husband.

While the election dominated, there were other things that also needed to be dealt with. Under the new Constitution, the Nigerian civil service had ceased to be one unified body. It was to be split into four. Some functions (and of course the staff needed to carry them out) like the Police, Prisons and Posts & Telegraphs would remain under the control of the Federal central government in Lagos. Others, including the Administration, would be divided between the Federal Government and the governments of the three regions into which the country was now split. Each civil servant had the right to choose under which government he would choose to serve; this, incidentally, included all the Nigerian civil servants of whatever grade (maybe 90 per cent of the total).

Now, obviously, I had no knowledge at all on which to make any rational choice. There was, however, a general feeling that the 'loyal' thing to do was to stay with your colleagues and, indeed, it would have taken more self-assurance than most cadets possessed to start their career by choosing so flagrantly to step out of line. It was not understood, at least in the bush, that the choice, apparently so easy and obvious, would have very considerable financial and career implications (particularly for the middle-ranking officers: that by signing they were cutting themselves off from their fellow officers in the other regions and in Lagos).

There was also, naturally, normal routine work to be done although I think court work was left until after the election was over (this was inevitable given the use of courts as registration centres).

As the work of registration proceeded, so the job of typing up the roll began. Our typewriters were old-fashioned manual machines, our clerks untrained as typists and not necessarily originating from Uyo Division. Copying from the manuscripts was slow work and, although each page was meant to be checked, it was very easy to make mistakes and difficult to correct these[9] while the accuracy of the originals themselves was questionable. Then when all was done a copy of the relevant section of the roll was sent to each registration office where it could be viewed by anyone and copies of the full roll were available to the political parties and at the district office so that entries could be challenged. (There may have been a few challenges, I cannot remember. I am sure that many successful challenges could have been mounted quite easily by either side but maybe neither was anxious to open up that particular can of worms.)

Registration complete, candidates could be nominated – two by the NCNC and, I think, one by each of the Action Group and the UNIP (fighting in alliance). So we needed to have made four times the number of native courts, that is 84 ballot boxes. Each would be identified by the candidate's name, number and symbol, each would be securely padlocked,[10] the keys being kept by the DO in his safe. The election would be in three weeks' time, all over Nigeria.

I was in general charge of the southern nine or ten stations, and Michael Mann of the northern, including Uyo township. Lesley and I went off the preceding night to a rest house near her station (which had the disadvantage of being separated from the rest of the division by a wide river, the only crossing being on a rather 'Heath

Robinson'-type ferry).[11] The ballot boxes had been distributed; the precious ballot papers were in the care of the individual presiding officers to be checked before polling with the candidate's representatives; pen and paper, printing ink and pads for the thumb prints (and probably sealing wax too) had been issued to the court clerks. There was no more we could do.

In the morning I went with Lesley to the polling station and stayed with her for a time while the first few voters arrived. She and her helpers seemed to be coping quite well, but two potential causes of trouble became obvious almost immediately. One was almost comical. In order to preserve the secrecy of the ballot (on which we had made great emphasis during our public meetings of instruction), the court clerks had put the ballot boxes (four boxes per polling booth, a separate box for each candidate) in little cell-like rooms lit normally by a single window. To stop anyone looking through this and seeing into which boxes a voter had inserted his ballot papers the window shutters were kept securely closed. There was thus virtually no light to distinguish one candidate's symbol and photo from another! Indeed, there were occasions when, after a prolonged absence by a voter, it was felt necessary to open the door to see if all was well, perhaps to reveal a bemused old woman sitting in the middle of the room on the floor quite unaware of what she should do. Others, unable to find the slits in the top of the ballot box, put their papers underneath the box, behind the candidate's photo (only attached with drawing pins to the wood box), on the windowsill. Occasionally, giving up, they either put both their ballot papers in one box (thus wasting one) or came out still clutching them. This, of course, slowed things down.

The other snag was that the voters could not remember what name they had given to the registration officer, or sometimes what village name they had claimed to come from. The polling officer, himself barely literate, then took hours trying to search through dozens of 'Bassey Udoh's, 'Udoh Bassey's, 'Akpan Udoh's, etc. to try and find which corresponded to the man before him. Again time was lost.

Given these problems, however, Lesley's people seemed to be coping and so I went off to visit the other stations for which I was responsible. The story here was the same, except that as the day went on voters become more impatient, would not queue and formed querulous crowds around the polling officers, thus further confusing and slowing down these gentlemen. At one station, however, the district engineer reported that there had been some violence and his court had three times been overrun by impatient voters, for the most part good humoured although one had crept up behind him with a club! There were tales of similar problems in other courts in the northern part of the division and I decided that my duty now lay in getting back to my wife.

When I arrived the station seemed peaceful, though beset by large crowds. Lesley told me, however, that earlier she had had adventures. As at other polling stations, the polling officers had found it difficult to identify on their lists the voters who came along, perhaps not all to vote – registration had we estimated run at only about 50 per cent – but perhaps to watch, or to try to vote even if they had not registered. At first everyone was good humoured and obediently kept at a distance from the court so that one or two could come forward at a time. But, gradually, getting bored with waiting, they came closer, ignoring the remonstrance of the court messengers, until they lapped the chest-high mud walls of the court.

By this time, one of the candidates who happened to live in this area, his supporters and the supporters of his opponent, were all getting decidedly worried, a worry that grew greater as members of the crowd began to climb on the walls. As they did so, the messengers threw them back into the mass of people waiting outside, but there were too many. The mud walls themselves began to crumble and then, like a flood, the crowd burst in. The party representatives flew behind Lesley, 'Madam, Madam, save us'. 'I never knew before', she told me later, 'what colour an African went when he was frightened to death'!

There seemed little that could be done but Lesley climbed onto the table where previously the polling officers had laboriously been working and, using the Court Clerk as an interpreter, called out that there must be silence (she had not been a teacher for nothing!). Then, she said, unless the court was emptied at once she would not allow any of them to vote AND THEY WOULD NOT EVER BE ALLOWED TO VOTE AGAIN! At this awful threat (which, of course, she had absolutely no authority to make), there was a certain amount of shuffling of feet and backward ebb. Then, calling on some of the native court members, and any chief village elders that could be found, she got the crowds organised into village groups at intervals around the court. Then, instead of waiting for the voter to come forward, she told the polling officer to call out the names from the list which the court messengers repeated in a stentorian voice until someone came forward in answer.

It was still slow, but faster than before, and as the day went on, the crowds thinned as people got hungry or thirsty or tired of waiting until at last darkness came and the polling was declared closed. Potentially it could have been nasty, not from malice but simply because crowds out of control are always dangerous. I was proud of the way she handled it, especially given the fact of her pregnancy, the heat and the fact that she had only been in Africa three months.

That night we slept at the nearby rest house as the ferry only worked during the hours of daylight, with the sacred ballot boxes, collected from the polling stations I was handling, all around us. Because the pontoon ferry did not work at night, however, the boxes from one station had not been brought in; the clerk therefore slept on them to prevent any tampering, while at my rest house old Bassie, the Uyo Station messenger, kept guard. The next morning the station lorry carried all the boxes back to Uyo.

There we found that disorders had been general[12] and that Uyo polling station itself had had to be closed long before the scheduled time because of the impossibility of polling properly. But the urgent task ahead was the count. This also was slow, as the ballot papers in each box had first to be assembled in numerical order to make certain that no voter had put both his papers in one box. No more complicated system could have been devised for Nigeria's (and maybe Africa's) first adult suffrage election.

Counting went on all day, scrutinised by the candidates. It was clear that it would be close and excitement in Uyo Township mounted. Finally, in the evening, Michael Mann, the district officer, read out the result: one seat for the NCNC, one seat for the Action Group/UNIP. This sounded eminently fair but was greeted with cries of disappointment, the Action Group/UNIP supporters being particularly vociferous. Later that night a crowd gathered to march on the station, being thwarted by our burly Superintendent of Police, Okafor, who drew a line on the mud road and had his men crack over the head with truncheons anyone who crossed it.

Naturally, there was a petition against the result, with claims that the election had not been conducted properly. In due course a High Court Judge heard this petition. He quashed the result. There could be no doubt that there had been irregularities: not all who had registered and had come to vote had been able to do so. The judge ordered a fresh election (by which time I had left the division). The result, however, was the same and, I am perfectly certain, reflected fairly the political views of the people of the division. They did not like Igbos but they had to live with them and, even if subconsciously, they had hedged their bets.

Chapter 16
Back to routine, 1954

Michael Mann must have been disappointed at the disorders that had taken place in Uyo during the election but, as I hope I have made clear, he was in no way to blame personally. Indeed, it was thanks to him and to Assistant Superintendent of Police Okafor that the disorders had been contained without any deaths.

I both liked and respected Michael, while Lesley was delighted to have in his wife Jill, a woman of great charm to whom she could talk, who was experienced, of a strong character, knowledgeable and with two young intelligent and energetic children. The previous three months must have been both lonely and difficult indeed for Lesley.

Michael told me that he had decided that a Colonial Service career was not for him. He had a vocation to be ordained in the Church and he and Jill were saving every penny that they could to help meet the costs of theological college. Under the terms of the new Constitution 'early retirement' was allowed (previously the minimum retirement age had been 45 and anyone who left before then did so with nothing; even now, the retirement terms were pretty minimal). So Michael applied to retire at the earliest possible date, 1 October 1955.[1]

The need to concentrate on arranging the elections had meant that other work – and particularly the direct contact with the people that district officers considered to be an essential feature of their job – had suffered. Moreover, under the new Local Government Law local administrative power rested with the councils: the DO could advise only if asked. So Michael decided that we would begin a concentrated spell of touring with one or the other of us staying in rest houses each week, visiting villages, hearing complaints, reviewing cases in the native courts.

In Uyo Division there were about six of these rest houses, sited first when there was little or no motor transport and when the only way of getting about was by bicycle or on foot, which gave the DO touring his division a local base where he would be easily accessible to the villagers. They were simple but not uncomfortable, usually a kind of open barn-like building with low walls, waist high. In one corner, though the walls went up to head height, to provide a sleeping area and a recess for an earth and bucket closet or thunder-box. (Refined people took along their own lavatory seat for this; others just used what was available.) In another corner there might be a smaller walled area for use as a store. That was all.

On alternate Monday mornings thereafter, the district lorry would come up to our house to be loaded with camp beds, a tin travelling bath, camp chairs, clothes, cooking utensils and food together with the servants' bedding rolls and impedimenta. We would then lead the way to the rest house where we had arranged to stay. While Lesley and the servants unloaded the lorry, arranged the furniture (the only item provided in the rest house, apart from the latrine bucket, was a big wooden table), saw that there was water and firewood and checked the oil lamps, I would go over to talk to the court clerk, hear what cases were coming up and collect the court records of the earlier proceedings.

As I have explained in an earlier chapter, there were 21 courts in Uyo Division, each with a panel of about 12 judges who sat in rotation and who dealt with all the everyday problems of village life, debt, minor breeches of peace, transgressions of village custom, divorce (with long drawn-out arguments concerning the refund of bride-price paid years before), occasionally rape and, always, land cases. These were often over the ownership of tiny strips of land but which were so bitterly contested that they would be raised again and again, sometimes even being referred all the way up to the Judicial Committee of the House of Lords.

The difficulty in such cases lay in part in the fact that there were no maps, no obvious boundaries, few man-made markers – a tree that a man claimed his grandfather had planted was the most one could usually expect, a complicated family structure and an attitude towards land which, while changing under the pressure of increasing population, certainly did not incline towards 'ownership' in the European sense. However, because of this increasing population the right to use land was becoming increasingly valuable and quarrels over it, increasingly bitter. If a land case were down for review, therefore, there would be little chance of hearing anything else.

The news that the DO was staying in the rest house would soon get about; village children would approach as close as they dared, round-eyed and ready to run off if challenged but curious to see what strange thing the *mbakara* or white people were up to. Towards evening there would usually be a group of people assembled with 'complaints'. These might concern an old man's request that he be exempt from tax; a request from a village that help be given to roof a village hall; a complaint that a teacher was forcing his girl pupils to have intercourse with him. On one occasion, Michael Mann told me a man said he had a headache. He was told not to waste time and to go away. Next day he reappeared and was again told to leave. A third time and Michael thought that he had better enquire 'where is the pain and what caused it?' 'A nail' was the reply and sure enough, a nail had been driven into the man's skull – an old punishment for thieves. Fortunately, he did not die. This, of course, was rather unusual but it was always necessary to listen, even if there was little practical assistance that could be given. Often, having had the opportunity to tell his tale and exchange a few remarks about his problem, the complainant seemed satisfied even if his difficulty remained unsolved.

With nightfall we would bath, sharing in the tin travelling bath a bucket (or perhaps two) of hot and (relatively) clean water. A drink while I read the court records, some supper and then to our camp beds and mosquito nets.

Court work itself I found interesting but never easy and I do not think I was particularly good at it – certainly I rarely finished a day, or even a case, confident that I was completely right in my judgements. A dozen or so cases was probably the most that one could hope to hear out of perhaps three or four times that number listed as awaiting review. The remainder would have to be left for another occasion, by which time the list would be back to its original length. In spite of one's effort there would still be some plaintiffs or defendants who were left unsatisfied and who decided to ask the Resident for a further review.

My visit to one rest house coincided with the funeral of a former head court messenger, a much-respected local worthy who was given a great send-off. There was a procession of some hundreds of people, the firing into the air of the cheap firearms known as Dane guns (he had been reputedly a mighty hunter in his day), the chanting of women. I was invited to go down to the grave shaft with the coffin (which was buried in an upright position so that the corpse was as if standing) and a few of the elders, and there some vintage palm wine was given as a kind of libation.

At another village (long unvisited), some innocent enquiries of mine about the palm harvest caused obvious concern. Fortunately, I realised before it was too late that my visit had been connected in the villagers' minds with the amount of tax they were paying (far too little) and they were worried that my questions were a prelude to a hefty upward hike in this sum (understandably unpopular). I had to do some hasty pacifying, as otherwise there could have been a small riot!

Although no formal title existed to the ownership of land outside townships, it had become customary to make a payment to villagers in 'compensation' if land was taken for building a road or some other similar public work. So when Shell, which had begun searching for oil in Nigeria in 1935, started to look at the geological formations in Uyo, it recognised that it would have to pay; and it soon became known that Shell paid well if it established a permanent base. Before this though, the first stage in prospecting was simply carrying out a seismic survey, explosive charges being set off at regular intervals on a straight line and their shock waves being plotted and measured so that the underlying geology of the land could be determined.

Normally, the amount of compensation that would be paid for this would be very small as there was no question of the permanent alienation of any land or the destruction of any trees or crops. One such line unfortunately went straight through a patch of *juju* bush and, even worse, a charge had to be exploded in the middle of it. The local villagers were perhaps concerned about the graves and souls of their ancestors; they may have had less worthy thoughts about the money they might get. Anyway they were up in arms. Michael Mann and I went out to talk to them with a view to explaining that their ancestors would sleep better if their descendants were enjoying money from oil – at least I suppose that is what we were doing. The village, however, was very upset. There was so much noise that we had no possibility of making our point. The older women in particular were being especially vociferous. Michael, therefore, suggested to me that we should divide into two. He would talk seriously to the older men; I should distract the older women. It was entirely sensible but when we came to it I began to wonder.

I talked, I hope soothingly, with one eye on Michael and a couple of policemen, a score of yards away. One old dear, at least, however, was not soothed. She waved a machete in ever descending circles about my head. I talked. The machete came lower. I talked the more desperately with an eye on how Michael was getting on. She screamed louder, and lower came the machete. It was clearly a question of time but before my nerve gave, and I am sure mine would have given before hers, there was an obvious expression of agreement from Michael and the elders, which gave me a way without loss of dignity of escaping from being scalped. I took it. No oil was found there.

Less out-of-the-way jobs that were referred to the District Administration included advising on future road bituminisation. Road traffic – and especially lorry traffic – had developed very rapidly over the past few years and once the number of vehicles using a road had passed a calculable point, the costs of maintaining an earth road became uneconomic. The only tarred road in Uyo in 1954 was the through link from Aba to Oron but there was an important road south also, to Opobo, used by lorries loaded with dried cod, the stench of which lingered after their passing, mixed with the billowing dust clouds that hung in the air behind them. A reliable traffic count of vehicle usage was needed, however every district officer was pressing for the bituminisation of a road in 'his' division and there had to be a rational allocation of resources to justify the cost.

It is, in fact, hard for the present-day observers of 'developing' countries to understand how short of funds colonial governments were. International development aid was almost unheard of and although in the district office there was the recently issued World Bank Report on the Development of Nigeria (which I remember reading with enthusiasm), there was general scepticism that even its modest – by the standards of these days – expectations could be achieved. Resources for new projects were hard to obtain so projects themselves had to be chosen with great care and executed with strict economy. This was reflected also in the amounts available to meet day-to-day expenses; the money for stationery was limited so draft envelopes were reused time and again, office furniture was basic and locally made, the typewriters were museum pieces. How often, later, have I heard colleagues remarking on how much we could have done if we, in those colonial days, had had a half – even a quarter – of the resources available to, and usually wasted by, the governments of independence.

But at the time the need to stretch resources was almost part of the fun. It was a challenge to one's ingenuity to find a way of doing something that was apparently undo-able. And so much more satisfying on completion than if one had had simply to sign a cheque: part of the mystique of being a bush DO. Just as another aspect of the work was its sheer variety, even that given to a very raw cadet such as myself.

Some tasks I have already mentioned, others included restoring the grave on Uyo Station of a district officer who had committed suicide some years before in a neighbouring district requesting that 'his bones should never lie in the accursed soil of Eket!'; the re-roofing of the station rest house at Uyo and designing a new house to replace the dilapidated one Lesley and I lived in. This was to be built of mud blocks as before, the blocks being made by prisoners and dried in the sun, then erected on a concrete raft in the hope that this would stop white ants (a vain hope). It was to be roofed with palm mats again, not 'pan' (corrugated aluminium) as, though the latter was much cheaper in the long run, the weight of a pan roof was much greater and so more money had to be spent straight away on roof supports. I had great fun with this design, but I was to be posted away from the division before the work on building was due to start; in fact it was never built.[2]

Leprosy was still prevalent at that time – the drugs that were soon virtually to eradicate the disease not having yet been discovered – and lepers were shunned as they had been in Europe in the Middle Ages. In the next-door Itu District, at a distance of some 25 miles from Uyo, an enormous settlement had been established in the 1920s for these unfortunate people, by a Presbyterian medical missionary, Dr MacDonald.

I had met the Rev. MacDonald (the younger brother of the settlement founder and presently in charge of the settlement) on the voyage out, and we were always pleased to visit there to worship in the vast mud-brick and mat-roofed church. This could seat 5,000 lepers at a time and was reputed to be the largest building of its kind in the world. But if, appropriately for a mission settlement, the church was the central feature, Dr MacDonald's Scottish Calvinism made sure that work was also emphasised. Fish bones and shells from the Enyong Creek, on the bank of which the settlement was built, were ground up and burned to make lime; palm-oil trees were not left simply to grow wild but properly spaced out and given fertiliser so that yields were several times as high as from the palms growing naturally in the bush. Fruit trees were planted and coconut palms – the trunks being useful for building, the nuts for oil as well as the white meat of the fruit. Vegetables were grown, chickens cared for and not just left to search for what feed they could find (with the result that they tasted quite different from the scrawny creatures which featured so large on our normal diet). There was a small herd of dwarf cattle as well, this breed being immune to tsetse fly, so that there was fresh milk available for the sick in the hospital.

Male and female lepers were kept segregated in separate 'villages', walled, and with their own 'police' and there was a school for the children. (There was also an equestrian statue in concrete of King Edward VIII – which must have been unique!).

At New Year we were particularly pleased to be asked by the DO of Itu to come with him to the settlement for a party.

There was church – the service was interpreted into four Nigerian languages – there was a brass band for musical accompaniment and whole throated singing from the 3,000 or 4,000 in the congregation – and afterwards there were games and races. There was a tug-of-war between the lepers on the one hand and the Administration and Church on the other (we lost). There was tea. There was a visit to the hospital to see any lepers from one's own division and to collect messages to take back to the invalid's home village.

But Itu, a kind of twentieth-century version of the Jesuits' Paraguayan Paradise, was already being affected by improvements in medical treatment of leprosy even if the major discoveries in the cure of the disease had still to be made. The numbers seeking refuge there had fallen, although they were still substantial. I am told though that it was bombed during the Biafran war and is now destroyed.

The short past history of British rule in Nigeria, the limited number of administrative officers and the small establishments of the Army, represented by four battalions of the West African Frontier Force (the WAFF) and the Nigeria Police, meant that a lot of importance was attached to the preparation by district officers of a monthly 'Intelligence Report'. This had once concentrated on the danger from some internal revolt – Mahdi-ism had been the former favourite subject – but the Cold War meant that the emphasis had shifted to the danger of Communism. Sometimes this had ludicrous consequences. An Afro-American woman education officer at a teacher training college in Uyo was reported by the police special branch to be a Communist agent; she was undoubtedly anti-British colonialism, naturally enough given her nationality and race, but if she was representative of the KGB's finest, I would have eaten my mosquito net!

There were 'secret societies' of course, and murderous ones too. Calabar Province had been the centre of the Leopard Society, *Ekpe Owo*, which had been very active less than ten years before and there was another similar murder cult in Abakaliki Division of Ogoja Province. Most 'palaver', however, was linked, inevitably with land and its ownership. I have referred once or twice already to the numerous land disputes that existed and to the passion with which these were pursued. One such, a quarrel between the Nyiongs of Uyo Division and the Nyas of Opobo, had dragged on for years, had gone through court after court and now, although a final judgement had been made in favour of the Nyiongs, the Nyas were still arguing. So it had been decided that the boundary between the land claimed by the two villages should be demarcated in such a way that there could be no further dispute, by sinking six-foot lengths of railway iron in cubes of solid concrete, each edge to measure a yard, and the pillars to be set up at 100-yard intervals.

We knew that the Nyas still felt bitter over the judgement – they had already chased off one team of surveyors – so it was agreed that we would make a show of force to demonstrate that the decision of the court had to be obeyed. Accordingly the DOs of Uyo and Opobo, their ADOs (I being one of these), a European assistant superintendent of police, about 40 of his men and court messengers from the nearest courts in the two divisions, assembled to enforce judgement. Out we marched. One pillar was erected. Then another. But we could see, through the bush, crowds of Nya assembling armed with bows, while further back were other men with Dane guns.[3] In front of all were women, screaming themselves into a frenzy, and who finally launched themselves on the two boundary pillars we had set up. The fact that the concrete had half set was no deterrent; it was scrabbled at with fingers until these were bloody and almost worn to the bone. The first pillar was uprooted with cries like those reputed to accompany the storming of the Bastille. Now what were we to do?

The women then started attacking the constables. They had their truncheons, of course, but it was pretty clear that if these were used, the Nya men would intervene. We were outnumbered, *and* they had both bows and arrows and guns, while (as was normal policy) we had no firearms. Nor did we wish the Nyiongs to come in to support us, as that could have meant a rather bloody little village affray. All we could do then was to form square(!) and retreat, with the women screaming insults and jabbing their bleeding fingers into the faces of our suffering constables. It was not very heroic but fortunately both DOs had given sufficient evidence of their courage in the past not to feel any need to prove it in a bush squabble![4] Two months later (after I had left Uyo Division), a really overwhelming force of police was brought in, equipped with tear gas, and the boundary was marked. But I wonder whether it still is?

Just before Christmas some missionaries came to see Michael to express their worries about education finance. The various Christian missions had originally set up most of the primary schools in Eastern Nigeria and, in the first instance, they paid the teachers. The missions had then claimed reimbursement for these expenses. In the past they had claimed this from the Native Authority but under the new Local Government Act the Native Authorities (which had been under the control of the DO) had been abolished. A county council had replaced it, but when the missions approached the county council they were told that, 'Yes, there would be money. It would be collected, but none was available now'.

Meanwhile the teachers had to be paid. So the missions had to borrow by overdraft from the bank. This overdraft was growing. The bank was worried. The missions were worried. So they had come to the DO who was there to settle all such problems. However, on this occasion, the DO could do nothing. Under the Local Government Act he had no *locus standi*. He could talk to the County Council Treasurer and to the Chairman of the Council but that was all.[5]

Our friends Brian (the district engineer) and Paddy Clark, who lived in the next house to us, asked us to join them for dinner on Christmas Eve. We had an enjoyable and convivial evening, and then we walked back to our house and went straight to bed. The next morning when our steward brought us in morning tea, he told us that one of the shuttered windows had been left open during the night. Lesley noted that her sewing machine – essential as she had to make all clothes and curtains herself – was missing. We told the police immediately and they gave us their view that it was almost certain to have been an 'inside job'. Their suspicions fell on the steward, a young man who had come to us from the American Lutheran Mission. We were very reluctant to believe that he could have been the guilty party. He was not a particularly efficient man and a bit glib but we took his strongly stressed Christianity at its face value. In any event there was no proof.

This was to be the last matter in which I took part in Uyo Division. In early January 1955, at short notice (as was always the case in a perennially short-staffed service), I was transferred to Calabar to work in the Resident's office, partly because Lesley was expecting her baby in four months and would be able to get medical treatment. We were sorry in many ways to go – I suppose one always looks back on one's first station with some nostalgia. We would also miss the Manns; with them we had made a life-long friendship; I have written above of what I learned from him. At the same time, I welcomed the prospect getting from the Resident's office a rather broader view of what was going on. There were also material things like electricity, proper running water, the availability of (albeit) frozen butter, bacon and other delights, all of which suddenly seemed very attractive.

So, we packed our possessions – already depleted by breakages after only four months, and not only by the servants as sudden and violent gusts of wind would blow vases to smash on the concrete floor. Our steward, the young man suspected by the police, asked if he could have a few days' leave to see his family as Calabar was – to him – a long way off. This we readily agreed to, as we would be staying in the catering rest house there for the first few days. Then we set off in the Nigeria Marine Service launch that took us on the two-hour voyage from Oron, down the Cross River, to Calabar.

Chapter 17
The crash of the Bristol Wayfarer

Calabar was by colonial standards an 'old' town. It had been a prominent trading port for some hundreds of years, and in the nineteenth century had been a focal point for the Royal Navy Anti-Slavery Squadron. Towards the end of that century (1884), when Britain was taking its first reluctant steps towards territorial control of the African mainland, it had been the administrative centre of the Oil Rivers Protectorate, the Consul being a quasi-Governor.

The importance of this position had been emphasised by a suitably imposing home and office for the holder. It was a two-storey building that avoided the depredations of the white ant (eating unseen through brick or timber) by having a cast-iron frame shipped out from England. The living quarters were on the airier first floor with views out over the town and the wide Cross River; offices were below. The furniture and fittings of the Residence had also been shipped out from England, heavy Victorian. From India, though, would have come the enormous leather punkah suspended over the dining table.[1] There was a croquet lawn and tennis courts while terraced gardens fell away (by 1955 it was no longer possible to maintain these in their former glory).

There were other features of the station that reminded of its former importance. The Presbyterian Mission was based in Calabar and Hope Waddell Institute (one of the earliest secondary schools in Nigeria) showed the importance that the missionaries had attached to educating 'the heathen'. The major trading companies, the French-owned CFAO and SCOA[2] and the British United Africa Company (UAC),[3] had factories (as shops were known on the coast).

There was also a graveyard. A visit to this was a melancholy event, full as it was of the graves of young men, 'died aged 20 after three months, of fever' read a typical headstone. It was not for nothing that the West Coast was known as the 'White Man's Grave' or that the jingle ran,

Beware, beware the Bight of Benin.
One came out where Forty went in.

Nowadays, though, it was no more than normally unhealthy. There were government medical officers, a fairly big hospital for the African population and a small cottage hospital on stilts for the European.[4] There was electricity and running water. The 'factories' had a large selection of tinned food; there was a cold store where meat and butter could be bought.

Other amenities included the normal golf course and tennis courts. There was a club with a bar, dining room, billiard room, magazines and a library. There was also a catering rest house. This institution was really just a small government-run hotel with about five or six individual chalets comprising of a sitting room, bedroom and bathroom. The rest houses – built by government when it was realised that district officers had neither the rooms nor the money to put up casual European visitors – were usually run on a part-time basis by a wife anxious to augment the family income. The rest house at Calabar was surrounded with casuarina trees and the wind whispering through their leaves sounded peacefully nostalgic.

It was here that we stayed for the first three or four days, although this was longer than we had planned. Our steward – the young man suspected by the police of theft – who had promised faithfully to appear after two just did not turn up. We had no news of him, so all we could do was assume that he had decided to take himself off. Fortunately there was quite a pool of servants available at Calabar and we were able to find a replacement without difficulty. Later we heard from the police that they had arrested our former steward when he had been seen wearing a pair of European socks of mine – proof that he had been involved in the burglary at Christmas; he had assumed that he would be safe to wear the socks when I was at a distance.

The house that we had been allocated was on the edge of a cliff looking out over Calabar harbour and the Cross River, a beautiful view. It would, however, be difficult to say anything about its design save it was 'functional'. It resembled a shoebox. All rooms opened out of one another. At one end there was a lavatory and bathroom, next was the bedroom, then came a living and dining room and at the far end there was a kitchen and a store. There was no glass in the windows, of course, but wooden shutters that could be used to provide shelter from the sun's glare and to keep out the rain. The main entry to the house was in front, but was too close to the edge of the cliff – there was a tale that when the then ADO was once away on tour a suitor of the latter's wife had visited one night. Carelessly he had neglected to put on the handbrake; this later slipped free and his car rolled over the cliff. Accordingly it was normal to come in and out through the bedroom! However, there was electricity and running water and the house was considerably more comfortable than the broken-down house we had left behind in Uyo. It was also within five minutes' walk of the Residency.

My job there as ADO, Resident's Office, was to be a kind of private secretary. I was responsible for keeping all confidential and secret files, for typing all confidential letters. I had the combination to the great safe and was responsible for coding, encoding and decoding secret or confidential telegrams. No doubt it could have proved dull in time but I found that just reading the files and reports from all over the province to be absorbing – then came an 'Event'.

On Saturday 5 February 1955 at about midday the phone rang. The young Nigerian in charge of Calabar airport was telephoning to say that he had been in radio contact with the scheduled flight from Enugu when the pilot had been cut off in mid-sentence. He had not been able to raise the plane since. It was now overdue. He felt that the Resident should be informed immediately. As the Resident was away seeing the Governor in Enugu, I decided that the DO, Calabar, should be told. He was in the middle of conducting a wedding and was at first furious at my interruption of the ceremony – he was a rather excitable man of adequate ability – but, once he listened to what I had to say, he acted sensibly, phoning Enugu (the Resident had already left and was on his way back), and then following the drill laid down in advance, as a precaution against any disaster.

All went smoothly. The Civil Aviation Department and the offices of the West African Airways Corporation in Lagos were informed. The local hospital and medical services were alerted. Police in Land Rovers were sent up to the north by the only road to the area where the plane should have been when contact was lost; the DO, Itu, (whose division was adjacent) was told to search south-eastwards; the Marine department launch started up-river. We were advised that two small aircraft were being sent to help in the search.

On the basis of estimated speed, time of departure from Enugu, 150 miles away by air, and expected time of arrival in Calabar, it seemed likely that whatever it was that had happened to the plane had taken place about 70 miles north. This would have put it over one of the least inhabited and least accessible parts of Calabar District. Moreover, given the thickness of the bush the area of last contact was calculable only approximately, and the odds were enormously weighted against finding anything quickly.

In view of my training with Cambridge University Air Squadron it was thought that I should help the young Nigerian at the airport. So we two spent the afternoon in wireless contact with the two search aircraft, directing them from the rather inadequate map that was all we had. However, with every minute that passed it seemed more and more certain that a disaster had taken place. Our only hope was that there might be some survivors. (The Nigerian although only recently qualified rose well to the occasion; this was recognised in the subsequent official report.) However, with the onset of dusk the aerial search had to be abandoned for the day. By this time the Resident had got back and the Director of Civil Aviation and his assistant had arrived by plane from Lagos. They, of course, knew the crew of the missing aircraft personally and were understandably worried and anxious to get closer to the scene of what seemed almost certain to be a tragedy. Accordingly the Resident directed that I should take them up by road at first light in the morning.

During that night, by good chance and within 12 hours of the loss of radio contact, one of the police Land Rover teams, operating 60 to 70 miles to the north, heard of a villager reporting something falling from the sky. The team, in the dark, in very broken and densely wooded country, had located the site of the crash, even though it was some five miles from the nearest road.

Thus, when we left Calabar at dawn the next morning we were already aware that the plane had crashed, as we had come to fear was the case. A constable was waiting for us on the road-edge when, two hours later, we reached the nearest point on the road, and, after a stiff walk up and down the steep hills, through small streams and always through thick bush and under an already hot sun, we in our turn arrived at the site about 10 a.m. Already the smell of rotting flesh was overpowering and it was immediately obvious that there had never been any hope of survivors. The plane, a Bristol Wayfarer, had come down almost perpendicularly – one palm tree head being sheared off like a knife at an angle of about 10 degrees – into the side of a steep hill, half burying its nose and engines in the earth and scattering passengers in small pieces all over the clearing made by the crash. It was bad, even those in the party who had fought in Burma found the heat, the heavy, sweet sickly smell and the flies more than their stomachs could endure. It was, naturally, even more upsetting for the two from Lagos who had known the crew and their wives intimately and who would have the distressing task of letting the latter know of their husbands' death. Photos were taken, a quick examination made. This showed that one engine was on full power at the moment of impact, the other off, and that a wing appeared to be missing, but for the moment there was nothing more we could do except retrace our steps to the road and return to Calabar.

Two immediate issues faced the Resident. First, we had to find out why the plane had crashed. This required expert help, which was soon provided by the British Ministry of Transport and Civil Aviation. Second, but more immediate, was the question of whether the bodies be buried where the plane crashed or be brought to Calabar. This had some political implications, as among the victims was a member of an important Rivers Province family, an area that did not support the ruling NCNC Government of the Eastern Region. If he were to be buried there, at the scene of the crash, it could have provoked speculation that he had not really died but had been got rid of, as the British had got rid of King Jaja all those years ago: farfetched, very probably, but these points had to be considered. So it was decided that the bodies of all the passengers and crew, 13 in all, would be brought back to Calabar for burial. The next day I drove the party up the earth road again and on the now well-trodden path to the scene of the crash.

Of course to talk of 'bodies' being brought back was very much a euphemism. What we had were bits of flesh and bone, already decomposing in the extreme heat, from which we made up approximately 13 equal stretcher loads. The sweet-sour death smell hung over everything as did the clouds of flies attracted to it. The stretcher loads were then carried back to the road, to wait for a lorry. It was a horrid job, especially as the slopes were steep and 'bits' were liable to slip off the stretchers. The bearers, local villagers, were understandably not very happy with their task.

I was excused having to go up to the crash scene on the next day, my friend Robert Graham (ADO, Calabar Division) taking my place. Lesley provided him with makeshift facemasks soaked in antiseptic to minimise the gut-turning smell. On his return that evening he called in at my house to let me know how he had got on, dust-stained, weary and shocked by the sight. Even though most of the mortal remains had by then been removed, the smell of death had still hung heavily over the site, and still clung to him and to his clothes.

A suitably impressive public funeral had to be organised, my wife and other ladies making wreaths doused in scent to overwhelm the odour of putrefaction. My friend and fellow ADO, Robert Graham, began setting in train the arrangements for the retrieval of the plane's wreckage; my only remaining involvement was enciphering and deciphering the telegrams that were speeding between London, Lagos and Calabar about the possible causes and consequences of the disaster.

The previous year the British Aviation companies had been traumatised by the apparently inexplicable crashes of the De Havilland Comet. There had also been a best-selling novel by Nevil Shute about metal failure in a new British aeroplane. If the crash of the Wayfarer proved to be the result of a similar failure it could lead to a breakdown of confidence in British manufacturers. The commercial consequences could be disastrous. If, on the other hand, there was a failure to issue a necessary warning and there was another crash it could give rise to a worldwide outcry (as well as being equivalent to murdering any victims involved). The telegrams that we were sending and receiving covered all these points. In view of the sensitivity of the subject, these were being sent using a code known as 'Double Playfair' that required great accuracy. A single mistake could 'botch up' a whole message. At the end of the day such a mistake was all too easy, so it was a question of checking and double-checking. There were no machines in those days!

Every piece of wreckage had to be searched for to assure the thoroughness of the investigation. The missing wing was found some miles away and, by great efforts, the plane's fuselage, wings and broken fragments were dragged to a site where the accident inspector could reassemble them. His initial report revealed metal fatigue in one of the main struts as the cause, leading to the wing breaking off in mid-air and the plane's uncontrollable headlong dive to earth. To make doubly sure, the Nigeria Marine shipped the wreckage to England for metallurgical examination; this confirmed the preliminary finding. The speed with which the cause had been identified would, it was hoped, prevent further accidents. Sadly, however, it did not.[5] The subsequent report paid tribute to the government departments involved in one way or another in this incident. It had been a model of inter-departmental co-operation.

Chapter 18
Polio, 1955–6

I have explained that the Colonial Service course had included a lecture on hygiene. Lesley, also, had been warned by the ladies of the Women's Corona Society of the precautions to be taken, no doubt my mother also had contributed her experience, so that Lesley was very insistent on this. I know our kitchen was infinitely cleaner than that of my bachelor colleagues, but whatever precautions were taken, fevers and 'tummy trouble' were endemic in the country. The water we drank came from streams in which thousands had washed, urinated and defecated. One could boil one's drinking water to be sure, and the water for the ice put in the whisky soda too, but the glass from which one drank would itself have been washed in water likely to contain every kind of horrid germ.

So, we were not unduly surprised when, a few days after we had arrived in Calabar, Lesley had a sudden and undiagnosed mild fever. In view of her pregnancy, she was taken into the little 'Senior Service' cottage hospital for a few days, but it was not thought by anyone to be a matter of any moment. I was worried, naturally. So, I am sure, was she, although she hid it well. However, nothing came of it and she was discharged quite well – a 'pyrexia of unknown origin (PUO)' as were so many such.

We were then both fully occupied with the plane crash as I have described in the previous chapter but at some stage – I cannot remember exactly when – Peter Trevorrow visited Opobo to discuss a by-election with the DO, Robert Varvill. For some reason he told me to join him there. I did, I was keen to see as many places as possible and Opobo was an interesting old town. The next day as we drove back to Calabar Peter suggested that we have a swim in the pool at Abak, a pool that Lesley and I had swum in just after Christmas when we were still in Uyo.

A few days after this, Peter Trevorrow, the Resident, with whom I got on well, had to return to England unexpectedly on some urgent family matter. His replacement was the DO, Calabar, who wished for his own nominee to run the Resident's Office, while

I was to take over from Robert Graham as ADO, Calabar Division, a move that in many ways I welcomed, especially as no change of house was involved.[1]

I was anxious to make sure that I left nothing outstanding for my successor and so, on Sunday morning (13 March)[2] I walked over to the office to do some final clearing up. In particular, the Colonial local cypher was due to be changed the next day and the old codebook had to be destroyed by burning. I was not feeling well, but carried on until I suddenly realised that the codebook I was throwing page by page into the incinerator was the new, not the old version! It was not in my view terribly important as the cipher had never been used, but it was distinctly unfortunate and as I was beginning to feel increasingly dizzy I went home.

During the day things got worse, my temperature rising and then falling, while my bones ached so that I was not able to settle. The next day Lesley telephoned the office to say I was ill and then to the senior medical officer, asking if he could see me. He was, of course, heavily occupied at the African hospital but eventually came and diagnosed malaria, leaving with both of us the clear impression that he thought I was something of a *malade imaginaire*.

The next day, however, I was worse; he came again and repeated his diagnosis. That night there was a most terrible thunderstorm and, to keep out the rain, which was driving under the eaves into the bedroom, I climbed on the window edges to close the heavy wooden shutters. I had almost finished when my right leg gave way underneath me and I fell to the floor. As it happened, it was only a temporary loss of muscular power and I was able to get back on my feet and into bed, but for the rest of that night the fever was worse than ever. The next day when walking to the loo, my leg again gave way and the servants had to pick me up and carry me to my bed. By this time my left leg and right arm were both paralysed and – as there was no ambulance – I had to be half walked, half carried by two friends to their car and then up the stairs to the little hospital.

I am far from clear about the events of the next few days apart from a general impression of helpfulness from the African orderlies and of care from the two European nursing sisters. My lungs were pretty badly affected – even at the peak of my recovery I never regained more than a third of 'normal' lung capacity. It is just as well for me that they were not worse as the nearest 'iron-lung' would have been over a hundred miles away. My urinary muscles also went (albeit temporarily) and I remember having to have a catheter, while not only were my right arm and left leg almost completely paralysed, but the other limbs were also very weak.

The doctors, however, seemed quite unable to make up their minds – I remember one doctor seeming particularly surprised that I had feeling in the sole of my foot although without any movement. The Acting Resident (though it was no business of his) seemed to feel that I had had a mental breakdown due to overwork, a diagnosis that the doctors appeared prepared to go along with (although the nursing sisters had, as they later told my wife, privately agreed that it was polio, but they felt they could not contradict their superiors).[3] It was decided, however, that I should have a lumbar puncture before being evacuated to Lagos.

Lesley, helped by some of the ladies on the station, hastened to pack up house and dispose (temporarily we assumed) of our goods, and then, laden with suitcases and six months pregnant, was driven with me to Calabar airport (24 March). Fortunately the DC3 – the ordinary routine flight with a few seats taken out to accommodate my stretcher – does not fly very high, as my breathing capacity was very small at that time. So it was that we returned to Lagos, which we had left so full of anticipation only seven months before.

The next few weeks were amongst the most miserable of our lives. Lesley had been 'wished' upon a couple in the Commerce and Industry Department whom we did not know and who were under the impression that they were putting her up only for a night or two (government housing did not run to much in the way of spare bedrooms or bathrooms, being still designed basically for single men). Nevertheless, they could not have been kinder to her. The real trouble lay with me. The Creek Hospital was hot and humid. I lay alone in a room with no understanding of what had happened to me. The words 'infantile paralysis', seriously depressing though they sounded, conveyed nothing to me. All I knew was that I was virtually unable to move and able to summon assistance only if the ward orderly had remembered to leave the bell push in reach of the fingers of my left hand. If he had not, as was quite often the case, I just had to lie there until someone came in – on one occasion I was left on a bedpan for several hours, aching, uncomfortable and upset. This particular state of affairs must be blamed on the matron, an entirely unsympathetic person, but no good purpose is served by enlarging further on it. Even if she had been nice we would still have been in trouble.

I was an Eastern Region civil servant; Lagos was Federal territory. I had no one to 'fight my corner' so to speak. As a cadet my salary, including expatriation pay, was only £790 p.a. before tax and deductions, and we had nothing behind us. We could not afford to rent any housing, even if there had been any to rent.

There was a shortage of government housing and, in any event I had no claim on a Federal Government quarter as I was under a different jurisdiction. Lesley could not stay much longer with her kind hosts and it was approaching the time when airline restrictions on the carriage of pregnant women would rule out her returning to England. However, she refused to leave me alone and helpless in that frightful hospital, not knowing when we might meet again. Nor did any doctor bother to try to explain what the long-term effects of my illness might be. We were in despair, and, on at least one occasion, we wept.

Finally, seeing no other way out, Lesley telephoned the Officer Administering the Government (the Governor-General being on leave) and, penetrating the bureaucracy that exists to shield the great, she explained our problem. Then, and much, apparently, to the annoyance of the Medical Department, things began to happen very quickly. A Medical Board was summoned and virtually ordered to pass me fit for invaliding home. A government MO, Doctor Dickie, who was being transferred to be Director of Medical Services in Sarawak, was asked to accompany me together with a nursing sister; four seats were taken out of the rear of the first-class cabin of the BOAC Argonaut passenger plane for a stretcher and a seat was provided for Lesley. Within a couple of days we were on the plane flying home (4 April).

It had of course fallen to Lesley to let my parents – and hers – know of what had been happening to me. Some letters from my father to his brother, Jim, passing on what she told him, have survived. One dated 31 March reads 'we had an air letter from Lesley to say that Ken had developed a limp and felt a bit giddy. He got no better and after the doctor had been dosing him for malaria fever he decided to send him into hospital. By this time Ken had lost the use of his left leg and right hand. In hospital they made a lumbar puncture and drew off some fluid from his spine. He was better after that.' Lesley concluded her letter saying, 'Don't worry – the worst is over and he is beginning to recover'. A second letter told them of my being invalided and that polio had been diagnosed.

Another letter from my father, dated 7 April, told my uncle that my parents had met us at London airport, 'Lesley looked haggard and thin – not at all well, I thought but I suppose it is all worry and strain of the past three weeks taking its toll. Saw Ken in ambulance – in himself, he says, he feels well, he is in no pain – but his paralysis is a little worse than I had expected. His shoulders and his stomach muscles, in addition to his left leg and right arm, are affected.'

Our problems, of course, were not over but the very fact that we were back in England, out of the heat and humidity and 'foreignness' of Nigeria – for all that it was a British colony – this was a relief in itself. I remember that I had a craving for cold, fresh milk which, of course, had been unobtainable: to be able to satisfy this desire – and oh how good that milk tasted – was marvellous. At first, though, we had to be separated. My parents, who had come to Heathrow to meet me, took Lesley back with them to their house outside Birmingham while an ambulance took me to the Royal National Orthopaedic Hospital at Stanmore where I was to spend nearly four months.

Hospital routine is, well, just routine, and, in an orthopaedic hospital with patients whose average stay lasted many months, there was not much to differentiate the days. The danger in such a place is of boredom and apathy, or, even worse, of despair. This is demoralising and it is very much to the credit of the hospital staff at Stanmore that this was never allowed to take hold and that a sense of purpose was maintained. The young probationer nurses were keen and sympathetic; we men could flirt with them and their giggles kept up our spirits, although the work was physically arduous and their hours long. The sisters and staff nurses, also, were outstanding, training their young charges while also making sure that we patients, some almost totally helpless, were cared for. Finally, there were the physiotherapists and their helpers who coaxed any muscle that showed a flicker of life back to its maximum strength. The medical staff, in all this, seemed to us patients to be virtually irrelevant; they appeared on their rounds, followed by a worshipping train, but they did not seem very pertinent.

My fellow patients were a remarkable lot. There was a young doctor whose arms and legs were so paralysed that they were almost useless; a former ballet dancer turned teacher whose only still-working muscles were those in her neck, with even these being much weakened; a young woman, six months pregnant, had caught polio in Nyasaland and – although the baby had been born without any blemish – she, the mother, would have to spend her life in a wheelchair;[4] there was a young woman hairdresser with both arms paralysed; a girl named Susan whose age I cannot recall, 10 perhaps? I could easily go on listing them and their differing degrees of disability, but all had two traits, some days when they found the future hopeless and others when they forced cheerfulness and a determination to make the best of their situation. There was also much comradeship.

In the first two or three weeks after arriving at Stanmore I was rested, my limbs being moved only gently. In these first few weeks there is a very considerable amount of pain as muscles deprived of stimulus 'die', but this is normal and passes, however unpleasant at the time. Then it became clear that, given the extent of my paralysis, its pattern was as good as one could hope for. My left leg was almost totally paralysed, but there were some muscles still working in the toes and the calf, which could maintain a little circulation (although in cold weather the whole leg rapidly turns icy and takes hours to warm up again). Similarly, although my right arm was paralysed, I retained some grip in the hand. My lungs were both affected as I have already mentioned, but there was sufficient breathing capacity left for most day-to-day living. The fact that I retained the use of my left arm and right leg (even though some quite important muscles in each were lost) meant that I retained some symmetry. As a result my own recovery process was to be reasonably fast.

Easter fell on 10 April in 1955. The ward sister asked which of her charges wished to take Communion, arranged for the hospital chaplain to attend and had the beds of those who wished to wheeled into the TV room at the end of the ward. I found the familiar words of the Prayer Book to be comforting.

I have sometimes been asked whether the misfortune of paralysis has led me to rail against God. On the first occasion I was asked this I was somewhat surprised at the question – the matter had not occurred to me. Since then I have often reflected on the subject but, with all honesty, I must say that my attitude to Him has not changed; indeed I consider that it would be presumptuous to do so. I am not a fervent believer, in the words of the hymn, 'My Love is weak and faint', but I cannot accept that Love and Belief can be dependent upon some kind of contract between Man and God, revocable if Man is not satisfied with what he is getting out of it. God is. Man may see Him imperfectly, may worship inadequately, may understand little or nothing of 'Why', but must still accept His supremacy.

While I was safely ensconced in hospital, though, Lesley still had problems. She did not wish to stay for long with my parents, as the long journey from Sutton Coldfield to Stanmore in her advanced state of pregnancy would have meant her hardly seeing me. Fortunately, one of the nursing sisters helped us out by arranging for Lesley to stay with her mother. Lesley also had to be 'booked in' to a hospital – something that apparently was normally done months in advance. NHS admissions staff did not appear to understand that her 'failure' to have secured a bed was not the result of fecklessness but of circumstance! However, at last they were persuaded, she went in at the first apparent sign of labour only to find after a day that nothing further was happening. She was then discharged and arrangements made for her to go in to the Edgware hospital a week or two later. There the baby, a girl, was born on 20 May.

Five days later the nursing staff washed me with more even than usual thoroughness, put me in clean pyjamas, into a wheelchair and an ambulance and, without letting me know what was planned, delivered me to Lesley's hospital for a brief visit to see her and our baby daughter – an extremely kind and thoughtful action by the sister in charge of my ward. It was actions like that which kept up the morale of her charges.

In Lesley's hospital the nursing care was not of such a high standard. The milk ducts in one of her breasts became blocked, the breast became painful and swollen and our baby, Caroline, was not getting enough milk. Eventually there had to be an operation and Lesley was given drugs to stop lactating – much to her distress as she had wanted to feed Caroline herself. She, of course, was alone there with no family or friends of her own to visit her (my aunt who lived on the other side of London was her only visitor). It is not surprising that she had occasional fits of acute depression – indeed it would have been surprising if she had not. We were less than two years married, she had a crippled husband whose future earning capacity was doubtful, no home of her own and a baby.

When one is badly afflicted one is terribly dependent upon the help and encouragement of others and in this, as in so much else, I was very fortunate. For example, very early on I received a letter from my brother, which he, normally right-handed, had written with his left. 'If I can write with my left hand', he wrote, 'Why can't you?' Obviously, my younger brother could not outdo me, so I tried, and, although the first efforts looked rather like drunken spider trails, eventually I was able to write an adequately legible hand – although writing was always to be a slow process.

From beginning with simple stretching movements I progressed to exercises with the physiotherapist on the bed, and then – on 25 April, a great day – to exercises in the gymnasium which was fitted up with slings and pulleys, wall-mounted parallel bars and other floor standing bars where walking could be practised. This achievement, however, was still some way off.

I wrote almost daily to Lesley and the following extracts from these letters show my progress.

23 May 1955: I am now officially sitting in a chair only of course for a short period each day – it is lovely to see the grounds from a sitting position. I can also use the lavatory properly which is far more satisfactory and gives me my first moments of privacy since I went to the Creek (hospital in Lagos).

27 May 1955: I have started walking at last, admittedly only in the pool, but it is a start. I wear a long polythene splint more or less shaped to the back of my left leg tied on with tape. My walking was quite good for a cripple, and Miss Gowan (my physiotherapist) was very pleased. My left leg does not follow straight through instead I have to hitch up my left side and swing my leg forward in a half circle. A bit peculiar isn't it? However, with practice it will be much more normal.

2 June 1955: I can take off my pyjamas while seated and put on my bathing costume, and from a sitting position on a bed I have unaided got up and got into my wheelchair. When one can do so little this is a great achievement in one's life.

8 June 1955: This morning I had a plaster cast made for my calliper.

It had been decided that I would need a full-length calliper with a bucket top encircling my thigh and on which my buttock could rest. Two struts then helped transmit my weight to spurs that fitted into the heel of my shoe. At the knee these struts were hinged and fitted with a catch to secure them in an upright position or to allow the calliper to be bent at an angle when sitting. At the knee, also, there was a leather cap to hold the kneecap in place. The fitting of all this required from the technician skills similar to those of a Saville Row tailor! Very fortunately for me the head of the orthopaedic workshop, Mr Tuck, was a master of his craft and nothing was too much trouble for him. Only when he was satisfied with the fit was I to be allowed to walk and then at first only between exercise bars to which one could cling.

10 June 1955: Tomorrow morning I hope to be given permission to walk on dry land.

This was the great moment and the timing of this first walk was also a test of the physiotherapist's skill and judgement. No wonder Miss Gowan[5] hovered anxiously when the time came to launch my first steps between the parallel bars. After months in bed and with the need to learn a new muscular rhythm, I was as unsteady as a 1-year-old.[6]

14 June 1955: Yesterday I continued walking, this time outside the bars and around the gym. I didn't find it any more difficult than inside the bars. I walked twice, the second being watched by Mr Nicholson, the house surgeon. He was very pleased.

16 June 1955: Yesterday I tried some stairs – only four and they were shallow ones, but I did them quite well. I also went for a stroll(!) outside. This was difficult as outside the physio block the grounds are uneven and slope in about three directions, but I managed it.

19 June 1955: Miss Gowan and I walked back from the physio block to the ward. I was holding her hand like a balance, but not putting any weight on it, so it can be claimed as almost all my own work. However, I still have a long way to go before I can walk in the bush.

21 June 1955: I have practised going up and down stairs and can do sixteen at a time so the stairs at home[7] will not present any difficulties. I have asked for a long weekend on 1 July to 4 July.

Poor Lesley was herself still in hospital, as a second incision had had to be made in her breast. Her only comfort was that Caroline was well and, after the initial feeding problems, was putting on weight. She was, however, now nearing the end of her long stay in hospital and was to be discharged within the next week.

22 June 1955: This afternoon I went for a long walk (at least for me) about 500 yards or so. I must have taken nearly one and a half hours with a few little stops on the way, but I did do it all on my own with just a stick in my left hand, and for a lot of the time there wasn't anyone with me not that I am entirely safe.

23 June 1955: Walking today was erratic – in the morning I did my best yet, very little dipping on my left foot, but afterwards was not so good. I was walking on the grass and I found it much more difficult partly the function of the grass and partly that it is more bumpy.

My surgeon,[8] who had taken a keen interest in my progress, agreed that I could go home for a weekend, travelling by myself on the train to Birmingham. Lesley, who had been discharged from her hospital at the beginning of June and was waiting for me on the station, looking radiant and carrying my daughter, Caroline, now two months old.

My joy at being at 'home', out of hospital and – above all – at being reunited with my wife for the first time after 16 weeks is indescribable. Equally thrilling, but also a bit frightening, was getting acquainted with my daughter. The first time I held her I was scared that – with only one hand – I would drop her! On the whole I managed quite well over the weekend. Stairs were no problem but all the easy chairs at home were low and I could not get out of them unaided. I also needed help in getting my calliper on, and tying my shoelaces was quite beyond me (although I was to learn later how to do so).

I was also able to see the car that Geoff had bought for us, a 1928 Austin 12, named 'Mine Own' by its last owner[9] as it was a 'poor thing'. However, it had leather upholstery (that Lesley had polished up) and with some new tyres and repaired brakes was to be invaluable.

Having managed on this first outing, I think that I was allowed a second home visit a fortnight later that went equally well. Although at the time I did not realise it, Professor Seddon had clearly regarded these outings as a kind of 'dummy run'. When he did his rounds the next week he announced quite unexpectedly that I could be discharged the next day. I was overwhelmed. I had been at Stanmore for four months and when I had been admitted a stay of as long as a year had been mentioned. That it was so much reduced was due mainly to the help I had received, and especially to my physiotherapist, Miss Gowan.

Returning to my parents' home, to be reunited with my wife and child was wonderful, but it also brought home to me the reality of my situation. It was one thing to feel that one was almost back to normal in the protected atmosphere of the hospital, with most other contacts being with men and women worse affected than oneself; it was very different when one was living in an ordinary home, without the special, full-time care that nurses on a rota could provide, where chairs, comfortable for fit people, were so low and engulfing that emerging from them was a struggle and when mats and carpets were inclined to ruck up under the drag of a crippled leg.

My new calliper also let me down. The metal struts that ran from the heel to the bucket top had been made from duralumin to reduce the weight of the instrument, but there had been a flaw in the casting and one day in the main street of Birmingham it buckled and I fell to the pavement. My brother, who was with me, drove me to the nearest orthopaedic hospital, but they helped make a temporary repair only with reluctance, making it plain that as I was not 'their' patient, they were not very interested. Nor was the repair satisfactory, the strut buckled again the next day and we tried a local blacksmith. He did his best, but as soon as I put any weight in my leg, down I went again. We had our car and my brother offered his services as driver and back I went to Stanmore, although not as the triumphal hero as I had hoped to be. Mr Tuck, however, rose to the occasion magnificently and the calliper was mended that same day.

It is appropriate here to record how much help my brother had been to both of us during these three months. He was in his last year at Cambridge, the part II of the tripos exams had been at the end of May, but he had been incredibly helpful from the date of our return to England at the beginning of April. He had also been meticulous in visiting both of us in our two separate hospitals and Lesley's letters to me of this time are full of the help he had given.

However, this accident brought home to me once more the limits of my recovery and forced me to think again of my future. Would I be able to go back to my job? If not what could I do then?

There was no question in my mind that I felt I had to make every effort to return to my job in Nigeria, as much as a demonstration to myself as because of my belief in the service to which I belonged. However, I was sufficiently realistic to recognise that the Colonial Office might invalid me out, as soon as I had used up my period of sick leave. The uncertainty gnawed at my mind throughout the hours of dark and was never far from the surface during the day.

Nowadays, of course, there are support organisations, trained counsellors, a whole back-up army. In the sixth decade of the twentieth century these supports did not yet exist. It was up to the man or woman to do what he or she could. I therefore asked about prospects of getting a job in the Home Civil Service, receiving a rather discouraging answer to the effect that I would be eligible to take the next open competition along with everyone else; no more than that.

At the same time I was daily increasing the amount of exercise that I was taking, walking once round the block to start with, then twice, until I was able to walk a mile without distress. So I made an appointment to call at the Colonial Office, where I was directed to see the Consultant Physician, Sir Brunel Hawes. Sir Brunel was a man of great experience, and he was (rightly with hindsight) dampening about my immediate chances of going back to Nigeria; however, he did not rule it out for the future provided that I continued to improve. To this end he insisted that first I should take a prolonged convalescence at Osborne House, on the Isle of Wight (Queen Victoria's loved home which her son Edward, who disliked it, had taken immediate steps to hand over as a convalescent home for officers, including both the Colonial and Home Civil Services) where I could be given sustained therapy and exercise. I was not best pleased to go back, as I thought of it, to 'hospital' but I had no choice.

Writing of these months I am aware that I have done so almost entirely egocentrically – 'my feelings', 'my worries' – in part because the other three main parties, Lesley and my parents, are now all dead. At the time, moreover, it was my own position, the sudden change of my position as an independently functioning adult to a broken halfling dependent upon others that dominated my own mind, thoughts and actions. Whether I was seen as that, I do not know; the belief, the fear that it was how I was seen was a sufficiently effective social sanction. Looking back, though, I can appreciate better the feelings of the other three.

Lesley, for example, was faced with the fact that her husband of less than two years was a cripple who might never be able to support her and our child. What would become of them if I was forever unemployed? And my parents, too, had had their dreams shattered. They had worked, had lived economically, had made sacrifices, to give Geoff and me a better start in life than they had themselves. The sufferings of my father in the internment camps of Sime Road and Changi Jail, the lonely war years my mother had lived not knowing whether she was still a wife or just a widow, were these now to be crowned in old age with looking after a crippled son? Thoughts such as these must have been in the minds of all three but they never gave voice to them although my prickly manner must have tried them sorely.

So it was in early September my wife packed clothes, the baby and myself into our car and drove us down to Osborne on the Isle of Wight. At that time wives were not allowed to stay at Osborne themselves; there was a kind of guesthouse for them at the gates but its cost was way beyond our means. Fortunately, however, there were some friends of Lesley's family living in Cowes. They very kindly agreed that she and Caroline could stay with them, an offer she accepted with gratitude.

For a time she was able to stay there, taking me out for drives around the island in the afternoon (for which the Osborne House kitchens would make enormous picnic hampers), or, with other convalescents, down to the private beach – as a passenger ferry the Austin with its running boards was marvellous and we once had a dozen in or clinging on to it.

The convalescent facilities at Osborne were very good: a physiotherapist, a retired Army gymnast, a delightfully patient occupational

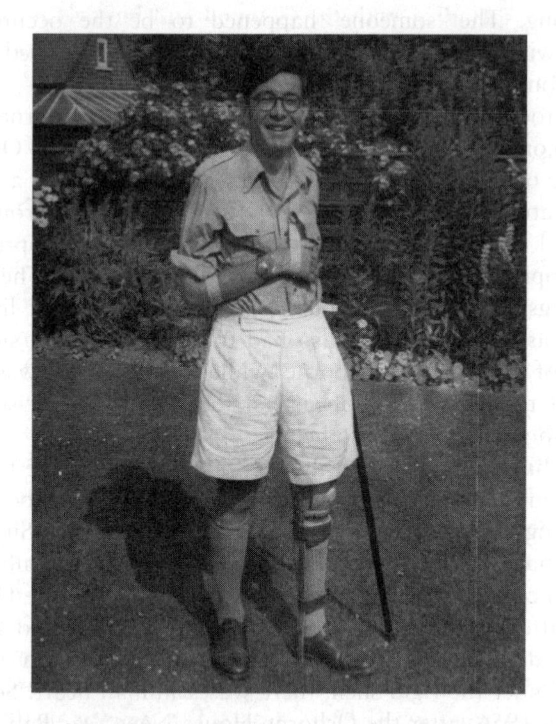

Figure 5 Ken after polio, 1955.

therapist and a high proportion of young and very well-qualified nursing sisters. Although I was becoming obviously stronger it was also becoming clear that my convalescence would not be quick and that I would soon be broke financially (my monthly 'half-pay' salary cheque would be only just over £30 and it cost 10 shillings a day merely to board at Osborne). Lesley, therefore, decided that she would return to my parents and get a job teaching so that we could manage until I was finally passed fit.

For the next three months she had the harder time of it, teaching, living with the 'in-laws', and having a six-month baby to look after, while I lived in the very considerable comfort of Osborne. There was interesting company – an admiral who had been Beatty's Flag Lieutenant at Jutland, a retired Resident from Nigeria who had left that country almost before I was born, a brigadier who was a Jockey Club Steward. There were wide grounds to explore under the mixed encouragement and strictures of nursing staff – as on one occasion when I had walked through the woods down to the sea I had fallen and, being unable to get up, had to wait until someone came along. The 'someone' happened to be the occupational therapist with a nursing sister and they were most surprised to hear a voice from behind a garden seat!

I, also, took longer walks outside the grounds of Osborne House itself – on one occasion I walked almost from Newport to Osborne, a distance of about five miles. Group Captain Bader[10] – a hero to my generation – used to play golf from the course around the house, so I tried too, but my particular muscle wastage prevented me developing any form of a swing; clock golf only! Then there were things like getting on buses, going shopping and living as normally as possible which also had to be relearnt and since the number of patients at Osborne while I was there was small compared to the number of sisters, there was always someone around who was prepared to help.

Meanwhile, at about monthly intervals I badgered the Colonial Office about going back to Nigeria, invariably being fobbed off by some young clerk or executive officer. At last, though, Sir Brunel told me that he was prepared to pass me as fit. This must have involved a certain amount of heart-searching amongst the Colonial Office staff. It must have been almost unprecedented to allow a crippled administrative officer to return to duty in a tropical country. Under the rigid shell, there was a human heart. So, early in January 1956, after the Osborne House New Year Ball, I went home.

Taken in all, I had again been fortunate in the speed and (relative) completeness of my convalescence. This resulted almost entirely from the continuing strong support of the staff of the Royal National Orthopaedic Hospital, to whom I have referred, to the staff at Osborne – particularly to Mrs Murray the occupational therapist and to Miss Maia Mathews, a young and very sympathetic nursing sister – and immeasurably most of all to Lesley, who had provided unfailing love and help throughout what must have been a most terrible year for her.

Chapter 19

Back to work, 1956

Naturally, having got permission to return to duty, my hope was to get back immediately. Equally naturally, this was not as easy as I had assumed. As usual, passenger ships were booked up for months ahead; planes also were full as the Queen was to pay her royal visit to Nigeria, the first such visit by a monarch to tropical Africa. All businessmen with interests in Nigeria, the press and others were very anxious to be present.

Moreover, I had to make some special preparations. Normally the 'bucket-top' of a calliper is made of leather, but in the context of Nigerian heat and humidity leather was obviously unsuitable – it would have been sodden with perspiration in half an hour and, thereafter, with repeated dryings out and re-soakings would soon have cracked and become very uncomfortable. So I was to have the top made of polythene, with little holes for the sweat to run out. It would be hot and might smell a bit, but it could be scrubbed!

I would have to learn to drive a car again. My own car was still almost new but, as was usual in those days, had manual transmission, which needed two legs while I had only the one that was usable. I was sure that someone must have had this problem before and made enquiries as to what might be done. I was told that a small firm, Feeny & Johnson, had developed a hand-operated clutch, mounted with a pistol trigger grip on the gear lever. This worked from a vacuum created by the exhaust manifold (I am totally uneducated in the mechanics of these matters, but I think I have it right); when the trigger was squeezed the clutch was engaged. The car could also be driven quite normally.

The Feeny & Johnson engineers were a bit dubious about their pet baby being fitted by a non-specialist, but there was no alternative unless I bought a car already fitted with automatic transmission. This would have been impossibly expensive. So they gave me a test drive on the old Brooklands racetrack where their office was located to check that I could drive safely using their device and, once satisfied, agreed to supply a kit with all the necessary parts and drawings. I cannot remember how I paid for it. I was back on full pay with effect from the date of the Colonial Office's formal approval that I was medically fit to resume my duty but the months on half-pay had left us very short. Still, somehow we managed.

This done and our passage booked in that most comfortable of piston-engined planes, a Stratocruiser, my parents drove us down to Heathrow early in February. We were heavily overweight with our baggage, of course, and at that time the 30 kilo per person regulation was strictly enforced, any excess being charged for at extortionate rates, so my daughter's carrycot was packed with weighty objects under her mattress; we had been told by a friend that this was the perfect way of escaping the weighing machines.

In a letter to his brother my father commented that he had never seen me as emotional as I was saying goodbye on this occasion. I was naturally worried. I had become more or less accustomed to being disabled but I knew that my appearance would shock my colleagues. I was concerned, also, at how well I would measure up to work. It was easy to appear outwardly confident in my ability to do a desk job at the very least, but I was equally aware that the actuality would present all sorts of challenges that could not be foreseen in advance. So I was scared. Thank God that I had Lesley with me to provide support and reassurance, although she too, no doubt, had her worries at returning to the unfriendly heat and humidity of Nigeria with a nine-month-old baby and a crippled husband.

This was not quite my first overseas flight – that distinction belonged to my medical evacuation from Nigeria the previous year – but it set a precedent which many of my subsequent journeys have followed: it did not adhere to the timetable. There was engine trouble at Rome and we had to spend the night there in a de luxe hotel (great comfort at BOAC expense) and be taken the next morning on a coach tour of the city before continuing our flight. At Kano we had to change planes; but because of the delay in Rome, we had missed the connecting flight to Enugu and so had to spend the second night in that famous old town.

The grandiloquently named Airport Hotel was a stark contrast to the comfort of Rome – 'first class' it definitely was not! In fact it consisted only of the wartime huts built then for the pilots of planes being ferried from America to the Middle East. It was hot (the harmattan[1] had failed to blow) and it was dirty. Service was non-existent. We asked for filter water. None came and I remember we cleaned our teeth in beer (which *was* brought when ordered). We were, no doubt, being unnecessarily fussy but we were tired. I was also worried about how I would be able to cope; it was all very well putting a brave face on my disabilities while cushioned in England – how would it be in West Africa?

There was also a brief, but panic-stricken, moment when a primus heating my daughter's tinned baby food flared up, with her on one side of it and ourselves on the other, making us fear that we would lose her to a fiery death! Somehow we managed to get to her but then we were still faced with the problem of how to put out the primus, which was still flaring alarmingly. We called to the rest-house servant to bring an empty bucket to up end it over the flame but, as he could not understand why we wanted an empty one, brought us one full of water instead. This we emptied out of the door to his patent astonishment and were about to put the bucket over the flame when it died down of its own accord! So we handed the bucket back, the servant by now clearly convinced that we were mad.

It was, however, only a day's additional delay; then, Enugu, where a very harassed administrative officer, a few years older than myself, named Frank Ashworth, was waiting to meet us – fed up because the delay in Rome had meant that he had no idea when we would arrive or from which direction. The Queen, he explained, had arrived the day before, Enugu was full of visitors and press-men, all administrative officers were on one special duty or another in connection with the visit and, to be frank, our arrival at this moment was a nuisance (to put it mildly). However, he had found somewhere for us to stay for a night or two, with a bachelor education officer who had a spare bedroom so he would take us there and leave us for a few days.

Our new host, although politeness itself, was clearly somewhat disconcerted with our arrival. His house was 'bachelor quarters', with the minimum of furnishings as he spent most of his time inspecting schools. A European woman in his house was unsettling enough, but to have a baby as well! He doubted if his cook could produce anything suitable for it to eat. Fortunately we still had tins and tins of baby food so that was no problem. His mind once relieved on this point, our host explained that we were welcome to stay for the next few days, that he was pretty busy but that he would try to take us to one or two of the functions being laid on for the Queen. After the visit was over, however, he was going on tour, taking his staff. It would then be up to us to make our own arrangements.

During the next two or three days we attended a number of the events but the one which sticks in my mind was one at Enugu airport to see the Queen on her return from Calabar. Her Majesty had

had a long day, travelling in small aircraft, numerous receptions and a regatta with African canoes racing[2] When the door of the DC-3 opened for her to step out one could almost see her physically wince from the sudden wave of heat, humidity and the smell of West Africa. Almost immediately, however, she discarded the weariness that she must have felt after a long day and the hours of travelling by car and in small planes. She acknowledged the cheers of the small crowd of well-wishers, smiled, came down the steps to the waiting car and was driven off waving to the onlookers. It was a triumph of royal discipline and training over physical tiredness. That evening, after the shortest of breaks, Her Majesty had to preside at a State dinner!

Sir James Robertson, who was Governor General of Nigeria at this time, has described the royal tour as a great success,[3] and, at some levels, it undoubtedly was. The Nigerian politicians who met Her Majesty experienced her charm; but on the other hand the person in the street who was expecting to see a figure in scarlet and ermine, wearing a crown set with jewels, and with an escort of mounted, steel-cuirassed and helmeted Life Guards, was perhaps disappointed, 'Nah, she be only young white madam' was one comment I heard. Whether for this, it was worth the discomfort she must have experienced, the weariness she must have felt, is perhaps worthy of question.[4]

The visit over, our host left on tour and we moved to the catering rest house. I had no instructions to report to anyone, no one appeared to be particularly interested in giving me any work to do; everywhere things were being returned back to normal after the disruption of the royal tour. For a few rather disheartening days I was left to kick my heels in idleness, while my baby daughter affected by the unaccustomed heat, cried without cease. At last we realised that she would be quite happy if, for most of the day, she were kept in her own small portable bath of cold water.

Then, one morning, a youngish administrative officer appeared at our chalet and told me that I had been posted to the Public Service Commission (PSC) and that he would drive me to their offices (where he himself also worked) and introduce me to the Secretary of the Commission. In haste I made myself ready. I had no idea what the Public Service Commission did – I had never heard of such a body. At least, though, it showed that my existence was known about, something about which I had been wondering rather anxiously in the past few days. There was no time then for my colleague to explain. He simply took me to a one-storey set of offices, knocked on a door and took me in to introduce me to the Secretary of the Commission. This gentleman, an Efik from Calabar named Tom Ikpeme, was totally unaware of my posting and was obviously a bit put out. My colleague explained that the Deputy Governor had arranged it, an explanation that did not either sooth or satisfy him. So Tom himself telephoned the Deputy Governor to find out what was going on. I felt greatly embarrassed, but happily the Deputy Governor buttered him up a bit, apologising for not having let him know personally of what was proposed, etc. Tom, mollified, now agreed to take me, explained that the passages officer was sick and that I could fill that 'seat'[5] temporarily.

My experience that morning, although I was not to know it, was not unusual. The Constitutional change of 1 October 1954 had greatly disorganised the civil service and it was to take more than another year to get things right. In the past there had been no overt political power from which the civil service needed to be insulated. Now, with a government of elected ministers, there was.[6] So, copying UK practice, each of the four successor services was to have its own Public Service Commission.

In the Eastern Region, however, various other tasks had been tied on to it. The Deputy Governor was the head of the Administrative Service but he had no staff and thus used those in the Public Service Commission that had formerly reported to him. The post of leave and passage officer (an anarchistic, dog's body job anyway) was attached to the PSC but had nothing at all to do with the responsibilities of that body. There was a blurred line between the functions of the Deputy Governor, those of the PSC and those responsibilities of the Ministry of Finance that related to staff numbers and salary grades. Finally, there was the job of 'Nigerianising' the civil service.

In this field, the difference between the situation in India and that in the African colonies could not have been more marked. In India there had been western-educated graduates in all professions for at least a century before political independence; there was no lack of trained indigenes to replace the British, indeed even in the ICS itself (the Administrative class) nearly half the posts had been filled by Indians before the war. In Nigeria there were still very, very few African graduates and the civil service was almost entirely composed of British officers – and of a substantial number of vacant posts. It had never been easy to recruit; the climate and poor living conditions had worked against that. Increasingly, too, salaries had failed to keep up with those being paid in Britain, let alone those offered in other more glamorous parts of the world.

Nigerian politicians, however, were suspicious. They believed, or it suited them to believe, that there were many Nigerians who were qualified for appointment to the civil service but whose qualifications were deliberately marked 'unacceptable' because, for example, they were granted by some unheard-of institution in the United States (where Zik himself had qualified)[7]. So a post of 'Director of Recruitment and Training' had been created in the office of the Public Service Commission[8] whose task was to Nigerianise the service as quickly as possible.

Almost immediately I was an interested observer of one of the personnel problems inevitable in this kind of situation (by this time, a week or two after my return, I had been moved into an Assistant Secretary post in the main PSC office). The Director of Recruitment was going on leave; the Secretary of the Public Service Commission proposed a Scot, able and popular who, on grounds of knowledge of the work and of seniority, clearly had every claim. But this post, the symbol of Eastern Nigeria's determination to establish its own indigenous civil service, required the approval of the Executive before it could be filled – even temporarily.

While no one doubted that Mr Kay would have 'Easternised' as well and as fast as anyone else, the politicians balked. The Scot did not blame them – he was a very fair-minded man – although no doubt he could have done with the additional 'acting allowance'. However, the Governor felt that this was one of those occasions when political realities required him to take the side of the politicians. Some of the British members of the Staff Association took the line

Figure 6 Efik women dancers.

Figure 7 Caroline and Nanny Katharine, 1956.

that the Governor had been insufficiently firm in resisting political interference in a civil service matter. Some non-Igbo Nigerians also wondered how they might have fared if they had been in the Scot's shoes and there was a rival Igbo candidate.[9] Neil Kay, however, accepted the decision with good grace. He was very soon to be promoted as a consequence.

To begin with, my main task in this office was to deal with another consequence of the break-up of the unified service, the transfer of the thousands of 'Junior Service' staff, clerks, messengers, clerical assistants and their technical service equivalents. Some were in the Eastern Region and wanted to stay. Some were serving in the East but were not from that region by tribal origin. They might, or might not, wish to go but some place had to be found for them. Many, many more were Easterners in Lagos or in the Northern Region. These might wish to stay where they were (as did most of those working in Lagos) or to transfer to the East (as did most of those in the North whose civil service junior grade staff were mainly Southerners). Every case had to be considered, salaries and conditions of service checked. Sometimes the information was inadequate, telephone calls had to be made, round holes had to be filled, if possible with round pegs. Then at last, a vacant post found, papers were forwarded, appointments made and the finished transaction published in the *Gazette*. It was the demolition of one civil service and the construction of four successors; then the men, occasionally women, and their families had to be moved.

There were British officers in the same position. Many of those in Lagos had served much of their career in the East. Once, they might have expected to return; in fact very few did so; salaries, 'perks' and working conditions were much better in Lagos. I noted, also, that both the nursing sisters who had cared for me when I had polio in Calabar had gone, one to the North, the other I do not know where.

I mentioned in Chapter 16 that the 1954 Constitution had provided for early retirement, a provision that Michael Mann in Uyo had decided to take. The young man who had just brought me along to the Public Service Commission was doing the same, as were others, not many, the terms were not generous, but still the beginning of what could be a haemorrhage.[10]

I have written above that salaries in West Africa had ceased to be attractive. Recognising this, the pre-1954 Government of Nigeria had appointed a Mr Gorsuch[11] as Sole Commissioner to review the salaries, conditions of service and structure of the Nigerian Civil Services. Mr Gorsuch had come; he had conducted a wide-ranging and thorough review (which is still in its way a model for this kind of thing). He had, just now, issued his report; it was for the four governments to decide what to do with it, to accept or reject it, but it had been assumed that whatever action was taken it would be in concert. Instead, to general consternation, only the Federal Government accepted the report in full; the others treated it as an 'À la carte menu', items from which they could pick and choose at will. Nothing could have brought home the changed situation more closely to civil servants than this action, which affected every employee in his pockets. Above all, the British staff who had chosen to stay with the East found themselves to be the worst affected since the Eastern Region government rejected most of the actions proposed to improve the lot of expatriates.[12]

As far as I was concerned, however, all seemed well financially (although in a few months we began to notice how much more it cost to live in Enugu that it had done in Uyo). My car had been well looked after during my convalescence, kept on blocks in the provincial garage at Calabar and with the engine turned over regularly. The DO there, Robert Varvill, arranged for it to be driven up to me. We had wheels of our own again! Actually, of course, *I* did not. *Lesley* did. I was dependent on her to take me to the office, etc., until the conversion kit arrived. This took a month or more and then an ingenious young English mechanic working for the local Ford agent set about installing it. To my delight (and his pride and pleasure), it worked.

I was able to drive immediately, but I thought that it wise to cover myself by asking the police to test me. I passed. Given the standard of driving by most Nigerians it would have been really disgraceful if I had not.

There was a housing shortage in Enugu caused by the creation of more ministries, requiring, of course, additional staff. Temporarily we were found a house rather like the shoebox we had occupied in Calabar. Later, Frank Ashworth (who had the unenviable job of housing officer)[13] found us another, of a new and imaginative design. This was built around three sides of a courtyard, a sitting/dining room making one wing with a side entrance to the garage. The kitchen and bathroom block faced the front entrance and the two bedrooms formed a secondary wing; a rear extension from behind the kitchen provided servants quarters.[14]

Our garden was uncultivated but purchase of composted 'night-soil' from the municipality gave some humus to the garden. The climate was so encouraging that a cutting (and we would steal cuttings unashamedly from the hedges of any house in Enugu) would produce a shrub in a matter of months. Outside our bedroom we had a great bush of African jasmine that filled the nights with scent; there were also morning glories and moonflowers running riot. We had 51 different sub-species of hibiscus in the hedge, a yellow alamanda, a poinsettia and an oleander and bushes of the reddish-yellow flowers known as Pride of Barbados.

We had to begin again with servants. We were very fortunate in that we heard that an exceptional African nanny was looking for work, one so good that her employers had even taken her to England on leave to carry on the care of their children. We waited not an instant and Katharine became a trusted friend and confidante for the next three years.

As if to make up for this, the men we hired – a cook and a steward – were dreadful, ignorant, idle, thieving layabouts. It was not surprising. An influx of businessmen had increased demand and by those who could pay over the market rate. The households of African politicians created another demand, this time where salaries might be lower but where a happy confusion would have meant little or no work. By contrast, we were not an attractive household. We were quite poor, a Madam at home meant no peace and there was no social cachet in working for a government officer when every political rag and party meeting proclaimed the end of colonialism and the coming of 'FREEDOM'.

A favourite trick was for the servant to behave so outrageously that he had to be sacked. He would then refuse to leave his quarter until he was paid compensation for being dismissed without notice, knowing that unless we had the quarter vacant we could not get a replacement. If he were not got rid of, however, he would get noisily drunk and abusive. One could not win. Igbos loved quarrels; they had a low ignition point and a capacity to proclaim their righteousness at length and at the tops of their voices without regard to anything as mundane as the facts of the matter. Both Lesley and I, by contrast, found such domestic shouting matches very upsetting.

These were also occasions when I was most aware of my physical weakness and that in any physical contest I would be an easy loser (not that any such event would ever have been wise). In general, though, although I had been inwardly worried about the reaction to my disabilities, I noticed none. This was in spite of the fact that the white shorts and socks gave prominence to the calliper on my left leg just as did the short-sleeved shirts to my withered right arm. Maybe growing up in a village lifestyle where disabilities were common and unconcealed meant that my appearance was not as strange as it was to Europeans in their sanitised society.

Anyway, we were back on track even if it was bumpier than we had expected and the destination less obvious.

Chapter 20
Turbulence, 1956–7

I had plenty to do in the office. I also had a great deal to learn about the workings of the regional government, the names of ministers, the internal organisation of the ministries, the names and positions of Administrative Service colleagues filling these – it must be remembered that I had had only just over six months' work experience before catching polio and that in 'the bush'. Naturally, also, I was anxious to learn what had happened in Calabar Province in the eleven months since I had left on sick leave.

At that time, the newly constituted system of local government had immediately shown its inadequacies, most obviously in financial mismanagement and – stemming from this – the inability to pay teachers' salaries. Here matters had got even worse. Uyo County Council had had to be dissolved and two units of police sent in to the division to 'persuade' the people to pay their tax arrears. In Opobo Division the position had been almost equally bad[1] and other divisions in Calabar Province had had the same problem (although none on the same scale). Throughout, the region councils had gone bankrupt through their own incompetence.[2]

Faced with this situation even this feckless government would be forced to amend the Local Government Act. The Premier, as Minister for Internal Affairs, agreed that all administrative officers (including Residents!) should be made local government commissioners in the division or province in which they were stationed[3] to restore some supervisory powers to administrative officers. In the meantime, the Regional Finance Law abolished the old Direct Taxation Ordinance and substituted a graduated system of income tax on all African males within the region,[4] district officers being responsible for its operation in their districts. This went a little way to returning their former authority. On the other hand, the government continued its declared policy of free universal primary education by 1957 without indicating where the resources for this were to be found, a conservative estimate being over £5m. per annum (while at the same time increasing this cost by extending to teachers the same salary increases proposed by Gorsuch to comparable civil service grades). There was also talk of a 'University of Nigeria' to be built at Nsukka.[5]

Amongst my colleagues, however, any discussion almost always came back to the difficulty of doing a satisfying day's work. Mr C. G. Eastwood (a senior Colonial Office official visiting Eastern Nigeria) wrote in a letter,

> in the Districts the Administrative Officers see the general standard of administration collapsing, bribery and corruption rife, being cold-shouldered and having their travelling allowances cut so that they cannot properly get round their districts. . . . The Permanent Secretaries suffer from the same things as the men in the Districts, but more intensively because they work at close quarters with ministers. They also find themselves being asked to do things that they find it hard to reconcile with their consciences. As one of the nicest of them said: 'it is really at bottom a moral question'.

Added to all this was the determination of the NCNC ministers to get rid of the Residents – their reason? Ostensibly it was because in a small area such as that comprising the Eastern Region there was no longer any need for the existence of provinces under a Resident. This, though, was just a cover. The underlying reasons were that ministers when on tour felt themselves eclipsed by a Resident with many years of experience. They also coveted the houses that the Residents occupied (indeed once these posts had been abolished the houses Residents had occupied were snapped up as guest houses for touring ministers!). Sir Clem, on the other hand, felt that at a time of unprecedented strain and when many district officers had far less experience than had been customarily thought necessary; it was essential to retain every experienced officer he could.[6]

The battles over this had continued throughout 1955. In the 1956 Budget Session of the House of Assembly the position of the Residents came up again. No financial provision was made for them. If this had been allowed to stand the effect would have been equivalent to their being sacked without notice or without payment of any compensation. Sir Clem could not, would not accept this. The Assembly was prorogued. There must have followed some behind the scenes negotiations between the Governor and the Premier. The upshot was that money was inserted for posts graded the same as the Residents but without using that title. They were not sacked as such; they could carry on working as administrative officers. They could not however officially continue to do the work that they had been doing and, lest it be thought that overemphasis was being placed on outward show, it must be borne in mind that there were many occasions when a single administrative officer might have to face an angry mob with no back-up but the prestige and authority of his office. It was worth rubies.

'How', it may be asked, 'could such a state of affairs be allowed?' Sir Clem was the Governor. He had all sorts of legal powers. But in any confrontation between Sir Clem and Zik, Sir Clem was on a hiding to nothing. Zik was an irresponsible politician. Sir Clem was the opposite. He was totally honest and open (too much so in the view of the Governor-General). In theory the Governor had recourse to law and, ultimately, the implementation of the law by force, but in fact (although this was known to less than a handful of the British staff in the Eastern Region so secret was it), Sir Clem had already decided against such a drastic step.

Almost a year earlier, officials in the Colonial Office in London, alarmed at the extent of the corruption prevalent amongst all members of the NCNC government, at the widespread breakdown in local government already referred to, at the determination of the politicians to obtain control of the civil service and at the profligacy with which the regions' limited financial reserves were being expended, had been toying with the idea that Britain had moved too fast along the decolonisation road and that consideration should be given to suspending the Constitution.[7] Sir Clem, on learning of this thinking, was appalled; he wrote on 8 August to Sir Thomas Lloyd:

> This does not mean that I consider this Region is fitted for self-government in 1956. In my opinion it will be quite unfitted nor do the great majority of the people desire self-government. . . . I am not being wise after the event. I gave the same advice in 1953 before the London Conference . . . if I thought it desirable to withdraw the promise of self-government, I should be predisposed to say so. *But the promise having been given, adequate reasons for its withdrawal do not exist while the disadvantages of doing so greatly outweigh the advantages of such a course.*[8]

Sir James Robertson wrote similarly on 7 August[9] while referring to 'The moral cowardice and irresponsibility of Zik himself and his complete incompetence as a leader' and to 'how far short Zik and his followers have fallen from what might reasonably have been accepted of them'. He went on to say,

> There can be no doubt that in justice they have merited the withdrawal of that promise (of self-government). But whether the world at large could be made to see the justice of that withdrawal and whether withdrawal would improve that state of affairs in the Eastern Region and not make it even worse are very different questions.

It was accepted by those advocating the repeal of the Constitution that this might lead to civil unrest and the need to use military force. When – at the highest level and under the greatest secrecy – the military were consulted, however, they were equally appalled. The (British) General Officer commanding the Nigerian Army stressed that his forces alone would be insufficient, considerable help would be needed from Britain and he pointed out the extensive military commitments that had had to be accepted in Malaya and Kenya.[10] This, added to the already expressed views of Sir Clem and Sir James, effectively put an end to talk of suspending the Eastern Region Constitution.

It was just as well. The Suez business in 1956 was to show up effectively how limited was Britain's ability to pursue an independent course of action that did not have the support of the United States; that support was likely to have been even less forthcoming in Nigeria than it was to be in Egypt.

However, ruling out the use of force left Sir Clem to continue his thankless task of trying by talk alone to persuade Zik to adopt more rational policies. This was to be Sir Clem's tragedy, a man who had spent almost all his 30 years of service in Eastern Nigeria, committed to the development of its people (with whom in the past he had always been on open and friendly terms) now compelled to do little more than watch the extreme corruption and financial fecklessness that the Eastern Region government, 'his' government, was displaying and that he feared might destroy all the benefits brought by British rule.

I have written at length on these events despite the fact that they took place while I was on convalescent leave and that, even had I been in Nigeria, the secrecy that surrounded them and my own junior status meant I would have had no knowledge of them. However, they form the essential if unseen backdrop to what went on in these last years of colonial rule. I must, however, return from these lofty matters to my own actions as a very junior assistant secretary where, because of the blurred responsibilities of the Public Service Commission and the Deputy Governor's Office, although certainly no actor in the unfolding drama, I was in a position to observe like a stagehand some of the scenes still to be played.

The new Staff List (which I was helping prepare) showed the number of civil service posts, the salaries attached, the names and qualifications of those officers holding them (and their relative seniority) and the number of posts vacant.[11] It was an essential man-management tool but, because it was a government publication, it could also be used in political argument. How did the officers formerly holding the position of Resident appear? And where? How many 'expatriate' and how many Nigerian officers were in each branch and grade of the civil service? Why were there not more of the latter? How many vacant posts were there? All these things had been shown in the Staff Lists published by the old unitary Government of Nigeria. Now we had to produce our own for the Eastern Region civil service.

I wrote in Chapter 15 of everyone having to opt for which service he (or she, of course, but the staff were overwhelmingly male) wished to be in, that the implications of this choice had never been spelt out but that ignorance and loyalty had meant that most expatriates had opted for where they were. The more senior 'long grade' administrative officers now recognised – but too late – the importance of the option they had been given. Posts in the Federal civil service for which they might have expected to be considered were now blocked to them because Sir Clem would not release Eastern Region officers to go to the Federal government in Lagos unless he could find a replacement. But no one in their right mind in the Federal Service would have transferred to the East on lower salaries and worse conditions of service. So men saw their former juniors being promoted into posts that they were not allowed to fill. Younger men might leave in exasperation[12] but the more senior had to consider future employability, the position of their wives and the education of children.

Some applied for posts in other parts of the Colonial Empire. The decision here lay with the Colonial Office and, although Sir Clem voiced his objections, a certain number were allowed.[13] In each case Clem's argument was the same. The staffing situation in the Eastern Region was critical. He was responsible for keeping the machinery of government functioning. It was touch and go whether it would. The departure even of one man reduced the chance of success. So, although he knew all 'his' officers by name[14] and understood their problems, his own sense of his duty required him to keep them in the East even against their wishes.[15]

Another matter that deeply worried Sir Clem was the financial position of the region.[16] The East was densely populated, its people traditional farmers, but only in the south-east (Calabar Province in fact) was there an export crop, palm oil. There were rumours of oil, oil companies were drilling (as mentioned in Chapter 16) but so far there had been no known really commercial strike.[17] Until oil was found, the Eastern Region government had to be modest in its plans, and economical, not to say miserly, in their execution. This did not suit the style of Zik and his colleagues (or that of any other African politician, come to that). They had fought elections with slogans like 'Freedom for All and Greater Abundance', claiming that the wicked colonialists had deliberately held Africa back, that the populace was entitled to the 'good life'. Now they found that the region's financial reserves were modest, new ways of raising money likely to be unpopular and, perhaps bitterest blow of all, that government accounting regulations and the caution of their accounting officers (the permanent secretaries in the ministries) limited the amount that they could siphon off to their own self-benefit.

To get round at least the last of these disappointments, new statutory corporations were set up. There was, for example, an Eastern Region Development Corporation, a Finance Corporation, an Industrial Corporation, a news service and others.[18] The legislation authorising these also allowed the government to finance them out of its general reserves but their expenditures were not subject to the same strict criteria as was normal with those of government. Meanwhile, ministers had much more of a direct say in choosing new staff for these parastatals, so that 'offices' could be sold or given to family members, not bothering with the procedures of the Public Service Commission. They needed office buildings; expensive new ones were built (by contractors chosen by and often related to the ministers themselves). It all gave a great impression. Even I, driving around Enugu and seeing all the new building going on, was taken in for a time by the surface impression of prosperity and development.

Ministers were not unaware that they were depleting the region's central reserves. It was, in part, a reversion to custom: 'the tradition of the people is one in which the public purse is exercised for private profit', as Sir James Robertson had written in an early despatch to the Colonial Office.[19] There may also however have been an element of calculation. Ministers were aware that when self-rule came expatriate civil servants would have to be compensated for 'loss of career'; the Secretary of State had made that plain to Zik. The ministers, indeed probably all Africans, thought this unjust. 'Why should Africa pay money to get rid of British Civil Servants when it had never asked them to come in the first place?'[20] So, logically, 'spend, spend'. If there was no money left in the reserves, compensation could not be paid!

As if this was not enough there was yet another matter for contention between Clem and Zik. Africans felt that the European banks discriminated against them. They would know of European firms, individual European customers having overdrafts, getting loans, being extended commercial credit. So whenever an African was refused these facilities he always ascribed it to race (I do not think they ever reflected that many women market traders had no such problem; these women were often incredibly shrewd, worked hard but never displayed their wealth ostentatiously). It was easier to blame the European banks. The next step was to set up an African bank. This, in fact, was what Zik had done many years before. He and his family held most of the shares in the African Continental Bank (ACB).[21]

I do not know how well run this institution was. My friends who were bankers thought it poor but that might have been professional jealousy. What was certain, however, was that it was undercapitalised and also that it did not have enough customers to make it viable. So Zik instructed all Eastern statutory corporations to use the ACB instead of the Bank of British West Africa (BBWA). The Eastern Region Production and Development Board[22] (which had substantial reserves) was obliged to move these to the ACB. In future the salaries of all Nigerian staff would be paid through the ACB.[23]

However, it very soon became clear to everyone that things were not going well. African staff salary cheques were not being met at the end of the month, sometimes not until the middle of the next even though the Accountant-General had authorised the transfer from the main government account with the BBWA to the ACB. There were rumours of corruption and embezzlement with the personal involvement of Zik himself.

Sir Clem consulted the Attorney General, Geoffrey Briggs. The Governor-General (because banking was a Federal responsibility) and the Secretary of State were consulted. The latter then appointed a judge, Mr Justice Foster-Sutton, to hold an inquiry in Lagos into the affairs of the African Continental Bank.[24] Zik inaugurated a policy of 'non-co-operation' (not that there had been much co-operation before) and orchestrated mass meetings of NCNC supporters, threatening violence. Nevertheless, the Foster-Sutton Inquiry began its hearings in Lagos and for many months the local newspapers were full of details of the proceedings.

As I wrote at the end of Chapter 19, we were satisfactorily housed. On either side of us were friends we had made while at Uyo. Hugh and Fiona Byatt, who had then been stationed in Opobo, now had a son, Lorne, almost exactly the same age as our daughter Caroline. (However, the Byatts were to leave in the latter part of 1956.) On the other side lived Brian and Paddy Clark (our PWD neighbours from Uyo). He was now helping to implement a major new water-supply project for Enugu, not before time. The Nigerian population of the town was growing rapidly as Igbos from all over the region flocked to it, expecting jobs and wealth (and most were to be disappointed). In the meantime water consumption had so far exceeded supply that during the dry season even in 'best' districts[25] water was not continuously available (not at all 'nice'; flush toilets can smell abominably when there is no water with which to flush them). Also, Angus Robin, who had been the supervisor on my Colonial Service course, was now in Enugu where he was Permanent Secretary for Health. He and his wife were very good to us and introduced us to their friends (see also below).

There were the usual domestic incidents. The house was on the edge of recently cleared bush and there were again snakes aplenty. One climbed up the waste pipe of the handbasin in my daughter's bedroom. Very fortunately it was seen by our African nanny, curled up at the bottom of the basin and unable to climb out. Katharine shouted for the cook who came in with a kettle of boiling water that killed the reptile immediately (and did no damage to the porcelain). It was a blessing; Caroline could so easily have got up before the nanny came in, have put her hands into the basin (she could not see over the rim) and been bitten. Another incident that could have turned out seriously happened to Lesley. She had gone into the kitchen to supervise some culinary operation and had knelt on the floor to check a dish in the oven (the stove, of course, was woodburning). An ember had fallen on the floor unseen and the back of her skirt caught alight. The cook shouted a word of warning but he did not know what to do, 'Throw water on Madam?', 'Rip off her skirt?' Fortunately I heard his shout, came in, saw the back of her dress afire and him standing paralysed but with a pail of water in his hands. I told him to throw it. Lesley's skin was only a little singed but the dress (recently made and one of her best) was good for nothing.

Figure 8 Lesley and Caroline, 1957.

Enugu, as well as electricity (nearly all the time) and water (subject to the interruptions I have mentioned) had shops and services. There was a modern branch of the Kingsway Stores, although sometimes even that might temporarily run out of staples like sugar or flour. There was a Cold Storage for butter, milk, bacon and meat from England (several times more expensive than meat from the market but not as tough and stringy). There was an Indian store, Chellarams, with spices, cottons and brassware, the staff infinitely obliging.[26]

Inevitably, too, there was a club, membership still being 'Europeans only', with a bar, a restaurant, lending library and open-air cinema. There had been a swimming pool as well but that had been closed because of fear of polio. We joined the club, of course, all Europeans did, but we found it expensive and our membership was rather intermittent.

We were in fact finding it hard to make ends meet as the cost of living rose steadily. We lived economically. Lesley made all her own and Caroline's clothes but there were many fixed costs over which we had no control; house rent was a proportion of salary, and electricity and water were nice to have but much more expensive than in England. I was the youngest member of the administration in Enugu as well as being married. It was nice to mix with permanent secretaries, interesting as well as being potentially helpful long-term in my job. But it cost.

There was a Church school in the mornings for young children up to the age of 7 or 8 (after that age children were normally sent to school in England, just as I had been). They were always looking (amongst wives) for qualified teachers so Lesley applied and was taken on immediately, earning £20 per month. She would have preferred to stay at home with Caroline but Katharine was a good and trustworthy nanny and we needed the money (only an unexpected legacy had enabled me to clear an overdraft).

I have several times referred to the loss of staff. There were also two new arrivals in 1956, both experienced and unusual men. Christopher Fogarty[27] (in his early thirties) was seconded from the UK Treasury to the post of Permanent Secretary, Finance – a most unusual action but one that presumably reflected Whitehall concern at the state of Eastern Nigeria's finances. Whether this was so or not, he was very definitely a positive acquisition. I liked him and judged him brilliant, not alone in so doing. He had a reputation for not tolerating fools or the over-pompous, but I found him patient and a willing and helpful instructor. He taught me, for example, how to write papers for ExCo,[28] that the main paper should never exceed 1,000 words (although appendices could be as lengthy as was necessary) and that they should always follow the same pattern: problem; background; considerations (arguments for and against); decision sought – which must be absolutely clear leaving no grounds for ambiguity. I hope I have always followed these; at least I know what I *should* do! Sir Terence Creagh-Coen, was a good bit older. A bachelor, he had been in the ICS[29] and after partition had stayed on in Pakistan as Establishments Secretary. In May 1956 he was recruited to Eastern Nigeria on contract as chairman of the Public Service Commission.

As I wrote earlier in this chapter there was much confusion as to what the status of the Public Service Commission should be and what its duties were.[30] This had been made worse by the fact that the first two chairmen (both able men incidentally) had been serving civil servants.[31] Both men had been and remained part of the normal civil service structure, a fact that helps to explain the confused relationships with the Governor's office and with that part of the Ministry of Finance which dealt with establishment matters. This was to change. Sir Terence, who had a nice idea of the importance of his post and the independence of the Public Service Commission, was concerned to find that his staff was also working for the Deputy Governor. Matters came to a head over some action of mine.

Arriving in Enugu as I did in the particular circumstances of the Queen's visit to Nigeria there was no one to explain to me how things were done. Lacking such guidance, it seemed to me that some things were not done very well. It appeared that administrative officers with a degree were often being used to carry out jobs that could be done by a responsible clerk. This situation had developed because 'Secretariat' staff were just district officers who had happened to be posted to a ministry; they were in no way trained to be desk-bound civil servants. In the field they were happy to trust native administration staff, or the clerks in the district office. In the Secretariat, however, clerks were 'Junior Service' and were not expected to take responsibility. Mr Gorsuch had proposed the creation of new intermediate grades, but in the East nothing had been done about this section of his report. I suggested that this be put right and that a new grade be created, of Nigerians naturally, who would be expected to carry responsibility and would be paid for it. With somewhat less than breathtaking originality I called this the 'executive grade'.

It may seem astonishing that this had not been done before, and my thinking was in no way original; indeed, I could easily have written a minute pouring scorn on the author for repeating such well-known management truisms as if they were a new discovery. However, brashly, I sent it direct to the Deputy Governor (Peter Gunning). He read it with approbation and passed to Christopher Fogarty in the Ministry of Finance. Christopher then spoke to Sir Terence assuming that the memo had initially been authorised by him. Sir Terence, though, had known nothing of it, and was not amused. However, he was a fair-minded man and, when the matter had been explained, realised that I had not deliberately gone behind his back: the system not me was at fault. The end result, however, was what I would have wished. The proposed executive grade was established and the process of Nigerianisation was effectively advanced.

Another area in which confusion reigned was that of 'General Orders'. Any public body needs such a framework. The former Nigerian civil service had its 'General Orders' the last edition of which had been published in early 1954. This was assumed to hold good, even though the unitary service for which it had been written had been broken into four fragments. Even more important, 'General Orders' assumed a service divided into two parts, a Senior Service that was composed of Europeans and a Junior Service of Africans (the fact that there were one or two Africans in the Senior Service did not matter very much). However, as the senior posts became more and more filled with Nigerians the anomalies between the two became more and more obvious.

For example, leave for 'Senior Service' posts was calculated at the rate of a week for each month of service. This was perhaps reasonable in the 1920s or 1930s[32] and might have been reasonable enough for expatriates but it was really excessive. Nigerian officers in 'Senior Service' posts, however, were also given this 'overseas leave' at the same generous rate.[33] In addition there was up to three weeks a year of 'local leave'[34] although how any distinction could be made between a Nigerian's 'overseas' (that he passed in Nigeria) and his 'local' leave (also passed in Nigeria) is beyond me. For the time being, however, wholesale reform of 'General Orders' was thought to be too much of a hot potato. Piecemeal amendments were made from time to time though, which probably did as much harm as good – certainly as far as keeping in step with the other three civil services was concerned.

Tony Shepherd, who had been on the London course and on the *Accra* with me, returned from leave at about this time (the second half of 1956) with a wife, Wendy. Wendy had also been a school-teacher in East Anglia and she and Lesley became fast friends. Tony (one of the few British officers who was really fluent in Igbo) had now been posted as ADO, Nsukka Division,[35] less than 40 miles from Enugu. Their house at Nsukka was spacious and in good repair and we were invited to stay whenever we wanted, an invitation we accepted with alacrity. I was delighted to feel in touch – even at one remove – with what was really going on in the bush. In return we were able to offer them a base when they wished to shop in Enugu.

In Enugu one was, of course, much more aware of what was happening in the world. There was an English newspaper in the club (sent by airmail) while wireless reception was also better. We were aware, therefore, of what was happening in the Middle East in the run-up to the Suez Affair. I do not think that Nigerians themselves were particularly interested in this or worked up by the rights-and-wrongs of it in the same way as were the chattering classes in England but I did gain two general impressions. I felt that the initial Anglo-French ultimatum followed by the successful assault on Port Said impressed them. 'Perhaps Britain was not such a pushover?' On the other hand the constrained withdrawal that followed so quickly must have reinforced any earlier view that Britain would not fight to retain its Empire.

Geoffrey Briggs, the Attorney General, was transferred at about this time to a judicial appointment in Malaysia (where my brother was to meet him). Sir Clem then went on leave (as we thought);[36] after a few weeks, however, it became known that he was retiring and that his successor would be Sir Robert Stapledon who was Chief Secretary in Tanganyika[37] but who had been a district officer in the East before the war.

The Administrative Service, in particular, regretted Clem's departure. They trusted him; they knew that he had given his all to Eastern Nigeria. A good brain accompanied his bluff, genial attitude, but perhaps there was insufficient steel in his dealings with Zik (Sir James Robertson seems to have thought so anyway).[38] Quite rightly, however, his experience remained valued by the British government; he was not simply discarded as governments so often discard their servants. He was appointed a director of the Commonwealth Development Corporation, an important post he continued to hold for many years. Perhaps, though, his departure was necessary. His aura was too associated with the past even though he himself was not wedded to it and was working for the future: nevertheless, this past both the good and the bad was inextricably linked to him.

It would be a totally wrong reading of the position, however, to think that there was any fundamental breach in Nigeria between the British and Nigerians. Ministers trusted their permanent secretaries; in the 'bush' the DO was still the voice of government (even if divested of much of his authority). Personal relations remained very good at all levels. The following incident is revealing.

The wife of one of my colleagues caught polio and her neck muscles were paralysed (fortunately for her this took place near Port Harcourt where there was the only iron-lung in the region). Medical advice was that she needed to be evacuated to England, the cost being several thousands of pounds. There was no appropriate item in the estimates to which this could be charged so it had to be approved specifically by the Executive Council (ExCo), still presided over by the Governor. Would they agree? After all Eastern Nigeria was poor, there were many other ways in which the money could be spent. However, I was told that when this item was reached on the agenda Zik simply observed that this was clearly essential and invited his colleagues to approve it without discussion: which they did.

We spent Christmas 1956 with Tony and Wendy. She had decorated the house with palm fronds and had made special efforts with the meal. There was a 'drinks party' at the DO's, other friends of the Shepherds dropped by, and all was happy and informal. A lot had happened in the year; there had been problems aplenty but, on balance, things had gone well. The next year could look after itself.

Chapter 21

Internal self-government, 1957–8

Almost immediately after we returned from Nsukka, the Foster-Sutton Report was published (3 January 1957). The report found that Zik's conduct with regard to the ACB had fallen 'short of the expectations of honest, reasonable people', scathing words perhaps in the context of Westminster at that time. Nigerians, however, accustomed to corruption, were not troubled by the implied condemnation and certainly found nothing particularly reprehensible in his actions.[1] Zik himself never saw the judgement as one that called for him to resign. Instead he called a General Election for the Eastern House of Assembly on 15 March 1957.

There was only one clear-cut election 'issue' within the normal meaning of the word. The opposition parties had no real hope of displacing the NCNC. The issue for them therefore was whether, relying upon fear of Igbo domination, they could secure sufficient seats in the new House of Assembly to justify a claim that there is genuine popular support for a Calabar–Ogoja Rivers State (ERPIN no. 9 of 10 March 1956). For Zik, the issue was to demonstrate that, whatever the British might think, he was the popular leader of the Igbo people.

The timetable for the holding of the election was almost as tight as that for the Federal Election in 1954. That experience, however, meant that all concerned – the electorate as well as the administration – were more aware of what they were doing and, from the standpoint of the district administration, what needed to be done in the time available. Even so no one underestimated the scale of the task, particularly as the total number of seats in the Eastern House was more than double the number of those elected by the Eastern Region voters for the Federal House of Representatives in 1954.

All Enugu-based staff were asked to help to the maximum extent possible. I was anxious to take part in the operation and Tony Shepherd obtained his DO's agreement to my coming up to Nsukka for the purpose. Nsukka (now the seat of the University of Nigeria) was at that time a fairly small town, although the division itself covered a large area, had a population of over half a million and would return five members. I knew the road to it of course from the weekend visits we had paid to the Shepherds, but of the district outside the government station I knew nothing.

After nine miles 'on the tar' the road was of laterite and heavily corrugated. If one went too slowly, one's car shook itself to bits, too fast and one was likely to skid; to find the happy medium was far from easy. I had no problem to begin with but about halfway I noticed that the temperature reading on the dashboard had shot up. On opening the bonnet I found that the radiator was almost dry. I stopped the engine to let it cool and then refilled the radiator from the thermos flask I always carried. Then I set off again. Within a few miles however, the radiator was again dry and now I had no water left, so I had to hunt up villagers to get them to give me some of their limited supplies, which on each occasion would get me forward a few miles. Darkness began to fall and finding villages and water became more difficult, but at last I could see the lights of Nsukka – just a few oil lamps only of course but as welcome as a beacon to a lost mariner. So some hours late, I arrived at my somewhat worried friend's house.

They were relieved to see me, but when I explained that because of the problem with my car I was virtually immobile, Tony must have wondered if I was not going to be more hindrance than help. However, he had a look at my car and determined that the rubber upper radiator tube had perished. To find a replacement was another matter, but it was done; in a lorry park – thronged and busy in spite of the darkness of the night – he found with the help of an oil lamp a piece of rubber tubing of about the right size, which would do. We – or rather they – could then get down to the election.

I had been asked to look after about five or six polling stations, and I duly checked each of them first thing next morning, the day of the election, to make sure all was well, and periodically again during the day. Everything was going smoothly and, indeed, the only mishap was another one to myself. At lunchtime, I went to the rest house to eat my sandwiches and looking round was told by the caretaker that a particular tree, covered in fruit, was very good for eating. I did not know the tree, but picked one fruit and bit it only to immediately spit it out. It was a cashew nut tree and the pulp surrounding the nut was very acid. My lips and the inside of my mouth felt as if they were raw, which in parts they were. I assume that it was just a language misunderstanding between the caretaker and me.

There had been no violence or party strife at any polling station throughout the division.[2] Nsukka was solid Igbo/NCNC country and, while the Opposition had put up candidates, there was no doubt that the NCNC men would get in with very substantial majorities. Nevertheless the votes still had to be cast and counted.

As had been the case in Uyo in 1954, the first thing to be done was to check the ballot papers from each box in each polling station to ensure that there was no duplication in ballot paper numbers. Any such would mean a voter had used his votes more than once for a particular candidate. A hundred thousand people had registered, I think, and, as there were five seats, this meant that up to 500,000 ballot papers had to be individually examined. Scrutinising and then counting went on for about 36 hours non-stop throughout the night by the light of oil lamps, throughout the day and again into the second night with relief counters available to provide sleep-breaks. Margaret Lawrence, the DO's wife, and Wendy arranged for sandwiches and tea to be ready as necessary. The result was that Nsukka's results – a walkover for the NCNC – were amongst the first in the region to be announced. Henry Lawrence was very satisfied. Every part of the operation had been well organised. I learnt a lot. The NCNC success at Nsukka was repeated throughout the region. It was only in Calabar Province that there was a significant 'anti-vote'.[3]

Back in Enugu I learned that there had at last been agreement on 'staff management' (if one can call it that). A proper Establishments Division in the Ministry of Finance would henceforward be responsible for staff numbers and conditions of service, leaving the Public Service Commission free to do the work for which it had been set up, appointing, disciplining and promoting staff. Of course in practice, it being Nigeria, the PSC was not 'independent' of political constraints. Nor would it remain free from corruption for very long. At least, though, it now had a proper structure. Neil Kay was promoted to take charge of the new division and I moved with him into the Ministry of Finance on 1 April 1957. Neil was a pragmatist and a good man to work for. I was to learn a lot from my time with him.

The election results meant that the British government had no reason to delay further the promise made in 1954 to review the Constitution. This memoir is not the place to examine this review in any detail. I confine myself to the two issues that were to affect me. The 1957 Constitutional Conference in London agreed that the Eastern and Western regions would move to full internal self-government on 1 October 1957. In all regions, however, there were substantial numbers of voters in reasonably clear areas that differed from the dominant political/ethnic party. (In the East these inhabited the non-Igbo provinces of Calabar, Ogoja and Rivers. There was no firm line of demarcation, however; substantial numbers of Igbos lived in all three of these provinces as well as overwhelmingly composing the population of those of Owerri and Onitsha.) In time-honoured fashion, a commission would be appointed to determine what should be done about this 'minority question'. This issue was to affect me in due course, but not immediately.

The second matter concerned the position of the civil service. As from 1 October 1957 the Governor would have no powers *vis-à-vis* the civil service. His protection and the more shadowy one of the British government would be gone. The government of the Eastern Region would be in control. Expatriate staff could then leave with earned pension and a lump sum in compensation[4] for their assumed 'loss of career'. This latter was calculated by a formula that took into account age, length of service and salary, with a maximum payment of £9,000. There were some other provisions as well, the most important being that if the officer had been promoted during the three years prior to leaving his salary would be averaged over that period. Such people would thus have an incentive to stay. If he/she were over the age of 41 (at which point the sum payable could decrease) his 'lumpers' would be calculated in such a way as to maximise the payment made. Once more this clause aimed at persuading staff to 'stay on'. There was also a completely new offer by the British government. If an officer applied to join a 'special list' his salary and pension would become UK responsibilities.[5] If, in the future, there was no place for him in Nigeria, a post would be found for him/her elsewhere; if no such post could be found he would receive the lump sum compensation then due to him under the formula.

What would happen now? How many British staff would go? In particular how many of the administration would go? It was they, after all, who constituted the frame of the civil service, they who staffed the upper echelons of the ministries, they in the last resort who ensured that the writ of government ran in the rural areas. Would enough remain to prevent disintegration and chaos?[6]

Sir Clem had warned repeatedly over the previous three years that there was a real danger that this last could happen. There had been 106 British administrative officers of all ranks from the Deputy Governor down when the Eastern Region Service started.[7]

In the two and a half years since, 15 had left. At the same time ministers had demanded more staff, more experienced staff of high quality in their ministries. The system was beginning to creak under the strain. Why were so many simply waiting to leave? Salaries were one reason. These were wretchedly low in spite of the Gorsuch increase. An officer with a degree and ten years of service would be getting less than £1,500 p.a., including expatriation pay. Wives were no longer prepared for long periods of separation from either their husband or their children. They knew that the Eastern Region had refused to pay the children's 'education' passages that the Gorsuch Report had recommended although the Federal government paid them. Naturally, they would meet women whose husbands were in the police or another Federal service and who would be receiving these; equally naturally they resented being always the worse off. Wives could see, also, that almost every European in the commercial sector was living in a better house, their wives dressed better and they had more money to buy imported food.

Most of the men had come out to Nigeria when the service appeared to offer the attractions of a career of service. They were no longer sure what they were working for. Nigerians might disregard the comments in the Foster-Sutton Report, the British saw it as simple confirmation of what they knew was going on. Ministers would try to 'fiddle' expenses. The pressure was continuous to award contracts other than on the basis of the best price. Why should they stay under the control of politicians whose chief activity had been to derogate and attempt to destroy everything for which they had worked?[8]

I was not at all sure what to do personally. Lesley and I were again finding it hard to manage. She had hoped to become head teacher at the Anglican primary school but, failing that, she got a job at the Roman Catholic Teacher Training College at a higher salary; so the immediate financial pressure was removed – although at the expense of time she could spend with our 2-year-old daughter. As for me, my 'lump sum compensation' would amount to less than £1,000, my earned pension to date to about £80 per annum. This would not keep us for long. Nor was there anything else I wanted to do. Finally, given my disabilities, I was not at all sure how I would find the job market in England.

So I put off taking any long-term decision. My friends Robert Graham (now Private Secretary to the Governor), Tony Shepherd, Michael Smith and Alan Ferguson also decided not to leave immediately (Tony and Wendy's first child had just been born which may have been a factor). The two women education officers who had come out on the *Accra* with us, though, decided to leave.

My 18-month tour would be completed in August but – as this was when the applications to retire would start to come in which would put extra pressure on the Establishments Division – I decided to extend it for three months. Lesley and Caroline, though, went home. To save money I moved out of our house into the catering rest house so that I need keep only one servant. Lesley, for her part, would stay with her mother.

Mathew, our cook/steward, looked after me well and I was well entertained by my married friends. The names of Robert Graham and Michael Smith, both bachelors who had come out with me on the *Accra*, also appear regularly in my letters to Lesley, usually rather like this, 'X came round and we had a drink. Several beers later we decided to call on Y', and so on, and on! We were, after all, still in our twenties.

During these three to four months my job was to process the notifications to retire, calculate the compensation and, under Neil Kay's supervision, to see that things worked smoothly. There was no sudden rush, rather a steady daily flow from all branches of the civil service until by the time of my departure on leave about 40 per cent of the total number of expatriates (and a bit more of the administration) had announced their intention to leave. This figure included almost all those who had held senior posts for three years and were about 40 years of age.

I have emphasised the departure of expatriates. As this was happening, of course – indeed even before the 1954 Constitution had hastened the pace of political change – every effort had been made to recruit Nigerians. There were 16 Nigerians in the Eastern Region Administrative Service when it was formed on 1 October 1954. Another 73 had been appointed by the time I went on leave in November 1957, bringing the number to about the same as that of the British officers still on the books.[9]

November came at last and I was able to take my leave. I could not wait to see Lesley; we had been separated for three months. She was pregnant again, we had hoped for it before she left but had not been sure. However we now knew that the baby would be born in May.

We could not afford to rent a house for ourselves so my parents agreed that we could spend my leave with them (my brother, also now in the service had been appointed to Sarawak). It was not particularly convenient for anyone, especially as we had no car. My father, though, allowed Lesley to borrow his car (naturally it did not have automatic transmission so I was unable to drive). Otherwise we had to use public transport (which I found difficult).

The Colonial Office required me to be examined by the specialists at the Royal National Orthopaedic Hospital. Here, the consultant recommended that I should have an operation to fuse the bones in my right wrist – the pattern of muscle damage was such that unless this was done the wrist and palm would be pulled down at right angles to the forearm, rather like a monkey's paw. Once done, though, the operation was irreversible. I was a little hesitant but I really had little choice but to take their advice. As it happened it turned out well, but there was an element of luck in this. The surgeon forgot to ask me until after I had had the 'pre-med' at what angle I wanted the hand to be fixed. It was not the best of times to be asked, as I was already drowsy; fortunately I was not too far under to explain. The result has been to give me a better grip in that hand than it would otherwise possess.

I also had to have the nail of the big toe on my left foot removed – since the foot had been paralysed the nail had shown a pronounced tendency to grow 'in', resulting in abscesses. For most people this operation would be a very simple affair, but not so in my case. Even at that time the circulation in the leg was very bad and so healing was slow. Moreover, I was not able to wear my calliper until the dressings on the toe had been removed so I had to spend a full week in hospital.

As soon as I had got over these things I asked the Crown Agents to arrange passages for us back to Nigeria. There were two reasons for haste. The first was Lesley's pregnancy. She was already in her seventh month and would soon not be allowed to fly. The second was that the news coming out of Eastern Nigeria was of widespread rioting and of what seemed to be verging on a collapse of government. How much of this was true? Were journalists exaggerating it? We did not know nor how to find out in England. By the time we arrived it was to discover that the unrest had largely died down. It had been very serious, however – not simply the product of gin and journalists.[10]

Why had this happened? In 1955 the Eastern Region government had promised free universal primary education (UPE).[11] In 1956 the government had realised that 'free' UPE would bankrupt the region within two or three years. It then introduced a system of fees. This was the immediate cause of the rioting. There were other reasons, also. The Nigerian peasantry were no fools. They could see how politicians were profiting with houses, cars, suits and high living and they resented it. They were also used to having white DOs whom they may not have exactly loved but whom they respected and trusted to be fair. Now these were going and being replaced by young Nigerians who seemed to be no better then they were. So they carried placards, 'Down with Black Rule', 'WE WANT WHITE DOs'. What perhaps was surprising was that it was in an Igbo Province, Owerri, that the authority of government had reached its lowest ebb.[12]

Fortunately for the government there were still just enough of these white DOs left to hold the line. But it had been a near-run thing and Federal police reinforcements had to be called in from Lagos. I understand that the ministers in Enugu had been in a state of panic.

It was good to be back with my colleagues and to learn that I was again going to work under Neil Kay in the Establishments Division. Christopher Fogarty had returned to England and been replaced as Permanent Secretary, Finance, by an Igbo, Oputa Udoji,[13] while our division had been moved to the Premier's Office (which had no effect on our day-to-day work). On the other hand, Lesley and I were disappointed that two of our house servants (to whom we had paid a salary retainer before departing on leave, with the promise of a further payment on our return) had not come back to work for us. I suppose that with the generally disturbed conditions they could not have been sure that we ourselves *would* be coming back – so many Europeans had left. Our nanny, Katharine, had kept her word, however, to Caroline's obvious pleasure.

I have little of much interest noted down for the next two months. One incident was the discovery of a great viper asleep in the kitchen. Unlike most snakes, this type was somnolent, not easily alerted, but with very powerful venom. It took refuge behind some boxes, and moving these so as to get at the creature, and its eventual noisy despatch, involved the servants from half a dozen houses, all shouting noisily as African servants do on any occasion. At least this was in a good cause and I 'dashed' them with pleasure.

The Eastern Region was settling down again after the disturbances caused by the 'education riots', but they were still to cause an unlikely repercussion. The Cabinet was unable to agree on the 1958 budget so that when the House of Assembly met to consider it, nothing was ready. Zik took the obvious but cowardly way out, making a speech to the effect that he had always been in the van of those emphasising the ability of Nigerians and their ability to rule themselves, that therefore it gave him exceptional pain to have to say that having appointed a Nigerian to be Permanent Secretary,

Finance, the man had fallen down on his job and that, as a result, no budget was available for the legislators to consider.[14] It was all absolute lies, of course – the fault lay entirely with the ministers who had shilly-shallied – but it saved Zik's face which was all that worried him.

Oputa was deeply upset at this attack, to which he could make no reply. He certainly discussed his position with Neil Kay, pointing out that he had been appointed by the Secretary of State after the same kind of education and on precisely the same terms as expatriate officers of the Administrative Service. He reckoned that his career had now been ruined and that he should be entitled to compensation on the same terms as that given to his white colleagues.

Neil gave sympathy but advised caution. He was sure that time would wipe clear the quite unjustified slur and that then the episode, deeply hurtful as it was, would be forgotten; Oputa just had to keep a low profile for a time and all would turn out well. He accepted the advice, reluctantly. And Neil was right. Next year Oputa Udoji was back in favour and was appointed head of the Eastern Region Civil Service, a position for which he was pre-eminently qualified and which he filled with great distinction.[15]

Lesley's time was now up and, after a long and painful delivery, our son, Nicholas, was born on 6 May at the 'Senior Service' hospital at Enugu. Lesley was most impressed by the sister/midwife, an Igbo named Okonkwo.

The time was coming for Neil to go on leave and I was desperately hoping that I might 'act' for him in his absence (this would have meant receiving an 'acting allowance' almost as great as my normal salary). Normally it would have been unthinkable that a junior should even think of such a thing, but times were not normal. Lesley and I were also finding it impossible to manage – prices were still rising fast and with a baby she could not get a job as she had done on the last tour. Neil was asked whether he considered it 'essential' that his replacement had experience in Establishments work (in which case I would have been given the post), but, being honest, he had to say that while it was desirable it should not override other normal factors. He was quite right – and, in any event, my 'experience' was really pretty limited, but it was a big disappointment, nevertheless.

There was a continuing inflow of notifications to retire although the pace was slowing as the almost total departure of British 'super-scale' officers had left a lot of vacancies. The Public Service Commission had stuck by the rules of seniority in filling these which meant that there had been a lot of promotions for officers in the 'long-scale', men in their late thirties with about ten years service. To obtain full benefit from their promotion, they would have to remain for three more years.

We then learned that there was an administrative problem about paying the pensions of those who had retired. Colonial Service Pensions Regulations required that where an officer had served in more than one territory his pension would be borne by the countries in which he had served according to the total salary he had drawn in each. The Federal government, however, had found this work too much for them (all of the Eastern Region officers were deemed to have been 'Federal' as far as their pre-1 October 1954 service was concerned). They could not calculate how much had been paid by them, the pension could not be apportioned and therefore it could not be paid. For some reason this came to me. It seemed to me that that those retiring should not be penalised and that as they had left from the East it was up to us to deal with it. So I authorised the Crown Agents to pay up to three-quarters of the amount due as an advance on pension.

No one queried this until the Accountant-General, Jack Bridget, returning from leave drew Christopher Fogarty's attention to the swelling volume of 'advances'. Unfortunately I had had no authority to authorise these so theoretically I could have been personally liable for perhaps two or three hundred thousand pounds of unauthorised expenditure. I got off with a verbal reprimand. Christopher was a reasonable man and he acknowledged that if I had put the matter to him he would have granted the authorisation. Still, I could have been in very hot water.

At about the same time I asked for a posting to a bush station in Calabar Province. This had always been my intention, to demonstrate that having had polio was not going to hold me back; but now money troubles added to the insistence of my request. I quite understood that asking for a posting at that particular moment might appear as if I was being petty and refusing to work under the Nigerian who had been chosen to act for Neil; this was not at all the case – my relations with this chap were perfectly good and I would have supported him loyally. But I could not afford to stay in Enugu.

I also understood the reluctance of my superiors to take the risk, 'after all', as one of them put it, 'pretty dodgy things sometimes happen in bush, a riot can get out of hand and the best of men may have to run for it. Where would you be then?' This was true, of course, but in itself it changed nothing. Either I got my posting or I retired. I got it. Finally, it was agreed but then, at the last moment, illness nearly stopped me. I caught mumps, very badly, with a high fever and all the complications (testicles swollen to the size of melons) that are associated with the illness in popular scatology. Only, it was not funny at all, it was very painful. Fortunately the doctor, Savage – one of the well-known Sierra Leone Savages – looked after me well, recognised my wish to get back to bush urgently and passed me as fit. So, with anticipation, in August we set off for Abak.

Chapter 22
Abak, 1958–9

I had visited Abak on several occasions during my time at Uyo, the townships of Ikot Ekpenne, Uyo and Abak all being on the edge of the Divisions named after them, and each being only about 15 miles from the other. While Ikot Ekpenne and Uyo were now 'on the tar', there was still only an earth road connecting Abak to the other two stations and to the rest of the region, potholed and dusty during the 'big' and 'little' dries, potholed and muddy during the other nine months of the year, never impassable but needing care if one thought of one's pocket or of the car's shock absorbers!

Coming from Uyo, from which I first saw Abak and is the view of it that I remember best, the road emerged from fairly thick bush as the ground fell away to a shallow but steep-sided valley through which the Abak River ran. On the other side of the valley, at the brow of the facing slope, the district officer's house stood, the Union flag flying prominently from the staff before it, a suitably romantic and impressive site which had appealed to me from the first.

I am sure that every administrative officer remembers with nostalgia 'his' first full charge, and in my case my pleasure at taking over was reinforced by my recognition of how lucky I had been to be left with sufficient physical strength to do so. I was determined, too, not only to run the division, but also to do so at least as well as, if not better than, any of my predecessors. This I can recognise now was wrong; I was looking at the post with a view to glory: it should have been with the aim of service. Although I was still young, I knew that time was short; I would be the last British district officer.

Indeed, although the Union flag flew bravely before the house, two large modern complexes were dominant architecturally. One of these was a teacher training college and the other a secondary school, both were run by Irish Roman Catholic fathers. No government building was half as impressive. At night, they stood forth even more, since both were brightly lit, shining modern temples against the solid backcloth of the African night; they stood for the 'new', as the flag did for the 'old' in Nigeria. Moreover, while I was the only British officer on the station, there must have been some 20 European missionaries resident in the division, Protestants as well as Roman Catholic (although the latter were the largest single denomination). There was a young married English doctor in the semi-mission hospital about 20 road miles away, a Nigerian agricultural officer with his English wife who lived on a government farm about ten miles off and, occasionally, a scientist at an oil palm research station, again about the same distance away. So, I cannot pretend to any real 'isolation', particularly as Lesley accompanied me.[1]

Even so, there was a lot to do. At the time the population of the division was estimated at about 250,000, but was certainly more than that. There was no gazetted police officer on the station, supervision being exercised rather lightly from Uyo, but one had to handle the police carefully as they were a Federal service (the files showed a long record of friction over the years between the DO, Abak, as the local Superior Police Officer and the Assistant Superintendent of Police at Uyo or Ikot Ekpenne). The prison, also a 'Federal' service, was under the supervision of the DO. This was normal and never caused any trouble. Other services, education and so on, in the absence of any local departmental representative, were also looked after by the DO.

Figure 9 Erosion on an earth road, Abak.

The division resembled in shape a rough horizontal diamond, bisected by the Kwa Ibo River, a wide and swiftly flowing stream, with a new concrete bridge at Ibritam (replacing the wire and pulley contraption I remembered from my earlier visits) and an old but satisfactory one at Utu Etim Ekpo, where there was a considerable expanse of swamp, foul smelling from its use as a place where cassava was rotted.[2] A third bridge at Ikot Okoro, midway between these two, had been broken by the excessive weight of a Shell oil-drilling rig – just as they had broken the bridge at Etinan in Uyo Division. (I do not know whether Shell paid compensation for the damage they caused in this way, but it certainly did not come back direct to us, and the inconvenience was disproportionate, adding about 15 miles or almost an hour's driving to my average journey to the far side of the division).

Abak, like the other mainland divisions of the province, was part of a fairly level plain about 150 feet above sea level, intersected by numerous streams and watercourses that had so eroded the light soil that they ran in narrow steep-sided valleys. The land was fertile, the rainfall about 90 inches per annum falling over nine months of the year with two dry spells, one of about a month and the other

Figure 10 Etinan Bridge over Kwa River.

of two months' duration. Humidity was always virtually at the maximum, except for a few weeks in the longer dry spell. The palm oil tree dominated the landscape, providing thick shade and allowing dense undergrowth, with its fruit supplying the cash crop on which the people relied.

Certainly agriculture could never have fed the average of 650 persons per square mile who lived in the district. These were all Annangs,[3] a sub-tribe of the Ibibio who are, ethnographically, a semi-Bantu race. Small in stature, they speak a tonal language with the limited vocabulary required for an agricultural, forest-dwelling people. There was no structured tribal system, the basic unit being the *ekpuk*[4] – from which young men could hive off at will if they could – while groupings of *ekpuks* were called a village and the villages in an area might be termed a clan, but that was all.

There was no recognised village authority, no such concept as that of a 'clan chief': every Annang felt himself as good as any other, and with his cutlass in his hand he was prepared to show it, a chop with its sharp blade being almost an instinctive reflex. Other Annangs were accepted as being kin of a kind; other Ibibios, who could at least be understood, were accepted; Igbos, more numerous in the Eastern Region as a whole, more industrious, were hated, and perhaps feared, although no Annang would have admitted this.

Abak (with Opobo to the south) had been the area where the 'Leopard Men' – the *Ekpe Owo* – had been most powerful in the 1940s, and maybe before. The society had probably at one time been no worse than many similar anthropomorphic cults, paying tribute to the leopard as an earthly incarnation of the power and cruelty of the spirits, initiates making offerings to placate them. Then, at some stage its leaders had recognised the potential power they possessed, power arising from villagers' fear of the power and savagery of the leopard and the belief that the *juju* could transform an ordinary man into a killing beast. From then on, it was a simple progression until the society became an organisation killing for money, for influence and for power, its members protected by the terror of its reputation and the profound belief that men did not simply wear leopard skins or put on iron-clawed gloves, but actually changed into the beasts.[5]

The power of the *Ekpe Owo* had been destroyed pretty effectively by the hangings held at Abak and Opobo jails in 1949, and, probably, also by the rapid growth of the human population which had left no bush where leopards could lie up, no game on which they could live. Without the real thing to back it up, the story lost some if its power. It was, nevertheless, still fresh enough in the minds, not only of the Annangs but also of outsiders, to give Abak a deserved reputation for violence.

Abak, unlike Uyo, had not initially been opposed to the NCNC and all three members in the Eastern Region House of Assembly (elected as recently as 18 months before) were of that party. One of these, Mr Afiah, was Minister of Works although not a man of any particular ability or local distinction. Since then though, and after the expenditure of large sums of money by the Opposition (who were financed, it was pretty certain, by the government of the Western Region), Abak had rather swung behind the rest of the Calabar Province in its support for the Calabar/Ogoja/Rivers Provinces Alliance. This body had agitated at the 1957 Constitutional Conference in London for the creation of a separate non-Igbo (COR) state to cover these three provinces, which would be separate from the Igbo-dominated Eastern Region.

At the conference the British government, which had come to the view that it should get shot of Nigeria as quickly as possible, had bought time. It had agreed that a commission should be established to look into the whole question of the future position of the minority tribes. (For it was not only in the East that these were protesting. In both the Western and the Northern regions there were substantial numbers who were opposed to the dominant Yorubas and Hausas who controlled these two regional governments.)

This type of problem was of course inevitable given the arbitrary manner in which boundaries had first been delineated, drawn on a map at a European conference without much regard to the physical features of the continent and none for tribal unity. In Ghana, the Ashanti and the backward peoples of the Northern Territories had voiced similar objections to being left to the (coastal) Convention Peoples Party; lip service had been paid to their concerns, but no more. Now it was Nigeria's turn.

Whatever justice was done, it could not be done for all. There were undoubtedly certain obvious practical difficulties in accepting the claims of the minority tribes – further fragmentation would increase the demands for trained indigenous manpower and also the costs of administration. Moreover, the creation of new states would be resisted by all existing politicians currently in power (who would not want their own fiefdoms disturbed, however much they might wish to kick over others), particularly in the 'Holy North'. Any fragmentation would disrupt the timetable for the granting of full independence to Nigeria in 1960 to which the Colonial Office was committed.

Nevertheless, it was thought necessary for the British government to give an outward impression that it was listening and hence the device of an appointment of a commission.[6] Behind the scenes, though, it was made clear to the members of the commission, all honourable men of course, that they were expected to find against the division of the three existing regions.[7] There would be no COR State.

This Minorities Commission Report was due to be published ten days after I took over Abak Division, indeed, a reason why my posting had been approved was so that all the Calabar Province divisions should have British district officers. A police 'riot unit' – a small but specially trained paramilitary body – had been stationed at Uyo and other police reinforcements were available at Aba, all just in case publication of the report was followed by rioting.

As I have written above, it was at this moment that I took over. My predecessor, a man from the Rivers Province tribe, had been reported on as being very much under the influence of one of the NCNC assemblymen. Under the circumstances of potential anti-Igbo trouble, I was (in retrospect, I think unjustly) a bit chary of having much to do with him.

Nigeria is, of course, now divided into far more 'states' than were ever then envisaged (and 'proved' to be impractical) but it took the bloody Biafran war to do this. It would be, I suppose, unfair to wonder if the consciences of the British policy formulators on this were ever troubled by the thought that a different finding in 1958 might have averted this later conflict.

I did not have much time to get to know my way around, just sufficient to visit each of the 19 courts, to meet their clerks and the secretaries of the four district councils. The day before the date of official publication of the report (whose contents, of course, we had not seen, but which, it was clear from the preparations made, were clearly against the creation of a COR State), a conference was arranged of all the surrounding district officers. A deputy commissioner of police (sent down from Enugu) also attended. We reviewed the likelihood of rioting. We were agreed that this was not expected. The people were sullen, but the knowledge that police were present in large numbers was likely to mean that there would be no violence. The long-term disaffection to the regional government, nevertheless, would remain.

So it turned out. There was a flurry of excitement when, early the next morning, I had a report of some shots being fired at Utu Etim Ekpo about 12 miles from Abak. Utu Etim Ekpo had been the village where the troops had shot a considerable number of people in the 1929 'Women's Riots',[8] and I drove out there with a small body of police feeling as if I was marching with Havelock to relieve Cawnpore! However, it turned out to be only an incident of petty theft, the shots having been fired by a Dane gun, a matter to be investigated to be sure, but not of 'crisis' proportions. As the area continued calm, the immediate tension ended, the police mobile group was withdrawn and we were all able to get back to work, or, in my case, to start getting a hold on my division.

There was a great deal to be done. The amount of tax collected in Abak – mostly coming from a 15-shilling per head assessment, although with an 'income' element for those thought to be earning more than £60 a year – was far less than it should have been (this was not new; Abak had a reputation for not paying). There was an appalling arrears list of native court cases awaiting review. More immediately there were district council elections to organise with nearly 200 candidates contesting the seats on the four district councils into which Abak was divided.

By this time Nigerians were getting used to voting and there were not quite the same problems stemming from ignorance of the procedures that I had met with in 1954; I had also had the benefit of observing Henry Lawrence and Tony Shepherd's arrangements for the 1957 elections at Nsukka. In these district council elections it was now basically a case of following an established pattern, only a rather more complicated one because of the increased number of candidates.

Fortunately the organisational side went smoothly. The elections were staggered over a number of days and each evening the presiding officers would come to the district office to be issued with the right number of ballot boxes, papers, indelible ink pads, party symbols and other impedimenta. The local Members of the House of Assembly at Enugu were of course very concerned as the council elections also affected their local standing. One, in particular, a Mr J. E. Eyo – a small rat-like man who had been the one involved with my predecessor – I had to warn against trying to interfere in the arrangements. He did as he was told, but thereafter I was to be his enemy.

During the days when voting was taking place I was out moving from one polling station to another, checking that voting was going smoothly and that the candidates had no complaints. There was no particular violence but on one occasion there was a squabble when voters were queuing and a chop with a cutlass took off a leg. Fortunately I arrived within minutes and was able to get the injured man to the small joint hospital at Ikot Okoro where the doctor was able to stitch him up; my car upholstery was washable. On another occasion, in our house at Abak, my wife received a note from a police constable: 'Madam, come at once, I am surrounded' – trapped in a church, poor chap. Lesley could not go – the car was with me – but she got a relief police detachment on their bicycles and the constable safe.

With our daughter just over 3 years old and a baby of less than six months, Lesley was busy. The DO's house at Abak, however, was large and comfortable. (The servants' quarters also were newly painted and in good repair. In modern houses these were usually built to reasonable standards but in bush houses they were often in a disgraceful state. To expect staff to be personally clean and well dressed and yet at the same time neglect the conditions under which *they* lived seemed to me to be quite wrong.) We had brought Caroline's nanny from Enugu with us and, although not an Ibibio, the land of her own tribe, the Aros, was not far off – so she was happy.

In front of the house was a covered veranda, with morning glories and moon flowers growing thickly up the supporting pillars, simple flowers without any scent that I remember, but colourful. The garden itself was quite large and well laid out with bushes of pride of Barbados,[9] while all over the station there were large flame trees, glorious when in season. There was a kitchen garden where tomatoes and various beans were grown, avocado pears, pineapple and the ubiquitous pawpaw, whose fruit was almost invariably served at breakfast (and very good it was too).

Altogether, we were really quite comfortable, although I was very busy trying, without much success, to reduce the arrears of court cases awaiting review, and pushing tax collection. I was anxious also, to see that the newly elected councillors settled in satisfactorily. As I have explained earlier, the government had recognised the initial mistake made in separating the district officer completely from the activities of district councils. Some authority, notably in the field of financial control, had been handed back to him.

A newly appointed Nigerian administrative officer, Christopher Chukwunyelu, was posted to me as assistant district officer to gain some practical experience in between his formal training courses. He had just graduated and returned from England, was a keen and likeable young man from Awgu in the Igbo country to the north, and we got on well together. I offloaded supervision of the prison on to him as soon as possible (as had been done to me) and generally tried to pass on the knowledge that I myself had so recently and imperfectly acquired.

He came out with me several times when I was hearing reviews of the cases in the courts – as an Igbo himself, the procedures would not be totally strange to him – and then suggested that he do some on his own. It so happened that amongst the cases listed for him was one concerning a claimed refund of dowry (or bride price as it was generally called). Following the divorce by a man of his wife the bride price he had paid initially to the woman's parents was refunded (less perhaps something for fair wear and tear). These cases were generally ill-tempered and were difficult to decide since the original transaction (of which naturally there was no written record) had taken place many years before.

This was what Christopher found. There were witnesses on both sides. They did not agree. The woman had more, and more convincing arguments. So, having patiently heard all that had to be said, he ordered only a partial restitution of what the plaintiff claimed he had paid. This was the last case he was hearing that day and having given his judgement he left the court for his next appointment, the aggrieved plaintiff standing there sullenly. I do not know the exact details of what happened next but I surmise that the woman or her relatives may have laughed at the man and jeered at him as village women can. Anyway, there in the open space around the court, he lashed out with his cutlass, almost severing her head from her neck before running for the bush.

The next morning the man presented himself to me at the district office. He admitted the killing (of which, until his appearance, I was unaware), saying simply: 'that when I heard all the lies that woman told my heart grew big inside me and I could see nothing. I would not let that woman have my money'. He had to be sent for trial by a magistrate – I did not have the powers to hear cases of manslaughter or murder – but I sent a strong recommendation for a light sentence as there was no premeditation or malice involved; simply an understandable (if his story was true) sudden loss of temper.

Christopher, when he heard of what happened after his departure from the court the previous day, was understandably shocked. I did not see however, that he could incur any blame. He had made his decision in the light of the evidence available; that was all he could do; the outcome was bad luck.

Apart from unfortunate incidents such as this, things seemed to be going quite well until I received a telephone call from Dicky Floyer, a senior administrative officer of many years experience whom I had met on my first voyage out. He was telephoning from Uyo District and asked if he could come over to see me. I was a bit surprised since I knew he was stationed in Enugu but naturally I agreed. When Dicky arrived about an hour later he explained that he had rather a difficult task. The Premier Dr Azikiwe had received a letter signed by the member in the Federal House of Representatives and the three members in the Regional House of Assembly. They alleged I had been guilty of corruption, political partisanship and other offences and demanded that I be moved to another division. Naturally, my first reaction was to say it was all nonsense but, looking at it carefully, it was not so easy as that. By a careful selection from my words and actions over the previous four months, ignoring their context, it looked all too horribly plausible. Although I denied the substance, and was supported by Christopher insofar as he was able to do so, I felt very worried as to how the interview with the four signatories would turn out on the morrow. I went to bed that night very sick at heart.

The next morning we all met in my office, all that is to say except for one of the members of the Regional House of Assembly, Mr J. E. Eyo (the man I had some trouble with on my arrival in the division). He had been told to come; the Member of the Federal House of Representatives confirmed that Mr Eyo knew of the meeting; no one knew why he was not there. So, after a wait, Dicky began without him. He went through each of the charges in turn and asked each of the three signatories present what they had to say. To each query they said they themselves had nothing: 'Mr Eyo said it was so.'

In the end, Dicky asked why, in the light of their having no evidence to substantiate the claims, they had signed the letter? 'Mr Eyo said to'. Did they wish to pursue the matter of my being moved? 'No'. Then, as all were about to leave, Mr Eyo arrived, very jaunty and explaining that he had found his car tyres flat which had caused his delay. We sat down again and Dicky pointed out that his fellow politicians had stated that the letter came entirely from him, what did he wish to say? His self-confidence suddenly deserted him 'It was what he had been told. He had no complaints against Mr Barnes – none at all. All a misunderstanding.'

That was that. Our meeting broke up with hypocritical expressions of good will. Dicky wrote a report to the Premier recommending that the letter be totally disregarded and I carried on. Nevertheless, I could not forget that my every move and word must have been the subject of malicious observation by one or more people (who must have included some staff from the district office) right from my first arrival. All I did or said in the future would have to be considered in this light.

I have wondered, too, very often about the providentially flat tyres of Mr Eyo's car. I cannot believe that this was pure chance;

I suspect one or more of the other signatories may have wished him to be discredited and had dug a trap for him to fall into. If so, they had succeeded, even if in so doing they gave me many hours of deep anxiety and hurt. However, outwardly I just had to carry on as before. Christopher left to take part in a training course organised for the newly appointed administrative officers at Man o' War Bay in the Southern Cameroons and this meant that there was even more to do than usual.

We spent Christmas at Abak – a charming group of young Annang girls came and danced on the front veranda. We had been asked to spend the New Year with Frank and Dorothy Ashworth at Owerri, an important District about 60 miles away where Frank was DO. This we were very pleased to do; Frank was a very good DO, a little older and more experienced than me and with bags of common sense.[10] Lesley liked Dorothy as well, while we thought it would be good for Caroline to be able to play with other European children – she had met none since we had arrived in Abak. As some compensation Caroline had invented an imaginary friend, 'Goosey', to whom she talked constantly and on whom I was always sitting or standing.

On our return to Abak we found it buzzing with activity and full of police, headed by the European Assistant Superintendent Humphries from Uyo. He told me that over the New Year there had been something of a scrap between two villages ten miles distant, with a man alleged murdered, a church and a school burnt down and several injured. Accordingly, he had brought over all the available police in Uyo to reinforce my own small detachment and proposed to descend on the aggressor village and arrest the malefactors. I agreed, on the understanding that I went first accompanied by the district interpreter[11] and a police orderly, while he followed close behind me with the two lorry loads of constables.

There was a rather overgrown earth track leading to our destination – it did not deserve the name 'road' – and when I arrived at the village there was no sign of the following lorries. This put me in a bit of a dilemma, but on balance I decided that it would be unwise to wait for the police; to do so would give the advantage to the villagers. Therefore, I got out of my car and, through the interpreter, demanded that a chair be brought for me and that the village heads be told that the DO wished to see them.

After a few minutes a rather rickety chair was brought. I sat down carefully (I *would* have looked a fool if the chair had broken under me and I had been sent sprawling to the earth!). Then three or four rather raggedly dressed old men came out from the huts.

Hoping that the police would turn up, I sat in silence for some further minutes, keeping the old men waiting, but, to my inward concern, there was no sound of lorries, so I told the old men I had heard of the previous day's riot with great anger. They might have had a grievance against the other village, but they knew that the correct action was to see me or to take an action in the court. They had not. They had taken the law into their own hands. I was not going to have it. I was not going to have the law broken. They had burnt another village's buildings. Did they want their own burnt? They had a choice. They could bring out the men who had done the damage, or they could take the consequences. The people who had attacked the other village would all go to prison and so would the leaders for having aided them.

Silence.

However, if the young men came forward voluntarily and gave themselves up I would see that the village was treated mercifully, there would be no collective fine and only those actually guilty would go to jail.

Then I sat back and waited. After a time the elders began to mutter amongst themselves, a long and heated discussion during which I tried to appear self-confident and relaxed, which I was not! Where had those stupid police got to? I was probably quite safe personally, but still our only arms consisted of the young constable's truncheon and my walking stick! Meanwhile the leaders had finished their discussion and the head began a long explanation of how they had suffered at the hands of the other village, how they had helped pay for the building and had not been allowed to use it, how their lands had been taken, their palm oil nuts stolen and that really *they* were the aggrieved parties. 'All very well', I said, 'but why didn't you come to see me? You know the law. The law says you do not attack another village. Government will be angry. Now, I want the young men who fought'. 'They have gone away'. 'Get them'.

More mutterings. Then one old man summoned a middle-aged one from the audience and whispered something to him at which the latter slipped away into the bush. We waited some more. After a time I saw one young man after another coming out of the bush, three, six, about a dozen. 'Were these all?' 'All!'

I was sure that it was not true, but it was better than nothing. Anyway, there was little more that I could now do, so I told them to stand in line, sat back in my chair and looked at the elders, hoping that sooner or later the police would turn up. What I would do with my prisoners otherwise I just did not know. Fortunately after a time I heard the sound of lorry engines. The ASP arrived, the police arrived, all ready for action and carrying rifles. The ASP was also full of apologies. He seemed a bit disconcerted, however, when I pointed out the line of young men and said that they were his prisoners and that now we could go back to the station. The young men were loaded into the back of a lorry, I made a final speech to the elders pointing out how many police had come and that more still would come if there was any further trouble. I then got into my car and went home.

My recollection is that it was impossible to prove any individual case of murder or manslaughter, that the young men all received jail sentences of a couple of years and that the village elders were bound over to keep the peace. However, I expect the feud went on for many future generations (just as it would have done in early medieval England). More serious, to my mind, was the next incident.

I had heard that a group calling itself 'Ama Uke?' ('You like which?' i.e. 'Your money or your life?') was operating on the Uyo/Abak/Ikot Ekpenne borders where the boundaries of the three divisions met, robbing small traders and the like, but no specific instance of their activities had come to my attention. Then, late one evening, an Igbo trader coming from Uyo to Abak was attacked coming down the hill from Uyo Division and only about half a mile from my house. He had either resisted or attempted to flee and had been cut with a machete, his bicycle and money stolen, and he himself left in the roadway. Some locals who had heard the noise had brought him into the station: prudently they had waited until the thieves had made off before showing themselves and rescuing the victim.

Lesley and the Nigerian dispenser, Mr Uko, did their best to provide immediate aid – the victim's arm was bleeding very badly and indeed appeared half-severed. I told the police sergeant to send all his men out in pairs on bicycles while I with one constable explored in my car all passable roads and tracks (not that I had any hope of actually seeing the gang, nor indeed what I and a single constable would do if we had, but because I thought it important from the point of view of morale for there to be a swift reaction). We found no one, of course, and when I returned to the station it was to find that the victim had been bandaged as well as the dim light of the oil lamps permitted, that Lesley had given him codeine (the only painkiller we had), and that a lorry had been obtained to carry him to the hospital at Ikot Okoro 20 road miles away.

For the next few weeks I made sure that the police kept to an increased schedule of night patrols while I myself drove around for two or three hours each night calling on as many villages as possible.

Ama Uke? had clearly terrified the area, roads into villages were blocked at nightfall, and when men came out of their huts they were now always carrying a weapon. This preventive action may seem pitifully inadequate but it was all that could be done given my limited resources; and it appeared to have had the desired effect: there were no more such flagrant attacks by this gang in Abak Division.

As for the Igbo trader, well, Dr Rowden, the young mission doctor at Ikot Okoro, told me that he had been able to save the man's life and, by some feat of skill, his arm. The doctor told me, whether jestingly or not, that the codeine Lesley had given the man had been sufficiently strong (for someone unused to such a sedative) to ward off the ill effects of shock during the bumpy ride to the hospital. Some months later, at 'complaints' at the district office one morning, a man appeared with a stiff arm. It was the trader who had come to thank me. His arm would never be perfect, but at least it was usable and he had his life. I was touched at his gesture but in truth

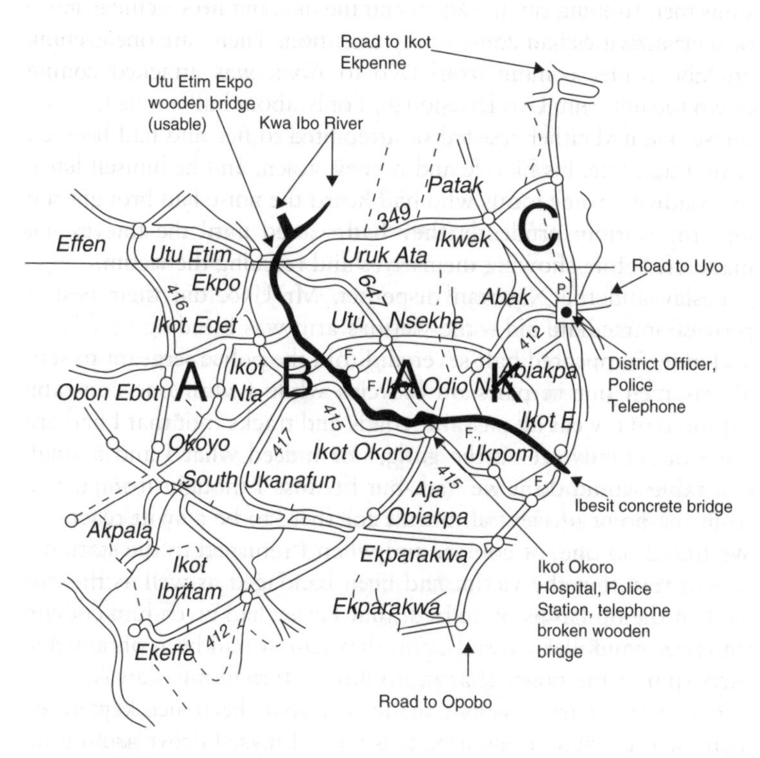

Map 3 Abak division, 1959.

his thanks were more appropriately directed to Dr Rowden, to the dispenser and to Lesley, rather than to me.

Dr Rowden was a young recently qualified English doctor who, with his equally young wife, had come out from England under the auspices of the Kwa Ibo Mission, an austere Irish Presbyterian order (although they themselves were both Anglican, so far as I can remember). The hospital was new, the brainchild of one of my predecessors who thought that the establishment of a 'county council' in 1954 would result in the existence of a body large and wealthy enough to meet the running costs of a small hospital acting as a centre for the rural health services in the division.

Such a service was undoubtedly needed. However, the county council, along with all other such creations in the region, had become bankrupt and incompetent: certainly incapable of employing a qualified doctor and nursing staff or financing the recurrent costs of even a small (60 beds) hospital. Some other sponsor had to be found and, after some negotiation, it had been agreed that the Kwa Ibo Mission would supply a medical officer, nursing sisters and administrative support. (The regional government would reimburse the mission for these costs and, with the four district councils that had replaced the abolished county council, would together meet the costs of medical supplies, drugs, etc.).

It was not very tidy perhaps, but the mission had been fortunate in its recruitment of Dr Rowden who was keen and enthusiastic. (He needed to be, being on call 24 hours each day, seven days a week, performing all operations with limited equipment and no specialised anaesthetist, examining the scores of patients presenting themselves each day, as well as running the hospital.) Lesley and I both liked him and his wife immensely.

His remit, though, did not extend to the supervision of the eight dispensaries and nine maternity centres scattered over the division whose costs were met by the district councils. In theory the government medical officer in Ikot Ekpenne looked after the centres but in practice he never came to Abak.[12] Accordingly I, and Lesley if she was with me, would call in whenever I passed one of these centres. They were very simple units, inadequately equipped, poorly maintained and insufficiently supplied with even the simplest medicines. Nor was the training level of the dispensers and maternity midwives very high, although they still met a need. (According to my handing-over notes written when I left Abak in August 1959 there were about 200 deliveries each year compared with my rather crude estimate of a total of 10,000 plus births each year in the division.)

There were also five small leper settlements in the division, each housing between 50 and 100 lepers. Supervision was exercised by the Kwa Ibo Mission and by the CMS at Uzuakoli in Owerri Province.

My calls were simply to make sure that the staff were on duty and not simply busying themselves with their own affairs (which otherwise, almost unsupervised as they were, was all too likely), and that they were as clean as possible. It had to be accepted, though, that there were difficulties in maintaining standards of hygiene when there was no piped or safe water and when after dark the only light probably came from their own oil 'bush' lamp. Occasionally, too, I was able to take a particularly sick person to the hospital; once we supplied a new rubber container for the ink of a fountain pen as a dropper to help feed a premature baby (it did not live).

Generally, African women would suckle a child for two years or more, with the consequence that their breasts rapidly became pendulous. A woman in her late twenties might well be taken as being twice that age. The children though, in general, seemed happy enough, constantly with their mothers as they were, although infant mortality was appallingly high and life expectancy at birth was no higher than the mid-thirties. There was, of course, no cow's milk available as a supplement (as there were no cows). Dried milks such as Klim were heavily advertised – as was Nestlé evaporated milk, but in the rural areas there was no money available for such luxuries (themselves now the subject of attack on the grounds that they can help spread disease as they were not usually prepared with boiled water).

The long period of suckling and an insufficiency of milk due to their own inadequate diet may well have, originally, given rise to the belief that twins resulted from a woman copulating with an evil spirit and that therefore twins were bad *juju*. As such, they could, perhaps should, be done away with. This was easily done putting them in the bush to die or be eaten by animals. Certainly this was the custom and there was almost nothing that could be done about it – neither births nor deaths were generally registered just as they were not in England until the 1830s. An American missionary couple working on the borders of Abak and Ikot Ekpenne heard that twins had been born in a nearby village and notified me in an attempt to save the babes. The couple offered to take the babes and bring them up but the family, exhorted by an elderly woman, would have none of this. I warned that if the infants died enquiries would be made and charged the two missionaries to keep an eye on the twins' well-being. However, I had no confidence in their long-term survival – death by natural causes was all too common not to be difficult to simulate.

As in Uyo, there were a large number of missionaries living in the division on whom I would call when I was passing. The Roman Catholics, in addition to two big institutions at Abak to which I have referred, also ran a large elementary teacher training college at Urua Inyang. They were easily the most numerous and influential, having long overtaken the Kwa Ibo Mission[13] although the latter had been the earliest in the field.

I had, one day, a call from one of these latter, a pastor in his late forties accompanied by his wife. They told me with some slight embarrassment that they had been married at Abak District Office many years before. Recently they had been burgled and the thieves had stolen a bundle of personal papers that the thief had presumably thought might be valuable. They were not, except to the couple as amongst them was their marriage certificate – the only proof that they had not been living in sin all these years! 'Did I have a copy?'

There were no filing cabinets in Abak District Office; files were kept on wooden shelves, at the mercy of damp (for the roof was not good) and white ant. The 'file retrieval system' depended on the memory of the district clerk, which was usually prodigious and for most things adequate. In recent years, however, there had been so many staff changes that there was no longer the old continuity. None of the current staff had been present at the time the marriage certificate was issued.

I wrote to the Federal authorities in Lagos in case a copy had been sent there, but they had no records. The only thing I could suggest was that I remarried them and gave them a document telling their story, with statements from various members of their flock to the effect that they had been living together as man and wife for as long as was known. This, with my district seal – the royal coat-of-arms above the words 'District Officer, Abak' in red wax, might look official enough.

The couple thanked me for my suggestion, but explained that having spent years exhorting their flock to live a married Christian life they did not wish to admit that they had no proof of their own marriage and were dependent on others' reports of their lengthy co-habitation as proof of their relationship. I could understand and sympathise with this, but I had no other suggestion to offer. So they went away, rather disconsolate, to brood upon their situation.

A few weeks later I began to reflect upon the implications of their loss, not so far as it affected them, but upon the district records as a whole. It was all very well in the past relying on the chief clerk's memory, but in the future there was likely to be much more staff mobility. A clerk was unlikely in the future to be recruited and stay on one station throughout his career; files should be reorganised according to a clear and logical system.

I drew up a beautiful new index, explained its logic to my staff and set them to the task of going through every piece of paper we possessed (which they did cheerfully enough, although I could tell from their facial expressions that they thought I was stricken in the brain; I think I probably was). However, there was an unexpected but satisfactory side effect. At the bottom of one heap, stained and ragged, but legible, was the pastor's wedding certificate! He and his wife were overjoyed.

A second incident involving a missionary was less happy. I was told that an American missionary was taking an inordinate number of photographs of young girls as they washed, swam and gambolled naked in the many streams that criss-crossed the division. One could not be unaware of these nymphs, just driving around they could be seen from any bridge, and undoubtedly they presented a charming sight. However, like many African peoples, the Annangs were somewhat fearful of photographs – prisoners would also object to being photographed while carrying out such routine and normal tasks as cutting grass or carrying water. In addition, to linger, watching naked young girls bathing was – at the very least – stupid.

The American was horrified when I explained that he was being accused of an improper interest in these creatures. 'I'm a married man. Why should I be interested? Sure, I have taken photos but these were art and for the information of folks back home who didn't have any idea of Africa.' This last was not an explanation that would have been well received by the objectors who would have been even more vehement had they been told that pictures of their young women were being circulated in the USA. I accepted his expostulations that he had acted in all innocence – after all I had been the victim of a malicious report myself only a few months before, but I told him to be more discreet in future and not to take any more photos. There was no need for his mission authorities to be informed; he should keep his head down and I would try to make sure that there was no sequel. Indeed, there was no further trouble, at least while I remained in the division.

A few weeks before this incident I had had a fall, not noticing in the dark one of the concrete rainstorm drains that encircled the house. I did not think anything of it at the time, but by the next morning my left foot was so painful that I was unable to walk on it and the pain showed no sign of decreasing – the reverse if anything. I drove to see the Roman Catholic sister/doctor at Anua in Uyo Division. She told me that I had broken a couple of small bones in the foot for which a small plaster cast was essential, rest desirable and that it should knit very quickly.

There was, however, a problem. A cast on my left foot meant that I was unable to wear the calliper that supported that leg. Without the calliper I could only shuffle unsteadily and that only on a smooth surface. Within the house it was possible to get about (although not easy). I had a division to run, though. I had to be mobile. So I had one of the heavy wooden PWD armchairs with which our house was furnished adapted so that it could be carried on two long bamboo poles. Four prisoners could support these and thus I could get around the station.

I could also visit the courts, having warned the clerk in advance to have bearers available, so that getting out of my car I could shuffle to the chair and then be carried up to the dais on which I would remain until the day's work was done. (It was effective, if inelegant: it had to be, as one of Mr Eyo's charges had been that my paralysis prevented me getting about and I felt I had to demonstrate that even with this added, if temporary, drawback I could still work!). In fact, once the bones had knitted a bit and with the plaster removed, the extra support given by the calliper meant that I was back to normal (even if only my 'normal') more speedily than is usual.

I have written of the large total rainfall but for those who have never experienced tropical rain, I must emphasise that it was not the gentle wet that we experience in England, it was fierce, blinding sheets of water as if

> The cataract of the cliff of Heaven fell blinding off the brink,
> As if it would wash the stars away as suds go down a sink.[14]

Except in the height of the rains, the downfall would cease as abruptly as it had begun, and the sun in blazing scorching fury would emerge. Puddles would steam and evaporate as quickly as they had formed. Roads a quagmire 15 minutes earlier would revert to their normal condition of dry reddish dust.

Often one would see snakes crossing the road. It was meant to be dangerous to run over these, they would not be killed but had been known to wrap themselves round wheel axles, ready to bite when the car stopped and an unsuspecting leg appeared. The trick to avoid this was to brake hard if one could not avoid the reptile so that the locked wheels gripped the dirt surface more closely and were more likely to crush the snake.

In this memoir I have referred repeatedly to tax collecting, to elections and general administration, to work in the courts and to the need to maintain some degree of law and order. The district administration was also deeply concerned in 'development', whether this was the building of roads and bridges (as described so vividly by Joyce Cary in *Mister Johnston*, based on his own experiences in the North) or by encouraging self-help 'community development' projects as filmed in *Daybreak at Udi*.[15]

Community development never really took off in Calabar Province in the same way as it had done in the Igbo provinces, possibly because the villages were even more fragmented. I had an allocation of money to help – the theory was that the village provided land, labour and such things as timber (for roofing) or sand (to mix with cement to make concrete) while the government, through the DO, supplied pan (corrugated aluminium, used for roofing), nails or cement. I can remember one 'community hall' being built in this way – it was, fortuitously, to be useful to me later, but as the end of the financial year approached a considerable amount remained unspent.

A few miles away from Abak at Ukpom a side road had a particularly steep descent to a narrow bridge with an equally sharp climb on the far side, both the 'down' and the 'up' being made the more dangerous by heavy erosion during the rains. The villagers were in fact quite good at filling in the fissures, but it was a work of Sisyphus, one downpour and the previous day's work would be washed away. Some form of tar-coat was needed and I experimented, vainly, with a Shell product called 'Colas B' which, while I knew it would not take heavy or repeated traffic was, I was assured by the local Shell manager, suitable for what I had in mind. Certainly it looked fine when first put down, but it turned out not to bind satisfactorily with the earth so that when I drove my car (gingerly) over the laid surface, the backward spin of the wheels lifted it off in strips from the red laterite beneath! I felt rather a fool, as may be imagined, and complained bitterly, so bitterly in fact that Shell offered to supply a little proper bitumen *free* to the Public Works road engineer (who had started surfacing the Abak/Ikot Ekpenne road for the government) so that it could be done professionally. The villagers got their road done in the end and my face was at least partially saved!

'Development' was reaching Abak. The tar road to Ikot Ekpenne, completed about the time I left the division, would make access easier and more comfortable. Work had started on building a modern bridge at Ikot Okoro to provide another crossing of the Kwa Ibo. There was a Colonial Development and Welfare Project for rural water supplies from which Abak 'township' was scheduled to benefit and I spent much time with a visiting water engineer walking the terrain and drawing up plans of the lines the pipes would follow. The benefits of this would be for my successors. For the present I was glad to obtain authorisation to build some new quarters for the district office staff and to haggle with the local contractors so as to get the best I could for the money available – in which of course I had the full support of the staff themselves! I doubt if the contractors on this occasion managed to get away with their usual tricks of using too low a sand/cement mix or unseasoned wood.

It should be noted, however, that an accompaniment to this activity was a marked increase in the number of non-British cars and lorries. In 1954 one saw the occasional Volkswagen 'Beetle' driven by a RC missionary; otherwise British Fords, Austins and Morris's dominated the market. Now, the smart car for the Nigerian lawyer or up-and-coming civil servant was an Opel Kapitan (or for those very sure of their future a Kommodore). British cars looked dowdy by comparison. The days of the 'Wa-Benz', as the 'big men' were known in East Africa because of their predilection of the excellent Mercedes cars, had not yet fully dawned but was clearly on the way.

Similarly, the new road projects that seemed to be under way all over the region were not being carried out by the PWD, the government's direct labour organisation. Slow and inefficient, its central initial stood for 'Waste' according to its detractors – even by British contractors. The new road projects were carried out by *French* firms (oh, the shame of it, 'Frogs' in our colony) which seemed to possess unlimited equipment (but not British, you know) and which surely only got the contract as a result of large 'dashes' – which was sometimes true!

Where all the money was coming from was not clear. Partly it was from past savings – the regional government was spending the sums accumulated by the Palm Oil Marketing Board to protect produce prices against international price falls such as occurred pre-war.[16] Local government authorities were similarly dissipating their 'reserves' (much to the despair of long-serving British DO's who prophesied that such profligacy would have to be paid for later and that money was being wasted).[17] An increasing amount of 'aid' was also becoming available, both from the British government and from international agencies. I have already commented on the fact that it was only when British political control was ended that large sums became available for economic development (when initially at any rate there was also a decline in the degree of rigorous financial control). As may be readily understood, this is something which my colleagues never cease to regret: 'If only', they say, 'we had had a tenth of the money now available what could we have done?' Indeed, looking at the way the country had been developed without external resources during the 50 years of British rule, one cannot but agree.

It was oil that was changing everything. After years of prospecting and innumerable failures (thus causing the Colonial Office to be ultra cautious) it was now certain that oil was there in commercial quantities. The revenue would transform Nigeria's economic future, so that it was now eminently credit-worthy. An ever-increasing number of Shell's employees were arriving, bringing with them an increased demand for local goods and services (and forcing up prices as a consequence) and demanding standards of amenities which were as unheard of to us government employees as ours were to a bush villager!

Thus, following my foray into road surfacing with 'Colas B', Lesley and I, when on a shopping trip to Aba, were invited to the house of a Shell employee. It was full of wonders. It was a 'storey' house, with an upstairs and with mosquito proofing such as my parents had had before the war in Malacca but which was rare in Nigeria. It also had air conditioning in the main bedroom! Visitors who were favoured were allowed in to this room to experience the sudden chill. No doubt our hosts could have made a tidy increase to their salary by charging a small entry fee! The awe we felt at this modern marvel was somewhat tinged with jealously. When a few weeks later an electrical fault resulted in a fire that completely destroyed the house there was in some quarters a feeling that this was proof that one was not meant to be cool on the equator!

Even in the bush the oil employees lived well. Lesley and I visited a camp on the far side of the division, sorry for these newcomers so far away, and prepared to be of any help that we could. We found a comfortable camp, a bore-hole supplying fresh, clean water, a generator for light and power, modern caravans with air conditioning and refrigerators and freezers full of cold store such as we could neither afford nor keep. We came away feeling like slum dwellers allowed a glimpse of a royal palace.

These were the living standards that would be thought essential in the future and that would be provided without question to expatriates and Nigerians alike by commercial firms (and by the British Foreign Office to its own staff). For the time being though, the government had no money to spend on this kind of thing and its servants, from being a privileged caste, would gradually fall further behind in the comfort and affluence stakes.

This created many problems for the newly qualified Nigerians who were entering the Public Service, particularly if, like the agricultural officer at Obio Akpa, they had married an English woman and brought her back to Nigeria. In such a case, the wife would often find herself resented by the Nigerian wives of her husband's colleagues and even more by those of his relations. All would be sharp to see if she was putting on airs; all would make certain that she did not escape (because she was white) such wifely chores as communal cooking and cleaning and the carrying of water. While on duty – to start with a Nigerian worked the same 'tours' as expatriates earning long leave in the same way – he would have a government house on the government station just as did his white colleagues; there, to some extent, his wife would be shielded. On 'leave' however, he would have to vacate his official quarter and would go back to his native village where his wife would be fully exposed to sarcastic jibes from old crones or jealous rivals. There would be no 'expatriation pay' – small though that was – to meet the costs of 'white men's' comforts. At the market, being a 'stranger' and not used to the art of bartering, she would be cheated and her husband would then complain that his 'chop' was worse and cost more than that of his friends. In the case of the agricultural officer's wife, she was isolated on the government farm, with no transport and with no one of her race to speak to except Lesley, if the latter was with me when I was touring that area. Lesley, however, although she listened with sympathy and understanding to what she was told knew that there was no way in which we could be of help in her domestic problems; indeed, to try to do so, would make matters worse.

All through these early months of 1959 my principal official task was organising in Abak the registration of voters in preparation for the Federal Elections that would be held later that year. This was no 'rush job', such as had preceded the 1954 Election. There was time to prepare and there was money.

In the East, five million copies of Form 1 (the application to register) were distributed, and there were three and a half million registration cards available to hand out to the individual electors once their names had been entered in the register. Four thousand ballpoint pens were issued as well, most of which failed to work!

(This piece of information along with much else is derived from Post's excellent and comprehensive study.) Of equal or even greater value to us in the field, however, was that a blind eye was turned to purchases 'for the registration' of all kinds of office equipment that we had read about in glossy magazines but could never have otherwise obtained, things like filing cabinets and adding machines, typewriters and duplicators that were not pre-war, in some cases even office chairs and tables. Luxury indeed, and enough extra money was available under the 'transport and travelling' sub-head to allow proper supervision of the registration process.

Training of the registration clerks had begun before Christmas and the process itself began in January. There was intense publicity. Although the circulation in Abak Division of the *Daily Times* (published in Lagos) was perhaps only two score copies it would be read aloud so that each copy might reach a hundred people or more. Similarly with the wireless; only a few owned radio sets but these few were affluent and influential. Finally, there was word of mouth; the party political machines being now far more highly organised than they had been five years earlier. The people, to whom elections were no longer another strange white man's *juju*, reacted well, and turned out in strength. (In Abak North West, one of the two single member constituencies into which the division was divided, registration was to total an astonishing 51.3 per cent of the total census population, one of the highest in the country.)[18]

This intense enthusiasm to register meant that there was pressure to include many who were manifestly underage. There was, of course, no system of registration of births and hence there were no birth certificates; the clerk had to rely upon appearance and local repute. In a rural area, though, where there still existed the customary classification of age-grades, this was not such a problem as in the towns. Nor did we have the problem of 'strangers', i.e. non-residents, to the same degree – a few Igbo traders in Abak, lorry drivers and prostitutes at Ika-na-Annang on the far side of the division where it was traversed by the Aba/Opobo road.

The question of what name to write in the register was to cause universal difficulties, just as it had in 1954 and for the same reasons. There were not many names in use at all – every family would have an Akpan (meaning eldest son); the name known in the village might not be the same as that a man had in his age-grade, while neither might accord with his private given 'family' name which might offend the spirits.

No particular problems arose but, nevertheless, I was not surprised to hear that there had been a complaint to the chief registration officer that I was favouring the Action Group/UNIP Alliance at the expense of NCNC. A Northern official, an Alkali (judge) I think, duly visited Abak. He made some enquiries and visited two registration centres selected by him (one of which happened by chance to be located in a village hall whose building I had assisted with community development money; the villagers were rather full of my praise as a result). The Alkali left quite satisfied that there was nothing improper. He was the first Northerner I had met (except for the Sardauna), tall, white robed, and, to my mind, most impressive.

Registration complete, the next task was to type out on wax stencils the manuscript lists of names, this typing being the justification for the expenditure on typewriters and duplicators to which I have referred. But even though we now had the necessary physical equipment, there remained the problem of finding the typists themselves, which was not easy in a relatively backward division. Eventually the task was done, but not as well as I would have liked and a number of minor errors were spotted in the checking carried out in Enugu and Lagos, which, while easily correctable, offended my pride in doing a job well.

Unfortunately, during this period I fell ill. We could not diagnose the trouble ourselves, but Lesley noticed that my stools were very pale while my urine was dark (this latter had led us to suspect black water fever). She described the symptoms on the telephone to the sister/doctor at Anua who decided that it was hepatitis and so Lesley drove me to the government hospital at Port Harcourt where the government medical officer, Dr Holgate, confirmed the diagnosis and had me put to bed.

Hepatitis has a depressive effect and I am by nature depressive so that my morale was pretty low. Fortunately Christopher had returned from his course so that the division would be looked after and Lesley was thoroughly capable, although I worried a bit about her being on her own with the two small children. However, there was nothing I could do – I was left feeling as weak as a kitten – except to wait for the illness to take its course. Fortunately the DO at Port Harcourt, Frank Kennedy,[19] I knew slightly and was a good chap. He called and brought books for me to read – I was bored to tears and this added to my melancholy – but he had young children of his own and he wished to take no risks of getting hepatitis himself. He was, also, packing up his own effects as he had decided to leave Nigeria. At last my urine stopped being dark brown and my stools began to return to that colour. My skin was still pretty yellow and I felt washed-out but I was pronounced fit to go home, with warnings about my diet, the need to avoid alcohol, to rest (!) and to be careful about possible long-term damage to my liver.

Tax collection, which had had to take second place during the period we were registering the population (not least because people might have assumed that the whole registration exercise was no more than another attempt to check on taxpayers), now came to the fore. Abak had always had a miserable record for this (recently confirmed to me by Mr G. Hennessy, one of my predecessors), having a far lower proportion of its population paying than any of the neighbouring divisions and I was determined to get this put right. The Acting Chief Secretary, Hugh Elliot, promised me any funds I needed to pay for temporary tax clerks. So heartened, we began a blitz, both on non-payers for the current tax and those who were in arrears for previous years – I did not differentiate much between the two; what I wanted was money and I did not care whether it came from current or back taxes.

I had a good Nigerian staff officer to rely on and we had recently been supplied with a Volkswagen Kombi van – the first official transport we had had in the division. This made our tax collectors much more mobile and enabled half a dozen or more defaulters at a time to be arrested and brought back to prison until such time as their relatives produced the amount owing *plus* a fine. On some occasions we found we got the best results by arriving at a village in force at dawn before the men had dispersed to set about their daily tasks. I would go out myself on these occasions as I wanted to make sure that the tax collectors behaved; I did not wish there to be any danger of allegations that they were indulging in punitive raids or improperly ransacking houses.

The tax we were collecting was a 'head' tax of 15 shillings on each adult male. It had been an important source of revenue and while in terms of total yield it had long since become of less importance compared with indirect taxes, such as customs and excise duties, or even conventional income tax, it retained a symbolic importance. It represented the recognition by every male inhabitant of government's sovereignty. In return for this acceptance, the government provided peace, communications and the opportunity to sell their produce. Such was the political theory but the actual mechanics of tax collecting remained an unpleasant business. I was never happy sending an old man to jail even if I knew his family would bring the money owed within 24 hours.

Every week the takings from each tax centre were collected, counted and paid into the Treasury immediately. On the occasions the takings arrived late or the sub-accountant was unavailable, they would be kept in the little safe in my office, the key to which I kept on a string around my neck. I would have a police constable on guard throughout the night but I still slept uneasily until they could be officially handed over when morning came.

The result of this pressure was satisfactory. Each week the total take was in excess of that of either the two previous years and when I left the division I recorded that tax collection was in excess of £52,000 by comparison with £39,000 the year before (substantial then, but a miserably small sum to modern European eyes).

'Zik', Dr Azikiwe, the Premier of the Eastern Region and the founder and leader of the NCNC, chose to visit Calabar Province about this time and there was a big reception for him at Ikot Ekpenne, to which we were invited. I was somewhat concerned as to how I would be welcomed – Zik was after all the leader of the party to which Mr Eyo belonged, but to my relief, Zik could not have been more charming. The Premier in his long white flowing robes was standing in the centre of a large clearing with crowds gathered respectfully around the edges. He saw me and called me over for several minutes of friendly conversation in full view of the several hundred present. I felt confident after that that there would be no more open trouble from the local party, nor indeed was there. (I have had a soft spot for Zik ever since!)

Abak had been the centre of the powerful Idiong society which itself had had close connections with the Aro's whose 'Long *juju*' had been destroyed by the Arochuku expedition of 1906. Idiong itself appeared to be in abeyance but 'Ekpo', a related society was still very active. It was a male society whose members wore elaborately carved and painted wooden masks. While intruders on its ceremonies might be 'roughed up' I never received any complaint that warranted action to be taken against it. Lesley, though, used to object to their howling in the valley of the little river that ran a few hundred yards from the station. She found it disturbing as this occurred only when I was absent from the station and she was on her own.

Another incident that alarmed her was that fairly early one night (again when alone) she heard the sound of someone walking on the gravel paths that surrounded our house and then of a man jabbering at the front. Somehow she managed to alert the servants – not easy, for Africans generally went early to bed and were thereafter very difficult to arouse – and they in turn called the police. A constable was put on watch but as Lesley later commented, 'the noise of him marching around in his boots on the gravel was almost as disturbing as the previous sounds; but at least I knew

I was safe'. The guard was kept on until I returned but it became known that the culprit was a madman who wished to pray to the flag or the flagpole (at night there would have been no flag as it was lowered at sunset). He was arrested but prison was not the place for him; he was harmless even if disturbing, and I persuaded his village to take him back and keep him under control – somewhat reluctantly on their part.

My son Nicholas had been three months old when we arrived in Abak and bringing him up had not been easy. The medical mistreatment Lesley had had when Caroline was born had affected her own ability to feed Nicholas satisfactorily although she had tried to do so. Moreover, keeping milk and bottles sterile in the damp and heat was difficult, and nappy rashes were easy to develop. As a result he had always been a rather peaky, thin baby; then, shortly after his first birthday he developed an acute enteric infection, combining diarrhoea and vomiting, which was rapidly dehydrating him, a condition made worse by the damp heat. His temperature was rising and we were sure that he would die,[20] but we managed to drive him to the sister/doctor at Anua who gave him a glucose drip feed to restore his bodily fluids and a combination of most of the antibiotics she had (she did not believe in half measures!). His temperature began to fall almost immediately, but it was not until the next day that he was out of immediate danger. He remained a skinny, anaemic-looking little boy while he remained in Nigeria.

My brother, Geoff, then wrote to us proposing that he should visit Nigeria while on his way back to Sarawak at the end of his leave in England, the cost of the journey being in part comprised in his return leave passage. We were delighted at the prospect (it was more than three years since we had seen each other, and it was in fact to be another three and a half before we met again), and I drove up to Enugu to meet him.

In the hours before Geoff's arrival I made my enquiries about the possibility of transferring to another colony. I was told there was a request in for a candidate as Administrator, South Georgia, which did not sound suitable and that administrative officers were urgently needed for Nyasaland where a State of Emergency had been declared a few months before.[21] This latter posting sounded interesting. The climate was clearly much better. The political situation, on the other hand, was a bit disturbing.

It must be remembered though that at that time (mid-1959) most of Africa – and all areas where there were any substantial numbers of European settlers – was still under colonial rule and that there was no apparent reason that this was likely to change in the near future. Moreover, the British government appeared to be committed to the success of the Federation of Rhodesia and Nyasaland. I asked if I could defer a decision until I had had a chance to talk to Lesley; this was agreed.

During his all-too-short stay Geoff kept a diary from which the extracts below are taken.

> 18th June, 1959. *We left (Enugu) about 1.30 for the sixty mile drive to Okigwi where Alan Ferguson*[22] *was District Officer. We arrived about 4.30 p.m. for lunch at 5 p.m. Ferguson offered us drinks, but took nothing himself. I asked him if he was not going to join us. He replied that he did not drink. Later, in a rather absent-minded manner, he reached out for a tumbler and three quarters filled it with Cointreau, which he drank while we chatted.*
>
> *We reached Abak, where Ken was DO, in darkness at 8.30 p.m. Lesley came out to greet us as we got out of the van. It was good to see her. She looked well, but a bit tired. I felt pretty tired myself. I remember having a bath, dinner and bed, but little else.*
>
> *The next day*, Friday 19th June, *I went with Ken to his office. The ADO, Christopher (Chukwunyelu), took me off to show me the prison. I was impressed by its size, cleanliness and organisation. Later I sat in a Native Court with Ken while he heard reviews (appeals?). In the afternoon Ken drove me with Caroline to a small, natural pool or waterhole where we swam.*
> Saturday 20th June. *Accompanied Ken to look over the Qua Ibo Mission Hospital (Dr Kenneth Rowden), after which we spent an hour at a committee meeting of the South Annang District Council. Lots of rain.*
>
> Sunday 21st June. *Bob and Jean Graham paid a visit; also a Margery someone who runs an occupational training school (shorthand and typing etc.). Rain, rain. We went to the RC Hospital to get medicines for Nicholas's dysentery. Later we called in on Don Dixon (Senior District Officer at Uyo) for beer. Home after dark for supper.*
>
> Monday 22nd June. *Rainy morning. I walked into Abak by myself while Ken was at the office. Everybody very friendly and each person I passed on the road said good morning. Later Ken drove me to Ibesit to see a leper village. The village was laid out in the shape of a keyhole with a well at the centre. From there we drove on to visit a palm oil factory, only to find that it had just closed for three months.*

The roads and paths are pretty rough in some places, mostly where the sandy surface has been rutted and ruined by lorries and rain, but on the whole they are good. Everybody seems to carry everything on their heads, whether it is merely an umbrella or an enormous load of fruit or vegetables. Enamel basins piled full of goods appear to be popular containers for carrying head loads.

Geoff, of course, was not only my brother; he was a fellow officer in the Administrative Service doing much the same basic job as I was. Sarawak, where he was serving, however, while also in the tropics had few similarities, population densities in particular being tiny when compared with those in Abak and the surrounding divisions. This enabled Geoff and the Sarawak Service to conduct a much more personal, almost intimate, style of administration. Geoff, I think, thought little of the Eastern Region.

Our house, for example, was '*fairly small by Sarawak standards and the Government furniture, such as it was, was typically chunky, functional and unlovely*'. It may be recalled that my initial reactions on arrival in Nigeria, based on my childhood memories of Malaya, were very similar. Geoff found the '*great many oil palm plantations . . . dull and depressing. I felt that it would not be difficult for a sense of isolation to become a problem, particularly if one were unmarried. Perhaps this feeling arose partly from our brief call on Alan Ferguson*'.

At the end of his stay I took Geoff back to Enugu where we were staying with our friends the Grahams (they were 'camping' in the Deputy Governor's house while he was on leave; no one else would have had the accommodation to put us up!). Geoff then writes:

We had been kindly asked to lunch by the Governor of the Eastern Region, Sir Robert de Stapledon-Stapleton. Lady Stapleton was present, and fellow guests included M. Claude Cheysson, which was then Commissioner of the Anglo-French Joint Commission for Africa South of the Sahara. My memories of this luncheon are chiefly ones of embarrassment. The Governor knew Sir Anthony Abell, the Governor of Sarawak, who had formerly served in the Western Region of Nigeria. During lunch he asked me how Tony Abell was, and what sort of house he had in Sarawak. Although my next posting was to be Sir Anthony's Private Secretary I had only met him once and hardly felt qualified to say much. However, I had stayed at the 'Astana' (palace in Malay) in Kuching, the old home of the

Rajahs of Sarawak, and now Government House of the new colony, and had been enormously impressed by its unique architecture, large airy rooms, imposing setting and sense of history. Tactlessly I extolled these virtues, adding that the house seemed rather bigger that G.H. in Enugu. This was greeted with a silence, which I needlessly attempted to fill by describing how some of the upriver tribes were accustomed to show their affection and respect for Sir Anthony and senior Government officials by the young girls of the longhouse daubing the faces of their guests with a mixture of soot and kerosene as they disembarked from their longboats on arrival. Too late I detected some frostiness around the table. The Governor changed the subject and I was left hoping that I had not given the impression of unseemly frivolity in far-flung outposts of the Empire!

I did not know at the time – nor have I learned subsequently – what the grandly named Anglo-French Joint Commission was for. As for the Commissioner, M. Cheysson, his command of the English language was already impressive but I thought him rather full of himself. Other qualities must also have been apparent – in addition to the beauty of his wife – as his name, Cheysson, stuck in my mind.[23] He was inclined to linger after lunch too, I remember, which the Governor, Sir Robert Stapleton, did his best to discourage, as he wanted to talk to me about the political situation in Abak.

The others having left, I was able to describe how I saw the political scene in Abak, now no longer solidly NCNC, but not necessarily Action Group or UNIP either. The Governor did not appear surprised and said that this accorded with his own information. He then passed me on to his Secretary Joe Widdell to discuss my proposed transfer. I confirmed that I was interested in the Nyasaland posting. The climate was much less humid (there was even a 'cold' season in the Highlands); there was schooling for white children. The recent 'Murder Plot', the proclamation of a State of Emergency, the arrest of the newly returned African leader, Dr Hastings Banda, and the critical Report of the Devlin Commission were admittedly disturbing features. However, as Nyasaland formed part of a Federation with European-dominated Rhodesia it seemed improbable that independence would come quickly. Indeed, I might even still have a 'full' career there. However, all had to await a formal offer from the Secretary of State.

Returning to Abak, and probably driving faster than was safe, we nearly had a disaster. Turning a bend I saw the road ahead completely blocked with cattle being driven south for slaughter. I blasted the horn and braked, but the slippery red earth did not hold the tyres and I ploughed, albeit slowly by this time, into the herd, one bullock finishing up with his rear on the bonnet, the dart shaped motif on it being almost up his anus. The animal turned and gave an astonished look as if to see who had perpetrated this outrage, slid off and lumbered away, astonishingly unhurt. We were as relieved as he.

Driving on earth roads was always a bit hazardous in one way or another. The road from Abak to Uyo, for example, was an important trade artery, and the earth road was used by several score lorries each day as well as by motorcars, cyclists and Africans walking between the two townships. In the rainy seasons (which lasted for about nine months of the year) this road became little more than a muddy track, although never quite impassable. However, there were numerous potholes filled with water and it was impossible to avoid these creating great splashes which showered any passer-by on foot with dirty muddy water.

I was always embarrassed when these sheets of water would descend on African women drenching their colourful cloths with muddy stains. I felt that one ought to stop and compensate them for the mess that had been made of their *lappas*. In fact it was not really possible because there were too many potholes and too many women, nor did these appear unduly upset. They were used to being splashed if not by me then by others who did so without any apparent consideration.

I have mentioned earlier in this chapter that there was an oil palm research station in Abak Division, part of the West African Institute devoted to the study of that crop.[24] At this station attempts were being made to develop improved strains of oil palm. The wild palm that was indigenous to the country had a low yield both in weight of fruit and also the oil content of that fruit relative to the strains in use in the East Indies. Oil palm there was a plantation crop, which made it easier for those countries to select and replant with higher yielding varieties than was possible with our peasant farming with its scattered stands, indeed individual trees. The controlled use of fertiliser was also simpler in a plantation economy. The scientists told me also that although climatic conditions appeared identical there was a greater intensity of ultra-violet light in the East Indies, which had a stimulating effect on growth. Indeed, the only reason why Nigeria was currently dominant in the market was the political instability of Indonesia under Soekarno. This advantage was likely to be only fleeting. It was important, therefore, that we took full advantage of it by developing higher yielding plants (I was pleased to hear that a Dutch botanist would shortly be stationed permanently at Ibesit), and that the Agricultural Department distributed free seedlings of the new strain. There was also the continuing and long-recognised need to maximise the quality and quantity of oil extracted from the fruit.

Fruit was cut by hand, men scrambling up the palm tree stem with the aid of a rope looped round their waists and also around the tree, with a cutlass in one hand. It was hard and dangerous work; falls were inevitable and broken limbs frequent. It was not surprising therefore that the heavy bunches of fruit, once severed from the tree by a cut from the sharp blade, should be allowed simply to fall to the earth, although the bruising that resulted set off a fermentation that could spoil the oil. Prompt processing was essential if the free fatty acid (FFA) level was to be kept low enough for the oil to be sold for margarine making.

Traditionally the oil was extracted by boiling the fruit in great cauldrons, releasing the thick, red, vitamin-rich oil, but to raise the extraction rate steam-powered 'Pioneer Oil Mills' had been developed before the war. Their introduction into common use, however, had been slow. After the war, their installation had provoked a number of riots; African women feared that they would lose their perquisite of the value of the kernels, not trusting their men folk to hand back to them that element in the total value of the sale that the kernels represented. So they had rioted! Those days were passed. The mills, with their tall chimneys belching forth smoke and the clank of their machinery, were now an accepted, if incongruous, feature of rural life. However, they were often not well maintained so that the quality and percentage extraction rate of oil was no higher than that achieved traditionally. When I left Abak Division only one was doing quite well, a second had managed to obtain sufficient produce only by raising the price it paid until it looked to me as if its operations must be uneconomic. The third was closed for lack of sufficient tonnage of fruit being brought in for purchase (the growers found that they could get a better price in the markets).

Fears that Nigeria would lose its dominant position in the world vegetable oil market have proved to be only too well grounded and indeed the country is now an importer. Whether greater government support for agriculture might have prevented this I cannot say, but certainly the establishment of the Agriculture Department was pitifully small. In Calabar Province there was only one qualified agricultural officer who not only ran the farm at Obio Akpa as

I have mentioned, but also had to supervise the work of his relatively unqualified agricultural supervisors and assistants in the other six divisions. It is not surprising then, that many schemes, such as those boosting food production through the distribution of subsidised fertiliser and attempts to improve the strains of chickens, failed. No one who has seen the scrawny African bird pecking everywhere for some sustenance can doubt the need of that: they were tough to survive in that environment and tougher to eat!

Pig rearing was also being encouraged and there was one man in particular whose piggery I remember as a model. Pigs, in general, however, were liable to infestation with worms, and one leg of pork (bought by me from another farmer one day when Lesley was sick with fever) was found by the cook to be full of cysts.

The government, partly as a gesture to the minority tribes, had decided to replace the old provincial structure with a new one. Calabar Province was to be no more; Abak was now to be part of a new Annang Province with Ikot Ekpenne, which also had a large Annang population. On the whole my own division was pleased at this partial reunification of the Annangs, although indignant that it had not been coupled with more boundary drawing to the south where other Annangs lived in Opobo Division. It was claimed they wished to be reunited with their blood brothers (this, so far as I can tell from the census figure, has since been done). There was, however, much dispute over where the new provincial offices should be built, the number of seats to be allocated to each of the divisions in the new Provincial House of Assembly and other such matters, none of which had been finally resolved during my time.

As part of this reorganisation new posts of Provincial Secretary were created, much needed to enable the dwindling number of experienced officers to supervise the very newly qualified men now entering the Administrative Service. Abdul Atta, a son of the Atta of Igala whose family was not in favour with the Muslim Hausa elite of the Northern Province, was appointed Provincial Secretary of Annang Province. He was well educated but his reputation was a bit chequered. However, I liked him personally and we got on well together. The Provincial Commissioner (a new and political post, ranking as a junior minister), however, liked neither of us and was glad when both of us left.[25]

Although there were no other European government officers in Abak Division there were some in other divisions and there was a certain amount of social entertaining. This normally took the form of lunch on Saturdays or Sundays at which the main dish was curry, groundnut stew or palm oil 'chop' (the difference being that the latter was made with palm oil, the former with crushed groundnuts). Side dishes of boiled egg, of coconut, of various hot peppers, of chopped fried onion and of banana would be served as an accompaniment. There would also be heaps of rice. Such a meal might in fact not be eaten until late afternoon, the time beforehand being spent in drinking beer or gin. It was a marvel that the cook could keep the food appetising given that he had no real idea when it would be eaten and the primitive nature of the kitchen: somehow they did.

My own time in Abak was now approaching its end. Oputa Udoji[26] had recovered from his temporary disgrace and was now Chief Secretary to the Premier and Head of the Eastern Civil Service. As such he made a tour of the region in the course of which he visited Abak. While there he told me that Neil Kay was being moved from his post as Establishments Secretary to that of Permanent Secretary, Agriculture. Oputa wanted me back in Enugu to take over the Establishments Secretary post. A Nigerian, Mr Emeghara, would be posted in as divisional officer (the initials DO being kept, but the full title being subtly, but quite logically, changed), and I should hand over to him as soon as possible.

There were a number of protests from the people of the division at the idea of having a 'black DO'. I do not think that these were intended merely as sycophancy. There was no idea of a 'Nigerian nationality': the country was of far too recent a creation for that. An Igbo was felt to be a potential oppressor. On the other hand an Ibibio or an Annang would have been in a difficult position vis-à-vis the government; the differentiation between public and private persona was (is?) no more perceived in modern Africa than it was until recently in most of Western Europe.

Our last days in Abak were a frenzy of activity. I had to write my handing-over notes and, when Emeghara arrived, introduce him round the division (fortunately Christopher[27] by now knew it well and would be able to fill in any gaps), and to make my own 'goodbyes'; Lesley had to supervise the packing. Then all was done, our loads were in the lorry and we were off.

It had been a hard but fascinating year, constantly busy – as I write this I am conscious of all the other things that were done, but which I have not had space to describe here. We had all had illnesses of varying degrees of severity. We had both had many frustrations, but we could also remember the drama of thunderstorms at night, the sky being lit like day with sheet lightning one moment, showing all the palm trees bent under the violent wind. Then there would be a deafening clap of thunder, and the sudden pitch black until the lightning came again, all to be climaxed by a 'cataract from the cliff of heaven', as the skies opened and the rains descended. Then there were the 'tick birds', buff-backed herons, as they are properly called, so many in numbers that the grass on the station compound looked white until they would take off all at once filling the sky with the noise of their wings. There was the rhythmic singing of the prisoners as they chopped the grass on the station while the warder dozed in the shade, and the scarlet of flame trees doubly brilliant against the dark dull green of oil palms.

Above all, there were the people, independent-spirited and hot-tempered, for whom I had felt responsible during the past year and whom I would never forget.

Chapter 23
Responsibility and a farewell to Nigeria

When we reached Enugu it was to find that my future was not as clear-cut as I had been led to believe. It was still intended that I should take over the Establishments Division, but the Public Service Commission had not actually given its approval. Nor was it even certain when it would be put to the Public Service Commission. All I could be assured of was that Oputa Udoji (Chief Secretary to the Premier and Head of the Civil Service) was in favour of it. So also was the Governor. The latter no longer had any official responsibility vis-à-vis the civil service, but he still had a certain amount of influence, as his relationship with Zik was much closer than that of Clem Pleass (his predecessor).

Sir Robert wanted a British officer with some past experience in Establishments work to take this job because a new inducement scheme (called 'Special list B') was about to start aimed at retaining British staff (especially the remaining administrative officers). I suited the requirements so he wanted me to make sure that it went off smoothly. The Colonial Office in London had fought hard for this scheme against the UK Treasury and the British tradition of financial non-involvement in colonial affairs. The CO, unusually, had won. It did not want its victory turned into defeat by any administrative hiccup in Enugu.

This still left Lesley and me uncertain. What to do? We had already served the normal 18-month tour during which Lesley had had the additional fatigue of bearing a second child who could very easily have died and I had been pretty ill with hepatitis. On the other hand I dearly wanted the glory of filling a senior post before I left, even if only in an 'acting capacity'. Moreover the extra money would be well worth having. Finally we decided that she should fly to England with the children and that if nothing were decided about my position I would follow in 2–3 weeks. If it were decided that I should 'act' I would stay on until the end of the year.

Lesley was not very happy about leaving me on my own again, but she found that Neil Kay's wife was also returning to England and the two wives agreed that Neil and I should share his house.

This would be a good deal less expensive for both of us. In theory, also, each would keep an eye on the behaviour of the other. Ironically, only a few days later, but just after Lesley had left, the approval of my acting appointment was given and I began work with the division whose staff I knew so well.

The new scheme in effect paid British staff immediately 90 per cent of the amount that they would have got if they had left on the understanding that they wouldn't in fact leave for three years. During these years an officer's pension would be increasing commensurately with his length of service; in addition, however, if he were promoted, the lump sum payable would be recalculated on the basis of his new salary and age; he would then receive 90 per cent of the difference between the 'old' and the 'new' 'compensation' totals. It sounded so good that everyone was suspicious of hidden snags. In fact there were not any. It was a very good scheme.

The British staff after years of virtual penury would have enough to live on. Eastern Nigeria was able to keep a cadre of experienced men who would be there for at least three more years and would be able to train up enough Nigerians to keep the government machine working. And Britain, what did Britain get out of it? Well, at a cost of less than a million pounds (most of which would eventually be spent in Britain) she escaped having egg all over her face as result of botching up de-colonisation. Also, and very much more important, it had now become clear that Nigeria's oil reserves were substantial: the oil was in the East, it was British firms who held the major concessions, their investments were in millions, and their potential profits even more. A relatively stable and prosperous Eastern Nigeria was worth many times more than a million pounds.

There were in fact no snags that I can remember, nor any difficulties. I think that everyone 'eligible' accepted the new offer and stayed the three years agreed; some stayed longer; some almost until the outbreak of the civil war in 1966. However, even before I had read the files and got the procedures going, there was another matter I was told to deal with. I have written in earlier chapters about the way in which, after 1954, the four civil services had gone their own way in such matters as staff gradings and conditions. Now the Federal government proposed a way to prevent things getting worse, perhaps even to smooth out what had gone wrong over the past five years. This meant a committee of ministers from all four governments with a sub-committee of officials.

Now, at that time, it was very difficult in the East to get ExCo to decide anything. No minister wanted to take any decision in case he upset Zik and Zik was interested only in the forthcoming Federal Election. However this proposal seemed to slip by without any discussion at all. Oputa simply gave me the file and told me to go to Lagos for the meeting, 'it's only a meeting, Ken. Let me know what happens', he said, and then he went off.

I was flabbergasted. The Permanent Secretary to the Federal Prime Minister would be in the chair of the officials' meeting and it was clearly thought by them that the regional civil services would nominate an equivalent (in our case that would have been Oputa). In fact they would get me – not even yet officially 'acting' – representing the East. Nor had I any instructions at all. I will not, of course, pretend that I was not also a bit flattered at the prospect of 'mixing (I would not go so far as to say "fighting") so much above my weight'. The arrangements, also, were flattering – a government car to meet me at Lagos airport and take me to the Mainland Hotel, the best hotel in Lagos. But I was also worried. I had read the agenda and it was clear that I was expected to have all sorts of position papers and 'government views' on the topics for discussion. I did not have anything.

In a letter dated 19 August I wrote 'the meeting was rather a disappointment . . . too formal and far too theoretical. I raised a few eyebrows I think when I said that my ministers would not read the principles underlying salary grading – all that they were interested in was the results. But then it is clear that they (i.e. those in Lagos) think that we in the East are a bunch of hicks, nice enough chaps but rather retarded in our mental processes'.

I do not think anyone read my report when I returned to Enugu, nor did I ever get any more instructions in the future. Papers about future meetings of the 'National Council on Establishments' continued to arrive, were marked to me, I dealt with them, attended their meetings in Lagos and reported back to Enugu, but all in a limbo. I might have been operating on a different planet.

Although (indirectly) it was made clear to me by the Governor's Office that the smooth working of the 'Special list B' scheme must be given top priority, I also had to deal with the ordinary day-to-day work with the Establishments Division. This had just been made harder by the appointment in the Premier's Office at Permanent Secretary grade of a man from Rivers Province to whom I was meant to report. This man, although nice enough, was of very moderate ability and with even less backbone; he did not want to take any decisions. So he simply 'sat on' files and would deny ever having received them, even if the office registry clearly showed them as being marked out to him. He was also jealous of Albert

Osakwe, an Owerri Igbo, and of Ikpi (from Ogoja Province), both of whom, he felt, were trying to muscle in on him, going so far as to tell me that if either ever asked me for information I was to refuse to give it!

As the approach of Federal independence grew nearer, the cost of living escalated. It was now plain that Nigeria would be able to export oil in commercial quantities and this increased the appetite of the circling commercial sharks, confidence tricksters and financial wide-boys. The sheer size of Nigeria also attracted the foreign offices of both major and minor powers, seeking influence in Africa's most heavily populated state. There was an influx in Lagos in particular, curbed only by the lack of first-class hotel accommodation and the non-availability of houses to rent. Still there was enough of an inflow to push up the cost of living, while builders were making a killing putting up new hotels and building fine houses. The demand for people with professional qualifications (whether these were European or Nigerian, indeed, perhaps, even more particularly the latter) was soaring. Government salaries, unchanged since Gorsuch five years ago, were becoming totally uncompetitive.

The Federal government accordingly proposed a new salaries revision. This was discussed at the next National Council of Establishments meeting, but I pointed out the difficulty this might cause the East (still the poorest region). All I could agree to was to put the case up. This I did on my return, sending, through my immediate boss, a draft Memorandum to Executive Council. So far as I can tell he acted as usual and did nothing about it. The Federal government – or at least some senior officials – got upset at the delay and I had a number of increasingly irate telephone calls from Lagos. I told my boss what was happening and that an immediate answer was wanted. He, suspecting trouble, became 'un-got-at-able'.

The Governor-General's Office in Lagos then phoned the Governor's Office in Enugu to complain that I was being unhelpful. As it happened I was with the Governor's Secretary (having a beer – it was Saturday lunchtime) when the call came, so I was able to explain what was going on. The Governor's Secretary and I found out where my man lived. There was no answer to a telephone call so we called at his house, roused him from his nap and 'persuaded' him to get the paper to ExCo. This really did not commit us to anything immediately; the paper recommended that we accepted the proposed new Salaries Commission while explicitly reserving the right not to be bound by the findings. It was a face-saving formula; in practice it would be impossible for any government not to go along with any halfway sensible proposals but Eastern Region ministers were not possessed of much backbone.

The next thing to do, though, was to work out what 'we' (the Eastern Region) would propose to the Salaries Commission. I worked closely with the Ministry of Finance (with another UK Treasury civil servant, Williams by name, who had replaced Christopher Fogarty as Permanent Secretary) in calculating how much a revision would cost and how much we could afford. We took various hypothetical increases, not necessarily a flat 'across the board' rate and agreed our responses when the Commissioner (a Mr Carlyle, formerly head of the Federal Treasury) came to Enugu. I think that the final recommendations were not sent out until after I had left Nigeria at the end of the year.

Meanwhile Lesley had stayed a few weeks with her parents and a few weeks with mine, both sides being concerned about how skinny Nicholas was. He was indeed little more than skin and bone, not having recovered fully from his illnesses at Abak. A few months in England however, was to put this right. Lesley was determined that this time we would rent a house of our own, and she found something suitable in *The Lady*. There were plenty of 'seaside-holiday lets' available, and their rents in winter were low enough even for us. So she took a house at Seaview on the Isle of Wight, which was to prove very satisfactory.

I had a minor problem of my own. While I was lying down one afternoon someone came to the door. I did not want to keep him waiting while putting on my calliper, so I tried hobbling through without it, as I was quite accustomed to do. Unfortunately, on this occasion I slipped and fell. Naturally, I made light of it at the time. The next day, however, my arm hurt like mad so I saw a doctor. He arranged for it to be x-rayed and this showed that it was fractured. The doctor, however, my good friend Savage, agreed that a simple sling (and some care) would be enough – no need for a plaster or elaborate bandaging.

The subject of ministerial organisation then came up again. When ministries had first been created in Eastern Nigeria it had been done by giving a minister, of Agriculture (for example), a permanent secretary and two or three administrative officers to form the ministry whilst the technical departments executing the policies of the ministry – the Department of Agriculture, the Department of Forestry and the Department of Fisheries, etc. in this particular case – remained virtually independent entities and carried on operating as they had done before. This had the great advantage of ensuring that ministerial interference in the technical departments was kept at a minimum. However some ministers were not satisfied. They wanted to be able to intervene directly when it suited them – not unknown nowadays in Britain either. So, there was pressure from ministers to integrate the technical departments more closely into the ministry headquarters. This would be a way, also, of enabling them to get plum jobs for Nigerian technical staff. It was one of those areas where there were in fact good arguments on both sides, but behind any rational arguments lay the wish of ministers to have their 'clients' around them, whom they could control and upon whom they could rely.

As on all occasions when we were separated I wrote every few days to Lesley but re-reading my letters to her and hers to me now show me how little I understood her problems. Trying to set up 'house' in England with two small children whose own lives had been disrupted by the move to that country, not knowing where to buy things, with no adult to talk to and, above all, with having to manage on a minimum amount of money, must have been very hard. It was not made easier by her local vicar. Lesley, only recently confirmed, had to take the children to church (some of the elderly congregation objected to the children being there). The vicar then called during the week and told Lesley that if she brought the children again he would preach against her from the pulpit. It sounded unbelievable. Lesley was terribly upset – and so was I when she wrote to me about it.

By about the middle of November virtually all work ceased pending the Federal elections of mid-December. Ronald Wraith (who had lectured on my Colonial Service course at London University) was the Federal Election Commissioner while 'Dicky' Floyer was overseeing the arrangements in the Eastern Region. The latter asked me to set up a small office to co-ordinate the results, staffed 24 hours a day from the time polling finished until the last result was proclaimed. I was glad to be involved (although it was perhaps not without irony that it had been Dicky who had been sent down to investigate my own conduct in Abak the previous year and that now I was helping to co-ordinate the running of the election throughout the region!).

The time and money available to prepare for the election over the past year now paid off. Counting in all the constituencies went smoothly and I cannot recall any incidents in the East. In my 'co-ordinating' office I had got a very big fridge out of the PWD, continually stocked with beer, and every available secretary manned the telephone lines. Not surprisingly we had a continuous flow of visitors and enjoyed ourselves enormously. More importantly, the NCNC held the Igbo heartland but, as I expected, most of the Calabar Province seats went to the UNIP/Action Group opposition.

With the election over and the Special list scheme working smoothly it was now time for me to depart. At the last meeting of the National Council on Establishments that I attended, the newly confirmed Federal Prime Minister presided for a short time. Peter Stallard, the normal chairman, introduced us all to him, taking the opportunity in my case to say that I was shortly leaving Nigeria on transfer. The Alhaji Sir Abubakar Tafawa Balewa was most gracious, thanking me for my services and wishing me well in my future career. I felt very honoured; I was after all not yet 30 and he was the newly elected leader of Africa's most populous state. The prime minister was a man of great presence and charm and his murder in 1966 precipitated the chain of unrest that dogged Nigeria for the next 36 years.

It had been Oputa's wish, incidentally, that at this last meeting I should be accompanied by Ben Odinamadu, a very capable young Nigerian, whom I think Oputa planned should take over from me. For some reason, however, he was not able to be with me so that this last meeting (for me) of the National Council was once again 'all white'. And yet within a year the country would have full independence.

Back in Enugu, Oputa was also very gracious. He tried to persuade me to stay, 'We want to keep you Ken', he said, but when I explained that the heat of Nigeria and my calliper made life more than just uncomfortable, he did not persist. He also bought my car from me for a (literally) knockdown price (I had been advertising it for sale at £150 and had been surprised to get no offers at all; he offered me a £100 in cash with a charming smile and, I am told, used it as a taxi for some years). I was to meet him again seven years later – during the Biafran war – when he was working for an international organisation and I for the Malawi government. Our meeting then was as friendly as had been this parting.

It was typically West African that I should leave with a tropical complaint. At an outside evening 'drinks party' I felt a sudden painful nip on my temple. The next morning I saw in the mirror two or three raised blisters that itched painfully. One broke and the white watery contents stung as they rolled down my face, raising blisters as they did. A cantharides beetle, a 'beastie' of which I had never heard, had bitten me. I have never heard of anyone else having been so unfortunate, the beetle (sometimes known as 'Spanish fly') is normally only used for its supposedly aphrodisiacal properties – see Robert Graves's 'Claudius' novels). I cannot say what effect it has in that way; indeed I would have thought the opposite.

So in December I left Enugu for the last time. The five and a half years I had had in Nigeria had taught me much. I had lost much of my initial starry-eyed innocence. The Empire that had still seemed so sturdy in 1954 was now visibly crumbling. I had lost an arm and a leg and gained a daughter and a son. I had experienced depths of misery that I had never expected. I had had moments of great pride and happiness. I had played a part in ensuring that the service I had joined with such pride in 1954 and which in 1957 and early 1958 looked as if it would be broken, had survived. The Administrative Service still provided a framework for government. The law was still obeyed; government still governed.[1] I have never returned but in spite of all its frequent awfulness I still have affection for Eastern Nigeria and the ebullient, noisy, vital people I had known.

The future for them was not going to be easy. Perhaps as many as a million were to die in the war at the end of which the East was devastated and the Igbos defeated. But since then there has been a resurgence, economically if not politically. As Sir Robert Stapledon wrote in a despatch,

> Any attempt to forecast the future must take into account one curiously obstinate feature of the Region's recent history – the fact that an erratic, spendthrift and incompetent Government has, despite its failings, contrived to muddle through without going bankrupt and without forfeiting permanently any appreciable degree of public support. This phenomenon which has mystified many observers is explicable only by reference to the tradition of Igbo solidarity; to the Igbos the N.C.N.C. is *their* party and its leadership is therefore sacrosanct (a negative but convincing proof of this explanation is provided by the non-Igbo areas of the Region where the people have no hesitation in giving formal expression to their dissatisfaction). It follows that much depends and must continue to depend upon the whims of a very few leaders and in particular upon the whims of *the* leader.[2]

And so it has continued.

Biographical notes

Arden, Donald, the Rt. Rev., CBE (b. 1916) Ordained Priest 1939, appointed Bishop 1961, elected Archbishop of Central Africa 1971. Retired 1981. Assistant Bishop, Diocese of London.

Armitage, Sir Robert (1906–90) Admin Off. Kenya 1929, Fin. Sec. Gold Coast (Ghana) 1948–54, Gov. Cyprus 1954–5, Gov. Nyasaland 1956–61.

Anderson, David (b. 1929) ed. Hale School, Perth, WA, Llb UWA 1951, Barrister and Solicitor 1953, Judge of Family Court 1977–99, Member of Order of Australia (AM) 1980, Deputy National President Royal Lifesaving Society 1979–82, WA president 1970–85.

Arrowmith, Keith (b. 1924) War Service 1943–7, Admin Off. Nigeria, MBE, 1949–57, Uganda 1957–65, Hong Kong 1966–9, Sec. R. Inst. Ch. Surveyors 1970–4, European Commission (Agriculture) 1974–89.

Ashworth, Frank (1925–2004) Admin. Off. E. Nigeria 1951–61, Chartered Accountant, France 1973–81, IoM 1981–92.

Atta, Abdul Aziz (1922–69) Admin Off. E. Nigeria 1948, S. Dist. Off. 1957, Perm. Sec., Fed. Min. of Fin.

Azikiwe, Namde ('Zik') (1904–96) ed. American universities. Newspaper editor and politician. A founder of the National Council of Nigeria and the Cameroons (NCNC) 1944 and President NCNC 1946–. Premier of the Eastern Region 1954–9, Governor General of Federation of Nigeria 1960, President 1963, ousted by coup 1966.

Baker, Colin, Prof., MBE (b. 1929) Admin. Off. Nyasaland/Malawi 1954, Asst Dist. Com./Dist. Com., Mpemba Col. Admin. Deputy 1962, Principal 1967–71, Dir. Admin., Ife Univ. Nigeria 1971–4, Professor and Founding Dir. Cardiff Business School, Univ. of Wales, Prof. Emeritus.

Barnes, Geoffrey, CBE (b. 1932) ed. Hollingbury Prep School, Brighton, Guildford Prep School, Perth, Dover College, Kent, St Catharine's College, Cambridge. Second Lieut. R. West Kents; Admin. Off. Sarawak 1956–67, Hong Kong 1969–91, Secretary for Security 1988–1991.

Barson, Derek (1922–80) Mentioned in Despatches, Burma, Admin. Off. Nyasaland, 1949–64, Asst Sec. RNLI 1964–6, Sec. and then Dir. Gen. Br. Red Cross 1966–80.

Barton, Philip (b. 1917) Capt. Burma Frontier Force 1940, Cadet Admin. Service Nigeria 1948, Perm. Sec. Eastern Nigeria 1958.

Blades, Derek (b. 19370 Statistician Malawi 1964, Director of Statistics 1969– ?, OECD.

Bourne, J. ('Jim') (b. 1917) War Service, Royal Signals (Captain), PoW, Colonial Off. 1947 (seconded Tanganyika 1953–5), CRO 1961 (sec. CAO 1962), Deputy High Commissioner Zanzibar 1963–5, Counsellor and Dep. HC Malawi 1966–70, Ambassador Somalia 1970–3, Consul-General Istanbul 1973–6.

Broadbent, Simon (b. 1942) Economist Malawi 1964–71, Econ. Adviser FCO, S. Econ. Adviser 1978, Ch. Econ. Adviser 1984–93, Visiting Fellow NIESR.

Byatt, Sir Hugh, KC, VO, CBE (b. 1927) Royal Navy 1945–8, Administrative Officer Nigeria 1952–7, Diplomatic Service (Bombay, sec'ded Cabinet Off. Lisbon, Mozambique, Inspectorate Nairobi, Ambassador Angola 1978, Portugal 1981–6).

Castle, Baroness Barbara (1910–2002) ed. Bradford Girls' Grammar School and St Hugh's College, Oxford, elected MP for Blackburn 1945, Chairperson of the Labour Party (1958–9), Minister of Overseas Development (1964–5), and subsequently held portfolios of Transport, Employment and Productivity (1968–70) and Social Services (1974–6), MEP (1979–89), joined House of Lords 1990.

Clarke, R. ('Reg') A. (b. 1921) Admin. Cadet Nigeria 1947, Asst Fin. Sec. 1954, Dep. Perm. Sec., Fed. Min of Finance 1959–63. IBRD 1963–72, Director of Personnel.

Codrington, John, KCMG (b. 1919) RNVR 1940–2, Royal Marines 1942–6, Admin. Off. Gold Coast 1947, Nyasaland 1968, Fin. Sec. Bahamas 1964–70, Fin. Sec. Bermuda 1974–7.

Cole, Sir David, KCMG, MC (1920–97) Foreign Office, First Sec. UK Del. UN 1948–51, First Sec. BHC New Delhi 1953–6, C'illor Ghana 1963–4, High Commissioner Malawi 1964–7; Minister India 1967–70, Amb. Thailand 1973–8.

Cole–King, Susan (1935–2000) Priest and Doctor. Medical Officer Malawi 1966–75, WHO, UNICEF, ordained 1988, Canon Christchurch, Oxford.

Collins, Chris, CBE (b. England 1920) Army 1939–46, Rhodesia Civil Service 1947–66, Undersec. Malawi Treasury 1966, Dep. Sec. 1967–73, Delegate of CEC to Sierra Leone 1976–80, Gambia 1980–5, retired to Alderney.

Cormack, Ian, MBE (1935) Administative Officer 1958, Principal Treasury 1967.

Creagh-Coen, Sir Terence Bernard, KBE, CIE (1903–70) ICS (Punjab) 1927, Indian Political Service 1935, transferred to service of Govt of Pakistan 1947, Chairman Public Service Commission, Eastern Region, Nigeria 1956–8. Author: *The Indian Political Service: A Study in Indirect Rule*, (London: Chatto and Windus, 1971).

Dale, Phillip, OBE (b. 1921) Admin. Off. Nyasaland 1949, S. Admin. Off. 1962, Ch. Estab. Off. 1966–70. Sec. for Public Service Solomons 1971–5, Ch. Sec. Turks and Caicos 1975–9, Government Sec. St Helena 1980–4.

Dewar, Robert, CMG, CBE (b. 1923) .Forestry Service Nigeria and Nyasaland 1944–64 (Ch. Cons. Forests), Perm. Sec. Min. Nat. Resources 1964–7, Econ. Affairs 1967–8, World Bank 1968–84.

Dickinson, Alan, MBE (1925–99) Admin. Officer Nyasaland 1950, Sen. Asst Sec. Finance 1962–5, retired, Asst Reg. Univ. E. Anglia.

Dickson, Hanmer ('Dicine') YWS (1923–2005) Sandhurst 1941, War Service Hodsons Horse and R. Artillery, Admin Off. Somaliland 1951–61, Malawi 1961–75.

Elliott, Hugh P., CMG (b. 1911) Cadet Nigeria 1934, Seconded Colonial Office 1946, Supervisor Colonial Service courses, London 1948–50, Admin. Officer Cl II 1954, Perm. Sec. Eastern Nigeria 1955, Adviser to Govt of Eastern Nigeria 1962–7.

Ferguson, Alan (1930–78) Admin. Off. E. Nigeria 1954–68, Asst Fin. Sec. Solomon Islands 1969–71, consultant.

Finniston, Sir 'Monty' (1912–91) Ch. Exec. Brit. Steel Corp, Chair 1973–8, Chancellor Stirling Univ.

Foot, 'Harry', MBE (b. 1935) Administrative Officer 1958, Principal Min. Econ. Affairs 1967, Treasury 1968, Undersec. 1970.

Franks, Robert, Economist Malawi 1970–3, IMF 1975–90.

Fricker, Geoffrey (b. 1919) Admin. Off. Malaya 1946, Nyasaland 1955, Ch. Estab. Off. 1962–4.

Fogarty, Christopher, CB (b. 1921) Admin. Service 1939–40, 1946–58 (RAF war service), Min. of Finance of Eastern Nigeria, 1956, Asst Sec. HM Treasury 1959, further Treasury posts culminating in Dep. Sec. Treasury and Dir. of European Development Bank 1972–6.

Graham, Robert, OBE (b. 1930) Admin. Off. E. Nigeria 1954, Private Secretary and then Secretary to the Governor 1962, Provincial Secretary Uyo, Sole Commissioner Okrika Riots, SDO Aba, Provincial Secretary Onitsha, retiredd 1965. Foundation Secretary to the University of Nottingham Medical School 1966–92.

Gunning, Sir (Orlando) Peter (1906–64) Cadet Nigeria 1931, Military Service 1941–5, S. Resident 1955, Deputy Governor E. Nig. 1956, Chairman Public Service Commission Uganda 1959–62.

Hardie–Bick, Peter

Hart, Baroness Judith, Min. Overseas Dev. 1969–70, 1974–5, 1977–9.

Hawes, Sir (Richard) Brunel (b. 1893) ed. Stonyhurst and St Thomas's, Military Service 1914–19, Med. Officer Kedah 1923, Prof. of Medicine King Edward VII Medical College, Singapore, Consulting Physician to Colonial Office 1943–61.

Hopkin, Sir (William Aylsham) Bryan (b. 1914) Dir. Nat. Inst. Econ. and Social Res. 1952–7, Economic Planning Unit Mauritius 1965, Min. of Dev. 1966–7, DG Econ. Planning, DM 1967–9, Dep. Chief Econ. Adviser, Treasury 1970–2.

Howard, 'Phil',Gen. Manager, Booker Bros., Malawi, Chair Air Malawi, Ltd.

Jaffu, George (b. 1938) Administrative Officer 1964, Undersec. Treasury 1968, Sec. to Treasury 1971, Sec. Pres. and Cabinet 1973–5, detention and retirement. Gen. Man. Lonrho's operations in Malawi 1978–2000.

Jones, Sir Glyn (1908–92) Admin. Off. N. Rhodesia 1931, Prov. Commissioner 1955, Sec. Native Affairs 1958, Ch. Sec. Nyasaland 1960, Governor Nyasaland 1961, Gov. Gen. Malawi 1964–6.

Kalilombe, Peter (b. 1935) Administrative Officer 1962, S. Admin. Off. 1966, Perm. Sec. Trade and Industry 1967.

Kay, Neal (1921–) Administrative Officer Nigeria (Eastern) 1948, S. Asst Sec. Estabs 1957, Permanent Secretary Ag. 1959, NHS Scotland 1962.

Kennedy, Sir Francis (Frank), CBE (b. 1926) Administrative Off. Nigeria 1953, Prov. Sec. Port Harcourt 1958–9, HM Diplomatic Service 1961 (Minister Lagos, Ambassador Angola, Consul-Gen. New York), British Airways 1986, Director 1987–96.

King, Sir Richard ('Dick'), KCB, MC (1920–98) N. Irish Horse 1940–6 (Major, Cassino), Min. Overseas Dev. Perm. Sec.

Lawrence, Henry (b. 1925) Admin. Off. Nigeria 1950, DO Nsukka 1956–7.

Lewis, Brig. Paul, Commander, Malawi Army.

Mann, Michael, the Rt. Rev., KCVO (b. 1924) War Service Dragoon Guards 1943–6, Admin. Off. Nigeria, 1946–55, Priested 1957, Vicar Port Harcourt, Nigeria 1962–7, Bishop Suffragen Dudley 1974–6, Dean of Windsor 1976–89, Chaplain to Order of the Garter, Asst Bishop, Diocese of Gloucester 1989 to present.

Michael. Ian, CBE (b. 1915) Prof. Ed. Khartoum Univ 1963–4, Vice-Chancellor University of Malawi 1964–73, Vis. Prof. Ed. Cape Town Univ. 1981.

Minford, Patrick, Professor, CBE (b. 1943) Tr. Economist Malawi 1956–9, UK Treasury 1971–3, Ed. NIESR 1973–4, Prof. Applied Econ. Liverpool Univ. 1976–7, Prof. Econ. Cardiff Business School 1997, Member Council Econ. Advisers 1993–6.

Morris, 'Terry', OBE (1918–2006) Colonial Audit Service 1949–61 (Sierra Leone, Gambia, Aden, Nigeria), Auditor-General Malawi 1964–76.

Moxon, Peter, Major, KAR, M Leg. Ass. Malawi.

Mullins, Patrick (1922–92) War Service Royal Navy, Admin. Off. Gold Coast 1951–3, Nyasaland 1953–64 (Sec. to Public Service Commission and Clerk to Leg. Ass.), Dep. Sec. BBC 1965–.

Munthali, Charles (b. 1935) Administrative Officer 1961, S. Asst Sec. 1964, Perm. Sec. 1966–72, World Bank 1972–95.

Neale, Kenneth, OBE (b. 1922) Lt. RNVR 1940–6, Home Civil Service, Colonial Office 1951 (Cyprus 1957/9), Central Africa Office 1962–4, FCO Counsellor Diplomatic Service, 1964–7, Home Office, Asst Sec. 1967–70, Dir. and Controller depts dealing with prisons, Council of Europe.

Norman–Walker, Sir Hugh, OBE (1916–85) ICS 1938–48, Admin. Off. Nyasaland 1949, Dev. Sec. 1954, Sec. to Treasury 1960–5, HM Commissioner Botswana 1965–6, Gov. Seychelles and BIOT 1967–9, Colonial Sec. Hong Kong 1969–74.

Osakwe, Albert (1918–) Dennis Memorial Grammar School, Onitsha, King's College Lagos and St Peter's Hall, Oxford, Admin Officer Nig. 1946, seconded as Industrial Relations Officer Nig. Coal Corp. 1952, Sec. Nig. Coal Corp. 1953, Dir. Recruitment and Training E. Nig. 1954, Perm. Sec. Min. of Agriculture 1957, Sec. to ExCo 1958.

Pallister, Michael (1930–2005) RAF (Medical) 1975, Air Commodore.

Phillips, Sir Henry, CMG, MBE (1914–2004) Commissioned Beds and Herts 1939–46, PoW of Japanese 1942 to end of war, Admin.Off. Nyasaland 1947 Dev. Sec. 1951, seconded Dep. Sec. Finance Fed. Rhodesia and Nyasaland 1953, Financial Sec. 1957, Min. Fin. 1963 to independence, Ch. Exec. Standard Bank Dev. Corp.

Pleass, Sir Clem, KCVO, KCMG, KBE (1901–88) Administrative Officer Nigeria 1924, Development Secretary 1949, Lt. Gov. (Eastern Region) 1952–4, Gov. ER 1954–7, Board Member CDC.

Purdy, 'Dick', OBE (b. 1927) Admin. Off. Nyasaland/Malawi, District Commissioner, S. Dist. Commissioner/ S. Asst Sec. 1965, Undersec. Dev. Div. 1967, retired 1974.

Rendel, Sir William, Kt (1908–95) FCA, Gen. Man. CDC 1953–73.

Richards, Geraint, Perm. Sec. Works Malawi, Ch. Capital City Dev. Auth., Head of Division, Eur.Comm. 1978–89.

Richardson, Philip (b. 1918) Admin Cadet Nig. 1940, seconded to Tonga, Sec. to Govt. 1947, seconded to BSIP 1951, seconded to CO 1953–5, Admin. Off. Nyasaland 1955, Sen. Asst Sec. 1959, Sec. to Gov. 1961, Undersec. 1962, Perm. Sec. 1964.

Roberts, Sir Brian, QC (b. 1923) Gray's Inn, War Service (RHA) 1943–5, Crown Council Northern Rhodesia 1943, Legal Asst Treasury Solicitor's Dept. 1951, Dir. Public Prosecution 1960, Perm. Sec. Min. of Justice, Solicitor-Gen. Nyasaland 1961, Attorney Gen. and Sec. for Justice 1964, Attorney Gen., Perm. Sec. to the PM and Sec. to the Cabinet 1965, stipendiary magistrate.

Robertson, Hamish, CB, MBE (b. 1931) Admin. Off. Nyasaland/Malawi 1954–63, S. Asst Sec. Treasury, 1964–7, Scottish Office 1967–92 (Undersecretary).

Robin, Angus H. (1917–?) Admin Cadet Nig. 1939, Military Service 1940–3, seconded CO 1952–4, Perm. Sec. E. Nig. 1954–8.

Seddon, Sir Joseph, Consultant CO, Professor RNOHospital.

Shepherd, Anthony (b. 1930) Admin Off. E. Nigeria 1954–60, Hong Kong 1960–71(Dir. Transport), independent transportation consultant and transportation projects promoter 1971–2003.

Smith, Michael (b. 1933) Admin. Off. E. Nigeria 1954–67 (Prov. Sec. Port Harcourt, Dep. Sec. Min. Health), NHS 1967–93, (Property Manager NW Thames Reg. Health Auth.).

Stallard, Sir Peter (1915–62) Cadet Nig. 1937, Military Service 1939–45, Sec. to PM, Fed. of Nig. 1957–61, Governor and C. in C. British Honduras 1961.

Thomas, Ambler, CMG (1913–96) Undersecretary Min. Overseas Development.

Tull, Thomas (1914–82) ICS 1938–41, Active Service India and South East Asia Commands 1941–6, Diplomatic Service 1947–71, High Com. Malawi 1967–71.

Trevorrow, Peter (1914–2000) Admin. Off. Nigeria 1938, S. Dist. Off. 1954, Class I 1956–7.

Udoji, Chief Oputa, CMG (b. 1917) ed. St Charles' Training College, Onitsha, UCL and King's Coll. Cambridge, Barrister, apptd. Admin. Off. 1948, Sen. DO 1954, Perm. Sec. E. Nig. 1958, Sec. Premier and ExCo 1959.

Varvill, Robert, DSC (1920–2003) War Service 1939–45 (Lt. C'dr, RNVR), King's Commendation for Gallantry, Admin. Off. Nigeria 1946, S. Dist. Off. 1956, retired 1958, CDC PE Consulting Group.

Wait, Rex, OBE (b. 1921) Administrative Officer MCS, Sec. to Treasury Malawi, appointments with ODM, IBRD and IMF in Afghanistan, Sri Lanka, Sierra Leone and Sudan.

Widdell, 'Joe', OBE (b. 1922) War Service (Royal Artillery, Captain 1940–6), Admin. Off. Nigeria 1949, Sec. to Gov. 1955–9, UK Civil Service 1958–87 (Principal, Col. Off., C. Af. Off., C'wealth Rel. Asst Sec. Dept. Transport/Environment).

Wilson, Geoffrey, Sir

Windsor, Ken, OBE (b. 1925) War Service 1944–8, Capt. RE, Colonial Office/DTC 1949–64, seconded Uganda Govt. 1955–8, Bechuanaland

Govt. 1962–5, Ministry of Overseas Development/ODA 1965–81, seconded BHC Malawi 1967–81, Head UN Department 1976–81, consultant UNIDO 1983–4.

Youens, Sir Peter (1916–2000) Cadet Sierra Leone 1939, Naval Service 1939–40, Asst Dist. Comm. 1942, Dist. Commissioner 1948, Com. HQ Judicial and Freetown Police Districts 1950, Asst Sec. Nyasaland 1951, Dep. Ch. Sec. 1953, Perm. Sec to PM and Cabinet 1963, Sec. Lonrho.

Young, David, MC

Notes

1 A childhood in Malacca, 1930–7

1 Sir John Martin, a civil servant in the Colonial Office, who had been seconded to the Malayan Civil Service (MCS). See Michael Jackson, *A Scottish Life: Sir John Martin, Churchill and Empire*, London: Radcliffe Press, 1999.
2 One of the first acts of the Dutch was to construct 'A Church for the exercise of the Reformed Religion', now the Anglican 'Christ Church'. It was here that my brother Geoffrey was christened.
3 The Malaccan ruler Parameswara had visited the Ming court in 1405 and the Enuch Zheng commanded the fleet that visited Malacca in 1409. Emperor Zhu Di had personally overseen the drafting of the text recognising Malacca as a state – see Louse Levathis, *When China Ruled the Seas*, Oxford: Oxford University Press, 1996.
4 I reckon that between 1928 (when my parents probably became engaged) and 1951 (when my father retired from Malaya) they were together for only about 12 years. They did not have a house of their own until 1951.
5 Stromboli is a tiny volcanic island lying off the coast of Italy on the same fault line marked by Vesuvius and Etna.
6 The Padang was a flat, grassy public space by the sea.
7 Mr Allen was my father's superior in the company.
8 The Tokay gecko – a species native to South East Asia and the best climber of all – owes its clinging power to the structure of its feet, each of which has a half a million tiny hairs. At the end of each hair are even tinier pads, called spatulas, numbering hundreds or thousands per hair. The intimate contact these spatulas – no more that ten millionths of an inch across – make with the surface enables the geckos to stick to it.
9 A short Malay sword.
10 Navy Historical Branch, D/NHB/22/2 (0626Q).
11 Lest it be thought that my memories of Malacca are unduly coloured by childhood nostalgia, I quote from a letter written by Sir John Martin to a friend in England, 'it is impossible . . . to see British administration at work . . . without believing that if the British Empire were to crumble it would mean taking the keystone from the arch of civilisation and the loss of powers for good which are tremendous beyond calculation and which could not be replaced' (Letter to Colin Hardie, Good Friday 1932).

2 England, prep school and the war, 1937–40

1 'What made coaling ship (in Aden) a misery was the sticky-black, gritty and pervasive nature of the material. Tipping coal raised choking clouds of dust, it got into the eyes, nose and mouth and it penetrated

every nook and cranny of the ship. Then "tubbing and shampooing" of both passengers and vessel.' Extract from Ian Morrison, *Passage East*, Charlottesville, VA: Howell Press,1997.

2 Her fiancé was rumoured to be serving on the North-West Frontier. I remember that she read the poem 'East is East and West is West' with particular sensitivity. It tells, of course, of peacekeeping amongst 'border thieves' by Queen Victoria's own Corps of Guides.

3 There was a small school chapel in the grounds to which we went every Sunday. So far as I recall, this was the only occasion on which we wore these suits – which we hated.

4 A letter from Vivian Marchiandi written in 2004 confirms this.

5 There is a statue to Peter Hajo, his two friends and their dog in Hoorn.

6 By chance an RNVR officer, Geoffrey Craven, DSC, then serving in *HMS Cossack*, the destroyer that effected this rescue, was to be a neighbour of mine in Hungerford.

7 Between the German frontier and Brussels this modern fort had been a key point in the Belgian defences.

8 Letter from the officer, Mr Robertson.

3 The *Viceroy of India* to Malaya, 1940

1 David and Stephen Howarth, *The Story of P&O*, London: Weidenfeld and Nicolson, 1986, p. 132. The first-class smoking room was of Scottish 'baronial' design.

2 All children, whether travelling First Class – like the two Barrett boys, Christopher and Roger, and John Coles, then aged 9, all three of whom were later to be at Guildford with Geoffrey and me – or Second Class as we were, ate together. Our mealtimes were earlier than those of the grown-ups.

3 Cape Town harbourmaster records incorrectly name the cruiser as *Cornwall*. I learned of the error from a neighbour in Hungerford, Vice-Admiral Troup who, at the time, was serving in *Cornwall* as a midshipman.

4 I had no contact with Anne Deveson after the ending of this voyage, but the memory of my ungallant behaviour weighed on my mind. When writing this chapter I made an effort to determine her present whereabouts from Devesons shown in the voters roll; none knew of her. Then, at the beginning of August 2005, I received an e-mail from New South Wales beginning 'I think I am the girl you didn't dance with'. It was almost exactly 65 years after the incident! Anyway, I was pleased to learn that I was forgiven. Her doings in this period included marriage and motherhood, authorship of a novel and much else, television programmes and appointment to the Australian Order.

5 The *Hindustan* had been built as a cruiser in the Royal Navy and transferred to the Royal Indian Navy of which she was flagship.

6 Side dishes such as grated coconut, sliced banana, and chilli, etc.

4 Malaya, 1940–1

1 Government schools were either Malay or Chinese. Europeans (or the better-off Eurasians, I suppose) would have been expected to be educated

privately. Indeed there was a European school in Cameron Highlands and another in Sumatra (to which my friend Michael Pallister went for a time).

2 Letter to author.

5 Australia, 1941

1 Alfred Holt's was one of the major cargo and passenger/cargo shipping lines operating out of Liverpool, the Blue Funnel Line (*Diomede* mentioned in Chapter 2), the Glen Line and the Straits Steamship Co. being subsidiaries.

2 F. K. Crowley, *Australia's Western Third*, London: Macmillan, 1960.

6 The invasion of Malaya, 1941–2

1 In Kathryn Tidrick's *Empire and the English Character* (London: I.B. Tauris, 1990, chapter 3) a section dealing with Sir Hugh Clifford, once Governor of the Straits Settlements, reads: 'On 18 December, the day he died, his compatriots were engaged in evacuating themselves – and only themselves – from Penang. Their abandonment on this occasion of those whom it had been their pride to protect destroyed at a stroke such loyalty to them as remained. Everywhere the Malays silently defected from the British cause; even the Malays rulers, the objects of such avowedly special concern, declined at this critical moment to identify their fortunes with those of the British empire.' It is only fair, however, to say that Robert Heussler (British Rule in Malaya, Westport, VG, 1981) indicates that the decision may have been taken as a result of British Military pressure.

2 Sir Shenton Thomas, the Governor, wrote in his diary on this day, 'Malacca had an air raid, it seems ridiculous that sleepy Malacca should have anything so up to date' – see Bryan Montgomery, *Shenton of Singapore*, London: Leo Cooper, 1984. It is surprising that my diary does not mention such an exciting event.

3 *Shenton of Singapore*, p. 104.

7 Australia, 1942–3

1 We never recovered these although I believe that the Japanese troops were meticulous in not looting. I have heard that the British troops who reoccupied Singapore in September 1945 were less scrupulous.

2 The school buildings were requisitioned for use as an American military hospital.

3 Hale flourishes. The school sold the land on which it stood when I was a pupil (near the WA Parliament) for a vast sum, bought a large tract of the Western Downs and built anew, all buildings equipped with every possible modern teaching aid and with extensive sports grounds.

8 The *Sarpedon*: back to England, 1943

1 Clay Blair, *Hitler's U-boat War the Hunted, 1942–45*, London: Orion, 2000, p. 553.

2 Ibid., p. 240.

3 Gerald Pawle, *The Secret War*, London: Harrap, 1956, chapter 8, 'Cables in the Air'.
4 The *Mars* Geoff and I had written in Perth had nothing SF about it save its name.
5 The need for a convoy may appear surprising given the distance of these waters from German or Japanese submarine bases but in fact a U-boat pack was operating in this area at the time. Kenneth Poolman in *Armed Merchant Cruisers* (London: Cooper in association with Secker & Warburg, 1985) writes that in August 1943, the Indian Ocean was considered to be the most dangerous area for shipping in the world, while the official history of the Royal Australian Navy (G. Hermon Gill, *The Royal Australian Navy, 1939-1942*, Australian War Memorial, 1957, p. 296) shows 12 ships sunk in June 1943 and 16 in the month of July. *War in the Southern Oceans, 1939–45* (L. C. Turner, H. R. Gordon-Cumming and J. E. Betzler, Cape Town; New York: Oxford University Press, 1971, xvi, p. 288) states that on 1 June U178, U196 and U198 were operating off Durban while on 1 July U177 was 700 miles east. The *Alice Palmer* (US), 7,176 tons, was sunk on 10 July and on 29 July the *Cornish City*, 4,952 tons, was sunk en route from Durban to Aden.
6 It was a peculiarity of all Alfred Holt ships, I have since learnt, normally to be crewed exclusively by their own men – they would never recruit from 'the pool' as was the custom of lesser lines. As a consequence their normal standards were far higher (*all* deck officers above the rank of cadet were required to have a Master's Certificate, for example). But in wartime even Alfred Holt had to take what they could get.
7 Convoys 'Outbound North 202' and 'Outbound North (Slow) 18' were under attack from 19–21 September. Three escorts and six merchant ships were sunk; three U-boats were sunk, a further three forced to abort: Blair, *Hitler's U-boat War*, pp. 421–6.
8 Blair, *Hitler's U-boat War*, p. 421, writes 'The German airmen ... remained under trained and inept at finding convoys. When they did find one, the position they reported was usually wrong.'
9 The arrival of our convoy – and such a large one – unscathed was unusual. Although the number of U-boats operating in the Atlantic had decreased over the past four months a considerable number of ships were still being sunk each month as shown below.

1943	*World*		*North Atlantic*	
	Ships	*Tonnage*	*Ships*	*Tonnage*
June	28	123, 825	4	18, 379
July	61	365, 398	18	123, 327
August	25	119, 801	2	10, 186
Sept.	29	156, 419	8	43, 775

Source: John Terraine, *Business in Great Waters, Wordsworth*, Editions, p. 768.

9 Dover College I, 1943–5

1 I was reminded at a reunion (22 July 2003) that, in the style of a New Zealand haka, I imitated the cry of a startled kookaburra and that I followed Australian Football rules, 'Never mind the ball, kick the man'.
2 This and other extracts are taken from surviving letters to David Anderson, which, by chance, were kept by him.
3 Billy cans are metal pots for putting on an open fire.
4 It was sad to see recently (2003) that the lovely building that had been Poltimore House is now badly decayed, the roof open to the sky, floorboards up, the marble fireplaces ripped out, and the gilding which decorated the saloon and other principal rooms now either faded or removed. Access to the grounds was not possible, and there is no trace of the water garden. A trust hopes to be able to raise enough funds to restore as much as possible; in view of the extent of the damage one fears that their hopes may be in vain. See Joselyn Hemming, *A Devon House: The Story of Poltimore*, Plymouth University Press, 2005.

10 Dover College II, 1945–9

1 The civilian internees were treated slightly better than were the military prisoners of war but on the other hand they were older, less fit and less able to endure what was still harsh and occasionally cruel treatment.
2 By some odd quirk of fate, the two boys who shared a study with me – Rex Berry and Tony Hall – after a separation of 50 years without even the exchange of a Christmas card found ourselves living within an hour's drive of each other.

11 National service: the RAF, 1949–50

1 The writer, David Hughes, was one of these (see obituary in *The Times*, 20 April 2005).

12 St Catharine's College, Cambridge, 1950–3

1 The system of 'tutorials', in which two or three undergraduates were tutored together by a don, reading their essays for discussion within the group and at liberty to speak and think freely about the problems of their subject – or any others – was peculiar to Cambridge and Oxford. 'It is a very intensive form of teaching and, when done well, a magnificent thing', commented Professor Collinson, Regius Professor of History, in the University Alumini Magazine of Michaelmas, 1993, 'some of the best supervisions are given by younger teachers who are fired up about their subjects.' MacDonagh, not much older than we, fell into this category. He was very likeable as well.
2 The name of the book of their travels through France, Spain, North Africa and Egypt to Lake Tana in Ethiopia. They returned via Jordan, Syria, Turkey and Yugoslavia. Later Geoff was a founder member of the Cambridge University Exploration Club.

13 A little interlude in London, 1953–4

1 At that time a well-known television and electronics firm, based in Cambridge.

2 Colonial Service courses for recruits to the Administrative Service had been established by Sir Ralph Furse and were run at Cambridge, London and Oxford universities, the choice between the three being dependent on the territory to which the probationer had been assigned and the local language which he would be required to learn. Thus recruits for Northern Nigeria learning Hausa went to Oxford, those for Eastern Nigeria learning Ibo or Efik/Igbo to London. There were none for W. Nigeria that year. It will be apparent that the 'tribalisation' of British entrants began very early! The 'official' name for the Colonial Service courses was the Devonshire Course 'A' for new recruits and Devonshire Course 'B' for serving officers.

3 George caught polio at about the same time as I did. Tragically he died leaving a young wife and child.

4 The Consumer Association magazine just launched to instant acclaim.

5 Sir Kenneth Bradley's own book, *Diary of a District Officer*, set in pre-war Northern Rhodesia is a classic description of the life of a 'bush' administrative officer of that time.

6 Her book *Women of the Grass Fields*, 1952, relates to their position in Bamenda (at that time forming part of the Trust Territory of the Southern Cameroons which was linked to Nigeria for administrative purposes). Angus Robin had served there at some stage, which may account for the happy choice of her selection as our lecturer.

7 The Secretariat was the name of the central government offices of each colony.

8 Sir Edward Wakefield (1903–69) had had a distinguished career in the Indian Civil and Political Services, was MP for West Derbyshire (1950–62) and was the first High Commissioner to Malta, receiving a baronetcy. He wrote of his Indian experiences in *Past Imperative*, 1966. His brother had been a great Captain of the England Rugby XV in the 1920s.

9 In Brussels, Hecqu, Congo, serving a similar purpose for Belgian officials and civilians going to the Congo (and also those of European Commission aid administrators), remained open until the 1980s; but British property developers eventually wreaked the same havoc there as they had earlier done in London.

14 The country and the job, 1954

1 The date of embarkation was also that of one's official appointment. Henceforward we were salaried and pensionable members of the service.

2 He was later to be permanent secretary finance for the Federation of Nigeria and subsequently personnel director in the World Bank.

3 I was interested to read in *Was it Only Yesterday?* (ed. Trevor Clark, Bristol: BECM Press, 2002) a similar comment by a contemporary (George Aitchison) going to the North, 'Apapa was a nightmare. The customs were uniformly insolent and unpleasant.'

4 As in all colonies, the offices where these worked was called the Secretariat, comprising one square, two-storey building with spacious, high-ceilinged rooms. However, as constitutional change brought African ministers and devolution of powers from Lagos to the three regions, one building became inadequate. A new one was needed,

the old, very imaginatively, becoming the 'Old Secretariat', the new the 'New Secretariat'. This, in accordance with Parkinson's law, was still not enough and temporary buildings were being put up everywhere.

5 Aba was a rapidly developing commercial centre, being on the railway and also on the region's only tarred road, one part leading north to Onitsha and thence by ferry over the river Niger to the Western Region, one south to Port Harcourt and the Atlantic (also the rail terminus) and another east to Calabar Province.

6 The civil service was split into two, the small 'Senior Service' consisting of what had once been posts for the 'British' but were now beginning to be filled with Nigerians and a very much larger 'Junior Service' of all other posts. The demarcation between the two extended into all aspects of life and work, including housing.

7 Most government housing outside the main towns was 'local', neither built by nor maintained by the Public Works Department. Only half-rent was charged.

8 General Orders set out the procedures governing appointments, transfers, promotion, discipline and retirement of civil servants, the allowances they could draw when travelling on duty, the rent that they paid, the amount of local and overseas leave that they would receive, indeed anything and everything that they did. It was a thick book and a new edition had just been issued.

9 Seeing Nigerians packed into these vehicles, apparently quite happily, sometimes made me wonder whether the indignation at the cramped quarters of slave ships is not sometimes excessive; although this is in no way to condone the general brutalities of that hideous trade.

10 It was from Opobo that Sir Harry Johnston 'shanghaied' King Jaja to the West Indies in a now forgotten (by Britain) act of peaceful trickery.

11 Although Uyo was first administered from Ikot Ekpenne (*c.*1900) and became a separate division only after the Arochuke Expedition of 1904.

12 The tale of the prisoner who got lost cutting wood in the bush, returned after the gates were closed and was found the next morning asleep outside, waiting to be let in, is undoubtedly true.

13 This was a kind of cutlass (indeed that was its name in the West Indies), often made out of an old car spring.

14 Fried flying ants were regarded by Africans as a culinary delicacy. I tried one once but, perhaps squeamishly, they were not to my taste.

15 Nevertheless, one was reported near Uyo in early 1955 and another young man and I had the rather silly idea of hunting it from a tree platform, using a goat as bait. I was posted before this came to anything; fortunately as we had no guns suitable for this kind of game and would have been more likely killed than killer!

16 In a division there might be 20 courts, each sitting two or three days per week and hearing between them a total of several thousand cases a year.

17 A native court building was usually a simple rectangular hall, walled up to waist height only on three sides with entries in the wall on these three. The fourth side consisted of two box-like little rooms for such things as court records, etc. One of the rooms could be used, if necessary, as a temporary – if very insecure – lock-up. The end of the hall nearest these would have a small dais with a table and chairs for the judges. When the DO was present he would sit here with the native

court judges seated on one side. A framed colour portrait of the Queen was hung behind him (the place which would be occupied by the Royal Coat of Arms in a British court).

18 Although the government gave great encouragement to the introduction of these, 'Pioneer Mills', believing that their use was essential if Nigerian oil was to be competitive in world markets, it now appears to be recognised that they were not very efficient.

19 These might perhaps have served the purpose of showing that the body being buried was whole and that no limbs or organs had been removed for *juju*. There was also a widespread belief, or maybe simply fear, of cannibalism: in some markets meat had to be sold with its hide or skin still attached as a proof that it was not human flesh that was being sold.

20 Twin murder, though, when one or both infants would be disposed of in the bush on the grounds that they must have resulted from the intercourse of the mother with an evil spirit, may well have originated because of the impossibility of a mother suckling two children, given her own diet.

21 A tour of service in West Africa usually varied between 18 months for cadets and a year for most senior and older men. In Malaya, by contrast, three to four years was the norm.

22 TNA CO: 554/1181, no. 2, Sir Clem Pleass to Williamson (Colonial Office), 18 October 1954. See also Lynn, p. 111.

15 Constitutional change and the Federal Election, 1954

1 Another account of this election but in Obubra Division of Ogoja Province is 'Nomination Day, November 1954' (in Ronnie Anderson (ed.), *Palm Wine and Leopard's Whiskers: Reminiscences of Eastern Nigeria*, Central Otago, New Zealand: R. G. Anderson, 1999).

2 Peter Trevorrow was actually only 'Acting Resident' but would always be addressed by others as 'Resident'.

3 Oron was in Eket Division, about an hour's drive on the tarred road from Uyo, on the west bank of the Cross River and the terminus of the ferry to Calabar.

4 Calabar Province had six divisions, Calabar itself, Eket, Uyo, Ikot Ekpenne, Opobo and Itu (to which was attached the sub-division of Arochuku).

5 I believe that in the Western Region there was also some kind of tax requirement.

6 NCNC – the National Council of Nigeria and the Cameroons, which had been founded by Dr Azikiwe and was the first national Nigerian party.

7 UNIP – United National Independence Party, representing the non-Igbo tribes of the Eastern Region and deriving its principal strength from Calabar Province.

8 Before a man/woman was allowed to vote their thumb was scrutinised to check that it had no ink mark. It was then pressed firmly onto the ink-pad. This was the only way of preventing multiple voting although some were put off, thinking that it was some kind of *juju*.

9 In those days typing for reproduction required the removal of the typewriter ribbon so that the key hit directly and perforated a thin paper.

Errors were corrected with some reddish substance. The document could then be run off on a Gestetner duplicator. Copies could get inky.

10 Finding 84 good padlocks presented quite a problem in itself.

11 A wire rope was strung across the river and firmly secured on each bank. Each end of the pontoon, on which the car was to travel, was attached by a shorter hawser running through a pulley that travelled on the wire rope spanning the river. The car was driven on to two planks resting on the pontoon. By angling the pontoon correctly the strength of the current would then propel the pontoon across the river. It was effective, but it always looked unsafe!

12 For example, Jill Mann, the DO's wife, had acted similarly to mine. Calling for a broom, she had climbed on a table and made brushing strokes, simulating that she would brush away like dust those who had improperly overrun her polling station.

16 Back to routine, 1954

1 Michael Mann had been an officer in the Dragoon Guards during the war (and many years later established their Regimental Museum in Cardiff Castle). His connection with Nigeria continued, however, after his ordination as a priest and he (with Jill) returned to Port Harcourt in the early 1960s as a missionary for the Missions to Seamen. They were there during the tense months preceding the Biafran war. Michael was ordained bishop at an early age and later became Dean of Windsor, Chaplain to the Order of the Garter and a Chaplain to the Queen.

2 The angle of slope of a mat roof was very important; too shallow a slope and the wind that accompanied a tropical rain storm would stand the mats vertical, letting the rain straight through. On the other hand, a steep pitch increased the total area to be roofed, thus needing more palm mats which, although made in the prison, still cost money.

3 Dane guns were primitive muzzle-loaders, presumably so called because Danish slave traders had once supplied such guns as 'trade goods' in payment for slaves. The guns in use at this time would have been locally made copies, mainly used for hunting and as dangerous to the user as to his prey.

4 The other DO (Robert Varvill from Opobo) had been a Lieutenant Commander in the Navy and, more recently, had been awarded the Queen's Commendation for Bravery. The ADO, Opobo, Hugh Byatt, was later to become an ambassador, while Colin Limb the ASP was to be involved in the (less serious) fracas outside Ryall's Hotel when Harold Macmillan visited Malawi in 1960.

5 The position grew steadily worse throughout 1955. Calabar Province was not, I think, alone in experiencing this problem, nor Uyo Division alone in the province, but I think it was worst affected. Eventually the regional government had to suspend the county council and, in several years' time, to amend fundamentally the Local Government Act. But this memoir is not the place to recount the whole story.

17 The crash of the Bristol Wayfarer

1 A punkah resembled a door on its side, suspended on its upper side from the ceiling. An ingenious contraption of ropes and pulleys

(operated by a labourer sitting outside the room) gave a sideways, rocking motion to this, producing a gentle disturbance to the heavy, still air.

2 *Compagie Francaise d'Afrique Ouestal* and *Société Commercial d'Ouest Afrique*.

3 UAC had taken over most of the old trading companies such as Millers and G. B. Olivant and was now the dominant British firm on the coast. See 'Trade Winds on the Niger'.

4 It reminded me of the old Malacca European Hospital where my brother had been born in 1932.

5 Mr R. Anderson, editor of *Palm Oil and Leopard's Whiskers*, made enquiries of the New Zealand Transport Accident Investigation Commission's Chief Inspector, Ron Chippendale, who advised: 'The accident involving structural failure of a main wing spar in a Bristol Freighter occurred at 11.33 hours on 21 November 1957, near Christchurch Airport. The aircraft ZK–AYH fell to the ground on the nearby Russley Golf Course. The aircraft was carrying a load of live cattle with two passengers and two crew. All lost their lives. There have been two RNZAF Bristol Freighter accidents involving loss of life, one in Malaya (as it was then) and one near Blenheim. I do not have the details but neither involved structural failure. The only difference between the Bristol Freighter and the Wayfarer, according to my adviser, was that the Bristol Freighter had nose doors for cargo loading and the Wayfarer did not.'

18 Polio, 1955–6

1 The shortage of staff had always been liable to mean that the change of one officer was likely to result in a general post. Readers of *Gentleman Rider* will recall that Joyce Cary had had similar experiences.

2 In my account *Polio and Me* (1998) I give this date in error as 6 March.

3 The polio virus was spread through contaminated water supplies, swimming pools being highlighted in Britain as a major source of infection. The virus attacked the motor nerves in the spinal cord and by severing these prevented commands from the brain reaching the muscles, which control all movements. In its early stages, polio is not easy to diagnose, but once paralysis appears the diagnosis should be obvious. While there is no *cure*, even now, once paralysis has set in it is generally considered that movement in any form will aggravate permanent muscular damage, and that patients should be kept perfectly still. As I was given the impression, however, that my loss of movement was caused by *will*, I felt that I should make every effort to overcome this weakness, efforts that almost certainly made my permanent state much worse.

4 With hindsight I think it more than probable that Lesley's unexplained illness in Calabar could have been mild polio.

5 My physiotherapist. For some reason all those physiotherapists I knew died quite young of cancer.

6 Somewhat ironically it was about this time that announcements were made of the discovery by Sabin and Salk of preventive vaccines against polio, too late for us in hospital but welcomed nevertheless as ensuring that others would not be affected as we had been.

7 Home was my parents' house at Sutton Coldfield.

8 Sir Joseph Seddon, who was a consultant to the Colonial Office. He had, deservedly, won an international reputation for his work in the Malta polio epidemic in the late 1940s.
9 A man named Carruthers who was going out to Kenya as an administrative officer. We were to meet many years later when, having left the service at Kenya's independence, he was working for OXFAM.
10 Although having lost both legs through enemy action, he continued to fly and fight.

19 Back to work, 1956

1 The strong cold dry wind from the north that blew in the months of January and February.
2 See article by Ann Grant in *Palm Wine and Leopard's Whiskers*, which describes the day from the point of view of one of the organisers/helpers.
3 *Transition in Africa*, the government documentary film of the royal tour received much praise in Britain: the women dancers of Calabar, the war canoe racing from the tribes of Rivers Province and a Durbar in the North all being vividly depicted.
4 Sir Clem Pleass, Despatch no. 23 of 18 October 1956, para. 33, disagrees, 'everywhere the Royal Party received spontaneous demonstrations of loyalty and affection'. He wrote also that 'the constant emphasis laid by Her Majesty on the subject of the unity of Nigeria will probably have a lasting effect politically'.
5 Nigeria-speak for post. If a man were not at his desk, one would be told that 'he not on seat'.
6 It was 'the declared policy of the N.C.N.C. to gain control of the Civil Service'. (Despatch no. 23 from Sir Clem Pleass, of 18 October 1956, para. 13).
7 'Zik', Dr Azikiwe, Premier of Eastern Region.
8 The post's relationship to that of the Secretary of the Commission was not defined. Was it subordinate to the latter? Equal to and independent of? The fact that the Secretary of the PSC was an Efik, recently promoted from the 'Junior Service' while the Director of Recruitment and Training was an Igbo graduate did not help their personal relationships.
9 The man eventually appointed, from Ogaja Province, was not even a proper Igbo; with Neil Kay's loyal help he performed adequately although his subsequent career was undistinguished.
10 'In the districts the administrative officers see the general standard of administration collapsing, bribery and corruption rife, themselves cold-shouldered, their travelling allowances cut so that they cannot properly get round their districts and indeed with the threat of disappearance, at least of Residents, hanging over their heads. At Enugu the situation is even worse.' TNA CO 554/1181, letter from C. G. Eastwood to Sir C. Jefferies, 30 May 1955.
11 I believe he had been an inspector of the UK Inland Revenue. It was his last task before retiring and I do not know what became of him. In Nigeria, however, for some years 1956 was known as the 'year of the Gorsuch'. Such is fame.
12 School holiday passages for children being educated in the UK was one of these; the refusal to agree payment alienated wives in particular.

On the general effects of this attitude of the ER ministers, see Governor's Despatch no. 23 of 18 October 1956, TNA CO 554/1164, para. 13.

13 The Secretary of the Housing Committee was the target of every woman entitled to a quarter either in her own right or because of her husband's position. They were quite unscrupulous in achieving their aims, using their husband's rank or their own charms and – if these failed – screaming abuse like a fishwife.

14 The design was by an administrative officer, Frank Bex, who, married with children, was uncomfortably aware of the drawbacks of existing accommodation (see Frank Bex, *Lucky Me*, privately published, 2003).

20 Turbulence, 1956–7

1 In a letter to the Secretary of State Sir Clem wrote of the 'almost complete collapse of effective local administration through the councils and repeated disorders'. TNA CO 554/1182 'Political Situation in Eastern Region, Nigeria' Pleass to Secretary of State, February 1956. See also letter from C. G. Eastwood (a senior Colonial Office official visiting Eastern Nigeria) about the suspension of many important town councils because of corruption and incompetence), TNA CO 554/1181, no. 12, of 30 May 1955.

2 Keith Arrowsmith in *Bush Paths* (Durham: Pentland Press, 1991), chapters 12 to 16, based on his diaries, describes vividly the insolvency of the councils in Eket Division.

3 TNA CO 554/1181, no. 14, *post scriptum* to letter from Sir Clem to Williamson of 22 June 1955.

4 Wealthier African women were also included – a bold move considering the events of 1929.

5 See Despatch no. 23 from Sir Clem Pleass, TNA CO 554/1164.

6 A file note prepared by the Colonial Office summarising the situation is at TNA CO 554/1337 dated 18–19 January 1956.

7 TNA CO 554/1181, no. 8, Minutes on a letter from Sir Clem Pleass of 14 May 1955.

8 TNA CO 554/1181, no. 26 of 6 Aug 1955, para. 4.

9 TNA CO 554/1181, no. 27.

10 TNA CO 554/1181, no. 60A of 27 September 1955 from Sir James Robertson forwarding letter of 26 September from Maj. Gen. G. H. Inglis.

11 The Foreign Office has inherited a copy of this document.

12 Hugh Byatt, for example, tried to transfer into the new Federal Diplomatic Service. He could not, left and joined the UK Foreign Office, finally ending his career as a Knight and Her Majesty's Ambassador to Portugal.

13 Keith Arrowsmith was allowed to go to Uganda having made it clear that he would leave anyway if permission to transfer were refused. Roy Somerset went to Aden, George Lewis to St Helena (although only on secondment).

14 My wife, when driving me up to the Deputy Governor's office would sometimes see the Governor and was always astonished that he knew her name, knew that we had a baby daughter, etc., and that he would go out of his way to greet her.

15 Paradoxically, personal relations between the politicians and individual administrative officers remained good at that time (and indeed later).

Indeed, Sir Clem wrote in his despatch of 28 October 1956, para. 13, 'When Members of the Parliamentary Delegation met Executive Council, the Premier took the line that not only were the N.C.N.C. anxious that British officers should continue to stay in the Civil Service after the achievement of self-government, but that it was indeed their duty to do so, and the duty of H. M. G. to encourage them to do so', TNA CO 554/1164.

16 See TNA CO 554/1181, no. 8, letter from Sir C. Pleass of 14 May 1955.

17 An appreciation of the oil-prospecting position in June 1957 was drawn up by the Colonial Office for the Secretary of State Lennox Boyd. It gives the impression that while there was definitely oil in commercial quantities there would be little financial return to governments for some time. TNA CO 1029/255, no. 5.

18 Sir Clem Pleass, despatch of 18 October 1956, para. 7, lists nine. TNA CO 5554/1164.

19 TNA CO 554/1081, 7 August 1955 and TNA CO 554/1125, no. 21A, 23 June/6 August 1955. Nigerian Government Political Intelligence Note no. 58.

20 It is hard not to sympathise with the Nigerians. The UK Treasury, however, had always stuck to the rule that colonies should be self-supporting during their life and was determined that this should apply also to their death. Later, opinions in Whitehall changed. First interest-free loans were given to meet the costs of compensation for loss of career, then, in the fullness of time, these were written off, but more than a decade was to pass before this happened.

21 TNA CO 554/1181, no. 58, CO note of Sept. 1955. For a full account of ACB matter see Martin Lynn, 'The Eastern Crisis of 1955–57: The Colonial Office and Nigerian Decolonisation', *Journal of Imperial and Commonwealth History* 30(3) (2002), pp. 91–109.

22 Marketing boards had been set up in all African colonies with the intention of ensuring a stable price for raw material producers irrespective of fluctuations in world commodity market prices. This meant that they had to have substantial cash reserves, sufficient to iron out any price fluctuations. It was good old paternalistic thinking but was inclined to lead to a conservative pricing policy that many economists thought did more harm than good.

23 See PRO CO 554/1181, no. 58 of Sept. 1955 and CO 554/1126, no. 105 of 5 July 1956.

24 See TNA CO 554/1127, no. 322 of 24 July 1956 and Lynn, 'The Eastern Crisis of 1955–57'. See also CO 554/1140, minutes from 31 Dec. 1956–2 Jan. 1957.

25 At one time entirely European but now multiracial they were tactfully called the Government Residential Area (GRA).

26 By contrast Kingsway would employ European women, the wives of lower grade officers, supplementing their husband's meagre salaries. They were less efficient, though, than the Indians in Chellarams, as if to make it plain that they were not accustomed to doing anything like working in a shop (except for hairdressing which was a lady-like thing to do).

27 *Who's Who* shows him as born in 1921.

28 Executive Council, 'the Cabinet'.
29 He subsequently wrote the history of the Indian Political Service, *The Indian Political Service: A Study in Indirect Rule*, London: Chatto & Windus, 1971.
30 A Public Service Commission (PSC) is intended to select impartially candidates for appointment to the Public Service, for subsequent promotion and for any disciplinary procedures necessary. Its membership should consist of the 'great and good' who should be able to carry out their duties without fear or favour and so prevent political interference in the conduct of civil servants. In practice it was almost impossible to find such paragons. The PSC should not be otherwise involved in governmental structures or organisation.
31 The first had held the post of Civil Secretary in the pre-1954 Eastern Regional government, and the second had been a Civil Service Commissioner in the former Federal government.
32 It was lavish, however, by comparison with the rates for Malaya and Borneo where one earned about six months' leave after a three-year tour (as Governor Clifford had pointed out in 1921!).
33 There was even a proviso that Nigerian officers could take 'overseas leave' in the UK every so often, passages for them and their families being paid.
34 Because of staff shortages and penury very few officers could take 'local leave'.
35 The sister of his district officer had been a patient at the hospital in Stanmore with me, having caught polio in Nyasaland.
36 Shortly before going on leave Sir Clem wrote to a senior Colonial Office official, 'from such information as is available to me, I should say that Nigeria is nearer at this moment to being split into three parts than it has ever been before' (CO 554/1140, no. 25–26 October 1956 letter from Sir C. Pleass to C. G. Eastwood). This appraisal was, of course, 'secret' at the time.
37 Not yet Tanzania.
38 See TNA CO 554/1182 'Secret and Personal' 8 Nov. 1956 from Sir James Robertson, Governor-General, Nigeria to Sir John MacPherson, Permanent Secretary to the Colonial Office.

21 Internal self-government, 1957–8

1 As Clem had written, 'The exercise of public power for private profit is well established in this Region as in many other under-developed areas and to expect people of this Region to judge politicians by the same standards as the British public now judge them is not only to court disappointment but to invite disaster. One might just as well have expected the Prime Minister of 1735 (Sir Robert Walpole) to have stopped bribing Members of Parliament.' TNA CO 554/1140, NO 8018, 27 September 1956. Nearly fifty years later we still see French and Italian politicians behaving as ours did then and with a similar tolerance by their electorates. See also CO internal minutes of 31 Dec. 1956–2 Jan. 1957 on the Report of the Foster-Sutton Commission.
2 Igbo villages formed much more recognisable units than did those in Calabar Province, moreover the electors were more sophisticated the

second time round. Certainly there were no such problems in identifying voters as we had experienced in Uyo.

3 See TNA CO 554/2128, no. 9, from Sir Robert Stapledon to Mr Secretary Lennox-Boyd.

4 'Lumpers' in popular parlance from lump sum compensation.

5 The UK Treasury had always insisted that colonies should not constitute any cost to the UK taxpayer. Staff salaries and pensions were a local responsibility.

6 Three years later the Belgian administration in the Congo collapsed almost overnight. Forty years later there is still no effective government.

7 ER Staff List no. 1.

8 See Sir Robert Stapledon, despatch no. 34 of 22 October 1957. TNA CO 554/1843, no. 3.

9 Many of these British officers were 'on leave pending retirement'. The 'active' number was a lot less. Three-quarters of the Nigerians, of course, had less than three years service, most of these a lot less. The number of British departures had moved Mr Lennox-Boyd to send Sir John Martin, a Deputy-Secretary at the Colonial Office, to visit Nigeria in Jan./Feb. 1958 and propose how the exodus could be staunched.

10 See contributions by Frank Kennedy and Tony Shepherd in *Palm Wine and Leopard's Whiskers.*

11 It had been realised immediately that this, in addition to other wild expenditures, would bankrupt the region – see Sir Clem Pleass's Despatches of 25 May 1955 and 18 October 1956 already cited.

12 See TNA CO 554/1955, no. 40, letter of 10 Feb. 1958 from Mr Eastwood (Colonial Office official visiting Nigeria) to Sir John Macpherson, Permanent Secretary at the Colonial Office and formerly Governor-General of Nigeria.

13 Oputa Udoji, an Igbo from Onitsha, had got his degree at Cambridge and had been appointed by the Secretary of State in the same manner as were expatriate administrative officers. He was the most senior Nigerian in the Eastern Region Service.

14 See Eastern Region House of Assembly Debates, 12 March 1958, column 39.

15 Udoji, after many years of service in Nigeria and then a further period of working for international agencies, regularly commuted between London and Nigeria attending reunions of his ex-colleagues who remained his good friends.

22 Abak, 1958–9

1 It is, of course, absurd to talk of being 'alone' in a district of some hundreds of thousands of people, but such is the usual tone of rulers. Roberdeau writes similarly of being an Englishman in eighteenth-century India. Although, one can get used to being on one's own. A bachelor friend who had been DO, Abak, three years before told me that at night he would get alarmed when he saw a car's headlights coming down the hill from Uyo. He would even tell his servants to put out the oil lamps to deter a potential (European) visitor.

2 Unrotted, cassava, an easily grown starch vegetable, contains cyanide and is poisonous. The soaking and rotting gets rid of this and makes

the plant edible, although it never becomes a 'prestige' food. Nevertheless, it was replacing yam, which is a hungry feeder.

3 'The Annangs are a strange people with a quality of awkwardness all their own, which it is difficult for those who have not mixed with them intimately to appreciate. It is a compound of suspicion, fear, insecurity, a tortuous seeking for motives in others, and the more unworthy these motives the better, of a temper at times sullen and bloody-minded and at others violent and bloody, of deceit, of a conspiracy of silence upon which crime flourishes, and also of a tenacity which enables, through and in spite of all these mixed elements, results, of a sort, can be achieved.' TNA CO 554/1182.

4 Household.

5 I have read the files of the interrogations held when the murders were investigated. One death, I remember, occurred when three men left one village in the dark to walk to another, but only two arrived; the two could not understand, were unwilling even to put the question to themselves, as to what had happened to their colleague. He had gone; that was clear. He had been with them when they set off, 'Yes'. However, of their actual journey they had nothing to say; darkness and fear so dominated the mind of the survivors that they were *unable*, not just unwilling, to make the connection that something must have happened to him. It is only fair, however, to point out that a district officer, John McCall, believed that the killings were by leopards NOT by humans. See p. 217 in *Palm Wine and Leopard's* Whiskers.

6 In March 1955 an internal Colonial Office working paper had read, 'A main aim of United Kingdom policy for Nigeria is . . . to prevent further fragmentation of the territory.' TNA CO 822/940, no. 3. See also Lynn, op.cit., p. 289.

7 Sir James Robertson certainly believed this.

8 See Susan M. Martin, *Palm Oil and Protest*, Cambridge University Press, 1988.

9 (Dwarf Poinciana) *Caesalpinia pulcherrima*.

10 Drinking a 'sun-downer' together one evening, Frank recalled that during the education riots of that January he had been surprised to find one village completely deserted. With some difficulty he managed to persuade some old women to come out of the bush where they had been hiding and he asked why everyone was hiding. 'In case the sailors come again', he was told, at which Frank recalled that it had been in that village that an English doctor had been murdered and eaten in 1905, for which a bloody retribution had been exacted. The memory had lingered and continued to deter.

11 Although all administrative officers had to pass language exams, very few (Tony Shepherd being one) were at all fluent – the tonal inflection was too difficult for most English people. The government accordingly employed interpreters. These naturally had great prestige as the voice of the white man. Intelligent and able men though they were, however, and human frailty being what it is, they could be tempted to abuse their office. This was rarely gross since the DO's language skills while not sufficient for independent speech might still be enough to stop an interpreter deliberately misrepresenting what was being said.

12 The government had great difficulty in recruiting Nigerian doctors to serve in the bush where living was hard and the legitimate financial

rewards were small. Having worked hard for many years to qualify most of them, understandably, wanted to earn their reward.

13 The Kwa Igbo Mission originated in Northern Ireland and was severely Presbyterian.

14 G. K. Chesterton.

15 Chadwick, the district officer at Udi, had the skills and interest to foster this and it deservedly made his reputation. With some, however, community development became a sacred cow, valued more as a way of enhancing personal promotion prospects than for the benefit to the people.

16 In fact the Marketing Board reserves in the past had been kept in 'sound' but low-paying British government securities so that the UK was the main beneficiary of the policy of price prudence. Investing *wisely and productively* in the country was a better use of these resources. The ER government, of course, had transferred most to the African Continental Bank.

17 Local authorities normally did not have much in the way of accumulated savings. What they had was likely to be kept in the Post Office Savings Bank whose 'reserves' were normally invested by the Crown Agents – cautiously and not very productively.

18 Post, op. cit., p. 204.

19 Later after a distinguished career in the Foreign Service, at the end of which he was knighted, he was appointed to the Board of British Airways.

20 In my distraught state due to my concern I shouted at our steward over something he had not done and which I thought he should have, getting the well-earned rebuke from him, 'Master, we know you are worried about the young master. We too are worried and are doing our best. There is no need to abuse us.' He was quite right, of course, and I apologised to him. He was a good servant and a good man.

21 I had read of this in the American *Time* magazine to which I subscribed and which was delivered by airmail. At the time it was almost the only comprehensive weekly news survey available, though not at all impartial.

22 Alan was a brilliant if eccentric colleague of my year. He died in his forties.

23 He was later to be a Foreign Minister of France and a potential Socialist candidate for the Presidency. He served two terms, also, as European Commissioner for Overseas Development during which he was my political master.

24 Britain had established a number of institutions to serve all four of her West African colonies. The research institutions in to the main crops, oil palm, cocoa and cotton, etc., earned an international reputation for their work. Sadly, when independence came to the colonies this regional co-operation ended for a time, although it recommenced under the auspices of ECOWAS (the Economic Community of West African States which is strongly supported by the European Union).

25 Abdul Atta later became Permanent Secretary, Finance, in the Federal government and we met again at the Commonwealth Finance Conference in London in 1968.

26 See Chapter 21.

27 I was not to see Christopher again. He was a nice and capable young man but I am told that he was killed when trying to put down a riot – as he was as black as they were, the rioters did not realise that he was an administrative officer.

23 Responsibility and a farewell to Nigeria

1 Hugh Byatt has told me that when many years later he was working for the UK Foreign Service as a Diplomatic Inspector, he visited Enugu. There he met Mr Israel Emelemadu, a colleague in Calabar and Enugu who had been in Warri at the time of the civil war, and had made his way back to the East with other Igbos from that district. I asked how they had fared, 'Oh', he said, 'it was alright. I said I was a DO when we were stopped and questioned, and the magic still worked'!

2 TNA CO 554/2393, no. 1, Despatch no. 5 from Sir Robert Stapledon of 14 April 1960, para. 27

Bibliography

Relevant files in the National Archives and documents in Cambridge University and Rhodes House libraries are cited in the notes to each chapter.

Australia and Malaya

Barnes, Geoffrey, *Mostly Memories*, Malaysia: Mulu Press, 1996.
Crowley, F. K., *Australia's Western Third*, London: Macmillan, 1960.
Haws, Duncan, *Merchant Fleets 6: Blue Funnel Line*, Hereford: TCL Publications, 1988.
Heussler, R., *British Rule in Malaya: The Malayan Civil Service and its Predecessors, 1867–1942*, Westport, CT: Greenwood Press, 1981.
Howarth, David and Stephen, *The Story of P&O*, London: Weidenfeld and Nicolson, 1986.
Jackson, Michael, *A Scottish Life: Sir John Martin, Churchill and Empire*, London: The Radcliffe Press, 1999.
Lee, Cecil, *Sunset of the Raj: Fall of Singapore, 1942*, Durham: Pentland Press, 1994.
Ludbrook, Juliet, *Schoolship Kids*, Perth, WA: Black Swan Press, 1998.
Montgomery, Brian, *Shenton of Singapore*, London: Leo Cooper, 1984.
Morrison, Ian, *Passage East*, Charlottesville, VA: Howell Press, 1997.
Shennan, Margaret, *Out in the Mid-day Sun*, London: John Murray, 2004.
Smith, Colin, *Singapore Burning: Heroism and Surrender in World War II*, London: Viking Penguin, 2005.
Tidrick, Kathryn, 'Hugh Clifford, Administrator', in *Empire and the English Character*, London: I.B. Tauris, 1990, chapter 3.
Thomas, David, *The Battle of the Java Sea*, London: Andre Deutsch, 1968.
Van Oosten, F. C., *The Battle of the Java Sea*, Shepperton, Surrey: Ian Allam, 1976.
Woodman, R., *The Real Cruel Sea: The Merchant Navy in the Battle of the Atlantic 1939–1943*, London: John Murray, 2005.

Nigeria

Proceedings of House of Assembly, Enugu: Government Printer.
Staff Lists 1955, 1957, 1958, 1959.
Anderson, Ronnie (ed.), *Palm Wine and Leopard's Whiskers: Reminiscences of Eastern Nigeria*, Central Otago, New Zealand: R. G. Anderson, 1999.

Arrowsmith, Keith, *Bush Paths*, Durham: Pentland Press, 1991.
Baker, Geoffrey L., *Trade Winds on the Niger: The Saga of the Royal Niger Company, 1830–1971*, London: The Radcliffe Press, 1996.
Bex, Frank, *Lucky Me: Memoirs of a Former District Officer in Nigeria*, East Sussex, privately printed.
Gailey, Harry A., *The Road to Aba: A Study of British Administrative Policy in Eastern Nigeria*, New York: SUNY Press, 1970.
Huxley, Elspeth, *Four Guineas: A Journey Through West Africa*, London: Chatto and Windus, 1955.
Jones, G. I., *Report of the Position, Status, and Influence of Chiefs and Natural Rulers in the Eastern Region of Nigeria*, Enugu: Government Printer, 1957.
Lynn, Martin, 'The African Continental Bank', *Journal of Imperial and Commonwealth History* 30(3) (2002), pp. 91–109.
—— *Nigérian Constitutionnel Documents, Vol. 2 Moving to Independence, 1953–1960*, London: The Stationery Office.
Martin, Susan M., *Palm Oil and Protest*, Cambridge: Cambridge University Press, 1988.
Nicolson, I. F., *The Administration of Nigeria 1900–1960*, Oxford: Clarendon Press, 1969.
Oliver, Michael, *Sir Harry Johnston and the Scramble for Africa*, London: Chatto & Windus, 1957.
Post, Kenneth W. J., *The Nigerian Federal Election, 1959*, Oxford: Oxford University Press for Nigerian ISER, 1963.
Post, Kenneth W. J. and Jenkins, George W., *Adelabu: The Price of Liberty*, Cambridge: Cambridge University Press, 1973.
Tutuola, Amos, *The Palm-wine Drinkard*, Atlantic Books, 1952.
Udoji, Oputa (Jerome), *Under Three Masters: Memoirs of an African Administrator*, Ibadan and Owerri: Spectrum Books, 1995.

Malawi

Baker, Colin, 'The Administrative Service: A Case Study in Africanisation', *Journal of Modern African Studies* 10/4 (1972), pp. 543–60.
—— *Seeds of Trouble: Government Policy and Land Rights in Nyasaland, 1946–1966*, London: I.B.Tauris, 1991.
—— *Development Governor: A Biography of Sir Geoffrey Colby*, London: I.B.Tauris, 1994.
—— *State of Emergency: Crisis in Central Africa, Nyasaland 1959–1960*, London: I.B.Tauris, 1997.
—— *Retreat from Empire: Sir Robert Armitage in Africa and Cyprus*, London: I.B.Tauris, 1998.
—— *Sir Glyn Jones: A Proconsul in Africa*, London: I.B. Tauris, 2000.
—— *Revolt of the Ministers: The Malawi Cabinet Crisis, 1964–65*, London: I.B.Tauris, 2002.
Bower, Tom, *Tiny Rowland*, London: Heinemann, 1993.
—— *Lonrho, Portrait of a Multinational*, London: Julian Friedmann, 1976.
Christiansen, Robert E. and Kydd, Jonathan, 'The Return of Malawian Labour from S. Africa and Zimbabwe', *Journal of Modern African Studies*, 1978.

Coleman, G., 'International Labour Migration from Malawi, 1875–1966', *Journal of Social Sciences*, 1973.

Cronjé, Suzanne, Ling, Margaret and Cronjé, Gillian, *Lonrho: Portrait of a Multinational*, London: Julian Friedmann, 1976.

Davidson, Ann, *The Real Paradise: Memories of Africa 1960–1963*, Durham: Pentland Press, 1993.

Giles, B. D., 'Economists in Government: The Case of Malawi', *Journal of Development Studies*, 1979, p. 217.

Guingand, Gen. Sir Francis de, *African Assignment*, London: Hodder and Stoughton, 1953.

Hedges, David, 'Notes on Malawi–Mozambique Relations', *Journal of Southern African Studies* 15/4 (1989).

Henderson, Robert d'A., 'Relations of Neighbourliness: Malawi and Portugal, 1964–1974', *Journal of Modern African Studies* 15/3 (1977).

Hewitt, A., 'Malawi: Eight Years Co-operation with the EEC', ODI Working Paper no.12, 1983.

Hewitt, A. and Kydd, J., *Effectiveness of Aid to Malawi*.

Howard, Anthony, *RAB – The Life of R. A. Butler*, London: Jonathan Cape, 1987.

Kydd, J and Hewitt A., 'Effectiveness of Structural Adjustment Lending: Malawi Evidence', *World Development* 14/3 (1986).

McMaster, Carolyn, *Malawi: Foreign Policy and Development*, London: Julian Friedmann, 1974.

Mhone, Guy (ed.) *Malawi at the Crossroads The Post Colonial Political Economy*, Harare: SAPES Books, 1992.

Mills, J. C., Price Responsiveness of Malawi Smallholder Farmers.

Minford, Patrick and Ohs, Peter, 'Supply Responses of Malawi Labour', *Eastern Africa Economic Review* (1970).

Morton, Kathryn, *Aid and Dependence*, London: Croom Helm in association with ODI, 1975.

Mullins, Patrick, *Retreat from Africa*, Durham: Pentland Press, 1992.

Newitt, Malyn, *A History of Mozambique*, London: C. Hurst, 1995.

Nyasaland Economic Symposium, *Economic Development in Africa: Papers Presented to the Nyasaland Economic Symposium held in Blantyre, 18 to 28 July 1962*, edited by E. F. Jackson, Oxford: Blackwell, 1965.

Paice, Edward, *Lost Lion of Empire: Ewart Grogan in Rhodesia and Kenya, 1900–1930*, London: Harper/Collins, 2002.

Perkin, J. O. N., *The Sterling Area*, Cambridge: Cambridge University Press, 1980.

Phillips, Henry, *From Obscurity to, Bright Dawn*, London: The Radcliffe Press, 1998.

Post, Sir Laurens Van der, *Venture to the Interior*, London: Hogarth Press, 1952.

Pryor, Frederick, *Malawi and Madagascar*, Oxford: Oxford University Press for World Bank, 1990.

Theroux, Paul, 'Malawi: Faces of a Quiet Land', National Geographic Society, Sept., 1989.

Snow, Philip, *The Star Raft: China's Encounter with Africa*, London: Weidenfeld and Nicolson, 1988.

Simon, Thomas, 'Economic Developments in Malawi since Independence', *Journal of Southern African Studies* (1975).

Southworth, Mr Justice, Commission Report, Nyasaland Government Printer, 1960.
Wilson, Amrit, *US Foreign Policy and Revolution: The Creation of Tanzania (Chicoms and the Railway)*, London: Pluto, 1989.
Wilson, Harold, *Purpose in Politics*, London: Weidenfeld and Nicolson, 1964.

Index

Note: page numbers in *italic* denote references to figures/illustrations.